GALA

'Recipes'

MY FAVOURITE RECIPES

NAYANA SHAH

Translated by

Riddhi K. Majmudar
B.H.Sc., Dietics

NAVNEET PUBLICATIONS (INDIA) LIMITED

Navneet House
Gurukul Road, Memnagar,
Ahmadabad – 380 052.

Phone : 6630 5000

Visit us at : www.navneet.com
e-mail : npil@navneet.com

Price : Rs. 160.00   G 3001

Published by :
Navneet Publications (India) Ltd.,
Dantali, Gujarat.

Type-setting :
Fotronics,
Bharwada House,
Nr. Old High Court Rly. Crossing,
Navrangpura, Ahmadabad – 380 009.
Phone : 2642 7448

Printed by :
Shreeji Offset
99, Amrut Industrial Estate, Ahmadabad – 4.

NAVNEET PUBLICATIONS (INDIA) LIMITED

Offices :
● Mumbai :
1. Bhavani Shankar Road, Dadar,
Mumbai – 400 028.
(Tel. 6662 6565 ● Fax : 6662 6470)
2. **Navyug Distributors :** Road No. 8,
M. I. D. C., Next to Indian Institute of
Packaging, Marol, Andheri (East),
Mumbai – 400 093.
(Tel. 2821 4186 ● Fax : 2835 2758)

● Ahmadabad :
Navneet House, Gurukul Road, Memnagar,
Ahmadabad – 380 052. (Tel. 6630 5000)

● Bengalore :
Sri Balaji's, No. 12, 2nd Floor, 3rd Cross,
Malleswaram, **Bengalore – 560 003.**
(Tel. 2346 5740)

● Chennai :
30, Sriram Nagar, North Street, Alwarpet,
Chennai – 600 018. (Tel. 2434 6404)

● Delhi :
2-E / 23, Orion Plaza, 2nd & 3rd Floor,
Jhandewalan Extn., **New Delhi – 110 055.**
(Tel. 2361 0170)

● Hyderabad :
Kalki Plaza, Plot No. 67, Krishnapuri Colony,
West Maredpalley, **Secunderabad – 500 026.**
(Tel. 2780 0146)

● Kolkata :
1st Floor, 7, Suren Tagore Road,
Kolkata – 700 019. (Tel. 2460 4178)

● Nagpur :
63, Opp. Shivaji Science College, Congress
Nagar, **Nagpur – 440 012.** (Tel. 242 1522)

● Nashik :
Dharmaraj Plaza, Old Gangapur Naka,
Gangapur Road, **Nashik – 422 005.**
(Tel. 231 0627)

● Navsari :
3/C, Arvind Nagar Society, Lunsikui Road,
Navsari – 396 445. (Tel. 244 186)

● Patna :
205, Jagdamba Tower, 2nd Floor, Sahdeo Mahto
Marg, Srikrishnapuri, **Patna – 800 001.**
(Tel. 254 0321)

● Pune :
Navneet Bhavan, 1302, Shukrawar Peth, Near
Sanas Plaza, Bajirao Road, **Pune – 411 002.**
(Tel. 2443 1007)

● Surat :
1, Ground Floor, Sri Vallabh Complex,
Kotwal Street, Nanpara, **Surat – 395 001.**
(Tel. 246 3927)

● Vadodara :
Near Hanuman Wadi, Sardar Bhuvan Khancho,
Vadodara – 390 001.

A Selective Glossary of Terms

1. **Icing Sugar** – Sugar which sets easily.
2. **Brown Sugar** – When sugar is heated it becomes brown. Instead of brown sugar one can also use half the amount of plain sugar and the other half amount of jaggery powder. Only plain sugar may also be used.
3. **Drinking Chocolate** – Chocolate Powder.
4. **Bread Crumbs** – Tinu bits of bread; Powdered Toast.
5. **Capsicum** – Big round Chilli.
6. **Canape** – They are small baskets made from maida. They are fried before using them.
7. **Vermicelli** – Very thin long strands or 'Sev' made from rice powder.
8. **Mackroni** – It is made from 'maida'. It is hollow inside like a pipe.
9. **Spaghetti** – It is made from 'maida' and is long and thin like sev.
10. **Noodles** – It is made from 'maida' we have two varieties of noodles – egg noodles and veg. noodles.
11. **Ajinomoto** – It is crystalline. It is mainly used in Chinese recipes. It helps the vegetables to cook faster and retain their taste.
12. **Chilli Sauce** – It is made from chillies. It is available in two colours, green and red. It is mostly used in Chinese recipes.
13. **Soya Sauce** – It is made from soya beans. It is dark brown in colour. It is mostly used in Chinese recipes.
14. **Vinegar** – It is also known as 'Saraka'. It is available in two colours i.e., white and brown. It is also used as a preservative. It is sour in taste. It is also used in Chinese recipes.
15. **Yeast** – It is used in the preparation of items such as breads, pizzas, nans, etc. We have two varietes of yeast, namely dry yeast and fresh yeast.
16. **Silver foil** – It is also known as 'Silver Varakha'. It is very delicate, paper thin like that used with butter-paper. It is used for decorating sweets and desserts and is spread on them along with the butter-paper. Then the butter-paper has to be carefully removed.
17. **Gelatine** – It is used for preparing puddings, salads, ice-creams, etc. It is used for setting these delicacies. One sachet is equal to 1 table spoon.
18. **Jelly** – It is a mixture of gelatine, sugar various colours and essence.
19. **Custard Powder** – It is used as a thickening agent in milk. It is used in items such as puddings, ice-creams, fruit-salads, etc. It is available in various flavours.
20. **Corn flour** – It is white coloured fine flour of corn. It is used as a thickening agent in soups, ice-creams and curries. It is also mixed with maida while making samosas and 'kachoris' to make them more crispy. It is also used while preparing pattices to make them delicious and crispy.
21. **Sodium Benzoate** – It is a kind of preservative. It is used in pickles and other items made from tomato. It is also used in various squashes and juices. For 1 kilo of food item, 1 gram of sodium benzoate is used. Too much use of the preservative should be avoided because it darkens the product.
22. **Potassium – Meta-Bi-Sulphate** – It is also called K.M.S. in short form. It is basically used in 'Sharbats' and tomato ketchup.
23. **Acetic Acid** – It is mostly used in products such as tomato ketchup, carrot pickle, sweet and sour chutney, etc.
24. **Citric Acid** – It is also called 'Limbu Na Phool'. It is used instead of lime Juice. Being in powder form it is used in items where lime juice cannot be used as it would moisten the item. It is used in dishes made from apple, mango, grapes, guava, etc. It can also be used in jams and jellies.

25. **Baking powder** – It is a mixture of corn flour, soda-bi-carb and cream of tartar. It is used as a raising agent in cakes and biscuits.

26. **Cream of Tartar** – It is also used as a raising agent in cakes and biscuits.

27. **Glazed Cherries** – It is prepared from cherries or Karamanda. They are soaked in red sugar syrup and then dried. They are used for decoration in cakes, biscuits, etc.

28. **Tuti-Fruiti** – Small pieces of raw papaya are soaked in coloured sugar syrup, and then dried. They are used for decoration in cakes and biscuits.

29. **Blackjeeri** – Take 1 teaspoon of jeera, and 10 pepper corns. Roast jeera and then grind jeera and pepper to a fine powder. This powder is used for dahiwada.

30. **Lai** – It can be made from maida or rice flour. Mix flour and water. Heat the mixture uptil it is thick. This can be used for pasting samosa covers puffs, etc.

31. **Aluminium Foil** – It is used to wrap lolipops. When the foils are tightly fitted over a bowl, the food inside remains hot.

32. **Eno's Fruit Salt** – It is a mixture of soda-bi-carb and citric acid. It is used in various dishes to make it soft and fluffy.

33. **China Grass** – It helps the ice cream to set faster.

34. **G.M.S. and C.M.S.** – These powders are used for making ice creams. They help to make the ice cream soft and prevent ice formation.

Note : For various recipes given in this book, variations can be made by using.

1. Raw banana instead of potato.
2. Bottle gourd or pumpkin instead of onions.
3. Lime juice in the same amount can be used instead of vinegar.

4. Margarine, ghee, or dalda ghee may be used instead of butter.
5. $1\frac{1}{4}$ table spoons of 'maida' may be used instead of 1 table spoon of corn flour.
6. If cheese has to be sprinkled and kept in the oven, cooking cheese can be used.

Weights and Measures

In most of the recipes the amount of the ingredients is given in the form of tea spoon table spoon and cup. For proper measurements measuring cups and measuring spoons are available in the market. While measuring any ingredient with a tea spoon, tea cup or table spoon measure full to the brim. Seive the flour before measuring. Do not press the ingredient into the cup while measuring or it will give false measurment. Weighing must necessarily be done accurately for all types of cakes and sweets. While for other recipes variation of a few grams is not critical.

1 cup=medium tea cup=210 ml

1 tea spoon	= 1 small spoon – 5 ml
1 table spoon	= 1 big spoon – 15 ml
1 table spoon	= 3 tea spoons
1 cup	= 16 table spoons
1 kilo	= $2\frac{1}{2}$ pounds
1 litre	= 1000 ml

Food Items that can be easily measured by a measuring cup.

Food Item	Weight in grams	Approximate mesurment in cup
Maida	250	2 cups
Rice	250	1 cup
Sugar	250	1 cup
Icing Sugar	250	$1\frac{3}{4}$ cup
Butter	250	1 cup
Paneer	250	1 cup
Grated Cheese	250	2 cups
Cream	250	1 cup

Point to be Remembered For Baking

Use alluminium containers for baking cakes, biscuits, bread, pizza base and baked dishes. Glass microvave containers should be used while using microwave oven. In various recipes the temperature may be given in F° or C°. For our convenience an 'Oven Temperature Chart' is given bellow.

Oven Temperature Chart

F°	OR	C°
225		110
250		125
275		140
300		150
325		165
350		180
375		195
400		210
425		220
450		235
475		250

Know Your Equipment

Fry pan – Tava.

Nutcutter – It is used to powder dry-fruits.

Chillicutter – It is used to grind chillies.

Chop-N-Churn – It is used for cutting vegetables into very small pieces.

Bowl, Casserole – A container in which the food remains hot for a few hours.

Hand Mixer – It is used for whipping and pulp-making.

Peeler – It is used to remove the skin of fruits and vegetables.

Kitchenmaster – It is used for straining soups and fruit juices.

Liquidiser – Used for grinding wet or liquid foods.

Mixer – Used for grinding dry foods.

Glossary of Terms Used in Cooking

To serve – To give.

To crush – To grind the ingredients into powder form.

To coat – To cover food with a thin layer of flour, egg, breadcrumbs or batter.

To beat – To introduce air into a mixture by a repeated vigorous motion, using a wooden spoon, wire whisk, fork or electric beater.

Starters – A small tasty portion of food or a drink served before meals.

Toothpick – It is used for holding small food items.

Grease – To coat the container from inside with any fat like butter, ghee, margarine or hydrogenated oils (like vanaspati) and then sprinkle or coat lightly with flour.

Beans – Green or dry Pulses.

Condensed Milk – A form of concentrated thick and normally sweetened milk.

Wrapper – Paper used to cover food.

Chiller – Place in the fridge having normal temperature where ice is not formed.

Un-mould – For un-moulding or removing a pudding, cake or jelly place the container up-side down.

Churn – Mixing slowly in the mixer.

Pulp – A smooth thick mixture of tomato, fruits or vegetables obtained by mashing them.

Stock – The liquid in which the vegetables are cooked.

Puree – Thick tomato pulp.

Coil – Wrap in circular motion.

INDEX

DISHES

1. SWEETS

1. Kansar — 19
2. Wheat Crack Lapsi (Porridge) — 19
3. Puranpoli (Stuffed Chapati) — 19
4. Tur and Chana Dal Puranpoli — 20
5. Potato Puranpoli — 20
6. Dates (Khajur) Puranpoli — 20
7. Cashewnuts Puranpoli — 21
8. Khajur-Figs Puranpoli — 21
9. Figs Puranpoli — 21
10. Ladava (Sweet Balls) — 21
11. Sweetened Wheat Sev — 22
12. Sev Biranj — 22
13. Sheera (Wheat flour) — 22
14. Rawa Sheera (Special for Satyanarayan Puja) — 22
15. Mung Dal Sheera — 23
16. Shrikhand — 23
17. Plain Mattha — 24

Various Types of Mattha

18. Mango Mattha — 24
19. Kesar Pista Mattha — 24
20. Figs Mattha — 24
21. Green Pista Mattha — 24
22. Strawberry Mattha — 25
23. Pineapple Mattha — 25
24. Dryfruit Mattha — 25
25. Rajbhog Mattha — 25
26. Gulab Mattha — 25
27. Custard Apple Mattha — 25
28. Dudhpak — 25
29. Custard Apple Dudhpak — 26

Various Types of Basundi

30. Plain Basundi — 26
31. Ghebar Basundi — 26
32. Sutarpheni Basundi — 27
33. Rasgulla Basundi — 27
34. Sitafal (Custard Apple) Basundi — 27
35. Indrani Basundi — 27
36. Pineapple Basundi — 27
37. Strawberry Basundi — 28
38. Navaratna Basundi — 28
39. Fruit Salad — 28
40. Dryfruit Salad — 28
41. Cream Salad — 29
42. Sitafal Custard Paneer — 29
43. Dudhpoha — 29
44. Carrot Kheer — 30
45. Sweet Pudla — 30
46. Sukhadi — 30
47. Kuler — 30
48. Panchamrut — 31
49. Penda — 31
50. Mathura Penda — 31
51. Mathadi (Petha) — 31
52. Mohanthal — 32
53. Magaj — 32
54. Mysore Pak — 33
55. Ghughara — 33
56. Sweet Puri (Suvali) — 34
57. Sweet Bundi — 34
58. Gulabjamun — 34
59. Bundi Gulabjamuns — 35
60. Kalajam (Black Jamun) — 35
61. Rasgulla — 36
62. Rasmalai — 36

9. INDIAN VEGETABLES

10. PUNJABI DISHES

+

Coloured Plates

ANERI

MY FAVOURITE
RECIPES

ANERI

MY FAVOURITE
RECIPES

ANERI

MY FAVOURITE
RECIPES

1 SWEETS

1. Kansar [Serves 2]

Ingredients

(1) 1 cup coarsely ground wheat flour

(2) $1\frac{1}{4}$ cup water

(3) 2 table spoons jaggery

(4) 1 table spoon oil + 1 tea spoon oil

(5) 2 tea spoons ghee

(6) Ghee and powdered sugar to taste for serving

Method

(1) For 1 cup wheat flour take $1\frac{1}{4}$ cup of water. Boil the water. Add jaggery.

(2) Add 1 table spoon oil to the flour.

(3) When the water starts boiling take out some water from it and keep it aside. Add 1 tea spoon oil and flour to the remaining water in the pan. Stir it properly with one end of a rolling pin. Cover it with a lid.

(4) Cook on a low flame. Stir with the rolling pin in between. When half cooked, add 2 tea spoons of ghee to it and mix well. Cook it until done.

(5) Extra water may be added if required. Also, extra flour may be added if required.

(6) Sprinkle powdered sugar and add ghee before serving.

2. Wheat Crack Lapsi (Porridge) [Serves 6]

Ingredients

(1) 250 gms wheat crack

(2) 200 gms ghee

(3) 300-350 gms sugar

(4) A few raisins

(5) Cardamom (powder)

(6) A few almonds

(7) A few charolis

(8) A little of khus khus (opium seeds)

Method

(1) Roast wheat cracks in a little ghee till they become light brown. Add hot water. For 1 cup wheat cracks add $3\frac{1}{2}$ cups of water.

(2) Add raisins and let it get cooked on a slow flame. When cooked add sugar and cook again till ghee is separated.

(3) Add a little cardamom powder. Spread it in a plate.

(4) Decorate it with boiled and chopped almonds, khus khus and charoli. Cut into square pieces of equal size.

3. Puranpoli (Stuffed Chapati) [Serves 3 to 4]

Ingredients

(1) 1 cup tuver dal

(2) 1 cup sugar or jaggery

(3) $\frac{1}{2}$ tea spoon cardamom powder

(4) $\frac{1}{2}$ tea spoon khus khus (opium seeds)

(5) $\frac{1}{4}$ tea spoon nutmeg powder

(6) Ghee

(7) $1\frac{1}{4}$ cup wheat flour

Method

(1) Cook Tuver dal in a little water in the pressure cooker, when cooked remove the excess water. Apply a little ghee to the kadhai.

(2) Pour the dal in that kadhai. Add sugar or jaggery in the required proportion and put the mixture on the flame.

(3) If the puran is very soft than add a little ghee to the wheat flour and add that to the dal mixture. Stir constantly. When the mixture is thick enough, i.e., When the spoon remains standing when placed in the centre. If it falls down it means the puran is yet not 'done'.

(4) Add the remaining ingredients of the person.

(5) Set it in a greased plate and allow it to cool.

(6) Knead the dough, a little harder than that for 'Phulkas'. Divide the dough into small balls. Take a ball of the dough and roll a little. Put a small amount of puran in the centre. Cover the puran by drawing up the edges towards the centre. Press the dough on the floured board and roll out into a round roti as large as a saucer. Put the puranpoli on a hot griddle, cook for a minute or two and turn once.

(7) When brown patches appear on both sides remove 'the puranpoli' from the griddle and apply a little ghee. Repeat the process for the rest of the dough.

4. Tur and Chana Dal Puranpoli [Serves 3 to 4]

Ingredients

(1) $\frac{1}{2}$ cup tuver dal
(2) $\frac{1}{2}$ cup chana dal
(3) 1 cup sugar
(4) $\frac{1}{2}$ tea spoon cardamom powder
(5) $\frac{1}{2}$ tea spoon poppy seeds
(6) $\frac{1}{4}$ tea spoon nutmeg powder
(7) A little ghee
(8) $1\frac{1}{4}$ cup wheat flour

Method

The method is same as given for Puranpoli (R. No. 3).

5. Potato Puranpoli [Serves 3 to 4]

Ingredients

(1) 250 grams potatoes
(2) 125 grams sugar
(3) $\frac{1}{2}$ tea spoon cardamom powder
(4) $\frac{1}{2}$ tea spoon poppy seeds
(5) $\frac{1}{4}$ tea spoon nutmeg powder
(6) A little ghee
(7) $1\frac{1}{4}$ cup wheat flour

Method

The method is same as given for Puranpoli (R. No. 3).

6. Dates (Khajur) Puranpoli [Serves 4 to 5]

Ingredients

(1) 250 grams dates
(2) 100 grams sugar
(3) 50 grams cashew nuts
(4) 50 grams mawa
(5) $\frac{1}{4}$ nutmeg (powdered)
(6) A little desiccated coconut
(7) 250 grams maida
(8) A little ghee
(9) A few pistas (powdered) for decoration

Method

(1) Remove seeds from the khajur and crush the pulp. Add and mix the sugar and heat the mixture.

(2) Remove it from the fire, when the mixture thicken's. To this add the 'mawa', cashew powder and nutmeg powder.

(3) If the mixture is soft than additional desiccated coconut or mawa may be added to it.

(4) Knead the dough using maida and ghee. Divide into small balls.

(5) Take a small ball of the dough and roll a little with a rolling pin using a little maida if required. Put a small portion of the mixture in the centre. Cover the mixture by drawing up the edges towards the centre. Press on the floured board and roll out into a thick and small roti. Put the puranpoli on a hot tava, cook for a minute, and turn once. After 1 minute, add a little ghee around the edges, turn again and fry the other side. When brown patches appear on both sides, the 'Puranpoli' is ready.

(6) Decorate with pista powder and serve with a little ghee applied on the 'poli'.

7. Cashewnuts Puranpoli
[Serves 3 to 4]

Ingredients

As per Khajur's Puranpoli. But instead of khajur take the same amount of the cashew powder.

Method

The method is same as given for Khajur's Puranoli.

8. Khajur-Figs Puranpoli
[Serves 4 to 5]

Ingredients

Take 125 grams of khajur and 125 grams of figs. The rest of the ingredients are the same as per Khajur's Puranpoli.

Method

As per Khajur's Puranpoli.

9. Figs Puranpoli [Serves 4 to 5]

Ingredients

As per Khajur's Puranpoli but take the same amount of figs instead of khajur.

Method

As per Khajur's Puranpoli.

10. Ladava (Sweet Balls)
[Makes 15 Ladoos]

Ingredients

(1) 500 grams wheat flour (coarse)
(2) 50 grams chana flour (coarse)
(3) 500 grams ghee
(4) 250 gms powdered sugar (coarse)
(5) 2 tea spoons cardamom powder
(6) 2 table spoons milk
(7) A few poppy seeds (khus khus)

Method

(1) Knead the dough of wheat flour and ghee (approx. 50 grams) using warm water for mixing. Divide the flour into small balls. Shape each portion like a muthiya and press slightly with your fingers.

(2) Fry them in ghee on slow flame.

(3) Crush them in the mixer or by hand. Sieve the mixture through a steel sieve.

(4) Take chana flour in a dish. Add 1 table spoon warm ghee and a little warm milk. Press the flour and leave for sometime. Sieve through a steel sieve. Heat the ghee and roast the chana flour mixture.

(5) When cool, add it to the wheat flour mixture. Add sieved powdered sugar, cardamom powder and a little warm ghee.

(6) Mix properly and make laddo's or balls roll the ladoos in khus khus.

(7) Coarsely powdered sugar can also be added to the ladoos.

(8) Rawa can also be used. Add 75 grams for rawa to wheat flour. For this 300 grams of powdered sugar should be used.

11. Sweetened Wheat Sev

[Serves 3]

Ingredients

(1) 4 servings (circles) wheat sev (200 grams)

(2) Oil

(3) Ghee

(4) Powdered sugar to taste

Method

(1) Add 1 tea spoon of oil to boiling water to prevent the sev from becoming sticky each other break the sev into large pieces and add it to boiling water.

(2) When the sev get cooked, strain it.

(3) While serving add ghee and powdered sugar.

12. Sev Biranj

[Serves 3]

Ingredients

(1) 4 servings (circles) wheat sev (200 grams)

(2) 4 to 5 table spoons ghee

(3) $\frac{1}{2}$ cup milk

(4) 1 to $1\frac{1}{2}$ cup sugar

(5) A little cardamom powder

(6) A few almonds (chopped)

Method

(1) Break the Sev into small pieces and roast in ghee till brown. Add hot water to it and cook on slow flame till sev is soft.

(2) Add $\frac{1}{2}$ cup of milk and sugar to it. Allow it to cook till all water evaporates and ghee is separated.

(3) Spread in a plate and decorate with chopped almonds and cardamom powder.

(4) If the ghee is more than it may be removed keeping the plate in a slanting position.

(5) Raisins may also be used for decoration. For boiling the sev, take water a little less than to cover the sev.

13. Sheera (Wheat flour)

[Serves 4]

Ingredients

(1) 1 cup wheat flour (coarse)

(2) 1 cup ghee (or little less can be used)

(3) 3 cups water

(4) A few raisins

(5) 1 cup sugar

(6) A little cardamom powder

(7) A few almonds

Method

(1) Roast the wheat flour in ghee till light pink in colour.

(2) Add boiling water to it. When the water evaporates add sugar and mix it well with the flour. Cook till it becomes dry and the ghee separates.

(3) Add cardamom powder and decorate with raisins.

(4) Soak the raisins in hot water and boil almonds, use these for decoration.

14. Rawa Sheera (Special for Satyanarayan Puja)

Ingredients

(1) 600 grams rawa

(2) 600 grams ghee

(3) 3 litres milk

(4) 650 grams sugar

(5) A few charoli

(6) A little cardamom powder

(7) A few almonds (soaked in water and grated)

Method

(1) Roast rawa in ghee till light brown.

(2) Add warm milk and cook well on low flame.

(3) When milk evaporates, add sugar and mix it well with the rawa. Cook till it becomes dry. Add cardamom powder.

(4) Decorate with charoli and chopped or grated almonds.

15. Mung Dal Sheera
[Serves 4 to 6]

Ingredients

(1) 1 cup mung dal (with skin)

(2) 1 cup ghee

(3) 1 cup milk

(4) 1 cup water

(5) Yellow food colour as desired

(6) $\frac{3}{4}$ cup sugar

(7) A few almonds and pistas (chopped)

(8) A few strands saffron

(9) $\frac{1}{2}$ tea spoon cardamom powder

Method

(1) Soak the mung dal over night for atleast 6 to 8 hours in water. Remove the outer skin of the dal and grind it in the mixer.

(2) Roast the dal paste in ghee till it is light brown in colour. Boil the milk and water together.

(3) Add the food colour to this boiled milk and water.

(4) Add this to the mung dal paste. Add sugar and mix it well with the mung dal. Cook till it becomes dry, and ghee is separated.

(5) Add some cardamom powder and decorate with chopped almonds, pistas and kesar (saffron) strands.

16. Shrikhand

Ingredients

(1) 1 litre milk

(2) 1 tea spoon fresh curd

(3) 200 grams sugar

(4) A few strands kesar

(5) A little cardamom powder

Method 1

(1) Add 1 tea spoon to luke warm whole milk. Place the bowl near the gas or over a hot bowl or any other warm place to basten the process of curd formation.

(2) Tie the curds in a thin cloth and let all the whey drain.

(3) You can also take a jute sac place a thin cloth over it. Spread the curds over the cloth and let all the whey drain.

(4) Thick 'chakka' would be obtained. About 400 grams of chakka would be obtained.

(5) Now take a little 'chakka' in a sieve or kitchen master and add little sugar. Pass this through the sieve. Repeat the same procedure for the remaining butter and sugar.

(6) Add cardamom powder and kesar (saffron).

Method 2

(1) Add 1 tea spoon curd and 2 tea spoons corn flour dissolved in a little cold milk to luke warm whole milk.

(2) Tie the curds in a thin cloth and let all the whey to drain.

(3) In summer there are chances of the 'chakka' getting sour. So to avoid this one can place the curds in sieve and put this on a bowl. Put this in the freeze to avoid souring.

(4) The amount of sugar should be half the amount of the 'chakka'.

Method 3

Add 1 tea spoon of curd to luke warm whole milk and put this bowl in a casserole. The curds sets faster by this method. Then complete the process as described in the earlier methods.

17. Plain Mattha

[Serves 3 to 4]

Ingredients

(1) 1 kg curd (not sour)
(2) 200 grams sugar
(3) A little cardamom powder

Method

(1) Tie the curd in a thin muslin cloth and let the water drain off. From 1 kg of curds 400 grams of 'chakka' would be obtained.
(2) It the curds are thick, more chakka would be formed.
(3) Sieve the thickened curds and sugar together through sieve or a kitchen master mix properly. Add the cardamom powder and refrigerate it.
(4) We can obtain approximately 550 grams of mattha from this.
(5) The amount of sugar is half the amount of the 'chakka'. Thus, almost 550 grams mattha would be prepared. The proportions of sugar may differ according to requirements and tests.

Various Types of Mattha

18. Mango Mattha

[Serves 4 to 5]

Ingredients

(1) 500 grams plain mattha
(2) 500 grams kesar mango pulp
(3) 2 drops mango essence

Method

(1) Mix all the ingredients and refrigerate the mixture.

(2) The amount of sugar would differ depending upon the sourness or sweetness of the mango pulp.

19. Kesar Pista Mattha

[Serves 4]

Ingredients

(1) 500 grams plain mattha
(2) 75 grams pista (chopped)
(3) A few strands of kesar
(4) 1 tea spoon milk

Method

(1) Dissolve kesar in 1 tea spoon of milk.
(2) Mix all the ingredients and refrigerate the mixture.

20. Figs Mattha [Serves 5]

Ingredients

(1) 150 grams dried figs (chopped finely)
(2) 500 grams plain mattha
(3) A few cardamom seeds

Method

(1) Add the chopped figs to boiling water. When lightly cooked strain the water.
(2) Allow the figs to cool, add them to plain mattha.
(3) Add cardamom and refrigerate the mixture.

21. Green Pista Mattha

[Serves 4]

Ingredients

(1) 500 grams plain mattha
(2) 75 grams pista (chopped)
(3) A few drops of green food colour

Method

Mix all the ingredients and refrigerate the mixture.

22. Strawberry Mattha

[Serves 4]

Ingredients

(1) 500 grams plain mattha
(2) 75 grams strawberries (chopped)
(3) A few cardamom seeds

Method

Mix all the ingredients and refrigerate the mixture.

23. Pineapple Mattha

[Serves 4 to 5]

Ingredients

(1) 500 grams plain mattha
(2) 500 grams pineapple (cut into pieces)
(3) 2 drops of pineapple essence

Method

Mix all the ingredients and refrigerate the mixture.

24. Dryfruit Mattha

[Serves 4 to 5]

Ingredients

(1) 500 grams plain mattha
(2) 75 grams kaju (chopped)
(3) 75 grams raisins
(4) A few cardamom seeds

Method

Mix all the ingredients and refrigerate the mixture.

25. Rajbhog Mattha

[Serves 4 to 5]

Ingredients

(1) 500 grams plain mattha
(2) 50 grams kaju (chopped)
(3) 50 grams raisins
(4) 50 grams strawberry
(5) A few strands of kesar (dissolved in milk)
(6) 100 grams fresh cream

Method

(1) Mix all the ingredients except the cream and refrigerate it.
(2) Just before serving add 100 grams of fresh cream to the mattha.

26. Gulab Mattha

[Serves 3 to 4]

Ingredients

(1) 500 grams plain mattha
(2) Gulabjal a little
(3) A few drops of red food colour
(4) A few cardamom seeds

Method

Mix all the ingredients and refrigerate the mixture.

27. Custard Apple Mattha

[Serves 4 to 5]

Ingredients

(1) 350 grams plain mattha
(2) 1 kg custard apple
(3) A few cardamom seeds

Method

(1) Remove the seeds from custard apple.
(2) Mix the pulp with all other ingredients and refrigerate it.

28. Dudhpak [Serves 2]

Ingredients

(1) 1 litre milk
(2) 1½ tea spoon rice (uncooked)
(3) 100 grams sugar

(4) A few almonds and pistas

(5) A few charolis

(6) A little nutmeg powder

(7) A few strands of keser

Method

(1) Apply a little ghee on the insides of the vessel for making dudhpak. Boil the milk.

(2) Add rice when the milk starts boiling.

(3) When the rice gets cooked, add sugar. Boil the mixture on slow fire with constant stirring till the colour changes. Remove from flame.

(4) Add boiled, chopped almonds. (Almonds can also be soaked for 6 to 8 hours in cold water) before chopping.

(5) Add charoli and cardamom powder.

(6) Dissolve the kesar and nutmeg powder in milk. Serve lukewarm.

29. Custard Apple Dudhpak

[Serves 3]

Ingredients

(1) 1 litre milk

(2) 400 grams custard apple (remove the seeds and take only the pulp)

(3) 80 grams sugar

Method

(1) Boil the milk.

(2) Add sugar. Heat on low fire with constant stirring till sugar dissolves completely.

(3) Cool the mixture. While serving add the custard apple's pulp.

Various Types of Basundi

30. Plain Basundi [Serves 2]

Ingredients

(1) 1 litre milk

(2) 100 grams sugar

(3) A few almonds and pistas (chopped)

(4) A few cardamom seeds

(5) A little nutmeg powder

(6) A few strands of kesar (dissolved in milk)

Method

(1) Apply a little ghee on the insides of the vessel for making basundi. Boil the milk on slow fire with constant stirring to avoid scorching of milk. Boil till it thickens.

(2) Then add sugar. Cook till the sugar dissolves completely.

(3) Remove it from the fire.

(4) Add the remaining ingredients. Serve chilled.

Note : Basundi can also be made first without adding sugar. After cooling powdered sugar may be added.

31. Ghebar Basundi

[Serves 2 to 3]

Ingredients

(1) 1 litre milk

(2) 50 grams ghebar

(3) 100 grams sugar

(4) A few strands of kesar

(5) A few cardamom seeds

(6) A few pistas

(7) A few almonds

(8) A little nutmeg powder

Method

Method is the same as for plain basundi. Only while serving, add small pieces of ghebar to it. Serve chilled.

32. Sutarpheni Basundi

[Serves 2 to 3]

Ingredients

(1) 1 litre milk

(2) 50 grams sutarpheni

(3) 100 grams sugar

(4) A few strands of kesar

(5) A few cardamom seeds

(6) A few pistas

(7) A few almonds

(8) A little nutmeg powder

Method

The method is the same as for plain basundi. Only while serving add small pieces of ghebar to it. Serve chilled.

33. Rasgulla Basundi [Serves 3]

Ingredients

(1) 1 litre milk

(2) 100 grams small rasgullas

(3) A few almonds

(4) A little nutmeg powder

(5) A few pistas

(6) A few cardamom seeds

(7) A few strands of kesar (dissolved in milk)

(8) 100 grams sugar

Method

(1) Put small rasgullas in plain basundi.

(2) Rasgullas can be made of various colours by adding food colour to the rasgulla mawa.

34. Sitafal (Custard Apple) Basundi [Serves 2 to 3]

Ingredients

(1) 1 litre milk

(2) 400 grams sitafal (remove the seeds and use only the pulp)

(3) 100 grams sugar

(4) A few almonds

(5) A little nutmeg powder

(6) A few pistas

(7) A few cardamom seeds

(8) A few strands of kesar (dissolved in milk)

Method

The method is the same as for plain basundi. Then remove the seeds from sitafal. Add this sitafal pulp to the chilled plain basundi.

35. Indrani Basundi

[Serves 2 to 3]

Ingredients

(1) 1 litre milk

(2) 20 grams nylon sev

(3) 100 grams sugar

(4) A few almonds

(5) A little nutmeg powder

(6) A few pistas, a few cardamom seeds

(7) Few strands of kesar (dissolved)

Method

(1) Roast the sev in ghee till it becomes light brown colour.

(2) Add this to the plain basundi.

36. Pineapple Basundi

[Serves 2 to 3]

Ingredients

(1) 1 litre milk

(2) 200 grams tinned pineapple

(3) 100 grams sugar

(4) A few almonds

(5) A little nutmeg powder

(6) A few pistas

(7) A few cardamom seeds

(8) a few strands of kesar (dissolved in milk)

Method

(1) Cut the pineapple into small pieces.

(2) Add them to the prepared plain basundi.

37. Strawberry Basundi [Serves 2 to 3]

Ingredients

(1) 1 litre milk

(2) 50 grams strawberries

(3) 100 grams sugar

(4) A few almonds

(5) A little nutmeg powder

(6) A few pistas

(7) A few strands of kesar (dissolved in milk)

Method

(1) After preparing plain basundi add kesar, pistas and nutmeg to it.

(2) While serving, add strawberry pieces to plain basundi.

38. Navaratna Basundi [Serves 2 to 3]

Ingredients

(1) 1 litre milk

(2) 100 grams chana flour

(3) 100 grams sugar

(4) A few almonds

(5) A little nutmeg powder

(6) A few pistas

(7) A few cardamom seeds

(8) A few strands of kesar (dissolved in milk)

Method

(1) Prepare bundi using chana flour in four different colours.

(2) Add this to plain basundi.

39. Fruit Salad [Serves 4]

Ingredients

(1) 1 litre milk

(2) 100 grams sugar

(3) 1 table spoon custard powder

(4) 100 grams grapes

(5) 2 bananas

(6) 1 apple

(7) 2 chikoos

(8) 250 grams alfanso mango

(9) Fresh cream or ice-cream (optional)

(10) A few kesar strands

Method

(1) Apply a little ghee all over in side of the vessel for making custard. Boil the milk on a low flame.

(2) Dissolve the custard powder in a little cold milk and add this to the boiling milk.

(3) Boil for few minutes. Remove from fire and let it cool.

(4) Add all fruits, cut into small pieces.

(5) Cream and ice-cream may also be added. Kesar ice-cream may also be added to give a fine colour to the fruit salad.

40. Dry Fruit Salad [Serves 5 to 6]

Ingredients

(1) 1½ litres milk

(2) 50 grams custard powder

(3) 150 grams sugar

(4) 50 grams kaju

(5) 20 grams raisins

(6) 80 grams figs

(7) 50 grams walnuts

(8) A few almonds

(9) A few cardamom seeds

(10) Few strands of kesar

(11) A few pistas

(12) 100 grams of vanilla ice-cream

Method

(1) Boil the milk with constant stirring. Dissolve the custard powder in a little cold milk and add it to boiling milk.

(2) Add sugar. Cook till the sugar dissolves completely. Remove from fires cool and refrigerate it.

(3) Chop kaju into small pieces. Soak kaju and raisins in water for 1 hour. Then strain them.

(4) Soak figs, cut into small pieces for 6 hours then strain and refrigerate them.

(5) Soak almonds for 6 hours in water. Remove the skin. If it does not peel off easily then boil the almonds for a few minutes.

(6) Chop the almonds and the walnuts and powder the cardamom. Dissolve kesar in little milk. Chop the pistas into small pieces.

(7) Add all ingredients except figs and ice-cream to milk.

(8) While serving add figs and ice-cream. Serve chilled.

41. Cream Salad [Serves 5]

Ingredients

(1) 100 ml milk

(2) 50 grams sugar

(3) 500 ml cream

(4) Bananas

(5) Apples

(6) Chikoo

(7) Pineapple

(8) Cherries

(9) 50 grams vanilla ice-cream

Method

(1) Boil the milk. Add sugar and cook it for sometime till sugar malts. Cool it.

(2) Then add cream and fruits cut into small pieces and ice-cream. For 500 ml cream add 1 kg fruits.

42. Sitafal Custard Paneer

[Serves 4]

Ingredients

(1) 1 litre milk

(2) 2 table spoons custard powder

(3) 100 grams sugar

(4) 50 grams paneer

(5) Ghee proportionally

(6) 2 sitafals

(7) A few pistas

(8) A few cardamom seeds

Method

(1) Boil the milk. Dissolve custard powder in a little cold milk. Add this to the boiling milk. Add sugar to it.

(2) Cut the paneer into small pieces and fry them in ghee. Add them to the boiling milk. Remove the seeds from sitafal.

(3) Crush sitafal pulp with a little amount of chilled milk. Add this sitafal pulp to cold milk.

(4) Add chopped pista and cardamom powder.

43. Dudhpoha [Serves 4]

Ingredients

(1) 1 litre milk

(2) 250 grams sugar

(3) 300 grams poha

(4) A few cardamom seeds (powdered)

(5) A few strands of kesar

Method

(1) Boil the milk. Add sugar and cook on low flame till sugar dissolves completely. Cool it.

(2) Wash the poha and add to the cooled milk. When the poha becomes soft, put in the refrigerator for some time.

(3) Add cardamom powder and kesar before serving.

44. Carrot Kheer [Serves 4]

Ingredients

(1) 1 litre milk

(2) 150 grams sugar

(3) 50 grams rice

(4) 100 grams carrots

(5) A few cardamom seeds

(6) A little ghee

Method

(1) Cook the rice separately. Boil milk and sugar together. Boil till it thickens. Then add the rice to the boiling milk. Boil the mixture for a few minutes and then remove it from the fire.

(1) Add some cardamom powder. Plain kheer is ready. For making carrot kheer.

(3) Grate the carrots and roast it in very little amount of ghee for a few minutes.

(4) Then add milk and sugar. Boil for some time till carrots gets cooked. Then add cardamom powder.

45. Sweet Pudla [Serves 4 to 5]

Ingredients

(1) 250 grams wheat flour

(2) 250 grams jaggery

(3) Ghee or oil

(4) A few pepper corn

Method

(1) Make jaggery water by dissolving the jaggery in water. Mix wheat flour, pepper corn and jaggery water. Keep the batter aside for 2-3 hours. Heat a griddle. Drop a spoonful of the batter and spread lightly.

(2) Add ghee or oil the edges of the pudla on both sides. Serve hot.

46. Sukhadi [Serves 3 to 4]

Ingredients

(1) 250 grams wheat flour (coarse)

(2) 250 grams ghee

(3) 200 grams jaggery

Method

(1) Roast the wheat flour in ghee on slow flame till it becomes light brown in colour.

(2) Remove it from the flame. Cut the jaggery into thin slices. Heat the remaining ghee. Add the jaggery to it when the jaggery melts, add the roasted wheat flour and cook for sometime. Grease a plate. Pour the contents into it. Press well by using a katori. Put cuts when it is hot cut into small square pieces when cool.

47. Kuler [Serves 3 to 4]

Ingredients

(1) 1 cup bajari flour

(2) $\frac{1}{4}$ cup ghee

(3) $\frac{1}{2}$ cup powdered sugar

Method

(1) Cream ghee in a plate by hand till it becomes light and fluffy. Add powdered sugar and continue creaming till light.

(2) Add the bajara flour and mix well. Make small balls (laddoo's).

(3) Instead of powdered sugar fine jaggery powder may also be used.

48. Panchamrut [Serves 10]

Ingredients

(1) 4 table spoons curd

(2) 2 table spoons powdered sugar

(3) 4 table spoons milk

(4) 2 table spoons honey

(5) 1 table spoon ghee

(6) A few tulsi leaves

Method

(1) Beat the curd and mix all the other ingredients except tulsi leaves.

(2) Lastly, add washed tulsi leaves.

49. Penda [Makes 10 Pendas]

Ingredients

(1) 250 grams mawa

(2) 125 grams powdered sugar

(3) A few cardamom seeds

(4) Kesar strands

Method

(1) Grate the mawa. Heat it for a few minutes and let it cool. Then add the powdered sugar and cardamom powder.

(2) For preparing kesari penda's add kesar dissolved in milk. Mix properly and make pendas.

(3) Various designs may be made on the pendas for decoration.

50. Mathura Penda [Makes 30 Pendas]

Ingredients

(1) 250 grams mawa

(2) 100 grams sugar

(3) 4 to 5 cloves

(4) A little cardamom powder

(5) 25 grams powdered sugar

Method

(1) Remove the mawa from the refrigerator one hour before preparing. knead the mawa well.

(2) Mix the sugar and again knead well for 10 minutes. Heat it with stirring constantly.

(3) When the ghee separates and the mawa is coffee brown in colour, add the cloves and cardamom powder. Remove it from the flame and add some powdered sugar. Spread the remaining powdered sugar in a plate.

(4) Make balls from the mixture when it is still hot. Roll the balls in the remaining powdered sugar. The balls will harden next day.

Note : The mawa has to be removed from the flame when it is still slightly soft enough even if the colour has not changed or ghee does not separates. Otherwise the penda's would turn out to be very hard.

51. Mathadi (Petha) [Serves 3 to 4]

Ingredients

(1) 100 grams maida

(2) 150 grams ghee

(3) 150 grams sugar

Method

(1) Add sufficient ghee to the maida and knead the dough well.

(2) Divide the dough into small equal parts. Roll out each part into a thick roti. Cut them into strips horizontally and then cut it from centre. Place the strips on a piece of paper for drying.

(3) Fry them on a slow flame till light brown in colour.

(4) Prepare the strips in the morning if the syrup has to be prepared in the evening, so that the strips are cooled completely.

(5) Mix the sugar and water. The amount of water should be just enough to soak the sugar. Make a thick sugar syrup. To test the syrup, place a drop on the plate. The drop should remain as it is i.e., it should not spread.

(6) Put the strip inside the syrup (not all) and mix very fast.

(7) The remaining syrup would separate out. Mix water to it and again prepare a thick syrup. Repeat the same procedure with the remaining strips.

52. Mohanthal [Serves 6 to 7]

Ingredients

(1) 250 grams chana flour (coarse)
(2) 200 grams ghee
(3) A little milk
(4) 300 grams sugar
(5) A few strands of kesar
(6) Few drops yellow food colour
(7) A few cardamom seeds (powdered)
(8) A few charolis
(9) A few almonds, a few pistas

Method

(1) Take the flour in a dish. Add warm ghee and warm milk. Press the flour and leave it for a few minutes. Sieve through a steel seive.

(2) Roast the flour on a slow flame in ghee till it becomes light brown.

(3) In other vessel prepare the sugar syrup using sugar and enough water. The syrup should form $1\frac{1}{2}$ thread.

(4) Add kesar, food colour, cardamom powder and roasted flour to this syrup. Stir properly, spread the mixture on a greased plate.

(5) Decorate with charolis, chopped pistas and almonds. Add a little warm ghee on it. Cool and cut it into pieces.

Note : The syrup has to be made properly for good mohanthal.

53. Magaj [Serves 6]

Ingredients

(1) 250 grams chana flour (coarse)
(2) 250 grams ghee
(3) A little milk
(4) 250 grams powdered sugar
(5) A few cardamom seeds
(6) A few almonds
(7) A few pistas, a few charolis

Method

(1) Take the flour in a dish. Add warm ghee and warm milk. Press the flour and mix it well and leave aside for sometime. Sieve through a steel sieve.

(2) Take a frying pan and roast the flour in ghee till it becomes brown. Remove it from the flame.

(3) When it becomes cool add powdered sugar, cardamom powder and mix well.

(4) Make small ladoo's or spread it in a greased plate and when settled, cut into small cut pieces decorate with chopped almonds, pistas and charolis.

54. Mysore Pak [Serves 5 to 6]

Ingredients

(1) 1 cup groundnuts
(2) 1 cup sugar
(3) $1\frac{1}{4}$ cup ghee
(4) A few cardamom seeds
(5) A little cardamom powder

Method

(1) If groundnuts are used then roast them, remove the skin. When cold, pound then in a nutcutter or in a grinder to a fine powder.
(2) If almonds are used instead of groundnuts then boil them, remove the skin, dry them and then powder them.
(3) Prepare sugar syrup using sugar and enough water. It should be $1\frac{1}{2}$ thread sugar syrup.
(4) Add groundnut powder and stir for some time.
(5) Add little warm ghee at a time to this.
(6) When the ghee separates add cardamom powder and set it in a plate. Decorate with cardamom seeds and sprinkle some water. So that a net like design is formed.
(7) Mysore can be made of various types like from kaju, almonds, pista, charoli, desiccated coconut etc.

Variation

Malai Mysore :

(1) Mix malai and sugar. Heat it while constantly stirring the mixture in one direction.
(2) When the ghee separates add cardamom powder.

55. Ghughara [Serves 6 to 7]

Ingredients

(1) 125 grams rawa

(2) 125 grams ghee
(3) A few cardamom seeds
(4) 150 grams powdered sugar
(5) A little khus khus (opium seeds)
(6) 250 grams maida

Method

(1) Roast the rawa in ghee till it becomes brown and cool it.
(2) Add the cardamom powder, khus khus and powdered sugar to the rawa.
(3) Add a little ghee to the maida. Rub it well. Knead the dough using cold water. Divide the dough into small balls. Take each ball of the dough and roll it into a small 'puri'. Put a small portion of the prepared mixture in it. Cover the mixture by drawing up the edges of the puri towards, each other press the edges lightly. If the edges do not stick then use a little milk for sticking it.
(4) Make the ghugharas in various shapes and fry them in ghee.
(5) Measure the sugar a little more amount than rawa (use 125 grams ghee for adding and frying).

Variation

(1) Instead of rawa, mawa can also be used. Roast the mawa for a few minutes. Remove it from the flame. Add cardamom, raisins and powdered sugar.
(2) Cool it.
(3) Roll out puris from maida dough (knead the dough with cold water). Fill the mixture in the centre. Cover it by drawing up the edges of the puri towards each other. Press the edges lightly. Decorate the edges using a fork or shape it like ghughara.
(4) For religious purposes milk can be used instead of water to knead the dough.

56. Sweet Puri (Suvali)

Ingredients

(1) 250 grams maida
(2) 125 grams sugar
(3) A little milk
(4) 1 tea spoon til (sesame seeds)
(5) A little cardamom powder
(6) 150 grams ghee

Method

(1) Boil milk and sugar. Add ghee to the maida and rub well. Add sweetened milk and knead into a hard dough.

(2) Add til, and cardamom powder. Knead well.

(3) Divide the dough into small balls. Roll each balls into thin puris and fry on a low flame. The puris should be white and crispy.

57. Sweet Bundi [Serves 4]

Ingredients

(1) 1 cup chana flour (very fine)
(2) 2 table spoons coarse chana flour
(3) 150 grams ghee, a few raisins
(4) 200 grams sugar (1 cup sugar)
(5) A few strands kesar and a few drops yellow food colour
(6) 1 tea spoon cardamom powder
(7) A few raisins

Method

(1) Mix 2 table spoons coarse chana flour, 1 cup fine chana flour and 1 tea spoon ghee. Prepare a batter with water.

(2) It should be little watery keep it aside for sometime. If the batter is too thick add extra water. If it is too thin, extra flour may be added. Melt ghee in a fry pan. When it is hot enough fry the bundi. Use a spoon and a frying spoon to make bundi's.

(3) Use the spoon to place the batter on the frying spoon. But the spoon should not touch the frying spoon.

(4) After each time clean the frying spoon.

(5) Prepare the sugar syrup by dissolving sugar in enough water. Make two threads sugar syrup. For testing the syrup place a drop in a plate, if it spread's lightly then the syrup is ready.

(6) Add kesar, colour and cardamom powder. If desired raisins may be added to the syrup.

(7) Add the bundi to a little warm sugar syrup. Two or three lots of bundi may be added at a time.

(8) If you find the bundi to be very sweet then put the bundi for a little less time in the syrup. Place the plate of bundi little tiled so that the extra sugar syrup separates out.

(9) Stir the bundi properly to prevent sticking. Ladoo's can also be made from this bundi.

58. Gulabjamun [Makes 35 to 40 Gulabjamuns]

Ingredients

(1) 250 grams gulabjamun khoya (mawa)
(2) 50 grams rawa
(3) 2 table spoons maida
(4) A pinch of soda-bi-carb
(5) A little few cardamom powder
(6) Ghee for frying
(7) 400 grams sugar
(8) A few drops rose essence
(9) A few rose petals for decoration

Method

(1) Soak the rawa in a little milk. Grate the mawa.

(2) Mix the maida, soaked rawa, soda-bi-carb and cardamom powder. Knead well. Divide the dough into small balls.

(3) Fry the balls on a low flame stirring them constantly for even browning. See that the balls do not crack. If they crack, add a little maida.

(4) For preparing sugar syrup add water to sugar and make a half thread sugar syrup. For the syrup after the sugar dissolves in the water, boil the mixture for a few minutes. The syrup is ready.

(5) Add the balls when they cool down completely. After adding all the balls to the syrup boil it for 5 minutes. Then add rose essence. Rose petals also may be added for decoration.

(6) After 5 to 8 hours delicious gulab-jamuns are ready. It requires 5 to 8 hours for the jamuns to absorb the syrup completely.

Variation

Instead of using 50 grams rawa, 50 grams of maida may be used for making good gulabjamuns.

59. Bundi Gulabjamuns

[Serves 6 to 8]

Ingredients

(1) 50 grams chana flour bundi (according to R. No. 57)

(2) 100 grams small gulabjamuns (according to R. No. 58)

(3) A few raisins

Method

(1) Make the bundi according to the recipe given above. Add raisins to it. Make very small gulabjamun according to the recipe given above. They should be a little bigger than the bundi.

(2) While serving, remove the gulab-jamun from the syrup. Mix them with bundi. Heat slightly.

60. Kalajam (Black Jamun)

[Makes 20 Kalajams]

Ingredients

(1) 1 litre milk

(2) 1 lime

(3) 250 grams gulabjamun mawa

(4) 50 grams rawa

(5) 2 tea spoons maida

(6) A pinch of soda-bi-carb

(7) 1 table spoon powdered sugar

(8) A few drops of yellow colour (or any other that may be preferred)

(9) Ghee for frying

(10) 500 grams sugar

(11) Desiccated coconut

(12) A few cherries

(13) A few pistas

(14) A few cardamom seeds (powdered)

Method

(1) Boil the milk. Cool it for 2 to 3 minutes. Add the juice of one lime to make paneer. If proper paneer is not formed, add some more lemon juice. Strain it and separate the paneer.

(2) Wash this paneer with plain water. Paneer should always be made one day before or atleast two hours ahead.

(3) Grate the mawa, mix the mawa and the paneer and knead well. Soak the rawa in very little milk for 10 minutes. Add this to the mawa.

(4) Add 2 tea spoons maida, soda-bi-carb, 1 table spoon powdered sugar knead well again. Spread this in a plate.

(5) Divide it into four equal parts.

(6) Take one part out of this and add a

few drops of yellow colour to it. Any other colour may also be used according to choice. Dark yellow or dark orange colour goes very well with the jamuns. Take the remaining three parts. Divide each part into smaller parts. Make a small ball out of each small part.

(7) Also divide the yellow dough into very small parts. Make a small ball out of each. Flatten the white balls between the palms.

(8) Put a yellow ball in the centre and roll again. Fry on a low flame while stirring constantly for even browning. See that the balls do not crack. If they crack, add a little maida to the white portion balls.

(9) For preparing sugar syrup add water to sugar. After the sugar dissolves, boil for a few minutes.

(10) Put the balls in the syrup when they are hot. After 5 or 6 hours remove the jamuns from the syrup.

(11) Roll the jamuns in desiccated coconut. Decorate with pistas (chopped), cherries or cardamom.

61. Rasgulla
[Makes 14 to 15 Rasgulla]

Ingredients

(1) 1 litre milk (cow's milk)

(2) Juice of 1 lemon

(3) $1\frac{1}{2}$ cup sugar

(4) 3 cup water

Method

(1) Boil the milk, cool and refrigerate it. Remove the malai the next day and again boil it.

(2) Take $\frac{1}{4}$ cup of water, to this add the juice of 1 lime. Cool the milk for 2–3 minutes. Then go on adding the lime mixture until paneer is formed.

(3) Strain it through a muslin cloth.

(4) Add 1 tea spoon of sugar to the paneer and knead it well until it becomes soft. Make small balls out of this.

(5) In a vessel take $1\frac{1}{2}$ cups of sugar and enough of water to make sugar syrup. Make a very thin sugar syrup. Put the balls in it. Boil for 15 minutes. Cover it with a lid for boiling.

(6) Remove from the flame. Add 1 cup of cold water and refrigerate it.

Note : Instead of lime juice $\frac{1}{2}$ tea spoon of citric acid or 2 table spoons of vinegar dissolved in a little water may also be used.

62. Rasmalai [Serves 5 to 6]
Ingredients

(1) $1\frac{1}{2}$ litres milk (cow's milk)

(2) 150 grams sugar

(3) 14 to 15 rasgullas

(4) A few almonds

(5) A few pistas

(6) A few strands of kesar (dissolved in a little milk)

Method

(1) Boil the milk till it is reduced to half of the quantity. Add sugar. Remove the syrup from rasgullas by slightly squeezing them.

(2) Add them to the boiling milk. Boil for 2 minutes.

(3) Remove from the flame and refrigerate. While serving decorate with chopped pistas, almonds and kesar.

63. Halwasan [Makes 20 pieces]
Ingredients

(1) 1 litre milk

(2) 3 tea spoons curd

(3) 2 table spoons gum

(4) Ghee

(5) 4 table spoons wheat flour (coarse)

(6) 300 grams sugar

(7) $\frac{1}{2}$ nutmeg

(8) A few cardamom seeds (powdered)

(9) A few strands of kesar

(10) A few charolis

(11) A few almonds

Method

(1) Boil the milk. Add curd till paneer is formed. Crush the gum to medium size pieces.

(2) On the tava, heat 2 tea spoons ful ghee and roast the gum till fully pops-up. Add the gum to the milk and stir.

(3) Roast the wheat flour in about 3–4 table spoons of ghee on a slow flame until they become light brown. Add this mixture to the milk and stir vigorously.

(4) Add about 150 grams of sugar to the milk. Heat the remaining 150 grams of sugar till it forms a brown liquid. Add this to the milk.

(5) When it starts thickening add powdered nutmeg, cardamom, kesar and almonds. When it further thickness, but it should not stick to the spoon remove the mixture from fire. Let it cool for sometime.

(6) Roll them into small balls. Flatten them little like pattice. Decorate with boiled, peeled and chopped almonds and charolis. (Two almond chips on either side and charoli in between.)

64. Jalebi [Serves 4]

Ingredients

(1) 1 cup maida

(2) 1 tea spoon curd

(3) 4 tea spoons chana flour

(4) A pinch of soda

(5) A little ghee

(6) $1\frac{1}{4}$ cup sugar

(7) A few strands of kesar

(8) A few drops of food colour

Method

(1) Make batter of maida and curd. Leave it for 24 hours. In winters leave it for $1\frac{1}{2}$ days before. The batter should not be too thin.

(2) Add chana flour and soda. Fill the batter in a special jalebi glass having a hole at the bottom.

(3) Heat the ghee in frying pan. When hot make jalebies in circular shape starting from outside and moving towards centre. If the glass is full of batter, thick jalebies are formed while if it has less batter thin jalebies would be formed.

(4) Make $1\frac{1}{2}$ to 2 threads thick sugar syrup. Put the jalebies in it.

(5) Let them soak the sugar syrup till another lot of fried jalebies ready. Remove the first lot of jalebies from the sugar syrup. Keep the sugar syrup hot by keeping it on a slow flame. If it thickens, a little water may be added. Remove the syrup from fire.

Note : (1) For 100 grams maida use 200 grams of sugar. For making batter about 130 ml of water can be used.

(2) A jalebi maker can be used for making jalebies. Do not store it in closed container or the jalebies would lose their crispness and soften.

65. Manbhavan Ladoo

[Makes 22 to 25 Ladoos]

Ingredients

(1) 100 grams mawa

(2) 125 grams desiccated coconut

(3) 100 grams powdered sugar

(4) A few cardamom seeds (powdered)

(5) 5 table spoons milk

(6) A few drops of red and yellow food colour

(7) A few tutifruiti pieces

Method

(1) Roast the mawa for 3 to 4 minutes. Cool it and add desiccated coconut, powdered sugar and cardamom powder.

(2) Add milk and divide the mixture into two parts. Add yellow colour to one part and red colour to other. Mix and make small ladoos out of it.

(3) Roll them in desiccated coconut.

(4) Decorate with contrast coloured tutifruiti.

66. Roller Coaster [Makes 24 pieces]

Ingredients

1. (1) 20 marie biscuits

    (2) 1 table spoon drinking chocolate

    (3) 1 table spoon coco powder

    (4) 3 table spoons malai

    (5) 3 table spoons icing sugar

    (6) A little milk

2. (1) 100 grams desiccated coconut

    (2) 3 table spoons malai

    (3) 3 table spoons icing sugar

Method

(1) Powder the marie biscuits in the grinder. Mix all the ingredients as mentioned in 1. Add a little milk if required and knead into a dough.

(2) Mix all the ingredients as mentioned in 2 and knead into a dough.

(3) Now divide both the doughs into two equal parts. Take one part of the biscuit dough.

(4) Place it on a sheet of plastic. Place other plastic sheet above it and roll it with a rolling pin.

(5) Remove the upper plastic and place a ball of desiccated coconut. Again place the plastic and roll.

(6) Remove the plastic. Start rolling it by slowly removing the plastic.

(7) Put these roll in plastic and refrigerate it for 1 hour. While serving cut them slightly slanting.

Note : (1) The rolled roti should be 4" thick. You can make 12 pieces from one roll.

(2) Avoid using too much malai to the Marie Biscuit Powder as will not be able to roll the roti properly. It would crack. If such thing happens then add additional 2 biscuits (powdered) to it.

67. Khajur Roll [Makes 25 rolls]

Ingredients

(1) 200 grams khajur

(2) 1 table spoon malai

(3) 5 marie biscuits

(4) $\frac{1}{2}$ cup dryfruits (almonds, pistas, walnuts)

Method

(1) Remove the seeds from the khajur, wash and clean them.

(2) Heat the malai in a pan and add the chopped khajur to it. Press lightly.

(3) When khajur softens add powdered marie biscuits. Keep some powdered biscuits aside.

(4) Add all nuts whole. Only almonds may also be added.

(5) When done, remove the stuff from the flame.

(6) Make small rolls out of the mixture. Decorate with almond pieces and roll them it in the biscuit powder. Put this roll in plastic or aluminium foil and refrigerate it. Cut into small pieces and serve.

Variation

(1) For fasting instead of biscuits groundnut powder or desiccated coconut may be used.

(2) Roll the rolls in the desiccated coconut or groundnut powder.

(3) Dry ginger powder, ganthoda and khus khus may also be added to make them tasty.

68. Coco Roll
[Makes 22 to 25 rolls]

Ingredients

(1) $1\frac{1}{2}$ packets glucose biscuits (or marie)
(2) 1 tea spoon cocoa powder
(3) 2 tea spoons drinking chocolate
(4) 100 grams mawa
(5) 100 grams powdered sugar
(6) 100 grams desiccated coconut

Method

(1) Powder marie biscuits, sieve biscuit powder together with the cocoa powder and the drinking chocolate.

(2) Grate the mawa. Mix powdered sugar and desiccated coconut to it. Keep some desiccated coconut aside.

(3) Knead a hard dough using little milk. Make small balls or rolls. Roll them in the desiccated coconut.

Note : (1) If you don't want to add mawa, a little milk, ghee or malai may be used to make the dough for the rolls.

(2) Instead of biscuits 125 grams of groundnut powder may be used. This can be consumed during fasting.

69. Kaju-Anjeer Roll
[Makes 12 to 14 rolls]

Ingredients

(1) 100 grams figs (Anjeer)
(2) 50 grams sugar
(3) 50 grams mawa
(4) 1 tea spoon ghee
(5) 5–6 cardamom
(6) Little nutmeg
(7) 150 grams kaju (cashewnut)
(8) 80 grams sugar
(9) 1 table spoon milk
(10) Silver foil for decoration (warakha)

Method

(1) Chop the figs into small pieces. Add a little water to it and soak for 1 hour. Add 50 grams of sugar and heat it for a few minutes.

(2) When it thickes add the mawa and a little ghee. When it is thick enough, remove it from flame, add cardamom and nutmeg powder. Make rolls.

(3) Powder the kajus finely and sieve the powder.

(4) Make sugar syrup using 80 grams of sugar and some water. Add 1 table spoon milk and remove the dirt of the sugar. Make $1\frac{1}{2}$ thread sugar syrup. Add the kaju powder to this.

(5) Mix properly. Remove from it the flame. Add cardamom and make big balls.

(6) Roll them into long rotis. Cut these into small rectangles.

(7) Take a rectangular piece and put the anjeer roll in the centre and roll it.

(8) Repeat the same with the remaining rectangular pieces and anjeer rolls. To make the kaju roti, it may be rolled between two plastics. Decorate with silver foil.

(9) Instead of making rolls, anjeer mawa can be stuffed in the kaju mawa and balls can also be made. Decorate them with silver foil.

70. Kaju-Anjeer (Khajur) Balls
[Makes 20 to 25 balls]

Ingredients

(1) 250 grams khajur (dates)
(2) 100 grams anjeer (figs)
(3) A little ghee
(4) $\frac{1}{4}$ cup milk
(5) 1 tea spoon sugar
(6) A little khus khus (opium seeds)
(7) 100 grams sugar (for syrup)
(8) 250 grams mawa
(9) 125 grams kaju powder
(10) A few cardamom seeds (powdered)
(11) A little arrowroot flour or milk powder
(12) Silver foil (warakha)

Method

(1) Wash the khajur and the figs. Remove seeds from the khajur and chop both of the dry fruits into small pieces.

(2) Heat a little ghee in a pan and roast the khajur and figs. When it becomes soft, add milk, 1 tea spoon of sugar and a little khus khus.

(3) When cooked properly, remove the mixture from the flame and allow it to cool. Grind it with a hand-mixer.

(4) Make syrup with sugar and milk. Roast the mawa with little ghee.

(5) When the sugar syrup is ready,

remove it from flame and add to it the kaju powder, mawa and cardamom powder. If it is soft, a little arrowroot flour or milk powder may be added. Make balls of khajur and figs mawa. Divide the kaju mawa into small portions.

(6) Take each portion and stuff the khajur, anjeer balls in the centre. Make a ball again.

(7) Decorate with silver foil. If the balls are very soft, refrigerate them.

71. Kajukatri
[Makes 20 to 25 pieces]

Ingredients for method 1

(1) 200 grams (2 cups) kaju powder
(2) 1 cup powdered sugar
(3) $\frac{1}{2}$ cup milk
(4) A little cardamom powder
(5) 1 tea spoon ghee
(6) Silver foil for decoration

Method 1

(1) Apply a little ghee inside the vessel and mix milk and powdered sugar. Boil it.

(2) After it boils for one or two times add the kaju powder and the cardamom powder. When it is thick enough like a dough, remove it from the flame. Add 1 tea spoon of ghee to the dough.

(3) Apply a little ghee to a plate and the rolling pin. Roll out the dough into a thick roti.

(4) When cool cut into small pieces. Instead of kaju, badam may be also used to make badamkatri. Decorate it with silver foil.

Ingredients for method 2

(1) 100 grams kaju
(2) 100 grams sugar

(3) 1 tea spoon ghee

(4) Silver foil for decoration

Method 2

(1) Make sugar syrup with sugar and enough water. Add little milk and remove the dirt of the sugar. Make three thread sugar syrup. Boil till it is thick, like a drop.

(2) Powder the kaju and add it to the sugar syrup. Mix properly, when it is thick enough like a dough. Remove it from the flame.

(3) Add 1 tea spoon ghee to the dough. Roll out into a roti between two plastics. Decorate with sliver foil. Cut into small pieces.

72. Chocolate Coconut Kajukatri
[Makes 25 to 30 pieces]

Ingredients

(1) 250 grams kaju powder

(2) 125 grams sugar for coating

(3) 1 table spoon drinking chocolate

(4) 1 table spoon cocoa

(5) 70 grams icing sugar

(6) 60 grams dalda ghee

(7) A few drops of vanilla essence

(8) Silver foil for decoration

(9) A few strands kesar

Method

(1) Make sugar syrup from the sugar and enough water. Add a little milk. Remove the dirt from the syrup. Make three thread sugar syrup.

(2) When ready, add the kaju powder. Remove it from the flame. Knead the dough well. Divide into big portions. Apply little ghee on the plate and roll them into a thick roti form.

(3) Sieve the drinking chocolate, cocoa and the icing sugar.

(4) Heat dalda ghee slightly in a pan. Remove it from flame. Add the mixture of icing sugar.

(5) When it cools slightly, add vanilla essence. Mix properly. Coat this properly on the kaju roti. Apply it in the form of a even layer on all sides.

(6) Cool, decorate with silver foil and cut into small pieces.

Note : A few kesar strands may be added to the kaju mawa, to make it yellow in colour.

73. Kaju-Pista Roll
[Makes 20 to 25 rolls]

Ingredients

(1) 250 grams kaju

(2) 125 grams sugar

(3) 1 tea spoon ghee

(4) 100 grams pista

(5) 50 grams sugar

(6) A few drops of green edible colour

(7) A little nutmeg powder

(8) Silver foil for decoration

Method

(1) Powder the kaju. Make sugar syrup from 125 grams sugar. Add a little milk to remove the dirt from sugar. Boil till it is thick like a drop. Make three thread sugar syrup.

(2) Add the kaju powder. Mix properly. When it is thick enough like a dough remove it from the fire. Add 1 tea spoon ghee. Mix properly.

(3) Crush the pistas. Make sugar syrup from 50 grams sugar. Boil till it is thick like a drop. Make three thread sugar syrup.

(4) Add the pista powder, a little edible green colour and nutmeg powder. Mix properly. When ready remove the mixture from the flame and add 1 tea spoon full of ghee.

(5) Divide the kaju mawa into big balls and roll the ball between two plastics. Make rolls from the pista mawa. Place a roll in the centre of the kaju roti.

(6) Roll the kaju roti into a roll form. Flatten it a little with hand. Decorate the roll with sliver foil.

(7) It can be served as a roll or cut into small pieces and served.

74. Kesar-Pista Roll
[Makes 20 to 25 rolls]
Ingredients

Mix kesar with kaju mawa.

Method

According to the Kaju-Pista Roll described above.

75. Badam-Pista Roll
[Makes 20 to 25 rolls]
Ingredients

According to the Kaju-Pista Roll, but use badam instead of kaju.

Method

According to the Kaju-Pista Roll given above.

76. Kaju-Pista Pan OR Pista Pan
[Makes 18 to 20 pans]
Ingredients

(1) 250 grams kaju
(2) 125 grams sugar
(3) 2 tea spoons ghee
(4) 50 grams pista
(5) 50 grams mawa (used for barfi making)
(6) 25 grams sugar
(7) A few cardamom seeds (powdered)

(8) A little of icing sugar
(9) A few drops of edible green colour
(10) A little nutmeg powder
(11) Silver foil for decoration

Method

(1) Powder the kajus. Make sugar syrup from 125 grams sugar and water. Add a little milk to remove dirt from the sugar. Boil till it is thick like a drop. Make three thread sugar syrup.

(2) Add the kaju powder. Mix properly. When thick enough like a dough, remove it from the fire and add 1 tea spoon of ghee. Mix properly.

(3) Powder the pistas. Roast the mawa in 1 tea spoon ghee.

(4) Make sugar syrup using 25 grams sugar. Add a little milk to remove the dirt from sugar. Boil till it is thick like a drop. Make three thread sugar syrup.

(5) Add pista powder, cardamom powder, icing sugar, mawa, nutmeg powder, a few drops of edible dark green colour.

(6) Take a small portion of the kaju mawa and roll it between two plastics into a small puri.

(7) Cut it into two parts. Put the pista filling on one part. Shape it like a pan. (samosa).

(8) Repeat with the other part.

(9) Decorate the pan with silver foil. Also decorate it with a small pista piece.

77. Badam-Pista Pan
[Makes 18 to 20 pans]
Ingredients

According to the Kaju-Pista Roll, but instead of kaju use badam (almonds).

Method

The same as given for Kaju-Pista Pan.

78. Pista Sandwich OR Kaju-Pista Sandwich [Makes 20 to 25 pieces]

Ingredients

Make the 'masala' stuffing the same as that for Pista Pan.

Method

(1) Roll out the kaju mawa between two plastics. Roll out two roties from kaju mawa.

(2) Place the pista masala on one roti.

(3) Place the other kaju roti on it. Press a little. Decorate with silver foil. Cut into small square or rectangular cubes.

79. Pista-Badam Sandwich [Makes 20 to 25 pieces]

Ingredients

According to the Kaju-Pista Sandwich, but take badam instead of kaju.

Method

The same as that for Kaju-Pista Sandwich given above.

80. Pineapple Sandwich [Serves 5]

Ingredients

(1) 10 pieces of big size rasgulla

(2) 1 small tin of pineapple or 3–4 rings of fresh pineapple

(3) 250 grams fresh cream

(4) 100 grams powdered sugar

(5) A few strands kesar

(6) 2 sheets of silver foil

(7) 5 pistas, 10 cherries

(8) 10 paper cups

Method

(1) Remove the rasgulla from syrup and cut each into two equal pieces. Press lightly with your palms and remove the syrup.

(2) If you making rasgullas at home then shape each like a pattice.

(3) Cut the pineapple into small pieces. If you using fresh pineapple, dip the pieces in the sugar syrup for sometime before use. If you use malai, then add a little milk to it.

(4) Take a few ice cubes in a vessel and place the bowl of cream on it. Now beat the cream in one direction only.

(5) Add the powdered sugar and kesar dissolved in little milk. Mix properly.

(6) Dip one piece of rasgulla in this cream and place it in a plate. Place pineapple pieces on it.

(7) Dip the other piece of rasgulla in the cream and place in on the pineapple pieces. Decorate the sandwich with silver foil. Cut the cherries into half. Place a piece in the centre of the top.

(8) Place pista chips around it. Place the sandwiches in paper cups. Serve chilled.

Variation

Instead of pineapple, orange, black grapes or mango (ripe) pieces may also be used.

Barfi, Halwa, Pak

Tips : Halwa or Barfi can be made from all fruits. When it is soft it is called halwa and when it is thick enough and cut into pieces it is called barfi. Fruits like banana, mango, apple, chikoo, papaya, pineapple, orange, sitafal etc. can be used.

Pak is made from dry fruits like badam, kaju, groundnuts, coconut, khajur, figs, pistas etc. For making any pak powder the dry fruit. Roast in a little ghee. Add enough milk. When thick enough add sugar. Cook till it thickens. Remove from the fire and add 1-2 table spoons of ghee. For making barfi or pak spread the mixture in a greased plate and cut into cubes.

81. Cadbury Chocolate Barfi
[Serves 3 to 4]

Ingredients

(1) 200 grams mawa
(2) 100 grams sugar
(3) 2 tea spoons ghee
(4) 6 tea spoons cadbury drinking chocolate
(5) 1 tea spoon cocoa
(6) Silver foil for decoration

Method

(1) Roast the mawa in a little ghee for 5 minutes. Then add sugar. When it is soft like sheera add cocoa and drinking chocolate powder.
(2) Mix properly. Spread the mixture in a greased plate.
(3) Decorate with silver foil. Icing can also be done.

82. Khakhara Barfi

Ingredients and Method

(1) Make khakhara's out of roti. Powder them. Take approximate quantity sugar and make three thread sugar syrup.
(2) Add khakhara powder and some cardamom powder. Spread in a greased dish and cut into cubes when it is settled.
(3) For making khakharas, place the roti on the hot griddle. Press it with a katori. Turn and press it on the other side. Roast on both sides until the roti is hard and crispy.

83. Paneer Barfi [Serves 3 to 4]

Ingredients

(1) 1 litre milk
(2) 1 lime
(3) 1 cup sugar
(4) 5 strands of kesar (dissolved in a little milk)
(5) 5 cardamom pods
(6) A few almonds, a few pistas
(7) Silver foil for decoration

Method

(1) Boil milk. Add lime juice till paneer is formed. Strain and tie it in a muslin cloth. Place some weight on it. Keep aside for 2 hours. All the water will be removed.
(2) Knead the paneer well. Make sugar syrup with sugar and enough water. Make one thread sugar syrup.
(3) Add kesar, paneer and the cardamom powder. When it is thick enough remove from flame and spread in a greased dish. Decorate with chopped almonds and pistas. (If you like chocolate taste sprinkle grated chocolate.)
(4) Make balls from the thickened mawa.

Variation

(1) Cut the silver foil into square shape. Decorate the balls. The balls will seem to be of two colours, white from above and yellow below.
(2) Decorate with cardamom or pista powder.

84. Kesar-Pista Barfi
[Serves 4 to 5]

Ingredients

(1) 100 grams pista powder
(2) $\frac{1}{4}$ tea spoon crushed kesar

(3) 200 grams mawa

(4) 2 tea spoons ghee

(5) ¼ tea spoon cardamom powder

(6) 125 grams sugar

(7) 1 drop of edible green colour

(8) 5 cherries

(9) Silver foil for decoration

Method

(1) Grate and roast the mawa in a little ghee. Add the cardamom powder.

(2) Make three thread sugar syrup using sugar and enough water.

(3) Boil till it becomes thick like a drop. Stir properly. Divide the mawa into two parts. To one part add the pista powder and green colour. Add ½ of the sugar syrup to this mixture. Spread the mixture in a greased dish.

(4) To the other part add kesar and the remaining syrup. Spread this mixture above the pista barfi.

(5) Decorate with silver foil. Cut them into round pieces with a round bottle lid or cutter.

(6) Arrange them in paper cups. Decorate it with sliced cherries.

Note : Instead of kesar, pista colour essence may also be used.

85. Shahi Tukada

[Serves 5 to 6]

Ingredients

(1) 5 to 6 bread slices

(2) Ghee for frying

(3) 3 to 4 cups milk

(4) 1 cup sugar

(5) ½ cup or 100 grams mawa

(6) ¼ tea spoon rose essence, a few drops of yellow edible colour

(7) Few strands kesar

(8) 1 tea spoon gelatine powder

(9) A few charolis

(10) 8 cardamom pods (powdered)

(11) A few tutifruiti

(12) A few almonds

(13) A few kajus

(14) A few pistas

(15) A little of nutmeg

Method

(1) Remove the edges of the bread slices. Cut them into triangles. Fry in ghee till they are golden brown. Mix milk and sugar.

(2) Boil till the milk thickens.

(3) Add grated mawa, rose essence and kesar. Mix gelatine with 3 tea spoons full of water and soak it for 5 minutes. Heat on a slow flame till it dissolves. Add this to the thickened milk.

(4) Add cardamom and other nuts. Arrange bread slices in a bowl.

(5) Pour the mixture on the bread, place another layer of bread slices over it. Again, pour the mixture on the bread slices.

(6) Decorate with chopped nuts, charolis and tutifruti. Refrigerate and serve chilled.

86. Walnut Fudge

[Serves 6 to 7]

Ingredients

(1) 1 tea spoon butter

(2) 1 tin milkmaid (400 gms)

(3) 250 grams walnut (coarse powder)

(4) 100 grams desiccated coconut

(5) 3 tea spoons cocoa powder

(6) A few drops of vanilla essence

(7) A few kaju

(8) A few magatari seeds

Method

(1) Heat the butter. Add the milkmaid or milk. Instead of milkmaid, 500 ml milk with sugar (thickened like basundi) may be also used.

(2) When the mixture thickens, add walnut powder, desiccated coconut and cocoa powder. Mix well.

(3) Remove it from the flame. Cool it. Add essence and make small balls. Roll them in desiccated coconut. Decorate with kaju bits, magatari seeds or cherries.

87. Ghari [Serves 3 to 4]

Ingredients

(1) 100 grams maida

(2) A little pure ghee for the puri

(3) 10 grams badam-pista powder

(4) 1 table spoon milk powder (optional)

(5) A little cardamom, mace (javantri) and nutmeg powder

(6) 100 grams mawa

(7) 60 grams powdered sugar

(8) Dalda ghee for frying

(9) 10 grams powdered sugar, a little of pure ghee and a little of dalda ghee to pour on the ghari.

Method

(1) Add enough ghee to the maida. Rub well. Knead the dough using cold water. Divide the dough into small portions. Make a puri from each portion.

(2) Mix badam-pista powder, milk powder, cardamom powder, nutmeg and mace powder.

(3) Roast the mawa on slow flame. When ghee separates add almonds, pista, nutmeg, cardamom and mace powder. Cook for 1 minute.

(4) Cool and add powdered sugar.

(5) Cut the puri into a square shape. Stuff the mawa mixture in the puri. Cover the mixture by drawing up the edges towards each other. Water may be used to make the edges stick with each other.

(6) Fry them in ghee. Cool them. Heat some dalda ghee and a little of pure ghee. Remove it from the flame and add powdered sugar. For $\frac{1}{4}$ cup ghee add 1 table spoon of sugar. Dip the ghari in this mixture for 2-3 times and put it in a thali.

(7) If a thicker layer is desired than put the ghari in the refrigerator and then again dip it in ghee after some time.

88. Carrot Halwa [Serves 5]

Ingredients

(1) 500 grams carrots

(2) 2 table spoons ghee

(3) 150 ml milk

(4) 175 grams sugar

(5) 150 grams mawa

(6) A few kajus and raisins

(7) A little khus khus and a little cardamom powder

Method

(1) Wash, peel and grate the carrots.

(2) Take 1 table spoon ghee in a pan and roast the grated carrots in it for a few minutes. Add milk and cook for sometime.

(3) When the milk evaporates add sugar, kajus and raisins. Add 1 table spoon of ghee.

(4) When the ghee separates remove it from the flame. Add cardamom powder and khus khus.

(5) If mawa has to be added, add it when the water from sugar evaporates.

(6) Mix well. 600 ml of milk may be added instead of mawa.

89. Dudhi Halwa
(Bottle Gourd)
[Serves 3 to 4]

Ingredients

(1) 250 grams dudhi
(2) 3 table spoons ghee
(3) 3 cups milk
(4) 100 grams sugar
(5) A few cardamom seeds (powdered)
(6) 150 grams mawa
(7) Silver foil for decoration

Method

(1) Peel the dudhi and grate it. Add water and boil it in a pressure cooker. Strain through a muslin cloth.
(2) Roast it in a little ghee for some time. Add boiling milk and stir properly.
(3) When it thickens add sugar. Cook for sometime till the water from the sugar evaporates. Add a little ghee and remove the halwa from the flame.
(4) Add cardamom powder. Spread the mixture on a greased dish. Decorate with silver foil.
(5) If mawa has to be added, add it after all the water of sugar evaporates. The mawa has to be roasted a little.
(6) Green colour may be also added if desired. If mawa is used, milk is not required.

90. Dryfruit Halwa
[Serves 4 to 5]

Ingredients

(1) 500 grams dudhi (tender)
(2) 250 grams sugar
(3) 1 table spoon ghee

(4) 250 grams barfimawa
(5) Cardamom powder
(6) Few drops of edible lemon yellow colour
(7) A few kajus
(8) Raisins and almonds

Method

(1) Wash, peel, grate and boil the dudhi. Strain water and add sugar. Heat the mixture.
(2) When a little water evaporates, add 1 table spoon of ghee. When all the water evaporates remove from the flame.
(3) Sieve mawa and roast it a little. Add cardamom powder, lemon colour to it.
(4) Cool it a little and then, spread in a greased dish.
(5) Add 2 table spoons of ghee on the dish. Decorate with kajus, raisins and chopped almonds.

91. Milk Halwa [Serves 2 to 3]

Ingredients

(1) 500 ml milk
(2) 1 table spoon sour curd
(3) 100 grams sugar
(4) A few drops of edible brown colour
(5) A few almonds and kaju

Method

(1) Mix milk, curd and sugar. Stir properly. Put on the flame for heating. Stir constantly.
(2) When mawa starts forming in the milk add a little brown colour.
(3) When very little syrup remains in it remove it from the flame and remove the halwa to other dish. Decorate with nuts.

92. Chikoo Halwa

[Serves 4 to 5]

Ingredients

(1) 4 chikoos

(2) 2 table spoons ghee

(3) 1 litre milk

(4) 100 grams sugar

(5) A little cardamom powder

Method

(1) Peel the chikoos and cut them into small pieces. Roast the pulp in very little ghee.

(2) Cook for some time. Add milk. When milk starts boiling, add sugar. Cook again.

(3) When it thickens, add 1 table spoon of ghee. Remove the halwa from the flame. Add cardamom powder. Spread in a greased dish.

93. Chikoo-Chocolate Halwa

[Serves 6 to 8]

Ingredients

(1) 250 grams chikoo

(2) 3 table spoons ghee

(3) 500 grams mawa

(4) 200 grams sugar

(5) 5-6 tea spoons drinking chocolate

(6) Cardamom powder as desired

(7) Silver foil for decoration

Method

(1) Cut the chikoos into small pieces and roast in 1 table spoon of ghee.

(2) In another frypan roast the mawa in 1 table spoon ghee. When the mawa is roasted add sugar. When the sugar dissolves and it thickens, add it to the roasted chikoo pulp.

(3) When the pulp thickens add 1 table spoon ghee and remove it from the flame. Add the drinking chocolate and cardamom powder.

(4) Spread in a greased dish.

Note : If the halwa has to be made in large quantity grated dudhi may be roasted with chikoo. To obtain the desired brown colour cocoa powder may also be added to it.

94. Apple Halwa [Serves 4]

Ingredients

(1) 2 apples

(2) 2 table spoons ghee

(3) 1 litre milk

(4) 150 grams sugar

(5) 1 lime

(6) Cardamom powder as desired

Method

(1) Wash, peel and chop the apples. Roast the pulp in 1 table spoon of ghee till it gets cooked. Add the milk.

(2) When it thickens, add sugar and lime juice. When it thickens, add 1 table spoon ghee and the halwa remove from the flame.

(3) Add cardamom powder. Spread the mixture in a greased dish.

95. Banana Halwa

[Serves 5 to 6]

Ingredients

(1) 3 bananas

(2) 2 table spoons ghee

(3) 1 litre milk

(4) 100 grams sugar

(5) Cardamom powder as desired

(6) Few crushed charolis

(7) Silver foil for decoration

Method

(1) Peel and cut the bananas into small pieces. Roast the pieces in 1 table spoon of ghee for some time. Add milk.

(2) When milk starts boiling and it thickens little, add sugar. Cook on a slow flame.

(3) When it thickens add 1 table spoon of ghee. Remove the halwa from the flame. Add the charolis and the cardamom powder and spread it in a greased dish.

(4) Decorate with silver foil.

Note : Reduce the quantity of milk and add a little mawa to reduce the cooking time.

96. Kaju-Walnut Halwa

[Serves 4 to 5]

Ingredients

(1) 100 grams kaju

(2) 100 grams walnuts

(3) 2 table spoons ghee

(4) 100 grams sugar

(5) 50 grams mawa

(6) A little cardamom powder

Method

(1) Powder the kajus and the walnuts in the nut cutter. Make a coarse powder. Roast it in 1 table spoon of ghee.

(2) Add roasted mawa to this. Then add the sugar and the cardamom powder. Cook for some time.

(3) When it thickens add 1 table spoon of ghee and remove the halwa from flame. Spread in a greased dish.

97. Fresh Coconut Halwa

[Serves 5 to 6]

Ingredients

(1) 1 coconut

(2) 125 grams ghee

(3) 175 grams mawa

(4) 150 grams sugar

(5) Few strands kesar

(6) Nuts as desired (kajus, raisins, almonds)

(7) Cardamom powder as desired

Method

(1) Crush or grate the coconut. Heat the ghee and roast the grated coconut in it till it becomes light pink.

(2) Add roasted mawa to it.

(3) Prepare two thread sugar syrup and add it to the coconut mixture.

(4) When it thickens add a little ghee. Remove it from flame. Add cardamom powder and the kesar. Decorate the halwa with chopped nuts. Kesar may be added to the syrup.

Note : For five persons 500 gms grated coconut is required.

98. Anjeer Halwa

[Serves 3 to 4]

Ingredients

(1) 5 to 6 pieces anjeer (figs)

(2) 250 grams dudhi

(3) 2 table spoons ghee

(4) $\frac{1}{2}$ cup milk

(5) 100 grams mawa

(6) 100 grams sugar

(7) 50 grams raisins, kajus, almonds, khus khus and cardamom powder

Method

(1) Boil the anjeer in some water. Crush when cool.

(2) Grate the dudhi and roast it in 1 table spoon ghee till dudhi is cooked.

(3) Add the mawa and anjeer mixture to it. When heated properly add sugar.

(4) When all the water from the sugar evaporates remove the halwa from flame. Add 1 table spoon of ghee. Add nuts and cardamom powder.

99. Banana-Coconut Halwa
[Serves 6 to 7]

Ingredients

(1) 5 to 6 bananas

(2) $\frac{1}{4}$ cup ghee

(3) $\frac{1}{2}$ cup sugar

(4) $\frac{1}{2}$ cup grated coconut

(5) $\frac{1}{2}$ tea spoon cardamom powder

(6) Few kaju and raisins

Method

(1) Heat 2 table spoons of ghee in a fry pan and roast the grated bananas in it with constant stirring, to avoid it from sticking to the pan and burning.

(2) When colour changes add a desired amount of sugar and coconut. When mixed properly, add the remaining amount of ghee, cardamom powder and nuts.

(3) When ghee the separates remove from fire. It can be served as pieces. It tastes well, hot or cold.

100. Groundnut Pak
[Makes 10 to 12 pieces]

Ingredients

(1) 2 cups groundnut powder

(2) $\frac{1}{2}$ (a little less than $\frac{1}{2}$ cup) cup milk

(3) 1 cup sugar

(4) 1 table spoon ghee

(5) Silver foil for decoration

Method

(1) Boil the milk and sugar.

(2) Boil it until a thick mixture is formed. i.e., The drop of the milk mixture should remain like that when placed in a dish. Then add the groundnut powder. Stir constantly till thickens.

(3) Add ghee and remove it from the flame. Spread in greased plate. Decorate the pak with silver foil. Cut into small pieces.

101. Khopara Pak
[Makes 10 to 12 pieces]

Ingredients

(1) 100 grams desiccated coconut

(2) 100 grams sugar

(3) 100 ml milk

(4) 1 table spoon ghee

(5) A little cardamom powder

(6) Silver foil for decoration

Method

(1) Boil the milk and sugar till it becomes a thick syrup like a drop is formed.

(2) Add desiccated coconut. Cook for some time. Add ghee and remove the mixture from the flame.

(3) Mix well. Add cardamom powder. Spread in a greased dish. Cool and decorate with silver foil. Cut into small cubes.

102. Khajur Pak
[Makes 4 to 5 pieces]

Ingredients

(1) 100 grams khajur (dates)

(2) 100 ml milk

(3) 2 table spoons ghee

(4) Silver foil for decoration

Method

(1) Cut the khajur into small pieces after removing the seeds. Add milk and crush the mixture.

(2) Roast it in 1 table spoon of ghee cook it till it thickens. When done add 1 table spoon of ghee. Spread in a greased dish. Decorate with silver foil. Cut into small pieces.

103. Khajur-Groundnut Pak
[Makes 12 to 15 pieces]

Ingredients

(1) 300 grams khajur

(2) 100 grams groundnut

(3) 2 table spoons ghee

(4) A little cardamom powder

Method

(1) Wash and grind the khajur after removing the seeds from them.

(2) Roast, cool, peel and powder the groundnuts.

(3) Roast the khajur and groundnuts powdered together in 1 table spoon of ghee.

(4) When thick enough, add 1 table spoon of ghee. Spread in a greased dish. Decorate with cardamom powder. Cut into small pieces.

104. Mango Raspak
[Makes 8 pieces]

Ingredients

(1) 2 cups mango pulp

(2) 2 table spoons ghee

(3) 1 cup sugar

(4) $\frac{1}{2}$ tea spoon cardamom powder

(5) 2 tea spoons dry ginger powder

(6) Silver foil for decoration

Method

(1) Heat the ghee in a fry pan. Add the mango pulp to it. Stir constantly.

(2) When the mango pulp thickens a little add sugar. Add enough sugar according to the sweetness of the pulp.

(3) Add a little ghee. When it thickness add the cardamom powder and the dry ginger powder.

(4) Spread the pulp in a greased dish. Decorate with silver foil. Cut into small pieces.

105. Mango Pulp Barfi
[Makes 5 pieces]

Ingredients

(1) 1 cup mango pulp

(2) A little ghee

(3) $\frac{3}{4}$ cup milk

(4) $\frac{1}{2}$ cup sugar

(5) A small piece baras

(6) A little cardamom powder

(7) A few strands kesar

(8) Silver foil for decoration

Method

(1) Put the ghee in a fry pan and keep it on fire. When it melts, add the mango pulp and stir constantly.

(2) When it starts boiling add the milk. When it thickens add sugar, ghee and cardamom powder. Kesar may also be added.

(3) When it becomes thick enough, spread it in a greased dish. Decorate with silver foil. Cut into small cubes when settled.

106. Aadu Pak (Ginger Pak)

[Makes 15 to 20 pieces]

Ingredients

(1) 100 grams ginger
(2) 300 ml milk
(3) 200 grams sugar
(4) 2 table spoons ghee
(5) A little dry ginger powder
(6) Silver foil for decoration

Method

(1) Wash, peel, cut into pieces and grind the ginger.
(2) Add the milk and sugar. Mix properly. Heat 1 table spoon of ghee in a fry pan and roast the mixture. Cook till the milk evaporates.
(3) This pak is slightly softer as compared to the others.
(4) When it thickens add the dry ginger powder and remove the mixture from fire. Add 1 table spoon of ghee. Spread in a greased thali.
(5) Decorate with silver foil and cut into small cubes.

107. Til Chikki (Sesame Seeds)

Ingredients for method 1

(1) 1 cup til (sesame seeds)
(2) $\frac{1}{4}$ cup ghee
(3) 1 cup jaggery
(4) 1 tea spoon glucose

Method 1

(1) Roast the til. Heat a fry pan. Melt the ghee, add the jaggery and cook to hard ball stage (test with cold water).
(2) Add the roasted til to it and mix well. Remove the mixture from flame. Add 1 tea spoon glucose. Spread the mixture on greased thali.

(3) Add til little at a time. The amount of til required would depend upon the quality of jaggery.
(4) Glucose helps to keep the colour of the chikki's white. Cut the chikki into small pieces.

Ingredients for method 2

(1) 1 cup til
(2) 1 cup jaggery (cut into small pieces)
(3) A little powdered sugar

Method 2

(1) Mix jaggery and water. Make a thick syrup. Boil the syrup until it thickens like a drop. Add til.
(2) Don't add all the til at a time. Add little at a time. Sprinkle some powdered sugar on the kitchen platform. Spread this mixture on the platform. Roll out the mixture with a rolling-pin into a thin roti while the mixture is still hot.

Ingredients for method 3

(1) 1 cup til
(2) 1 cup sugar
(3) A little ghee
(4) A little powdered sugar

Method 3

(1) Roast the til. Heat the ghee in a frying pan. Add sugar. Stir constantly. Boil the mixture till it thickens like a drop.
(2) Add til. Sprinkle powdered sugar on the platform. Roll out into a thin roti while it is still hot.

Variation

By these methods various chikkis from desiccated coconut, groundnut, kaju, almond can be made. Groundnuts, almond and kaju have to be powdered.

Note : (1) From remethod 2 and 3 you can make 4 rotis of til chikki.

(2) For making one chikki roti take 1 small katori of til and 1 small katori of sugar.

108. Mamara Chikki (Rice Puff Chikki) [Makes 35 to 40 pieces]

Ingredients

(1) 100 grams rice puffs (mamara)

(2) 2 table spoons ghee

(3) 200 grams jaggery

(4) 1 table spoon glucose

Method

(1) Roast the mamara. Heat a little ghee in fry pan. Add chopped jaggery.

(2) Boil till it thickens a little. Add the roasted mamara. Add a little glucose. Glucose helps to make the chikki white and crispy.

(3) Add mamara just enough for jaggery. Spread the chikki on a greased dish while the mixture is still hot. Cut into square pieces.

109. Methi Ladoo [Makes 35 to 40 pieces]

Ingredients

(1) 100 grams dried methi powder (fenugreek seeds)

(2) 350 to 400 grams ghee

(3) 250 grams wheat flour (coarse)

(4) 300 grams jaggery

(5) Dry coconut (grated)

(6) A few almonds

(7) 250 grams powdered sugar

(8) A little khus khus

(9) A little dry ginger powder

(10) A little ganthoda powder (pepper root)

(11) A few magatari seeds (pounded)

Method

(1) Take enough ghee in a fry pan. Roast the wheat flour in it. Cut the jaggery into small pieces. Remove the wheat flour from the flame.

(2) Mix dry coconut, almonds (powdered), magatari seeds, dry ginger powder, ganthoda powdered sugar and khus khus.

(3) Mix the jaggery and the wheat flour. Cool it and mix all the other ingredients. If ghee is less additional ghee may be added. From mixture make the ladoo (small balls).

Note : (1) If ladoo's are made for men 150 grams of gum (pounded) may be added.

(2) If you desire to add more methi flour then reduce the wheat flour by the same amount. If urad flour is added, add warm milk and warm ghee to the flour. Rub and press the flour. Leave aside for sometime. Sieve through a steel sieve. Roast in ghee till light brown. Add this and then form ladoos.

(3) If you want to add more amount of methi, then reduce the amount of wheat flour.

110. Gundar Pak (Dry Gum Pak)

Ingredients

(1) 100 grams gum (pounded)

(2) 100 grams ghee

(3) 1 litre milk

(4) 200 grams sugar

(5) A few almonds (pounded) and a little khus khus (pounded)

(6) $\frac{1}{2}$ katori dry coconut (grated)

(7) 100 grams magatari seeds

(8) 1 large spoon dry ginger powder

(9) 1 large spoon ganthoda powder (pepper root)

Method

(1) Heat the ghee in a fry pan. If the gum is soaked in water before using, less ghee is required.

(2) Add the gum to the heated ghee. Stir constantly. Add more ghee if required. Roast the gum till it becomes light brown in colour.

(3) Add milk slowly and stir constantly. Add sugar. Cook till all milk evaporates.

(4) Add khus khus, almonds and coconut. When thick enough, add the remaining ingredients. Store in a container.

Note : (1) This is very good for health particularly after delivery. It is eaten one month after the delivery. After delivery grind gum to small pieces and soak in ghee and refrigerate.

(2) It is also very good, for everybody in winter. For that it can be used immediately after soaking or also without soaking.

111. Peda

Ingredients

(1) 100 grams gum (pounded)

(2) 100 to 150 grams sugar

(3) 50 grams ghee

(4) 1 litre milk

(5) 50 grams dry coconut (2 katoris)

(6) 10 grams gokharu (pounded)

(7) A few almonds, pistas, khus khus, mace and a little nutmeg powder

(8) 30 grams dry ginger powder

(9) 20 grams ganthoda (pepper root)

Method

(1) Apply a little ghee to the inside of a vessel. Pour in milk. When it starts boiling, add sugar. Add gum powder.

(2) When it starts thickening, add coconut and other ingredients. Add a little ghee.

(3) Remove it from the flame when the ghee separates.

112. Adadiya
[Makes 25 to 30 pieces]

Ingredients

(1) 250 grams urad flour (fine)

(2) 350 grams ghee

(3) A little milk

(4) 125 grams gum (pounded)

(5) $\frac{1}{2}$ cup desiccated coconut

(6) 10 to 15 almonds

(7) 10 pistas

(8) 10 cardamom pods

(9) 3 table spoons dry ginger powder

(10) 3 table spoons ganthoda (pepper root)

(11) $\frac{1}{4}$ nutmeg powdered

(12) 150 to 200 grams powdered sugar

Method

(1) Add warm ghee and warm milk to the flour. Press the flour and leave aside for some time. Sieve through a steel sieve.

(2) Roast the flour in ghee till it becomes light brown. Add gum.

(3) Roast for sometime. Remove the mixture from the flame. Add all the ingredients except sugar.

(4) Cool it. When it is cooled, add sugar and 3 to 4 table spoons of ghee. Spread it in a greased dish. After two hours cut into small cubes and serve.

113. Sobhagasutha

Ingredients

(1) 600 grams dry ginger powder

(2) 150 grams ghee

(3) 2 litres milk

(4) 800 grams sugar

(5) 100 grams almonds

(6) 15 grams pistas

(7) 50 grams magatari seeds

(8) 10 grams muskmelon seeds (dried)

(9) 15 grams ganthoda (pepper root)

(10) 15 grams white pepper (or black pepper)

(11) 4 grams cinnamon

(12) 5 grams peper (long pepper)

(13) 5 grams vanskapur

(14) $2\frac{1}{2}$ grams cloves

(15) 1 small nutmeg

(16) $2\frac{1}{2}$ grams kesar

(17) $2\frac{1}{2}$ grams cardamom

(18) 3 grams mace

(19) 3 pieces baras

(20) Silver foil for decoration

Method

(1) Grind all the masalas separately.

(2) Roast the dry ginger powder in 3 to 4 tables spoons of ghee till it has coffee colour. Remove in a dish.

(3) Make mawa from milk 3 to 4 hours earlier. Knead the mawa well and roast it in ghee.

(4) Add dry ginger. Add water to sugar and make three thread sugar syrup. Add dry ginger powder and mawa to the syrup. Remove it from the flame and stir constantly. Spread it in a thali.

(5) Let it cool and see that balls can be formed out of the mixture. If it is still soft, again heat it till it becomes thick enough.

(6) Add the remaining masalas except baras powder. See that no lumps are formed.

(7) Cool it and add the baras powder. (More amount of baras powder would give a bitter taste.)

(8) Spread it in a greased dish. Decorate it with silver foil. Cut into cubes and store in a box. It should be stored in an airy place or refrigerator.

114. Amala Jeevan

Ingredients

(1) 1 kg amala

(2) 7 table spoons ghee

(3) 2 kg 200 grams sugar

(4) 1 nutmeg

(5) 10 grams nagkesar

(6) 25 grams bay leaves (tamal patra)

(7) 5 grams cloves

(8) 25 grams charoli

(9) 10 grams kali musali

(10) 10 grams pepper (long pepper)

(11) 20 grams almonds

(12) 10 grams cardamom

(13) 10 grams mace (javantri)

(14) 5 grams kesar

(15) 25 grams asan (ashawagandha)

(16) 10 grams cinnamon

(17) 25 grams salom

(18) 10 grams white musali

(19) 30 grams ganthoda (pepper roots)

(20) 10 grams pistas

Method

(1) Grind into coarse powder all the ingredients. Mix and sieve all the ingredients.

(2) Grind almonds, pistas, charolis, nutmeg separately. Do not sieve if finely pounded.

(3) Choose big amala. Steam them in the pressure cooker like muthiya.

(4) Cool and then remove the seeds. Crush it and pass it through a strainer to get pulp.

(5) Heat 7 table spoons of ghee and roast the amala pulp for a few minutes. Add sugar.

(6) When it becomes transparent and is a little dark in colour, spread and see in a dish and water.

(7) The pulp should be thick enough like a drop. Add all the spices slowly. Keep stirring. Remove it from the flame, when it thickens. Spread in a dish and let it cool. If it is soft reheat it till it is loose.

(2) SNACKS

115. Bhajiya

Ingredients

(1) 1 cup chana flour (fine)

(2) 1 tea spoon red chilli powder

(3) $\frac{1}{4}$ tea spoon turmeric powder

(4) 1 tea spoon sugar

(5) 1 tea spoon rice flour

(6) A pinch soda

(7) 1 tea spoon dhana-jeera powder

(8) $\frac{1}{4}$ tea spoon garam masala

(9) Vegetables such as potatoes, green chillies, onions

(10) Bananas, pumpkin, mangoes

(11) Brinjal, sweet potato

(12) Poi leaves, ajwain leaves

(13) Oil for frying

(14) Salt to taste

Method

(1) Mix all masalas with chana flour and make a batter.

(2) For banana and green chilli bhajiya, the batter should be a little thick.

(3) Potatoes, onions should be cut into thin slices. Banana should be cut into big pieces or thick slices.

(4) Heat enough oil in a frying pan. Dip the slices (vegetables or fruits) of which bhajiyas have to be made in the batter and fry them.

(5) Hot and crispy bhajiyas are ready to serve.

(6) Slit the green chillies, (remove the seeds) and fill in a mixture of dhana-jeera powder, salt and sugar. Cut the alfanso mango into square pieces for making mango bhajiya.

116. Batatawada [Serves 5]

Ingredients

(1) 500 grams potatoes

(2) Oil for frying

(3) $\frac{1}{2}$ tea spoon cumin seeds

(4) 1 tea spoon til

(5) 2 tea spoons chilli-ginger paste

(6) 3 table spoons coriander leaves (finely chopped)

(7) $\frac{1}{2}$ tea spoon citric acid

(8) 2 tea spoons sugar

(9) 2 tea spoons arrow-root flour

(10) 1 tea spoon garam masala

(11) A few cashewnuts

(12) A few raisins

(13) 150 grams chana flour

(14) $\frac{1}{2}$ tea spoon red chilli powder

(15) $\frac{1}{4}$ tea spoon turmeric powder

(16) 4 tea spoons rice flour

(17) Salt to taste

Method

(1) Boil, cool and grate potatoes. Do not pour cold water on the potatoes.

(2) Heat 2 tea spoons of oil in a kadhai, add cumin seeds and til for seasoning. Then add chilli-ginger paste, coriander leaves, citric acid, sugar and arrow-root flour.

(3) When it cools down, add mashed potatoes. Add salt, cashewnuts, raisins and spices. Make small balls from the mixture.

(4) Make batter of chana flour. Add a little salt, red chilli powder, turmeric powder, and rice flour. Dip the balls in this batter and fry them, in hot oil.

117. Kajuwada [Serves 5]

Ingredients

(1) 500 grams potatoes

(2) 2 tea spoons chilli-ginger paste

(3) 2 tea spoons sugar

(4) 3 table spoons finely chopped coriander leaves

(5) $\frac{1}{2}$ tea spoon citric acid

(6) 1 tea spoon garam masala

(7) 1 tea spoon til (sesame seeds)

(8) A few cashewnuts, raisins

(9) Bread crumbs (dried bread powder)

(10) Oil for frying

(11) Salt to taste

Method

(1) Boil, cool, peel and mash potatoes. Add all ingredients except kaju, raisins and bread crumbs. Divide the mixture into small portions.

(2) Take each portion and flatten it with your palms. Stuff in pieces of kaju and raisins. Again roll out into balls. Roll in bread crumbs to form the upper crust. Fry them in hot oil.

118. Dalwada [Serves 5 to 6]

Ingredients

(1) 500 grams green gram dal (skinned mung dal)

(2) A small piece of ginger

(3) 12 to 15 green chillies

(4) 10 cloves garlic

(5) A pinch hing (Asafoetida)

(6) Onions

(7) A few green chillies to be fried (for serving)

(8) Oil for frying

(9) Salt to taste

Method

(1) Soak the dal for 6 to 8 hours in water. Grind it coarsely in the mixer.

(2) Add all the ingredients except onion. Mix well, make balls and fry the wadas in hot oil.

(3) Cut the onions into long slices. Add salt to them. Fry the whole green chillies in hot oil. Serve them with hot dalwadas.

Variation

(1) Instead of only mung dal, some amount of urad dal may be also added.

(2) Wadas can also be made from plain mung dal, urad dal and cow's pea dal (chawla dal).

(3) A little amount of rice flour may be added to make the wada's crispy.

119. Dahiwada [Serves 5]

Ingredients

(1) 1 cup cow's pea dal

(2) 1 cup urad dal

(3) $\frac{1}{4}$ cup mung dal

(4) Oil for frying

(5) 1 litre milk

(6) Sweet chutney for serving

(7) A little red chilli powder

(8) Salt to taste

Method

(1) Soak all the dals for 6 hours. Grind them coarsely in the mixer. Add salt and water to make thick paste and fry wadas in hot oil from this mixture. Soak these wadas in luke warm water. Remove them from water. Press very lightly to drain off the water. Place them in a dish.

(2) Pour curds on it. Sprinkle salt, red chilli powder, roasted cumin seeds powder and sweet chutney.

Variation

(1) You can also take 2 cups of cow's peas dal and 1 cup of urad dal for making wadas.

(2) **Stop Dahiwada :** Make wadas from the stuffing used to fill kachoris. Dip them in Dahiwada mixture and fry them. Before serving treat them like dahiwadas.

120. Large Dahiwada

[Serves 5 to 6]

Ingredients

(1) $2\frac{1}{2}$ cups green gram dal with husks (mung dal)

(2) 2 tea spoons ginger-chilli paste

(3) $\frac{1}{4}$ tea spoon hing

(4) Oil for frying

(5) 1 litre curd

(6) A little red chilli powder

(7) A little black salt

(8) Dates chutney

(9) Salt to taste

Method

(1) Soak the dal for 4 to 6 hours. Remove the husks. Grind coarsely. Add asafoetida, ginger-chilli paste and salt to it.

(2) Dip a large spoon in water. Place some batter in it and drop the wada into hot oil to get large wadas.

(3) Soak them in luke warm water. Remove the wadas and press them lightly to remove excess water.

(4) Pour beatened curd (should not be sour) on it. Sprinkle salt, red chilli powder, black salt and add sweet chutney to it.

121. Vegetable Dahiwada

[Makes 35 to 40 wadas]

Ingredients

(1) 100 grams french beans

(2) 100 grams chawli

(3) 200 grams carrots

(4) 300 grams potatoes

(5) 1 tea spoon ginger-chilli paste

(6) 3 table spoons coriander leaves (finely chopped)

(7) 1 tea spoon cloves, cinnamon powder

(8) 3 tea spoons sugar

(9) A few cashewnuts

(10) A few raisins

(11) 1 tea spoon garam masala

(12) 200 grams chana flour

(13) $\frac{1}{4}$ tea spoon turmeric powder

(14) Oil for frying

(15) 1 litre curd, sweet chutney

(16) Chilli powder

(17) 1 tea spoon sesame seeds

(18) Salt to taste

Method

(1) Cut and steam all vegetables. When cool add all the masalas and make balls.

(2) Make a batter of chana flour, salt and turmeric powder like batatawada. Add salt.

(3) Dip the balls in the batter and fry them in hot oil. Top the wadas with curd, sweet chutney, salt and red chilli powder.

(4) Instead of chana flour, maida can also be used.

122. Bread Dahiwada

Ingredients and Method

(1) Shape the bread slices into round shape. Take one slice and fill the mixture of vegetables (according to R. No. 121) in it. Place an other slice over it. Press properly and fry them. If they crack than they may be dipped in maida flour batter and then fry them.

(2) Soak them in thin butter milk to which salt is added. Remove and then top each wada with curds. Sprinkle salt, red chilli powder and add sweet chutney.

123. Macaroni Wada

[Makes 25 wadas]

Ingredients

(1) 100 grams macaroni

(2) 125 grams green peas

(3) 250 grams potatoes, (cut them into small pieces)

(4) 125 grams french beans (cut them into small pieces)

(5) $\frac{1}{2}$ cup chopped coriander leaves

(6) $1\frac{1}{2}$ table spoon chilli paste

(7) $\frac{1}{2}$ tea spoon ginger paste

(8) Oil for frying

(9) Salt to taste

For white sauce

(1) $\frac{1}{2}$ cup maida

(2) 250 ml milk

(3) $\frac{1}{2}$ packet butter (50 grams)

(4) 125 grams capsicum (chopped finely)

Method

(1) Melt butter, add the flour and cook for 2 minutes. Stirring constantly throughout till it is very light pink in colour. Gradually add milk.

(2) Add capsicum.

(3) Cut the macaroni into small pieces, add a little salt and boil it. When sauce thickens, add macaroni. Boil the potatoes, french beans and peas.

(4) Add them to the white sauce. Mix properly. Divide them into small portions. Roll each portion into a ball. Fry them in hot oil.

124. Rice Dahiwada

[Makes 5 to 6 dahiwadas]

Ingredients and Method

(1) In 1 cup of rice add salt, 1 tea spoon red chilli powder, $\frac{1}{4}$ tea spoon turmeric powder and 1 tea spoon garam masala. Mix properly. Make small balls of the mixture. Make a thin batter of urad flour and water. Dip the balls in the batter and fry them.

(2) Top them with curds, sweet chutney, salt and roasted cumin seeds powder. Decorate with coriander leaves.

125. Gota [Serves 5 to 6]

Ingredients

(1) 2 cups chana flour (coarse)

(2) $\frac{1}{2}$ cup wheat flour (coarse)

(3) 2 bunches methi bhaji (chopped finely)

(4) 1 tea spoon ginger-chilli paste

(5) 2 table spoons finely chopped coriander leaves

(6) 1 cup curd

(7) 4 table spoons sugar

(8) A pinch soda

(9) 1 tea spoon sesame seeds

(10) 10 pepper corns (coarsely pounded)

(11) 1 tea spoon coriander seeds (coarsely pounded)

(12) 1 tea spoon garam masala

(13) Oil for frying

(14) Salt to taste

Method

(1) Mix chana flour, wheat flour, pepper, a little curd, coriander seeds and all masalas.

(2) Add methi leaves chopped finely and washed. Make a thick batter.

(3) Add enough sugar. Mix little oil, water and soda. Heat for sometime. Add it to the batter just before making the gotas. Add a little hot oil.

Variation

(1) Mix well. Fry the gotas in hot oil. Serve hot. Gotas can be made by using only fine chana flour or coarse chana flour, and little rawa.

(2) Gotas can be made of coriander leaves, curry leaves, poai leaves or spinach.

(3) Crushed onions may be also added. Pakodas can also be made from grated bottle gourd, pumkin, cabbage and grated cucumber.

126. Dahi Pakoda [Serves 3 to 4]

Ingredients

(1) 125 grams chana flour (fine)

(2) 25 grams wheat flour

(3) 25 grams rice flour

(4) 1 tea spoon red chilli powder

(5) $\frac{1}{4}$ tea spoon turmeric powder

(6) $\frac{1}{4}$ tea spoon soda

(7) Oil for frying

(8) A little curds

(9) A little sweet chutney

(10) A little green chutney

(11) Salt to taste

Method

(1) Mix all the flours, salt, red chilli powder, turmeric powder and soda.

(2) Add enough water to make a thin batter.

(3) Fry the pakodas in hot oil. Soak them in water for some time.

(4) Press lightly to remove the excess water. Top with curds, sweet chutney, green chutney, salt and a little red chilli powder. Decorate with chopped coriander.

127. Rice Pakoda
[Makes 10 to 12 pakodas]

Ingredients

(1) $1\frac{1}{2}$ cups rice (cooked)

(2) 1 cup chana flour

(3) $\frac{1}{4}$ tea spoon turmeric powder

(4) 1 tea spoon sugar

(5) 1 tea spoon ginger-chilli paste

(6) 1 cup boiled vegetables (french beans, carrots, potatoes, peas)

(7) Oil for frying

(8) Salt to taste

Method

Mix all the above ingredients. Make a batter and fry the pakoda's in hot oil. Pakodas can be made without vegetables also.

128. Wada Pau
[Makes 20 pieces]

Ingredients

(1) 500 grams potatoes

(2) Oil accordingly

(3) $\frac{1}{2}$ tea spoon mustard seeds

(4) 2 tea spoons urad dal

(5) A few curry leaves

(6) $\frac{1}{4}$ tea spoon turmeric powder

(7) 1 tea spoon sesame seeds

(8) 3 onions (finely chopped)

(9) 1 tea spoon ginger-chilli paste

(10) 2 table spoons finely chopped coriander leaves

(11) 1 lime

(12) 2 tea spoons sugar

(13) A little sweet chutney

(14) A little green chutney

(15) Garlic chutney

(16) Nylon sev

(17) Ghee and butter

(18) 20 pieces paubhaji bread

(19) A little chana flour

(20) $\frac{1}{2}$ tea spoon red chilli powder

(21) Salt to taste

Method

(1) Boil, peel and grate potatoes. Heat 2 table spoons oil in a vessel and add mustard seeds, urad dal, curry leaves, sesame seeds, turmeric powder and onions. Fry it until onions are light brown in colour.

(2) Add grated potatoes and the remaining masalas. Shape like wadas. Flatten a little, dip the wadas in chana flour batter and fry them in hot oil.

(3) Slit the bread from the centre, spread the sweet chutney, garlic chutney, coriander chutney, inside both the sides. Put the wada in the centre and close the bread.

(4) Heat a little ghee or oil on tava and shallow fry the pau-wada on both sides. Decorate with sev and finely chopped coriander leaves.

129. Patara [Serves 6]

Ingredients

(1) 250 grams colocasia leaves (patara)

(2) 225 grams chana flour

(3) 2 tea spoons red chilli powder

(4) A pinch asafoetida

(5) 1 tea spoon garam masala

(6) 5 table spoons sugar

(7) 1 cup curd

(8) 1 lime

(9) $\frac{1}{4}$ tea spoon turmeric powder

(10) 1 tea spoon dhana-jeera powder

(11) 1 banana

(12) Oil accordingly

(13) 1 tea spoon mustard seeds

(14) 1 tea spoon sesame seeds

(15) $\frac{1}{2}$ cup butter milk

(16) A few coriander leaves chopped

(17) Grated coconut

(18) 1 tea spoon clove-cinnamon powder

(19) A few khus khus seeds

(20) Salt to taste

Method

(1) Remove the veins from colocasia leaves. Wash and wipe them. Mix all the masala in chana flour.

(2) Add 2 table spoons oil, 3 table spoons sugar and mashed banana to it. Make a thick batter.

(3) Spread the batter on the leaves and roll them tightly. Steam the rolls.

(4) They can be steamed in the cooker also. But without the (weight) whistle and put the rolls on the seive.

(5) When they are done separate them and apply oil when they are still hot. This would keep their colour green and help to keep them soft.

(6) Heat more amount of oil in a vessel and add mustard seeds, sesame seeds, butter milk, salt, sugar and cinnamon-clove powder in the seasoning. Cut the patara into pieces (not very small).

Add them to the seasoning shallow and fry them for some time before removing. Garnish with grated coconut, chopped coriander and sprinkle some khus khus on them.

130. Patara Bhajiya (Samosa)

[Makes 25 samosas]

Ingredients

(1) 150 grams colocasia leaves

(2) 250 grams potatoes

(3) 100 grams dried peas

(4) $\frac{1}{2}$ tea spoon turmeric powder

(5) 1 tea spoon ginger-chilli paste

(6) 1 tea spoon garam masala

(7) 1 lime

(8) 2 tea spoons sugar

(9) 2 table spoons finely chopped coriander leaves

(10) 2 table spoons rice flour

(11) A pinch asafoetida

(12) $\frac{1}{2}$ cup maida

(13) Oil for frying

(14) Salt to taste

Method

(1) Boil peas. Cut potatoes finely and fry them. Mix potatoes, peas and remaining masala.

(2) Remove the veins from colocasia leaves. Cut each leaf vertically into two parts.

Spread the masala on one side and roll like a samosa.

(3) Make batter of maida, salt, asafoetida and water. Seal the samosa with thick maida batter. Then dip the samosa in maida batter (not too thick) and fry them. Serve hot.

131. Kachori

[Makes 12 to 15 kachoris]

Ingredients

(1) 250 grams fresh beans (tuver)

(2) A small piece of ginger

(3) 8 to 10 green chillies

(4) Oil accordingly

(5) $\frac{1}{2}$ tea spoon mustard seeds

(6) 1 tea spoon sesame seeds

(7) A pinch soda

(8) 1 potato

(9) 50 grams rice flakes

(10) A few coriander leaves

(11) $\frac{1}{2}$ tea spoon citric acid

(12) 2 tea spoons sugar

(13) 1 tea spoon garam masala

(14) A few kajus and raisins

(15) 300 grams wheat flour or maida

(16) Sesame seeds

(17) 1 tea spoon powdered sugar

(18) $\frac{1}{2}$ tea spoon lime juice

(19) Salt to taste

Method

(1) Crush the fresh beans lightly. Grind ginger and chillies.

(2) Heat enough oil in a kadhai and add mustard seeds, sesame seeds, ginger-chilli paste and fresh beans. Add salt. Fry for some time. Dissolve soda into water.

(3) If needed add boiled and mashed potatoes. Add it to the mixture. Washed rice flakes also can be added. Fry for some time. When cooked properly, add all the masalas. If fresh beans are less than the proportion of potatoes can be increased.

(4) Knead the dough made of either wheat flour only or maida and little amount of wheat flour. To this add 1 tea spoon of powdered sugar, 2 tea spoons oil, and some lime juice. Knead the dough like that used to make puris. Divide the dough into small portions.

(5) Roll out each portion into a puri fill in the stuffing. Shape it again into a ball. Fry the kachoris.

Variation

(1) Green peas, cucumber, tendali can also be crushed and added for stuffing. Roast peas, cucumber and tendali before adding, them to the fresh beans.

(2) Mung dal and green peas kachoris also tastes good.

132. Dudhi-Poha Kachori
[Makes 10 to 12 pieces]

Ingredients

(1) 250 grams bottle gourd (dudhi)

(2) 100 grams nylon poha (rice flakes)

(3) Oil

(4) $\frac{1}{2}$ tea spoon cumin seeds

(5) A pinch asafoetida

(6) $\frac{1}{2}$ tea spoon citric acid

(7) 2 tea spoons sugar

(8) 2 tea spoons ginger-chilli paste

(9) 2 table spoons coriander leaves

(10) 250 grams maida

(11) Red chutney

(12) Salt to taste

Method

(1) Grate the dudhi and boil it. Strain to remove all water. Press lightly so that most of the water is removed from it. Add the rice flakes to it.

(2) Heat 2 table spoons oil in a vessel. Add cumin seeds, asafoetida, ginger-chilli paste, citric acid, sugar and coriander leaves. Add the dudhi-poha mixture, fry for some time. Remove it from the flame. Make small balls from the stuffing.

(3) Knead the dough of maida, salt and a little oil, like that needed for making puris. Divide the kneaded dough into small portions.

(4) Roll each ball of dough into a puri. Fill in the stuffing and shape it like a ball. Fry the kachori in hot oil. Serve with red chutney.

133. Mung Kachori
[Makes 10 to 12 pieces]

Ingredients

(1) 1 cup mung

(2) Oil

(3) A pinch asafoetida, ginger-chilli paste

(4) 2 tea spoons turmeric powder

(5) 1 tea spoon sesame seeds

(6) 2 tea spoons desiccated coconut

(7) 2 table spoons finely chopped coriander leaves

(8) $\frac{1}{2}$ tea spoon citric acid

(9) 1 tea spoon tea masala

(10) 1 tea spoon sugar

(11) 1 tea spoon garam masala

(12) 2 cups maida

(13) Salt to taste

Method

(1) Boil the mung. Do not over boil them other wise they will be very soft. They should be half cooked strain.

(2) Heat oil in a vessel. Add asafoetida and the mung. Fry for some time. Remove it from the flame. Add all the remaining masalas.

(3) Knead the dough of maida, salt and a little oil like that needed for puri. Divide the dough into small portions.

(4) Make small puri of each portion. Fill the stuffing in the centre. Shape like a ball or kachori and fry on a slow flame.

134. Samosa
[Makes 12 to 14 samosas]

Ingredients

(1) 200 grams potatoes

(2) 50 grams green peas

(3) Oil

(4) 1 table spoon ginger-chilli paste

(5) 2 table spoons finely chopped coriander leaves

(6) $\frac{1}{2}$ tea spoon cumin seeds

(7) $\frac{1}{2}$ tea spoon turmeric powder

(8) 1 tea spoon red chilli powder

(9) A pinch asafoetida

(10) 1 tea spoon finely chopped mint leaves

(11) 1 tea spoon citric acid

(12) $\frac{1}{2}$ tea spoon garam masala

(13) $\frac{1}{2}$ tea spoon sesame seeds

(14) $\frac{1}{2}$ tea spoon tea masala

(15) $\frac{1}{2}$ tea spoon anardana (pomo-granate seeds)

(16) 2 tea spoons sugar

(17) 100 grams maida

(18) $1\frac{1}{2}$ table spoons rawa

(19) $1\frac{1}{2}$ table spoons ghee

(20) 1 table spoon wheat flour

(21) Salt to taste

Method

(1) Boil and peel the potatoes. Boil the peas. Grate the potatoes.

(2) Heat a little oil in a vessel. Add cumin seeds, turmeric powder, red chilli powder, and asafoetida. Also add green chillies, garam masala, sesame seeds, coriander leaves (chopped) and mint leaves (chopped), lime juice, tea masala and anaradama. Fry for some time.

(3) Add potatoes, peas, sugar and salt. Mix them properly. Fry for some time. Remove it from the flame.

(4) Knead the dough like puri of maida, rawa, ghee, salt and wheat flour like that needed for puris. Divide the dough into small portions. Make a puri from each portion. Divide the puri into two.

(5) Fill the stuffing and shape like samosa. Fry them. While stuffing put one pea at the base to give it the proper shape.

(6) Serve the samosa's with garlic and sweet chutneys. Instead of boiling the potatoes, they can be cut into small pieces and then fried. This can be used for making the stuffing.

Note : (1) 1 cup maida, 1 table spoon rawa, 1 table spoon ghee, a little of wheat flour.

(2) This proportion can be used while preparing samosas, kachori and cone.

(3) Pomogranate seeds are known as anardana.

135. Punjabi Samosa
[Makes 12 samosas]

Ingredients

(1) 250 grams potatoes (peeled and cut into small pieces)

(2) $\frac{1}{2}$ cup green peas

(3) $\frac{1}{2}$ table spoon ghee

Ingredients for Dry Masala

(4) 2 cinnamon pieces

(5) 3 cloves

(6) 6 pepper corns

(7) 1 tea spoon coriander seeds

(8) 1 tea spoon cumin seeds, Roast, cool and grind all ingredients into powder form

(9) 250 grams maida

Ingredients for Wet Masala

(10) $\frac{1}{2}$ cup coriander leaves

(11) $\frac{1}{4}$ cup mint leaves

(12) A small piece ginger

(13) 4 green chillies

(14) $\frac{1}{4}$ tea spoon amachur powder

(15) 1 tea spoon sugar

(16) $\frac{1}{4}$ tea spoon turmeric powder, Mix all the ingredients and make a fine paste in the mixer.

(17) Sweet chutney

(18) Coriander chutney

(19) Oil

(20) Salt to taste

Method

(1) Heat $1\frac{1}{2}$ table spoons ghee in a vessel. Add potatoes. Cover the vessel with a lid with some water on it. Stir intermittantly for some time.

(2) Add the peas. Cook for some time. When potatoes and peas are cooked add the dry masala ingredients, paste, anaradana powder, salt, turmeric and sugar. Mix properly, cool the stuffing.

(3) Knead the dough with maida, 3 table spoons melted ghee and salt. Knead it a little softer than that of paratha. Keep the dough aside for some time.

(4) Knead again. Divide the dough into large portions. Roll out each portion into a big puri. Cut the puri into two.

(5) Take a part in hand and roll out like a pan. Fill in the stuffing. Stick the edges by pressing lightly.

(6) Heat the oil on a high flame. Then fry the samosas on a slow flame. They can be half fried and kept aside.

(7) Then when ever required re-fry them. In this way the samosas will be very crispy. If they are full fried once only then they will become soft very fast. So frying them twice is advisable.

(8) Serve them with spicy chutney and dates chutney mixed together.

(9) Also coriander chutney can be mixed with sauce for serving.

136. Patti Samosa
[Makes 25 pieces]

Ingredients

(1) 250 grams potatoes

(2) 100 grams peas

(3) 100 grams maida

(4) 2 table spoons wheat flour

(5) A little rice flour

(6) $\frac{1}{2}$ tea spoon red chilli powder

(7) $\frac{1}{2}$ tea spoon chilli paste

(8) $\frac{1}{2}$ tea spoon garam masala

(9) $\frac{1}{2}$ tea spoon ginger paste

(10) $\frac{1}{2}$ tea spoon anardana (dry pomogranate seeds powdered)

(11) 2 table spoons finely chopped coriander leaves

(12) $\frac{1}{4}$ tea spoon citric acid

(13) 1 tea spoon sugar

(14) Oil

(15) Salt to taste

Method

(1) Mix maida, wheat flour and 1 tea spoon salt. Knead a soft dough like phulka. Divide the dough into small portions. Roll out into very thick and small roti.

(2) Take 2 rotis. Apply a little oil to both the rotis, sprinkle little flour. Place the other roti on it i.e. place both rotis on each other. Roll out on to phulka. Roast like a roti on both sides on the tava. Separate both the rotis from each other. Make all such rotis in the same way. Keep them in a closed container. Do not roast them for long or they would become hard.

(3) Make the samosa stuffing by boiling potatoes and peas. As given in the above recipe.

(4) Cut the rotis into long strips. Mix 1 table spoon maida or rice flour and 4 table spoons water properly. Heat the mixture till it thickens. Put the stuffing at one end and roll like samosas. Stick the edges with the prepared maida mixture.

(5) Fry the samosas in hot oil. If the samosa has to be stored for a longer time, place a thin muslin cloth in the box. Place samosa at the base. Again put other piece of muslin cloth on it, then place other layer of samosa. Put the box in the refrigerator.

Ingredients for Chutney

(1) 25 grams chana dal

(2) A small piece of ginger

(3) 5 to 6 green chillies

(4) $\frac{1}{4}$ cup finely chopped coriander leaves

(5) $\frac{1}{4}$ cup finely chopped mint leaves

(6) $\frac{1}{4}$ tea spoon citric acid

(7) Salt to taste

Method

Soak the chana dal for 6 hours. Grind it coarsely. Add ginger-chilli paste, coriander leaves and mint leaves. Also add citric acid and salt. Mix well.

Variation

(1) Samosa can be made by soaking the papads in water and then filling them with the stuffing.

(2) Stuffing can be made of peas, fresh beans, tendali, cucumber, chawli and chana dal.

(3) Stuffing can be made by mixing tendali, cucumber and chawli. Crush the chawli in chilli-cutter and then roast it.

137. Tri-colour Bread Samosa
[Serves 4]
Ingredients

(1) 16 slices sandwich bread

(2) Butter

(3) Green coriander chutney

(4) Tomato ketchup

(5) 1 to $\frac{1}{2}$ cup chana flour

(6) Oil

(7) 1 tea spoon red chilli powder

(8) Salt to taste

Method

(1) Apply butter on one slice of bread. Then apply coriander chutney on other slice. Put the buttered slice on it.

(2) On the upper side apply butter and ketchup. Put on other slice with butter on it. Again apply butter and coriander chutney on the top side.

(3) Again place a slice with butter above it. Place 4 slices of bread like this.

(4) Make a batter of chana flour, salt and red chilli powder. Heat plenty of oil in a fry pan.

(5) Dip the bread into the batter and slowly put it into the fry pan for frying with the help of a tavetha. (flat spoon with a long handle)

(6) Turn it with the help of the tavetha. Remove it from oil when done. Cut into 4 pieces.

(7) Serve hot with chutney or sauce.

138. Cheese-Paneer Samosa

[Makes 15 samosas]

Ingredients

(1) 250 grams paneer

(2) 100 grams cheese

(3) 10 green chillis

(4) 1 small piece of ginger

(5) Oil

(6) $\frac{1}{2}$ tea spoon cumin seeds

(7) A pinch asafoetida

(8) 4 pieces cinnamon (powdered)

(9) 4 cloves (powdered)

(10) $\frac{1}{2}$ lime

(11) 2 tea spoons sugar

(12) $\frac{1}{2}$ tea spoon turmeric powder

(13) 4 table spoons finely chopped coriander leaves

(14) 2 tea spoons desiccated coconut

(15) 250 grams maida

(16) Coriander chutney

(17) Tomato sauce

(18) Salt to taste

Method

(1) Grate paneer and cheese.

(2) Heat 1 table spoon of oil in a vessel and add cumin seeds asafoetida, cloves and cinnamon. Fry a little. Add ginger-chilli paste, paneer and cheese. Fry for one minute. Remove it from the flame.

(3) Add lime juice, sugar, salt, coriander leaves and coconut.

(4) Mix properly. Mix 1 table spoon oil, and salt to maida and knead a puri like dough. Then make rotis out of it as in patti samosa. Cut into strips and fill the stuffing of paneer and cheese. Roll like samosa and fry them.

(5) Also puris can be made and cut into 2 and stuffed and shaped like samosa. Fry them.

(6) Serve hot with green chutney and sauce.

139. Cheese-Paneer Ghughara

[Makes 15 pieces]

Ingredients and Method

(1) Prepare stuffing like that prepared for cheese paneer samosa. Give the stuffed puris, a semi circular shape like ghughara instead of triangular samosas.

(2) Fry the ghugharas in hot oil.

140. Cheese-Paneer Roll

[Makes 20 rolls]

Ingredients and Method

(1) Prepare the same stuffing as required for cheese-paneer samosa. Boil, peel and grate 500 grams potatoes.

(2) To that add 100 grams of powdered toast and 50 grams of arrow-root flour. Add salt. Divide this potato mixture into small portions. Take one portion flatten a little by pressing with hand and fill in the cheese-paneer stuffing and shape like roll. Fry the rolls in hot oil.

(3) You can also make cheese-paneer pattice by shaping the balls like pattice.

141. Onion Samosa
[Makes 5 to 7 samosas]

Ingredients and Method

(1) 250 grams of onions finely chopped. Heat oil in a vessel, add mustard seeds asafoetida, 1 table spoon sesame seeds. Fry for a minute. Add finely chopped onions and saute for a few minutes.

(2) Add 3 table spoons of roasted chana dal powder (daliya), salt, ginger-chilli paste, 1 tea spoon of clove cinnamon powder, 2 tea spoons of coconut, coriander leaves, juice of 1 lime and 2 tea spoons of sugar.

(3) Cool the stuffing. Make the rotis as in patti samosa. Cut the rotis into strips and fill them with the stuffing. Shape the pattis (strips) like samosa and fry them.

Variation

Parathas and bhakharwadi also can be made with this stuffing.

142. Rice Flakes Onion Samosa
[Makes 10 to 12 samosas]
Ingredients

(1) 100 grams rice flakes
(2) 250 grams onion
(3) Oil for frying
(4) 1 tea spoon urad dal
(5) 2 tea spoons green chillies
(6) 1 lime
(7) 2 tea spoons sugar

(8) 1 tea spoon garam masala
(9) Rotis as in patti samosas
(10) Salt to taste

Method

(1) Soak rice flakes in water. Grate onions.

(2) Heat a little oil in a vessel, add urad dal. Add grated onion. Fry onions for few minutes. Add rice flakes and all other masala.

(3) Make strips from rotis. Fill in the strips with the stuffing. Shape (triangular) like samosas. Fry in hot oil.

143. Cutlet
[Makes 12 pieces]
Ingredients

(1) 50 grams french beans
(2) 50 grams carrots
(3) 250 grams potatoes
(4) 100 grams peas
(5) 50 grams chawli
(6) Oil
(7) 1 tea spoon sesame seeds
(8) $\frac{1}{2}$ tea spoon mustard seeds
(9) 1 tea spoon ginger-chilli paste
(10) $\frac{1}{4}$ cup coriander leaves
(11) $\frac{1}{2}$ lime
(12) 1 tea spoon sugar
(13) 2 table spoons arrow-root flour
(14) Toast (powdered)
(15) Salt to taste

Method

(1) Cut all vegetables into small pieces. Steam them. Boil potatoes, peel and grate them.

(2) Heat a little oil in a vessel and add mustard seeds, sesame seeds, ginger-chilli paste and coriander leaves. Fry a little.

(3) Add lime juice and sugar. Add arrow-root flour and stir constantly to prevent lump formation. Add toast powder.

(4) When arrow-root flour and coriander get roasted. Then add toast powder to the vegetables. Add salt and all other masala. Mix properly.

(5) Make cutlets using moulds while adding sugar during seasoning lower down the flame or lumps would be formed. Powdered sugar may be added at the end.

(6) Roll the cutlets in powdered bread crumbs. Fry on a high flame.

Variation

(1) Instead of bread crumbs powdered rice flakes can also be used. If the cutlets crack then a very thin batter of maida can be made. Dip the cutlets in the batter and fry.

(2) Cutlet roll – the stuffing can be shaped into rolls and cutlet rolls can be made.

144. Cutlet and Sev Roll
[Makes 20 rolls]

Ingredients and Method

(1) Shape the cutlet stuffing into rolls. Make a batter of 50 grams maida. Dip the rolls in the batter.

(2) Roll in vermecilli (broken). Fry them. Serve them with red chutney.

145. Burger, Hotdog
[Makes 4 pieces]
Ingredients

(1) 4 prepared cutlets
(2) 4 buns

(3) Green chutney
(4) Garlic chutney
(5) Sweet chutney
(6) Cucumber
(7) Tomatoes
(8) Onions
(9) Cheese
(10) Sauce
(11) Butter

Method

(1) Cut the bun from the centre. On one side at the bun, apply sweet chutney and on the other side apply green and garlic chutney.

(2) Slice all vegetables. Put sliced vegetables. Then put the cutlet and the cheese. Put the other slice of the bun shallow fry in butter or oil.

(3) For hot dog make long cutlets and use the long hot dog bun.

146. Vegetable Burger
[Makes 8 to 10 pieces]
Ingredients

(1) 100 grams capsicum
(2) 100 grams cabbage
(3) 100 grams carrots
(4) 200 grams cream
(5) 1 tea spoon mustard powder
(6) 2 tea spoons sugar
(7) 2 tea spoons pepper powder
(8) Cucumber slice
(9) Tomato slice
(10) Tomato ketchup
(11) Salad leaves (optional)
(12) 8 to 10 prepared cutlets
(13) Onion slice
(14) Oil

(15) 8 to 10 buns

(16) Salt to taste

Method

(1) Cut the capsicum into small pieces. Add grated cabbage and carrot to it. Add cream, mustard powder, sugar, salt, pepper powder. Mix properly.

(2) Peal and slice cucumber and tomatoes.

(3) Slice the bun horizontally into two parts. On the lower slice apply tomato ketchup. Place a salad leaf on it. Then place the cutlet. Place grated cabbage and carrot mixture on it.

(4) Arrange cucumber, tomato slices on it. Shallow fry onion slices on a non-stick pan. Place them on tomato slices.

(5) Place the other slice of the bun, press slightly. Shallow fry on both the sides on a non-stick pan. Or put in the oven for some time. Heat the oven from the upper side only.

147. Bread Rolls [Makes 15 rolls]

Ingredients

(1) 15 slices sandwich bread

(2) 250 grams stuffing made for batata-wada (According to R. No. 116)

(3) Oil

Method

(1) Make the stuffing as for batatawada or boil, peel and grate potatoes.

(2) Add onions, ginger-chilli paste, citric acid, sugar, salt, garam masala to it.

(3) Remove the edges from the bread slice. Moisten the bread slices. Press very lightly to remove the extra water. Fill in the stuffing and close the edges tightly. Roll into oval shape.

(4) Fry in hot oil on a high flame.

148. Dabeli [Makes 12 pieces]

Ingredients

(1) 10 to 12 dabeli buns

(2) 500 grams potatoes

(3) 100 grams roasted groundnuts

(4) 1 tea spoon red chilli powder

(5) $\frac{1}{2}$ tea spoon pepper powder

(6) 8 to 10 green chillies (paste)

(7) 25 grams sesame seeds (powdered)

(8) 1 tea spoon coriander seeds

(9) 2 table spoons coriander leaves (finely chopped)

(10) 10 grams fennel seeds

(11) 1 table spoon amchur powder

(12) 1 lime

(13) 1 tea spoon garam masala

(14) 1 tea spoon sugar

(15) Ghee

(16) Garlic chutney

(17) A little cumin seeds

(18) A little jaggery

(19) 2 onions (finely chopped)

(20) 100 grams pomogranet seed

(21) Nylon sev

(22) Oil

(23) Tomato ketchup

(24) Salt to taste

Method

(1) Boil, peel and grate the potatoes. Pound the roasted groundnuts into half bits.

(2) Heat a little oil, add groundnuts and fry for a few seconds. Add salt, red chilli powder and pepper. Fry again for a few seconds.

(3) Add all the masala in the potatoes like in batatawada.

(4) Cut the bun from the middle into two. Apply both chutneys.

(5) Add all the masalas pomegranate, groundnuts. Finely chopped onions can be kept separate and then added to individual buns.

(6) Put little ghee for heating on a tava. Roast the buns and then put the masala, or first put the masala and then the bun can be shallow fried.

Amchur sweet chutney

Mix amchur powder, jaggery, salt and red chilli powder. After adding essential water heat it.

Garlic chutney

Mix garlic with salt, red chilli powder, jaggery and cumin seeds and grind to a fine paste.

149. Cheese Toast
[Makes 8 pieces]

Ingredients

(1) $\frac{1}{2}$ cup maida
(2) 200 grams cheese
(3) $\frac{1}{4}$ tea spoon pepper powder
(4) 1 tea spoon baking powder
(5) 4 to 6 table spoons milk
(6) 8 slices of bread
(7) Oil
(8) Salt to taste

Method

(1) Grate the cheese. Mix cheese, maida, salt, pepper powder, baking powder and milk. Make a thick paste.

(2) Cut the bread slices into triangles. Apply the paste on the bread slice and fry them.

(3) The paste can be applied on both sides of the bread slice. Finely chopped onions, roasted in oil may be added.

Note : Finely chopped onions can be sauted and added to the paste. Also the amount of cheese can be reduced and increase the amount of maida accordingly.

Variation

For chilli cheese toast, add finely chopped capsicum.

150. Rawa Bread
[Makes 8 pieces]

Ingredients

(1) $\frac{1}{2}$ cup rawa
(2) 2 green chillies
(3) 1 table spoon coriander leaves
(4) $\frac{1}{4}$ tea spoon pepper powder
(5) 200 grams cheese
(6) 1 tea spoon baking powder
(7) Ghee or oil
(8) 8 slices of bread
(9) Salt to taste

Method

Mix all ingredients in the rawa. Make a thick paste. Apply the paste to the bread slice. Shallow fry in oil or ghee.

Note : If you want to add less cheese than add some more rawa.

151. Gold Coin [Serves 3 to 4]

Ingredients

(1) 100 grams potatoes
(2) 50 grams carrots
(3) 50 grams french beans
(4) 50 grams green peas
(5) 50 grams onions
(6) 2 table spoons oil
(7) $\frac{1}{2}$ tea spoon mustard seeds
(8) 1 tea spoon clove

(9) $\frac{1}{2}$ tea spoon lime powder

(10) 2 tea spoons sugar

(11) 1 tea spoon garam masala

(12) Bread

(13) $\frac{1}{2}$ cup maida

(14) Salt to taste

Method

(1) Cut potatoes, carrots, french beans peas into small pieces and boil them. Grate onions. Press to remove all water from it.

(2) Heat little oil in a vessel. Add mustard seeds, cinnamon-cloves powder and grated onions. Fry for a few minutes. Add finely chopped vegetables and peas. Add salt, lemon powder, sugar and garam masala. Remove it from the flame after some time.

(3) Cut the bread slices into triangles or round shape. Make a batter of maida and water.

(4) Moisten the bread slice from above, put the stuffing and dip the slices in the batter. Sprinkle some rawa on the stuffing and fry them.

Variation

(1) Sago can be coloured and kept on the sieve. This coloured sago can be sprinkled on the stuffing instead of rawa.

(2) Sago can be coloured in various colours like red, green, yellow etc.

152. Tip Top Pakoda [Makes 6]

Ingredients

(1) 5 to 6 slices of bread

(2) 250 grams potatoes (boiled)

(3) 1 tomato

(4) 1 onion

(5) 1 tea spoon chana flour

(6) 1 tea spoon ginger-chilli paste

(7) 1 tea spoon sugar

(8) 1 tea spoon garam masala

(9) Oil for frying

(10) Salt to taste

Method

(1) Cut the bread slices into 4 pieces or into round shape pieces.

(2) Boil, peel and grate potatoes. Add to the potatoes finely chopped tomatoes, onions, green chillies, ginger paste, salt, sugar, garam masala and chana flour.

(3) Make rolls from the mixture shaped like guava. Place them on the bread slices. Fry them upside down with the bread on the top.

153. Vegetable Sandwich

Ingredients

(1) Potatoes

(2) Peas

(3) French beans

(4) Sandwich bread

(5) Ginger

(6) Chillies

(7) Coriander leaves

(8) Lime

(9) Sugar

(10) Garam masala

(11) Omum (ajawain)

(12) Oil

(13) Mustard seeds

(14) Butter

(15) Fresh beans

(16) Cucumber

(17) Tendali

(18) Salt to taste

Method

1. (1) Boil potatoes and peas. Mash the potatoes and add all masala. Apply butter on two slices of bread on one slice put the stuffing.

   (2) Put the other slice on it. Apply butter on both the sides of the slice and toast it in the toaster.

2. (1) Cut french beans and potatoes finely.

   (2) Heat oil in a fry pan (take little extra oil). Add mustard seeds, omum, green chillies, french beans, potatoes and salt. Boil the peas.

   (3) Add the other masala when the vegetables are cooked. Add peas, fill this stuffing in the buttered bread slices and toast in the toaster as above.

3. Prepare the masala as that used in kachori. Stuff that stuffing to make fresh beans sandwich.

4. A mixture of coriander chutney, sauce and butter can be also applied on toast or sandwich.

5. Cut thin slices of onions, boiled potatoes, tomatoes, cucumber and capsicum. Apply butter on the bread slices. Sprinkle cheese and chat masala on the stuffing. Toast in the toaster.

6. (1) Cut cucumber, carrots, onions and tomatoes very finely.

   (2) Sprinkle chat masala and cheese (grated) on this stuffing place the stuffing between the two slices to bread. Apply butter on the outer side of the slices. Toast in the toaster.

154. Club Sandwich

[Serves 3 to 4]

Ingredients

(1) Sandwich bread

(2) 200 grams potatoes

(3) 100 grams green peas

(4) 1 tea spoon ginger (paste)

(5) 1 tea spoon chillies (paste)

(6) 3 table spoons corriander leaves (finely chopped)

(7) 1 lime

(8) 1 tea spoon sugar

(9) 1 tea spoon garam masala

(10) Butter

(11) Coriander leaves chutney

(12) Cucumber

(13) Tomato

(14) Jam

(15) Ketchup

(16) Salt to taste

Method

(1) Boil, peel and grate potatoes. Boil green peas. Mix peas potatoes and all other masalas.

(2) Take three slices of bread. Apply butter to them. On one slice apply chutney. Then arrange thin slices of cucumber and tomato.

(3) Put other slice on it. Put the stuffing on it. Apply jam and ketchup on it.

(4) Close it with the third slice. Toast it in a toaster or serve as it is in a folded paper napkin.

155. Ratalu Sandwich

Ingredients

(1) Ratalu (yam)

(2) Pepper

(3) Red chilly powder

(4) Oil

(5) Lime

(6) Salt to taste

Method

(1) Take the longer variety of yam.

(2) Peel and cut the yam into thick slices steam them. Then fry the slices, sprinkle salt, pepper, red chilli powder and lime juice on it. Make sandwich with two slices, one above other. Cut into two pieces. The same masala can be sprinkled above this sandwich also.

Note : You can also add chat masala.

156. Cutlet Sandwich [Serves 4]

Ingredients

(1) 16 bread slices

(2) Butter

(3) Sauce

(4) Sweet chutney

(5) Spicy chutney   (6) 8 cutlets

(7) Chat masala   (8) Cheese

Method

(1) Apply butter to bread slice. Apply sweet and spicy chutney and put the cutlet, in between.

(2) Apply butter to other slice of bread and put it on the cutlet.

Variation

Place tomato, potatoes, peas or any other vegetable or pulses on the bread slice, apply chutney. Place another slice of bread on it and toast it in the toaster. Apply a little butter to the toaster base before putting the sandwich on it.

157. Mung Dal Toast [Makes 12 pieces]

Ingredients

(1) 6 slices of bread

(2) $\frac{1}{2}$ cup mung dal

(3) 1 tea spoon ginger-chilli paste

(4) 1 tea spoon omum (ajawain)

(5) 1 tea spoon cumin seeds

(6) 1 onion

(7) 1 capsicum

(8) Green chutney

(9) Coriander leaves

(10) Oil for frying

(11) Salt to taste

Method

(1) Cut the bread slices into triangular pieces.

(2) Soak the dal for 2-3 hours in water. Grind it slightly coarse. Prepare batter like that used for dahiwada. Cut onions and capsicum finely.

(3) Add onions, capsicum, ginger-chilli paste, cumin seeds, omum and salt.

(4) Apply green chutney on the bread slices. Then place the stuffing and fry them up-side down.

Variation

With the mung dal batter dhokala's can also be made. Add a little water to the batter for making dhokala's. Season with oil, mustard seeds and sesame seeds.

158. Low Calorie Dahiwada [Makes 12 to 14 pieces]

Ingredients and Method

(1) Make batter of 1 cup mung dal (According to R. No. 157). It should be slightly thin. Add salt, a pinch of eno's fruit salt and ginger-chilli paste to it.

(2) Put the batter in the toaster and toast it soak the wada in luke warm water for some time.

(3) Remove from water and press a little to remove the excess water. Arrange them in a bowl. Pour some curds on it. Add salt and sweet chutney.

(4) In this way tasty dahiwada's can be prepared without frying.

Note : Instead of eno's fruit salt a pinch of soda and citric acid can also be used.

159. Hyderabadi Toast
[Makes 12 pieces]

Ingredients

(1) 200 grams batatawada masala
(2) 50 grams french beans
(3) 50 grams carrots
(4) 50 grams green peas
(5) 1 tea spoon ginger-chilli paste
(6) $\frac{1}{2}$ tea spoon lime
(7) 1 tea spoon sugar
(8) 1 tea spoon garam masala
(9) Sweet chutney
(10) Garlic chutney
(11) Spicy coriander chutney
(12) Nylon sev
(13) Onions (finely chopped)
(14) 6 bread slices
(15) Oil for frying
(16) Salt to taste

Method

(1) Prepare the stuffing as is made for batatawada. Chop french bean and carrots. Boil carrots, peas and french beans.

(2) Cut the bread into small triangular slices. Add all the masalas to the boiled vegetables. Spread the stuffing on the bread slices. Then spread the finely chopped vegetables on it.

(3) Prepare a very thin layer of maida. Dip the bread slices in the batter and fry them turned downwards. Arrange them in a dish. Add all the chutney's, sev and finely chopped onions before serving.

160. Vegetable Bread Roll
[Makes 15 to 20 rolls]

Ingredients

(1) 250 grams cabbage
(2) 250 grams carrots
(3) 100 grams cheese (grated)
(4) Salt to taste
(5) Pepper powder
(6) Green chillies
(7) Oil for frying

Method

Mix all the ingredients except bread to prepare the stuffing fill the stuffing in the bread slices and roll like bread rolls. Fry them in hot oil.

161. Spinach Paneer Peas Roll
[Makes 15 to 20 rolls]

Ingredients

(1) 250 grams paneer
(2) 250 grams green peas
(3) Oil
(4) 2 tea spoons ginger-chilli paste
(5) 3 tea spoons sugar
(6) 2 table spoons lime juice
(7) 2 tea spoons garam masala
(8) 500 grams spinach
(9) 200 grams chana flour
(10) 1 tea spoon cumin seeds
(11) A pinch asafoetida
(12) $\frac{1}{4}$ tea spoon turmeric powder
(13) 2 tea spoons green chutney
(14) Salt to taste

Method

(1) Grate the paneer crush the green peas. Heat a little oil in a vessel. Add cumin seed and asafoetida for seasoning. Add salt, ginger and chilli paste, sugar and lime juice.

(2) Add garam masala to the grated paneer. Add paneer and peas to the mixture. Fry for some time. Remove it from the flame.

(3) Prepare a batter of chana flour and spinach. Wash, cut and blende-rised in the mixture. Mix it with chana flour. Add water only if required. Add salt, cumin seeds and turmeric powder to the batter. Prepare rolls from the paneer and peas stuffing.

(4) Dip the rolls in the spinach batter and fry them. Serve with green chutney.

162. Fresh Beans (Tuver) Cone

[Makes 12 to 15 cones]

Ingredients

(1) 250 grams fresh beans (green beans of tuver)

(2) 100 grams maida

(3) 150 grams potatoes

(4) $\frac{1}{4}$ tea spoon turmeric powder

(5) 50 grams toast powder

(6) Red chutney

(7) A little rice flour (for making paste for sticking)

(8) Oil for frying

(9) Salt to taste

Method

(1) Prepare masala according to R. No. 131.

(2) Mix maida, salt and enough oil. Knead the dough for puri. Boil, peel and grate potatoes. Add salt, turmeric powder to it. Divide the dough into small portions. Roll each portion into a puri. Divide each into two.

(3) Make a cone from it. Seal the edges of the cone by maida paste.

(4) Fill the kachori masala in the cone.

(5) Now make small balls from the potato stuffing. Fit one small ball on the top of the roll. Press it lightly to cover the masala like a lid.

(6) Prepare thin batter of maida. Dip the bigger portion of the cone into this batter.

(7) Roll the mouth portion in the toast powder.

(8) Fry the cones in hot oil. Serve with red chutney.

163. Mung Dal Cone

[Makes 12 to 15 cones]

Ingredients

(1) Rice flour

(2) Prepared rotis as required

(3) Oil

(4) $\frac{1}{2}$ cup mung dal

(5) 1 onion

(6) 1 capsicum

(7) 2 table spoons potatoes (boiled, peeled, mashed)

(8) 1 tea spoon ginger-chilli paste

(9) 2 table spoons coriander leaves (finely chopped)

(10) $\frac{1}{2}$ tea spoon citric acid

(11) 2 tea spoons sugar

(12) 1 tea spoon garam masala

(13) Pomegranate

(14) 1 table spoon desiccated coconut

(15) Sev

(16) Salt to taste

Method

(1) Mix rice flour with a little water and boil it till it thickens like a paste. Remove it from the flame.

(2) Cut the rotis into 4 pieces. Take an aluminum foil cone and stick the roti on it. Seal it with the rice flour paste. Place the other pieces of roti's on it. Prepare 7 to 8 such cones and fry them.

(3) 1 big roti can also be rolled out and then it can be cut into 4 pieces. They can be used to cover the cone.

(4) Soak the mung dal in water for 3 hours. Grind it.

(5) Add finely chopped capsicum to it. Add all the other masalas also. Add the mung dal and potato.

(6) Fill the cone with mung dal masala at the base. Then put some pomegranate seeds, sev, desiccated coconut on top of it.

Variation

(1) Instead of mung dal, potato (washed boiled and mushed add all masala). It can be used as the stuffing.

(2) Sev, rice puffs, fine sev, onions, pomegranate seed, bundi, potatoes (boiled and cut to small pieces) can also be used for filling. Add the chutney over it.

(3) Seasoned rice, potato poha, upama, pulse bhel etc. can also be used.

164. Fresh Beans Roll [Makes 10 to 12 rolls]

Ingredients

(1) $\frac{1}{2}$ cup sago

(2) 300 grams potatoes

(3) 2 tea spoons arrow-root flour

(4) $\frac{1}{4}$ tea spoon white chilli powder

(5) 100 grams green peas

(6) 200 grams fresh beans

(7) Oil

(8) 1 tea spoon green chillies

(9) 2 table spoons coriander leaves

(10) 1 tea spoon garam masala

(11) 1 lime

(12) 2 tea spoons sugar

(13) Salt to taste

Method

(1) Soak the sago in water and strain. Boil, peel and grate the potatoes. Add arrow-root flour, salt and white chilli powder to the potatoes.

(2) Crush the peas and fresh beans. Heat a little oil in a fry pan and saute the peas and beans (crushed) for some time. Add all the masalas. Cool.

(3) Make a medium sized ball from the potato stuffing. On a greased thali place 1 spoon full of sago (shape like a puri).

(4) Shape the potato stuffing like a puri. Place it on the sago. Spread the fresh beans stuffing on it.

(5) Slowly roll it.

(6) Close the edges by pressing the potato stuffing. Fry in hot oil. Make such rolls with the remaining stuffing. Serve hot with tomato ketchup.

165. Pau Bhaji [Serves 6 to 7]

Ingredients

(1) 250 grams potatoes (chopped finely)

(2) 100 grams cabbage (chopped finely)

(3) 100 grams cauliflower (chopped finely)

(4) 1 brinjal (cut into big pieces)

(5) 250 grams green peas

(6) 250 grams onions

(7) 8 to 10 cloves garlic

(8) 250 grams tomatoes (chopped finely)

(9) 3 table spoons butter, ghee and oil

(10) A few cumin seeds

(11) A pinch asafoetida

(12) A small piece ginger

(13) 2 tea spoons chilli paste

(14) Finely chopped 2 capsicum

(15) A tea spoons red chilli powder

(16) $\frac{1}{2}$ tea spoon turmeric powder

(17) 2 tea spoon dhanajeera powder

(18) 2 tea spoon pau bhaji masala

(19) Lime

(20) Coriander leaves

(21) Chat masala

(22) Bread

(23) Salt to taste

Method

(1) Steam potatoes, cabbage, cauliflower, brinjal and green peas together.

(2) Chop onions finely.

(3) Heat 4 table spoons ghee or oil in a vessel. Add asafoetida, cumin seeds, onions and garlic paste. Cook for some time. Spring onions may also be used.

(4) Add finely chopped capsicums. Add the ginger and chilli paste and fry for 3 to 4 minutes. Add 2 table spoons ghee. Add red chilli powder, turmeric powder, dhana jeera and pau bhaji masala. Cook for 2 minutes.

(5) Add the tomatoes and very little water. Cook for 2 minutes. Add the mashed vegetables and lime juice. Decorate with coriander leaves.

(6) Cut the pau from the middle. Heat oil or ghee on the tava. Roast the bread slice for a few minutes.

(7) Chop onions, cabbage and tomatoes finely. Add salt, red chilli powder, lime juice, coriander leaves and chat masala.

(8) Serve hot bhaji with pau and onions.

166. Idli Takatak

Method

(1) Make the bhaji for pau bhaji and add small idlis to it.

(2) A few drops of colour can be added in the idli batter to have coloured idli's.

167. Bread Pattice

[Makes 15 to 20 pattice]

Ingredients

(1) 500 grams potatoes

(2) 1 lime

(3) 6 slices of large bread

(4) 1 table spoon corn flour

(5) 150 grams green peas

(6) Oil

(7) A small piece of ginger

(8) 1 tea spoon chilli paste

(9) 4 table spoons chopped coriander leaves (finely chopped)

(10) 1 tea spoon desiccated coconut

(11) $\frac{1}{2}$ cinnamon-cloves powder

(12) $\frac{1}{2}$ tea spoon sugar

(13) $\frac{1}{2}$ tea spoon red chilli powder

(14) 1 tea spoon sesame seeds

(15) 15 to 20 raisins

(16) $\frac{1}{2}$ tea spoon poppy seeds

(17) 1 tea spoon garam masala

(18) 1 tea spoon magtari seeds

(19) 3 table spoons rawa

(20) Salt to taste

Method

(1) Boil, peel and grate potatoes. Add salt, lime juice, bread and cornflour to the grated potatoes to prepare the stuffing.

(2) Remove the crust from the bread

slices and divide each slices into four small pieces. Fry them.

(3) Crush the peas coarsely. Heat little oil in a vessel and saute the peas for some time. Add fried bread slices, and all the masalas, mix properly.

(4) Stuff this stuffing in the potatoes. Shape like pattice.

(5) Make a very thin batter for rawa. Add salt to it. Dip the pattices in the batter and fry them.

168. Peas Atom Bomb Pattice
[Makes 6 to 8 pattice]
Ingredients

(1) 500 grams potatoes
(2) 1 lime
(3) 2 table spoons arrow-root flour
(4) 1 table spoon powdered sugar
(5) $\frac{1}{4}$ cup bread crumbs
(6) 150 grams green peas
(7) A small piece ginger
(8) 1 tea spoon chilli paste
(9) 2 table spoons oil
(10) $\frac{1}{2}$ tea spoon mustard seeds
(11) 1 tea spoon sesame seeds
(12) $\frac{1}{2}$ cup finely chopped coriander leaves
(13) $\frac{1}{4}$ cup desiccated coconut
(14) $\frac{1}{4}$ cup powdered groundnuts
(15) 2 table spoons sugar
(16) 1 table spoon garam masala
(17) A little rice flour
(18) Oil for frying
(19) Salt to taste

Method

(1) Boil, peel and grate potatoes. Add salt, lime juice of $\frac{1}{2}$ lime, arrow-root flour, powdered sugars and bread crumbs. Mix properly to prepare the stuffing.

(2) Crush peas, chillies and ginger together. Heat a little oil in a vessel. Add mustard seeds, sesame seeds for seasoning. Add the crushed peas. Cook for some time.

(3) Add coriander leaves, coconut, salt, sugar, powdered sugar and coarsely powdered roasted groundnuts.

(4) Cook for 3 to 4 minutes, when it gets cooked add 2 table spoons powdered sugar, $\frac{1}{2}$ lime juice and garam masala. Cool the stuffing. Divide the potato mixture into small portions. Sprinkle flour on the rolling board. Take each portion of potato mixture and roll it out. Put the green peas stuffing in the centre and shape like pattice.

(5) Fry one pattice at a time. Cut the pattice from the centre into two. Serve with tomato ketchup.

Variation

Instead of green peas stuffing, other stuffing can be made with grated coconut, coriander leaves and grated cucumber, thick curds, salt, green chillies, sugar, garam masala. Mix properly. Make pattice using this stuffing.

169. Rice Flakes Pattice
[Serves 4]
Ingredients

(1) 250 grams nylon rice flakes
(2) 250 grams green peas
(3) $\frac{1}{2}$ cup fresh grated coconut
(4) 1 tea spoon ginger-chilli paste
(5) $\frac{1}{4}$ cup finely chopped coriander leaves
(6) $\frac{1}{2}$ lime
(7) 2 tea spoons sugar
(8) 8 raisins
(9) Oil for frying
(10) 50 grams maida
(11) Salt to taste

Method

(1) Wash the rice flakes and remove all the excess water. Add salt and mix properly.

(2) Crush peas and roast in them a little oil. Add all masalas. Mash the rice flakes.

(3) Divide the rice flakes mixture into small portions. Flatten it slightly between your palms. Fill in the peas stuffing. Shape like pattice.

(4) Make a very thin maida batter. Dip the pattice in the batter and fry them.

170. Onion Pattice

[Serves 6]

Ingredients for outer layer

(1) 500 grams potatoes

(2) 2 slices bread

(3) 1 lime

(4) Oil for frying

(5) Salt to taste

Ingredients for inner layer

(1) 4 onions

(2) 100 grams rice flakes

(3) $\frac{1}{2}$ tea spoon green chillies

(4) 2 table spoons coriander leaves (finely chopped)

(5) $\frac{1}{2}$ tea spoon ginger paste

(6) 1 tea spoon garam masala

(7) $\frac{1}{2}$ tea spoon citric acid

(8) 1 table spoon sugar

(9) Salt to taste

Method

(1) Boil, peel and grate potatoes. Add salt, lime juice and bread. For the stuffing, grate onions.

(2) Add washed rice flakes (Remove water from rice flakes). Divide the potato stuffing into small portions.

(3) Fill the onion stuffing in the potato mixture. Shape like pattice. Roll in poppy seeds. Press in boiled peas. Fry them.

Note : The inner stuffing can be made by using only rice flakes if onions are to be avoided.

171. Ratalu Pattice

[Serves 5]

Ingredients for outer layer

(1) 400 grams ratalu (yam)

(2) 1 tea spoon red chilli powder

(3) 1 lime

(4) 2 tea spoons sugar

(5) 2 table spoons arrow-root flour

(6) 4 table spoons bread crumbs

(7) Oil for frying

(8) Salt to taste

Ingredients for inner layer

(1) 50 grams chakka (solid curds)

(2) $\frac{1}{4}$ cup fresh grated coconut

(3) 1 cucumber

(4) 1 tea spoon green chilli paste

(5) 2 table spoons coriander leaves (finely chopped)

(6) 2 table spoons powdered sugar

(7) 50 grams sev (fine)

(8) 1 lime

(9) 1 tea spoon sesame seeds

(10) Salt to taste

Method

(1) Cut the yam into pieces. Boil them in a pressure cooker in the sieve. When cool, grate them. Add all the masalas and mix properly.

(2) Refrigerate the chakka so that it does not get sour. If you want to make the chakka at home, add extra malai to milk and heat a little. Make curds of this luke warm milk. When the curds is set, tie it in a muslin cloth. Keep it hanging for a few hours. Let all the water drip off. Chakka is ready.

(3) Add grated fresh coconut, grated cucumber and all the other masalas to it.

(4) Take a small portion from the yam mixture. Fill the chakka stuffing in the centre. Shape like a pattice. Fry on low flame.

Note : If you are making yam pattice for fasting do not use sev and bread crumbs.

Variation

Yam roll : Instead of shaping the yam cover like a pattice, shape it slightly oblong and fry them.

172. Green Tikkiya
[Makes 25 pieces]

Ingredients

(1) 250 grams potatoes

(2) 250 grams peas

(3) Oil

(4) 4 to 5 cloves of fresh garlic

(5) 1 lime

(6) 1 tea spoon sesame seeds

(7) 2 table spoons desiccated coconut

(8) 1 tea spoon garam masala

(9) 4 table spoons finely chopped coriander leaves

(10) 1 tea spoon green chilli paste

(11) 1 cup chana flour

(12) 1 tea spoon red chilli powder

(13) $\frac{1}{4}$ tea spoon turmeric powder

(14) A pinch of asafoetida

(15) Salt to taste

Method

(1) Boil peas and potatoes. Peel and grate

potatoes. Heat 1 tea spoon oil in a vessel and fry mashed potatoes and peas. Fry for a few minutes. Remove it from the flame. Add all the masalas. Mix properly. Shape into small tikkiyas.

(2) Add salt, red chilli powder, asafoetida to chana flour. Make batter like that used to make bhajiya. Dip the tikkiyas in the batter. Fry on a slow flame. Serve with coriander leaves, chutney and curds.

Variation

Curds, dates chutney, coriander chutney, salt, red chilli powder, kalijiri can be added to make dahiwada.

173. Kurkuri Tikkiya
[Makes 25 to 30 tikkiyas]

Ingredients

(1) 6 potatoes (boiled, peeled and grated)

(2) 2 bananas (grated)

(3) 1 tea spoon red chilli powder

(4) $\frac{1}{2}$ tea spoon turmeric powder

(5) 1 tea spoon garam masala

(6) 1 lime

(7) 2 tea spoons sugar

(8) 1 cup soaked sago

(9) Oil for frying

(10) Salt to taste

Method

(1) Mix potatoes, banana and all masalas.

(2) Spread a few sago on a greased thali.

(3) Put a portion of potato mixture on it. Spread and shape like tikkiya. Sago will stick to it.

(4) Fry them. Serve hot with mint and coriander chutney.

Note : For fasting dish instead of turmeric powder and garam masala, add cinnamon-cloves powder.

174. Chana Dal Tikkiya
[Makes 25 to 30 pieces]

Ingredients

1. (1) 500 grams potatoes
    (2) 2 tea spoons green chilli (paste)
    (3) 1 tea spoon arrow-root flour
    (4) 1 lime
    (5) Oil
    (6) Salt to taste

2. (1) 150 grams chana dal
    (2) 1 table spoon amchur powder
    (3) 1 tea spoon red chilli powder
    (4) 1 tea spoon garam masala
    (5) Salt to taste

3. **For garlic chutney**
    (1) 3 tea spoons red chilli powder
    (2) 25 cloves garlic
    (3) $\frac{1}{2}$ lime   (4) Salt to taste

4. **For dates chutney**
    (1) 50 grams dates
    (2) 50 grams dry mango
    (3) 1 tea spoon red chilli powder
    (4) Black salt
    (5) 1 tea spoon cumin seeds (powder)
    (6) 50 grams jaggery
    (7) Salt to taste

5. **For coriander chutney**
    (1) $\frac{1}{2}$ cup coriander leaves
    (2) $\frac{1}{4}$ cup mint leaves
    (3) 2 tea spoons sugar
    (4) A small piece of ginger
    (5) 2 green chillies
    (6) $\frac{1}{2}$ lime   (7) Salt to taste

Method

(1) Boil, peel and grate potatoes. Add salt, green chillies, arrow-root flour, and lime juice.

(2) Soak the chana dal for 4 hours. Boil it in a pressure cooker. The chana dal should remain whole. Add salt, red chilli powder, amchur powder and garam masala.

(3) **Garlic Chutney :** Mix all ingredients and grind it. Add a little water while grinding.

(4) **Dates Chutney :** Remove seeds from dates. Boil dates, dry mango, and jaggery. Grind and strain it. Add salt, red chilli powder, cumin powder and black salt powder.

(5) **Coriander Chutney :** Prepare green chutney by grinding all ingredients. Add little water while grinding.

(6) Fill the chana dal stuffing in the potato mixture. Shape like tikkiya. Fry and keep them aside.

(7) Roast on a griddle till brown on both the sides by adding a little oil. Spread all chutneys and serve.

Variation

Curds can be added to make dahiwada.

175. Rice Flakes Tikkiya
[Makes 10 to 12 pieces]

Ingredients

(1) 250 grams rice flakes
(2) 2 tea spoons green chillies
(3) 4 table spoons finely chopped coriander leaves
(4) Lime juice
(5) 2 table spoons sugar
(6) 1 tea spoon garam masala
(7) Salt to taste

Method

Soak rice flakes for 2-3 minutes. Strain it to remove all excess water. Add all masalas. Shape like tikkiya. Fry them.

176. Spinach-Chana Dal Tikkiya
[Makes 12 to 15 Tikkiyas]

Ingredients

(1) 1 cup chana dal
(2) 200 grams spinach
(3) 5 to 7 green chillies
(4) A small piece of ginger
(5) 8 to 10 cloves garlic
(6) Oil
(7) Salt to taste

Method

(1) Soak chana dal for 4 hours. Grind it.
(2) Chop spinach finely, wash and add to chana dal. Mix all other ingredients.
(3) Shape like tikkiya. Fry them.

Variation

To make dahiwadas add curd, over it.

177. Chhole Tikkiya [Serves 5]

Ingredients

(1) 250 grams kabuli chana
(2) 400 grams potatoes
(3) Lime
(4) 2 table spoons arrow-root flour or corn flour
(5) 1 table spoon powdered sugar
(6) 150 grams green peas
(7) 2 table spoons desiccated coconut
(8) 1 table spoon cashewnuts
(9) 1 table spoon raisins
(10) 1 table spoon green chilli (paste)
(11) 1 table spoon sugar
(12) 1 table spoon garam masala
(13) Oil
(14) Salt to taste

Method

(1) Make chhole as in R. No. 370.
(2) For tikkiya boil, peel and grate potatoes. Add salt, $\frac{1}{2}$ lime juice, arrow-root flour and powdered sugar. Mix properly.
(3) Boil peas and add coconut, cashewnuts, raisins, salt, green chillies, $\frac{1}{2}$ lime, sugar, garam masala and mix.
(4) Fill the green peas stuffing in the potato mixture. Make tikkiyas. Fry them or roast on a griddle till brown on both the sides by adding oil.
(5) Serve with chhole.

178. Pattice
[Makes 20 to 25 pattice]

Ingredients

(1) 250 grams potatoes
(2) 200 grams peas
(3) 2 tea spoons chilli paste
(4) Coriander leaves chopped finely
(5) 2 tea spoons ginger paste
(6) 1 tea spoon garam masala
(7) 1 tea spoon citric acid
(8) 1 tea spoon sugar
(9) Rice flour
(10) Oil
(11) Salt to taste

Method

(1) Boil, peel and grate potatoes.
(2) Add all ingredients except rice flour. Shape like pattice. Roll in rice flour.
(3) Fry the pattice. If you are going to serve pattice with ragada. Then roast on a griddle till brown on both the sides by adding oil.

179. Ragada [Serves 4 to 5]

Ingredients

(1) 250 grams dry peas

(2) Oil

(3) ½ tea spoon mustard seeds

(4) 1 tea spoon sesame seeds

(5) A pinch asafoetida

(6) 3 onions

(7) 10 cloves garlic

(8) 2 tomatoes

(9) 1 tea spoon ginger-chilli paste

(10) 1 tea spoon garam masala

(11) 1 lime

(12) 1 table spoon sugar

(13) 1 tea spoon red chilli powder

(14) ½ tea spoon turmeric powder

(15) 1 tea spoon amchur powder

(16) 2 table spoons jaggery

(17) 2 potatoes

(18) 2 table spoons finely chopped coriander leaves

(19) Garlic chutney

(20) Coriander chutney

(21) Dates chutney

(22) 1 carrot

(23) 1 beetroot

(24) Salt to taste

Method

(1) Boil the peas. They should remain whole.

(2) Heat 2 table spoons oil in a vessel. Add mustard seeds and onions. Fry for 3-4 minutes. Add the garlic paste and tomatoes. Fry again for some time.

(3) Add all masalas and peas.

(4) Add boiled potatoes. Boil for 5 minutes. If you want to thicken the gravy, add a little chana flour, dissolved in water.

(5) Decorate with chopped coriander leaves. For serving, place the pattice in the serving dish. Add ragada over it. Add all the chutneys.

(6) Decorate with grated beetroots. Also add finely chopped 1 onion.

Note : Fresh Punjabi masala may be added to the ragada for better taste.

180. Sev Usal [Serves 4 to 5]

Ingredients

(1) Ragada (as R. No. 179)

(2) 150 to 200 grams fine sev

(3) 2 boiled potatoes

(4) 2 onions

(5) 1 carrot

(6) 1 beetroot

(7) Coriander chutney

(8) Khajur chutney

(9) Garlic chutney

(10) 2 table spoons finely chopped coriander

Method

(1) Prepare ragada. While serving add all chutneys and finely chopped onions, potatoes on the ragada.

(2) Decorate with chopped coriander leaves, grated carrots and beetroot. Sprinkle sev on it.

181. Sev Puri

Ingredients

(1) Panipuri

(2) Curds

(3) Sweet chutney

(4) Sev (fine)

(5) Mung or chana (boiled)

(6) Red chilli powder

(7) Coriander leaves

(8) Boiled potatoes

(9) Chat masala

(10) Salt to taste

Method

(1) Arrange the puris in a dish.

(2) Add curds, sweet chutney, sev, mung, salt, red chilli powder and potatoes (small pieces). Add chat masala. Decorate with chopped coriander.

182. Sev Khamani

[Serves 5 to 6]

Ingredients

(1) 500 grams chana dal

(2) 200 to 250 grams oil

(3) $\frac{1}{2}$ tea spoon mustard seeds

(4) 1 tea spoon sesame seeds

(5) 1 table spoon garlic paste

(6) 2 tea spoons chilli paste

(7) 1 table spoon sugar

(8) 1 lime

(9) 250 grams fine sev

(10) $\frac{1}{2}$ cup fresh grated coconut

(11) 1 pomegranate

(12) 4 table spoons finely chopped coriander leaves

(13) Salt to taste

Method

(1) Soak chana dal in water for 6 hours. Steam it in the pressure cooker.

(2) Pass it through the sieve. Heat oil in a vessel. Add mustard seeds and sesame seeds for seasoning.

(3) Add garlic, dal, salt, green chilli paste and sugar to it. Add a little water and lime juice.

(4) When it is roasted properly remove it from the flame. For serving, place it in the serving dish. Sprinkle sev on it. Decorate with grated coconut, pomegranate and chopped coriander leaves.

183. Green Mung

Ingredients

(1) 1 cup mung

(2) 1 table spoon oil

(3) Salt to taste

Method

(1) For making mung for panipuri, soak the mung for 2 to 4 hours.

(2) Boil some water. Add oil, salt and mung to it. When done remove from flame. Strain it to remove the excess water.

184. Panipuri [Serves 5]

Ingredients

(1) 600 grams potatoes

(2) 200 grams chana

(3) Khajur chutney

For dry masala

(1) 4 to 5 pieces cinnamon

(2) 8 to 10 cloves

(3) $\frac{1}{2}$ tea spoon cumin seeds

(4) 8 to 10 pepper corns

(5) 1 tea spoon garam masala

(6) 1 tea spoon red chilli powder

(7) 1 tea spoon omum

For paste

(1) A small piece of ginger

(2) 3 to 4 green chillies

(3) 1 small bunch of coriander leaves

(4) $\frac{1}{2}$ bunch of mint leaves

(5) 1 tea spoon black salt (powdered)

(6) 1 lime

(7) Salt to taste

Method

(1) Grind all the ingredients of dry masala to a fine powder. Blenderise all the ingredients for making the paste.

(2) Add the paste to chilled water. Leave it for 2-4 hours. Then add the dry masala, black salt, salt and lime juice. Strain and refrigerate it.

(3) Boil the potatoes. Add salt to chana and boil them. Mix both together and add some dry masala and salt to it.

(4) Prepare sweet chutney. Sprouted mung or green mung can also be used.

(5) While serving add chana, potato, curds, sev and chutney in the puri. Serve with the chilled puri (water) prepared.

Variation

Finely chopped onions, hot ragada, spicy bundi, dahiwada can also be added to the puri.

185. Bhel [Serves 4 to 5]

Ingredients

(1) 250 grams rice puffs

(2) Oil

(3) $\frac{1}{2}$ tea spoon mustard seeds

(4) 2 tea spoons red chilli powder

(5) $1\frac{1}{2}$ tea spoons turmeric powder

(6) 150 grams wheat flour (200 grams puri)

(7) 150 grams chana flour (200 grams sev)

(8) 1 pomegranate

(9) 4 table spoons finely chopped coriander leaves

(10) 1 beetroot

(11) 3 tomatoes (finely chopped)

(12) 3 potatoes (boiled, peeled and chopped)

(13) 3 to 4 onions (finely chopped)

(14) Dates chutney

(15) Garlic chutney

(16) Coriander chutney

(17) Salt to taste

Method

(1) In a big vessel, heat oil for seasoning rice puffs. Heat 2 table spoons oil and add mustard seeds, 1 tea spoon red chilli powder and $\frac{1}{2}$ tea spoon turmeric powder. Add rice puffs.

(2) Add salt, 1 tea spoon red chilli powder, $\frac{1}{2}$ tea spoon turmeric powder, a little oil to wheat flour. Knead the dough like that used for making puris (a little hard). Divide the dough into small portions. Roll each portion into a thin puri. Prick with knife or fork dry them for some time.

(3) Add salt and $\frac{1}{2}$ tea spoon turmeric powder to chana flour to make sev. Fry the puris. Instead of puri, shakar para can also be made.

(4) Break the puris into big pieces. Mix all the ingredients in the required proportion. Sprinkle sev and chopped coriander leaves on top of it. Serve immediately.

186. Fruit Bhel [Serves 3 to 4]

Ingredients

(1) 1 apple

(2) 1 chikoo

(3) 2 oranges

(4) 2 sweet limes

(5) 50 grams strawberries

(6) 50 grams grapes

(7) 1 cup sprouted mung

(8) 1 cup groundnut

(9) 1 tomato

(10) 1 cup rice puffs

(11) $\frac{1}{2}$ cup dates chutney

(12) Coriander chutney

(13) Juice of $\frac{1}{2}$ lime

(14) 50 grams sev

(15) 25 grams bundi

(16) $\frac{1}{2}$ cup grated carrots

(17) Chopped coriander leaves

(18) Chat masala

(19) Salt to taste

Method

(1) Peel and cut all fruits and tomatoes into small pieces.

(2) Boil groundnuts. Strain all the water. Cut tomatoes into small pieces.

(3) Mix all the ingredients. Decorate with chopped coriander leaves.

187. Bhel Sonjoli
[Makes 20 to 25 pieces]

Ingredients

(1) 50 grams rice puffs

(2) 200 grams potatoes (boiled peeled and cut into small pieces)

(3) 100 grams onions (chopped finely)

(4) 100 grams sev (fine)

(5) 300 grams wheat flour

(6) Sweet chutney

(7) Coriander chutney

(8) Oil

(9) Salt to taste

Method

(1) Season the rice puffs. Make puris of 100 grams wheat flour as given in R. No. 185. Prepare sev.

(2) Mix all ingredients in required proportion and prepare bhel.

(3) Take 200 grams of wheat flour and knead the dough like that of puri. Divide the dough into small portions.

(4) Roll out big puri. Cut into small puris with a katori. Put the bhel in the centre. Place another puri on it. Seal the edges with water.

(5) Fry them in hot oil. Serve hot with green chutney. After cutting the puris, remove the extra dough. Reroll the extra dough to make for other puris.

188. Bhel Ghughara
[Makes 20 to 25 pieces]

The same as R. No. 187, make shape only like ghughara.

189. Bhel Samosa
[Makes 25 to 30 pieces]

Ingredients and Method

The same as R. No. 187.

Roll the puris, cut into two shape each portion like samosa. Fill in the bhel stuffing. Seal the edges. Fry them in hot oil.

190. Golgappa
[Makes 8 pieces]

Ingredients

(1) 1 cup maida (plain flour)

(2) 2 table spoons wheat flour

(3) Oil

(4) $\frac{1}{2}$ cup mung

(5) 1 cucumber (chopped finely)

(6) 2 tomatoes

(7) $\frac{1}{2}$ pomegranate

(8) 50 grams bundi

(9) 50 grams sev (fine)

(10) 1 onion (finely chopped)

(11) Sweet chutney

(12) Garlic chutney

(13) Coriander leaves chutney

(14) Coriander leaves (chopped)

(15) Chat masala

(16) Salt to taste

Method

(1) Mix wheat flour, maida, salt and oil. Knead the dough like that kneaded for puri. Make big puris.

(2) Prepare mung as in R. No. 183.

(3) Fill all the ingredients in the puris. Add all chutneys and lastly chat masala. Decorate with chopped coriander leaves.

Variation

Canapes can be fried and the above stuffing can be served in them.

191. Khaman [Serves 8 to 9]

Ingredients

(1) 250 grams chana flour

(2) 1 tea spoon ginger-chilli paste

(3) A pinch of asafoetida

(4) 2 tea spoons oil

(5) $1\frac{1}{2}$ tea spoons citric acid

(6) 1 tea spoon soda-bi-carb

(7) 1 tea spoon mustard seeds

(8) 1 tea spoon sesame seeds

(9) 4 to 5 green chillies (cut lengthwise)

(10) 4 tea spoons sugar

(11) 1 table spoon kajus (cashewnuts)

(12) 4 table spoons coriander leaves

(13) 4 table spoons grated coconut

(14) Salt to taste

Method

(1) Add salt, ginger-chilli paste, asafoetida and oil to chana flour and make batter. Add a little citric acid to it.

(2) Boil water in a big container. Place the sieve at the bottom. Place a steel dish on it. Grease the dish.

(3) Add soda-bi-carb and mix well. Mix in one direction only. Pour the batter in the dish. Cover the container with a big dish or cloth so that the vapours do not escape. Put some weight on the dish.

(4) For vaghar heat oil in a vessel. Add mustard seeds, green chillies, $1\frac{1}{2}$ cups water, sugar, pieces of kaju.

(5) Boil the water.

(6) When the khaman is done remove and cool it. Cut into pieces. Add the seasoning. Decorate with chopped coriander and grated coconut.

192. Chutney [Serves 8 to 9]

Ingredients

(1) 1 cup chana flour

(2) $\frac{1}{2}$ cup sour curds

(3) $\frac{1}{2}$ tea spoon red chilli powder

(4) $\frac{1}{4}$ tea spoon turmeric powder

(5) 1 tea spoon sugar

(6) 1 tea spoon oil

(7) $\frac{1}{4}$ tea spoon mustard seeds

(8) Salt to taste

Method

(1) Mix chana flour and curds. Beat well so that lumps are not formed.

(2) Add water, salt, turmeric powder, red chilli powder. Boil the mixture with constant stirring. If the curds is not sour than add a little amount of citric acid.

(3) When done remove it from the fire. Add the seasoning of oil. Chutney is ready.

193. Rice Flakes Khaman

[Serves 2]

Ingredients

(1) 1 cup milk

(2) 1 tea spoon sugar

(3) $\frac{1}{2}$ tea spoon turmeric powder

(4) 2 cups rice flakes

(5) 1 tea spoon chilli paste

(6) 1 tea spoon garam masala

(7) $\frac{1}{2}$ lime

(8) 2 table spoons oil

(9) 1 tea spoon mustard seeds

(10) 2 table spoons coriander leaves (chopped finely)

(11) Salt to taste

Method

(1) Wash the rice flakes. Mix milk, sugar and turmeric powder together. Boil it.

(2) When it starts boiling, add washed rice flakes, salt, chillies, garam masala. When milk evaporates add lime juice. Mix properly. Remove it from the flame. Spread in a greased thali. When cool cut into pieces. Add the seasoning. Decorate with chopped coriander leaves.

Note : Instead of milk, sour curds can be used and instead of lime juice, citric acid can be used.

194. Crushed Dal Khaman

[Serves 5 to 6]

Ingredients

(1) 500 grams chana dal

(2) $\frac{1}{2}$ tea spoon soda-bi-carb

(3) $\frac{1}{2}$ tea spoon citric acid

(4) 8 to 10 green chillies

(5) 1 table spoon oil

(6) $\frac{1}{2}$ tea spoon mustard seeds

(7) $\frac{1}{2}$ tea spoon sesame seeds

(8) A pinch asafoetida

(9) 2 table spoons coriander leaves (for decoration)

(10) Salt to taste

Method

(1) Soak the chana dal for 4 hours. Grind it coarsely. Add salt, soda, citric acid in the batter.

(2) Pour the batter in a greased thali. Put the dhokala for steaming. When done, remove and make cuts.

(3) Add seasoning and green chillies cut into long strips. Add green chillies in seasoning and spread the seasoning on the khaman. Decorate with finely chopped coriander leaves.

195. Batata Poha [Serves 4]

Ingredients

(1) 200 grams potatoes

(2) 3 table spoons oil

(3) $\frac{1}{2}$ tea spoon mustard seeds

(4) 1 tea spoon sesame seeds

(5) 4 green chillies (finely chopped)

(6) A few curry leaves

(7) $\frac{1}{2}$ tea spoon cloves-cinnamon powder

(8) $\frac{1}{2}$ tea spoon turmeric powder

(9) 2 table spoons sugar

(10) 1 lime or $\frac{1}{4}$ tea spoon citric acid

(11) 300 grams rice flakes

(12) A few cashewnuts and raisins

(13) 4 table spoons coriander leaves (finely chopped)

(14) 2 table spoons grated coconut (fresh)

(15) Salt to taste

Method

(1) Heat a little oil in a vessel. Add mustard seeds, sesame seeds, green chillies, curry leaves and cloves-cinnamon powder.

(2) Fry for few seconds. Add potatoes and a little water. Add salt and turmeric powder. Cover it with a lid.

(3) When potatoes are done add sugar and lime juice.

(4) Wash and strain rice flakes. Add them to the potatoes. Add kajus and raisins. Mix properly. Remove from flame. Decorate with chopped coriander and coconut.

Variation

If you want to add onions, add them to the hot oil before potatoes. Fry for some time until the onions change its colour. Then add potatoes.

196. Cucumber Poha [Serves 3]

Grate or finely chop the cucumber. Make it as batata poha.

197. Rice Puff Chutpati
[Serves 5 to 6]

Ingredients

(1) 4 to 5 potatoes

(2) 4 to 5 onions

(3) 100 grams roasted chana dal (powdered)

(4) 100 grams salted peanuts (peeled and powdered)

(5) 500 grams rice puffs

(6) 5 to 7 green chillies (chopped finely)

(7) 4 table spoons oil

(8) 1 tea spoon cloves-cinnamon powder

(9) A few curry leaves

(10) 1 tea spoon sesame seeds

(11) 1 lime

(12) 2 table spoons sugar

(13) Salt to taste

Method

(1) Soak the rice puffs for a few minutes and strain.

(2) Heat a little oil in a vessel. Add clove, cinnamon, curry leaves, chillies, sesame seeds and onions.

(3) Fry for 5 minutes.

(4) Add potatoes, chana powder, peanuts and rice puffs. Add all the masalas.

198. Khandavi [Serves 3]

Ingredients

(1) 1 cup chana dal flour

(2) $\frac{1}{2}$ tea spoon citric acid

(3) $\frac{1}{4}$ tea spoon turmeric powder

(4) $2\frac{1}{2}$ cups water

(5) 2 table spoons oil

(6) $\frac{1}{2}$ tea spoon mustard seeds

(7) 2 table spoons sesame seeds

(8) 3 to 4 green chillies

(9) 4 table spoons coriander leaves (finely chopped)

(10) 2 tables spoons grated coconut for decoration

(11) Salt to taste

Method

1. (1) Mix chana flour, salt, citric acid, turmeric powder and make a batter.

(2) Put the mixture on the flame for boiling. Stir constantly. When it thickens spread on a plastic sheet or a thali or cooking stand.

(3) When cool, cut and make rolls of khandavi.

(4) Add seasoning. Sprinkle chopped coriander leaves and grated coconut.

2. (1) 1 cup chana flour, 1 cup curds, 1 cup water, salt to taste, $\frac{1}{4}$ tea spoon turmeric powder, $\frac{1}{4}$ tea spoon citric acid.

Mix and beat everything together to avoid lumps. Boil the batter in a pressure cooker for one whistle when the cooker cools, mix the boiled batter with spoon. Spread on the plastic sheet.

(2) Cut and make rolls of khandavi. Add seasoning.

Note : If the khandavi does not roll properly than boil the batter for some more time till it thickens properly.

199. Canapes [Makes 12 pieces]

Ingredients

(1) 12 pieces canapes

(2) 100 grams potatoes (boiled and grated)

(3) 50 grams peas (boiled)

(4) $\frac{1}{2}$ tea spoon garam masala

(5) 1 tea spoon sugar

(6) $\frac{1}{4}$ tea spoon citric acid

(7) 1 tea spoon ginger-chilli paste

(8) 4 table spoons finely chopped coriander leaves

(9) Coriander chutney

(10) Tomato sauce

(11) 25 grams sev

(12) 25 grams fried chana dal

(13) $\frac{1}{2}$ pomegranate

(14) Oil

(15) Salt to taste

Method

(1) Fry canapes in hot oil. Mix potatoes, green peas and all masalas to make the stuffing, heat it and then cool it.

(2) Fill 1 table spoon of stuffing in canapes. Add coriander chutney, sauce, sev, chana dal, pomegranate. Decorate with chopped coriander.

Variation

Various stuffings can be filled in canapes like bhel, fruit bhel, cauliflower-potato vegetable, rajama, corn, corn and rajama, potato poha, upama, grated cheese and paneer, samosa stuffing, fried bread pieces, golgappa, sev khamani etc.

200. Handava [Serves 4 to 5]

Ingredients

(1) 2 cups rice

(2) 1 cup tur dal

(3) $\frac{1}{4}$ cup chana dal

(4) $\frac{1}{4}$ cup urad dal

(5) 1 cup curds

(6) 4 table spoons wheat flour (coarse)

(7) 250 grams bottle gourd (dudhi)

(8) 2 tea spoons ginger-chilli paste

(9) 2 table spoons methiya masala (pickle masala)

(10) 2 table spoons jaggery

(11) 1 tea spoon red chilli powder

(12) 10 cloves garlic

(13) $\frac{1}{2}$ tea spoon turmeric powder

(14) 2 tea spoons pickle oil

(15) Oil

(16) A pinch soda

(17) 1 tea spoon mustard seeds

(18) 2 tea spoons sesame seeds

(19) Salt to taste

Method

(1) Wash rice and all dals, dry them and grind them into coarse flour.

OR

Soak rice and all dals for a few hours. Blenderise them. Add curds to it while grinding.

(2) Add 3 table spoons of curds to flour. Add all the masalas. Prepare a batter with luke warm water. Add grated bottle gourd. In winter, use a little more amount of curds. Keep the mixture aside for 6 hours.

(3) In summer add less curds and keep aside for 4 hours.

(4) While making handava heat a mixture of 2 table spoons oil, water and soda. Grease the cooker and put the batter in it. Add seasoning of oil, mustard seeds and sesame seeds.

(5) Keep the gas on high flame for 5 to 10 minutes. Then keep the gas on slow flame for 30 to 35 minutes.

(6) Handava can be prepared in a non-stick pan. When done from one side turn it upside down. It can be prepared in on ordinary oven or a microwave oven.

201. Vegetable Handava (1)

[Serves 3 to 4]

Ingredients

(1) 50 grams french beans
(2) 50 grams carrots
(3) 50 grams green peas
(4) 100 grams potatoes
(5) 50 grams bottle-gourd
(6) 50 grams cauliflower
(7) 50 grams cabbage
(8) 50 grams coriander leaves
(9) 1 cup handava flour
(10) 1 tea spoon sesame seeds
(11) All masalas required for handava
(12) 5 cloves garlic
(13) Oil
(14) Salt to taste

Method

(1) Wash and chop all vegetables finely.

(2) Mix them in the flour. Make handava as shown in the method of R. No. 200.

Note : Thick pudlas can also be made from this batter.

202. Vegetable Handava (2)

[Serves 4 to 5]

Ingredients

(1) 500 grams potatoes (boiled, peeled, grated)
(2) 500 grams yam (boiled, grated)
(3) 500 grams peas (boiled)
(4) 500 grams carrots (cut into pieces and then boiled)
(5) 200 grams groundnuts (powdered)
(6) 4 tea spoons ginger-chilli paste
(7) 4 tea spoons sugar
(8) A little citric acid or 4 tea spoons lime juice
(9) $\frac{1}{2}$ tea spoon turmeric powder
(10) 4 tea spoons garam masala
(11) 4 table spoons coriander leaves (finely chopped)
(12) 4 table spoons grated coconut
(13) Oil
(14) 1 tea spoon mustard seeds
(15) $\frac{1}{4}$ tea spoon asafoetida
(16) 2 tea spoons sesame seeds
(17) 50 grams toast powder
(18) Salt to taste

Method

(1) Keep all the vegetables in four separate bowls.

(2) Add groundnuts and all the masalas to all bowls.

(3) Add salt, sugar, ginger-chilli paste, lime juice or curds, turmeric powder, garam masala, chopped coriander leaves and grated coconut to all. Mix properly.

(4) Take four dishes of the same size. Add the vegetables and seasoning to them.

(5) Now first place the yam layer then the peas layer, then the carrots layer and lastly the potato layer.

(6) Sprinkle toast powder on the top. Add the seasoning again on top. Bake in an oven or in cooker without using the weight.

203. Khichado [Serves 5]

Ingredients

(1) 400 grams wheat

(2) 150 grams tur dal

(3) 30 grams dates (dry) (cut into four pieces)

(4) 30 grams peanuts

(5) 30 grams coconut (dry) (cut into long chips)

(6) 6 to 8 kajus

(7) 50 grams val beans

(8) 50 grams fresh tuver beans

(9) 50 grams green peas

(10) A pinch of soda

(11) $1\frac{1}{2}$ table spoons raisins

(12) Cloves-cinnamon powder

(13) Sugar and jaggery to taste

(14) Ghee accordingly

(15) 8 to 10 almonds

(16) $\frac{1}{2}$ nutmeg

(17) 1 tea spoon cardamom powder

(18) A pinch saffron strands

(19) 2 table spoons ginger-chilli paste

(20) Oil

(21) 4 green chillies

(22) $\frac{1}{2}$ tea spoon mustard seeds

(23) 1 table spoon red chilli powder

(24) $\frac{1}{2}$ tea spoon turmeric powder

(25) $\frac{1}{4}$ tea spoon asafetida

(26) $\frac{1}{4}$ cup finely chopped coriander leaves

(27) Salt to taste

Method

(1) Soak wheat for 6 to 8 hours in sufficient amount of water. Then wash and strain it. Boil in cooker or in a vessel. Grease the vessel, add water, when the water starts boiling, add wheat grains. Stir constantly.

(2) Wash tur dal.

(3) Add dates and peanuts and boil.

(4) Boil tuver and val beans in pressure cooker without the weight on. Add little citric acid and salt to it, to maintain its colour.

(5) Mix wheat grains, dal and beans. Add cashewnuts, raisins, $\frac{1}{2}$ tea spoon cloves-cinnamon powder.

(6) Remove the desired quantity of mixture to make sweet khichada.

(7) Add sugar and jaggery to it. Add saffron (dissolved in water), nutmeg powder, cardamom powder. Heat little ghee, add clove-cinnamon powder (2 to 3 cinnamon and 4 to 5 cloves) to it. Add this seasoning to the khichado.

(8) For spicy khichado add salt, chillies and ginger paste.

(9) Heat oil for seasoning and add kashmiri chilles, (whole), mustard seeds, turmeric powder, asafetida and cloves-cinnamon powder (2 to 3 cinnamon and 4 to 5 cloves). Khichado should be semi liquid. Decorate with finely chopped coriander leaves.

1 kg wheat khichado can serves 12 persons.

204. Aneri Special Chata-kedar Cake [Serves 3 to 4]

Ingredients

For Dhokalas

(1) 250 grams idli or dhokala flour

(2) $\frac{1}{2}$ cup curds

(3) 2 table spoons oil

(4) 4 table spoons water

(5) 1 tea spoon soda

(6) Salt to taste

For green peas stuffing

(1) 100 grams green peas

(2) 2 table spoons oil

(3) $\frac{1}{2}$ tea spoon mustard seeds

(4) 1 tea spoon sesame seeds

(5) 2 tea spoons ginger-chilli paste

(6) 1 lime

(7) 2 tea spoons sugar

(8) 1 tea spoon garam masala

(9) 50 grams coriander leaves

(10) Salt to taste

For corn stuffing

(1) 200 grams corn

(2) $\frac{1}{2}$ cup milk

(3) 3 table spoons ghee or oil

(4) $\frac{1}{2}$ tea spoon mustard seeds

(5) 1 tea spoon sesame seeds

(6) A pinch asafoetida

(7) 1 tea spoon cloves-cinnamon (powder)

(8) $\frac{1}{2}$ tea spoon turmeric powder

(9) 1 lime

(10) 2 tea spoons sugar

(11) 1 tea spoon garam masala

(12) 1 tea spoon chilli paste

(13) Tomato sauce

(14) Salt to taste

For Decoration

Shrikhand chakka (maska), carrots, beetroot, cucumber, tomato, capsicum.

Method

(1) Prepare dhokala batter from idli flour with luke warm water. Add salt and curds one hour before preparing dhokala.

(2) While making dhokala add boiled mixture of oil, water and soda. Make about 3 thalis of dhokala.

(3) Cool and cut into heart shaped pieces. (Shape can also be round)

(4) Crush green peas. Heat a little oil in a vessel. Add mustard seeds, sesame seeds, ginger-chilli paste, peas and salt.

(5) When cooked, add all masalas and cool it.

(6) Grate corn. Add milk to it and cook it. Heat a little ghee or oil in a vessel and add mustard seeds, sesame seeds, asafoetida, cloves-cinnamon powder and turmeric powder. Add grated corn to it.

(7) Add all the masalas and cool.

(8) Prepare the chakka from curds. Take one piece of dhokala. Spread a layer of chakka on it. Then place peas stuffing.

(9) Apply chakka to the lower side of the dhokala. Place it on peas stuffing. Place corn stuffing over it. Apply sauce and place third layer.

(10) Apply the chakka to all the sides with a butter knife. Decorate with carrots, tomatoes, and beetroot on all sides.

205. Aneri Special
Vegetable Lolipop [Serves 5 to 6]

Ingredients

(1) 250 grams boiled potatoes

(2) 250 grams cabbage (grated)

(3) 50 grams cauliflower (grated)

(4) 1 tea spoon red chilli powder

(5) 1 tea spoon amchur powder

(6) A small piece of ginger

(7) 10 green chillies

(8) 10 cloves garlic

(9) 4 table spoons coriander leaves (finely chopped)

(10) 5 table spoons mint leaves (finely chopped)

(11) 4 bread slices (remove crust and powder it)

(12) 1 tea spoon garam masala

(13) A few drops red edible colour

(14) Small ice-cream sticks

(15) Maida as required

(16) Bread crumbs

(17) Aluminum foil

(18) Oil   (19) Salt to taste

Method

(1) Mix potatoes, cabbage, cauliflower. Add salt, red chilli powder and amchur to it.

(2) Add ginger-chilli and garlic paste, chopped coriander leaves and mint leaves, powdered bread, garam masala, red edible colour.

(3) Mix properly. The stuffing should be lolipop colour.

(4) Shape like pattice. Place the ice-cream stick in centre.

(5) Mix salt and water to the maida flour and make a thin paste. Dip the pattice in this paste. Roll it in bread crumbs and fry them.

(6) While serving cover the ice-cream stick with aluminum foil. So that oil does not stick to the hand.

Note : (1) If you don't want to place the stick, fry only the cutlets or rolls.

(2) Tooth picks can also be used. This can be served as starters at a feast.

(3) Addition of garlic is optional.

206. Paneer Cutlets [Serves 5]

Ingredients

(1) 250 grams paneer (grated)

(2) 300 grams potatoes (boiled, peeled, grated)

(3) 2 onions (finely chopped)

(4) 100 grams cabbage (grated)

(5) 5 green chillies

(6) 50 grams coriander leaves (finely chopped)

(7) 1 lime

(8) 1 tea spoon garam masala

(9) 200 grams toast powder

(10) Oil

(11) Salt to taste

Method

(1) Mix all ingredients except toast powder.

(2) Shape like cutlets. Roll in toast powder. Fry them. Serve hot.

207. Chatpata Chana Poha
[Serves 3 to 4]

Ingredients

(1) 1 cup rice flakes

(2) 3 table spoons oil

(3) $\frac{1}{2}$ tea spoon cumin seeds

(4) A small piece of ginger

(5) 2 green chillies

(6) 1 cup chana (fresh)

(7) 2 table spoons coriander leaves

(8) 1 onion

(9) Salt to taste

Method

(1) Heat 2 table spoons of oil in a vessel. Roast rice flakes. Add salt. When it is slightly pinkish in colour, remove it from the flame. Keep aside.

(2) Heat 1 table spoon oil in a vessel, add cumin seeds, ginger-chilli paste, fresh chana and salt.

(3) Cover it with a lid. When the chana are done, add rice flakes. Mix properly. If onions are to be added saute them before adding.

(4) Decorate with finely chopped coriander leaves.

208. Mung Dal Dahiwada
[Serves 5 to 6]

Ingredients

(1) 2 cups mung dal

(2) 1 cup urad dal

(3) 2 tea spoons ginger-chilli paste

(4) A pinch asafoetida

(5) 1 to $1\frac{1}{2}$ tea spoons eno's fruit salt

(6) Curds

(7) Sweet chutney

(8) Red chilli powder

(9) Kalijiri

(10) Salt to taste

Method

(1) Soak mung and urad dal for 3 to 4 hours. Blexlerice the mixture to make a coarse batter like dahiwada.

(2) Add salt, chilli-ginger paste, asafoetida, and 1 to $1\frac{1}{2}$ tea spoons eno. Instead of eno's fruit salt, a pinch soda and $\frac{3}{4}$ tea spoon citric acid may be added. Mix properly.

(3) Apply a little oil in the sandwich maker. Spread the batter in it. When done, soak the wada in luke-warm water. Press lightly to remove excess water pour curds, sweet chutney.

(4) Add salt, red chilli powder and kalijiri.

209. Papadi Chat

Ingredients and Method

(1) Mix maida, salt, pawa and oil. Knead the dough. Make a big roti. Cut like shakkarpara and fry them.

(2) Soak and boil mung and chana.

(3) Make pakodas of wheat flour with a little salt and soda added to it.

(4) Dissolve jaggery in water. Boil for sometime. Soak pakoda's in it.

(5) Place the shakkarparas at the loose. Put pakodas on it. Then add dates chutney, curds, bundi, sev, mung, chana on it. Decorate with chopped coriander leaves.

210. Idli Chat [Serves 3 to 4]

Ingredients

(1) 1 cup idli flour

(2) 50 grams french beans (chopped finely and boiled)

(3) 50 grams carrots (chopped finely and boiled)

(4) 100 grams peas (boiled)

(5) Amchur chutney

(6) Garlic chutney

(7) Coriander chutney

(8) Sev (fine)

(9) Salt to taste

Method

(1) Ferment the idli flour for 5 to 6 hours as is done for making idli. Add all vegetable and salt to it.

(2) Make small small idlis.

(3) Add all chutneys. Decorate with chopped coriander leaves and sev.

Variation

Various (edible) colour may be added to make coloured idlis.

211. Cheese Bread
[Makes 3 pieces]

Ingredients

(1) Cheese cube

(2) 3 slices bread

(3) $\frac{1}{4}$ cup maida

(4) Oil for frying

(5) Salt to taste

Method

(1) Cut the cheese cube into 2 or 3 pieces (long strips).

(2) Remove the crust from the bread slice. Roll it with a rolling pin. Put the cheese strip on one end and roll. Shape like rolls.

(3) Make a thin batter of maida, salt and water. Stick the roll edge with this batter. Heat oil in a fry pan. Fry the rolls till light brown in colour. Like this roll the other bread slices.

212. Dhokali [Serves 3 to 4]

Ingredients

(1) 250 grams batatawada masala

(2) 250 grams wheat flour

(3) 2 cups tur dal

(4) $\frac{1}{2}$ tea spoon turmeric powder (for dal)

(5) 4 table spoons oil

(6) 1 tea spoon red chilli powder

(7) $\frac{1}{4}$ tea spoon turmeric powder (to be added to the dough)

(8) 1 table spoon dhana-jeera powder

(9) 2 table spoons jaggery

(10) 2 tea spoons amchur powder

(11) 1 tea spoon garam masala

(12) $\frac{1}{2}$ tea spoon mustard seeds

(13) 2 pieces cinnamon

(14) 6 cloves

(15) 2 sticks curry leaves

(16) Salt to taste

Method

(1) Prepare batatawada masala. Knead the dough of wheat flour, salt with a little oil and turmeric powder mixed with it. Divide the flour dough into small portions. Roll each portion into a puri.

(2) Put the stuffing in the centre of the puri and shape like ghughara.

(3) Prepare tuver dal, when the dal starts boiling, add these ghughara.

(4) Add salt, red chilli powder, turmeric powder, dhana-jeera powder, jaggery, amchur powder and garam masala. Season with mustard seeds, cinnamon cloves and sweet curry leaves.

213. Sweet and Sour Dhokali

Ingredients and Method

(1) Prepare the dough as in R. No. 212. Cut the rotis, bhakhari or puri into big pieces.

(2) Heat a little oil in a vessel. Add mustard seeds, turmeric powder, asafetida and red chilli powder.

(3) Add curds and water to prepare butter milk. Add this butter milk to the vaghar.

(4) Add pieces of bhakhari, puri or roti, salt, sugar, garam masala, water may be added if required.

214. Buffwada
[Makes 12 to 15 wadas]

Ingredients

(1) 25 grams sesame seeds
(2) 1 table spoon groundnuts (powdered)
(3) 25 grams grated coconut
(4) 15 grams raisins
(5) 1 tea spoon ginger-chilli paste
(6) 1 table spoon coriander leaves (chopped finely)
(7) 1 tea spoon powdered sugar
(8) ½ lime
(9) 250 grams potatoes (boiled, peeled and grated)
(10) 50 grams toast powder
(11) 2 table spoons arrow-root
(12) Oil
(13) Salt to taste

Method

(1) Mix sesame seeds powder, groundnut powder, coconut, raisins and all the other masalas (sufficient in quantity).

(2) Boil, peel and grate the potatoes. Mix potatoes, toast powder, arrow-root, 1 table spoon of oil and salt, for the outer layer.

(3) Stuff the stuffing mixture in the potato mixture. Roll like potatowada.

(4) Fry in hot oil. Serve with sauce.

Variation

(1) **Buff Pattice :** Shape like pattice.
(2) **Buff Roll :** Shape like rolls.

215. Limewada
[Makes 12 to 15 wadas]

Ingredients

(1) 750 grams potatoes
(2) 100 grams tuver or peas (fresh)
(3) Oil
(4) 1 tea spoon ginger-chilli paste
(5) ¼ cup finely chopped coriander leaves
(6) ½ lime
(7) 1 tea spoon sugar
(8) 1 tea spoon garam masala
(9) 1 tea spoon sesame seeds
(10) 150 grams chana flour
(11) 200 grams curds
(12) Khajur chutney
(13) Coriander chutney
(14) 1 table spoon roasted cumin seeds
(15) Red chilli powder
(16) Red, green, yellow edible colour
(17) Fresh coconut (grated)
(18) Salt to taste

Method

(1) Boil, peel and grate 400 grams of potatoes. Grate the remaining 350 grams potatoes. Soak in water. Strain after some time and spread on a cloth to dry.

(2) Divide this into four parts. Colour each part with red, yellow and green colours. Leave the fourth part white.

(3) Heat oil in a vessel. Fry them on slow flame. Mix all four together.

(4) Crush fresh beans or peas and make kachori masala.

(5) Make very small balls. Add salt to the potatoes mixture. Stuff the kachori masala in the centre.

(6) Prepare a thin batter of chana flour and salt. Dip the potatowadas in the batter.

(7) Add beaten curds, green and red chutney, roasted and powdered cumin seeds, salt and red chilli powder.

(8) Decorate with fried chips (coloured), coriander leaves and grated fresh coconut.

216. Tava Mehafil [Serves 6]

Ingredients

(1) 6 samosas, made from potatoes and green peas

(2) 6 kachoris, made from fresh beans

(3) 6 small wadas, made from dahiwada flour

(4) 150 grams spicy bundi made from chana flour

(5) 150 grams small puris made from maida

(6) 250 grams long potato chips

(7) 6 pieces gota

(8) 100 grams rajma (soaked and boiled)

(9) 100 grams paneer (cut into chips and fired)

(10) 250 grams onions (cut, boiled and crushed)

(11) 25 grams garlic (paste)

(12) 50 grams poppy seeds

(13) 100 grams magatari seeds

Method

(1) Soak poppy seeds and magatari seeds for 4 hours.

(2) Heat 125 grams dalda ghee. When hot add $\frac{1}{2}$ tea spoon cumin seeds, asafoetida, 1 tea spoon ginger-chilli paste, crushed poppy seeds and magatari seeds. Fry for some time till ghee separates.

(3) Add 150 grams of tomato sauce, 1 tea spoon garam masala and salt. The gravy is ready.

(4) On a griddle arrange all the snacks. Keep on slow flame, add hot gravy on it. Decorate with chopped coriander leaves and grated coconut.

217. Delhi Chat

[Serves 3 to 4]

Ingredients

(1) 100 grams dahiwada

(2) 50 grams bundis made from chana flour

(3) 100 grams potatoes (boiled and cut into small pieces)

(4) 100 grams maida puri (break them into small pieces)

(5) 50 grams sprouted mung (boiled in hot water)

(6) 50 grams black chana (soaked and boiled)

(7) 100 grams fine chana flour sev

(8) 25 grams cumin seeds (roasted and powdered)

(9) Add 1 table spoon chat masala to it

(10) 250 grams curds (beaten well)

Method

(1) Mix all ingredients a little at a time. Add curds, sauce, green chutney, cumin seeds and chat masala powder. Mix well.

(2) Decorate with chopped coriander and sev.

218. Pea Paneer with Chocolate

[Serves 4 to 5]

Ingredients

(1) 200 grams peas

(2) 200 grams paneer

(3) 2 tea spoons ginger-chilli paste

(4) 1 tea spoon garam masala

(5) 1 tea spoon sesame seeds

(6) 1 lime

(7) 2 tea spoons sugar   (8) Oil

(9) 4 table spoons coriander leaves (finely chopped)

(10) 250 grams maida

(11) Coriander chutney

(12) Salt to taste

Method

(1) Crush peas and prepare masala such as kachori.

(2) Add grated paneer.

(3) Mix well. Mix maida, salt and little oil. Knead the dough like puri. Divide the dough into small portions. Roll each portion like puri.

(4) Stuff the paneer stuffing and roll like chocolates.

(5) Fry in hot oil. Serve hot with coriander chutney.

219. Pulses Bhel [Serves 4 to 6]

Ingredients

(1) 100 grams chana

(2) 50 grams muth

(3) 50 grams mung

(4) 50 grams carrots (cut into small pieces)

(5) 100 grams tomatoes (chopped finely)

(6) 100 grams onions (chopped finely)

(7) 100 grams potatoes

(8) 50 grams sev   (9) 6 bread slices

(10) 3 pieces cinnamon

(11) 5 cloves   (12) 2 bay leaves

(13) Sweet chutney

(14) Coriander chutney

(15) Garlic chutney

(16) 4 table spoons coriander leaves (chopped finely)

(17) 1 table spoon red chilli powder

(18) Oil   (19) Salt to taste

Method

(1) Soak mung and muth separately overnight. Strain and tie in a muslin cloth next day for sprouting or place them in a sieve, soak chana overnight. Boil all three pulses.

(2) Heat a little oil in a vessel. Add cloves, cinnamon and bay leaves. Fry for a few seconds. Add all three pulses. Mix well.

(3) When done add potatoes, carrots and tomatoes.

(4) Cut the bread into small pieces and fry them till they become golden brown. While serving, add the pulse mixture, bread crumbs and chutneys in required quantity mix well. Decorate with chopped coriander leaves.

Crispy Snacks

220. Spicy Puri

Ingredients

(1) 1 cup wheat flour

(2) $\frac{1}{2}$ tea spoon omum (ajawain)

(3) $\frac{1}{2}$ tea spoon cumin seeds

(4) 1 tea spoon red chilli powder

(5) $\frac{1}{2}$ tea spoon turmeric powder

(6) Oil for frying

(7) 1 table spoon malai

(8) Salt to taste

Method

(1) Crush omum and cumin seeds a little. Add the mixture to wheat flour. Add 3 table spoons oil.

(2) Mix all ingredients and knead a hard dough. Divide the dough into small portions.

(3) Roll out each ball into a puri and fry the puris. You may prick the puri with a fork.

221. Khari Puri

Ingredients

(1) 125 grams rawa
(2) 250 grams maida
(3) 1 tea spoon cumin seeds
(4) Ghee
(5) Oil for frying
(6) Salt to taste

Method

(1) Roast the rawa in a little ghee till it becomes light brown in colour. Mix all the ingredients and ghee. Knead a hard dough. Knead the dough properly till it is little soft. Divide it into small portions.

(2) Roll out each portion into a small and thick puri. Fry the puris in oil or ghee.

Variation

Mix maida and a little wheat flour. Add extra ghee, malai, salt, cumin seeds, pepper powder to it. Knead a hard dough. Divide the dough into small portions. Roll out each portion into a small puri. Prick with fork or knife. Fry the puris in hot ghee or oil.

222. Farasi Puri

Ingredients

(1) 1 cup maida
(2) 1 tea spoon pepper dal
(3) 4 to 5 table spoons ghee
(4) Oil for frying
(5) Salt to taste

Method

Mix maida, salt, ghee and pepper dal. Knead the dough. Divide the dough into small portions. Roll out each portion into a thin and big puris. Prick the puris with a fork. Fry them.

Variation

You may also roll out small puri like paratha. Shape it like a samosa. Roll out a little and fry the samosas. This is samosa farasi puri.

223. Padwali Khari Puri

Ingredients

(1) 2 cups maida
(2) 1 cup wheat flour
(3) 4 to 5 table spoons ghee
(4) 3 table spoons malai
(5) 1 tea spoon pepper powder
(6) A little rice flour or maida for preparing the paste.
(7) Dalda ghee or ghee and oil mixed for frying.
(8) Salt to taste

Method

(1) Mix both flours, malai, salt, pepper powder and knead the dough like that needed for making puri. Divide the dough into large portions. Roll out each portion into a big roti. Mix ghee and flour and heat it for a few minutes. Cool it and make a paste. Apply this paste on the roti.

(2) Roll the roti. Cut it into small portions.

(3) Press each portion and roll into a square shaped puri. Fry in dalda ghee.

Variation

You may also make small portions and roll out with the layers on the top. Fry them to make jalebi shaped puris.

224. Mathiya

Ingredients

1. (1) 500 grams muth flour
   (2) 150 grams urad flour

(3) 50 grams cow's pea flour

(4) 1 tea spoon sesame seeds

(5) $\frac{1}{2}$ tea spoon omum (ajawain)

(6) 2 table spoons white chilli powder

(7) A pinch asafoetida

(8) 5 tea spoons sugar

(9) 1 table spoon ghee

(10) Oil for frying

(11) Salt to taste

2. (1) 500 grams muth flour

(2) 125 grams urad flour

(3) 75 grams sugar

(4) 20 grams salt

(5) 20 grams white chilli powder

(6) A pinch omum (ajawain)

(7) A pinch asafoetida

(8) Oil for frying

Method

(1) Take any one of ingredient as given above. Boil 1 cup of water. Add salt and sugar to it. When it boils remove it from the flame.

(2) Add 1 table spoon ghee to it. Mix flour, sesame seeds, omum, white chilli powder and asafoetida. Knead the dough with luke warm water. Knead a hard dough.

(3) Knead well till the dough is soft. Divide the dough into small portions. Cream ghee and muth flour together with light and fluffy (Do not heat the ghee). Roll each portion into this flour and ghee mixture.

(4) Roll out into thin roti. Keep aside uncovered for sometime. Then cover them with a cloth. Fry them in very hot oil.

Note : The addition of cow's pea flour is optional.

225. Thick Mathiya

Ingredients

(1) 250 grams muth flour (fine)

(2) Oil

(3) $1\frac{1}{2}$ tea spoons red chilli powder

(4) $\frac{1}{2}$ tea spoon omum (ajawain)

(5) $\frac{1}{2}$ tea spoon sesame seeds

(6) 1 table spoon powdered sugar

(7) 25 grams wheat flour

(8) Salt to taste

Method

(1) Mix flour, enough oil and all the masalas. Add wheat flour and knead the dough.

(2) Knead very well till it becomes soft and smooth. Divide the dough into small portions. Roll out each portion into small and thick mathiya. Fry the mathiyas in very hot oil.

226. Cholafali Fafada

Ingredients

1. (1) 500 grams chana flour

(2) 100 to 150 grams urad flour

(3) A pinch soda

(4) 1 table spoon oil

(5) Salt to taste

2. (1) 500 grams chana flour

(2) 100 grams urad flour

(3) 75 grams cow's pea flour

(4) A pinch soda

(5) A table spoon oil

(6) Salt to taste

3. (1) 2 cups chana flour

(2) 1 cup muth flour

(3) 1 cup urad flour

(4) A pinch soda

(5) $\frac{1}{2}$ tea spoon ghee (cream the ghee and add to the flour)

(6) Salt to taste

Note : In all the three combinations of ingredients include black salt to taste, red chilli powder to taste and oil for frying.

Method

(1) Select any one combination of ingredients from the three given above. Boil approximately 50 ml of water.

(2) Add salt and soda to it. Prepare the dough with luke warm water.

(3) Knead the dough thoroughly. Roll out into thin and large rotis using rice flour for rolling. Cover and keep aside.

(4) While frying cut them into long strips and fry them. Sprinkle black salt (powder) and red chilli powder on it.

Note : For making cholafali fafada using ingredients 1 and 2, add oil to water.

227. Fafada Chutney

Ingredients

(1) $\frac{1}{2}$ cup chana flour

(2) $\frac{1}{2}$ cup sour curds

(3) Oil

(4) Black salt

(5) 50 grams ginger

(6) 100 grams green chillies

(7) 50 grams coriander leaves

(8) 50 grams mint leaves

(9) Salt to taste

Method

(1) Mix curds, chana flour and 3 cups of water. Heat 1 table spoon of oil for seasoning. Add asafoetida.

(2) Add Chana flour mixture, salt and black salt. When the mixture starts boiling, remove it from the flame.

(3) Add ginger, chilli, mint and coriander paste.

228. Papadi

Ingredients

(1) 1 cup oil

(2) 2 cups water

(3) A pinch soda

(4) $\frac{1}{2}$ tea spoon omum

(5) 3 cups chana flour

(6) Oil   (7) Salt to taste

Method

(1) Beat oil and water well. Add salt, soda and omum powder to it. Add enough of chana flour to it. Heat oil in the frying pan.

(2) When the oil is very hot, make papadi using the frying spoon used for papadi. Reduce the flame to medium and fry the papadi. Serve with green chillies. If the chana flour is ready made, then do not add soda.

229. Gathiya (1)

Ingredients

(1) The same as for papadi

(2) 2 table spoons pepper

Method

(1) Method is the same as papadi but add pepper in the mixture and keep the batter a little thick.

(2) Make gathiyas using gathiya frying spoon. Press the mixture on the frying spoon.

230. Gathiya (2)

Ingredients

(1) 500 grams chana flour

(2) 1 tea spoon pepper (powdered)

(3) 1 tea spoon omum (powdered)

(4) 1 tea spoon soda

(5) Oil   (6) Salt to taste

Method

(1) Mix omum, pepper and flour. Heat a griddle and roast soda and salt on it.

(2) Boil $1\frac{1}{2}$ glass water. Add soda and salt to it.

(3) Add enough oil to the flour. Knead the dough hard enough using boiled water.

(4) Mix 2 tea spoons of oil to water. Use this water for softening the dough. Soften a little dough at a time and put it on the frying spoons used for making gathiya. Heat oil in a pan. Make gathiyas by pressing the dough on the frying spoon with holes on it. Fry well.

231. Phoolwadi

Ingredients

(1) 250 grams chana flour (coarse)

(2) 100 grams sour curds   (3) Oil

(4) $\frac{1}{2}$ tea spoon soda

(5) 10 pepper corns

(6) 1 tea spoon coriander seeds

(7) 1 tea spoon garam masala

(8) 2 tea spoons red chilli powder

(9) 1 tea spoon sesame seeds

(10) 50 grams sugar (11) 50 grams rawa

(12) $\frac{1}{2}$ tea spoon citric acid

(13) $\frac{1}{4}$ tea spoon turmeric powder

(14) Salt to taste

Method

(1) Beat curds, oil and soda well.

(2) Mix chana flour, rawa, enough oil, citric acid, sesame seeds, coriander seeds, garam masala, pepper, salt, red chilli powder, sugar and turmeric powder. Add beaten curds mixture.

(3) Add a little water and make a soft mixture that can be rubbed on the frying spoon with holes. Keep the mixture aside for 2 to 3 hours. Heat oil in a pan.

(4) When it is hot, add a little oil to the mixture. Beat the mixture well. Press the mixture on the frying spoon. Do not rub.

(5) Fry the phoolwadi.

Variation

(1) Phoolwadi can be made by using the ingredients in this proportion.

(2) 3 cups chana flour (coarse), 1 cup oil, 1 cup curds, a little less than 1 cup sugar, 1 cup rawa.

232. Coriander Bhakharwadi

[Makes 30 to 35 pieces]

Ingredients

(1) 1 to $1\frac{1}{2}$ cups chana flour

(2) 1 tea spoon turmeric powder

(3) 250 grams coriander leaves

(4) 50 grams sesame seeds

(5) 50 grams fresh coconut or cylone coconut powder

(6) Oil

(7) 3 table spoons ginger-chilli paste

(8) 2 tea spoons garam masala

(9) 1 table spoon sugar

(10) 1 lime   (11) Salt to taste

Method

(1) Mix chana flour, enough oil, salt and a little turmeric powder. Knead the dough. Keep aside for one hour.

(2) Heat a little oil in a vessel. Saute coriander. Add ginger-chilli paste and saute for a few minutes.

(3) Powder coarsely sesame seeds.

(4) Roast in a little oil till, it becomes light brown in colour. Roast coconut in a little oil till light brown in colour. Mix all three together.

(5) Add salt, garam masala, sugar and turmeric powder. Divide the dough into small portions.

(6) Roll out each portion into roti (not too thin about 8" diameter).

(7) Spread the masala on it. Apply lime juice at the upper edge. Roll it once. Apply lime juice and again roll it twice.

(8) Apply lime juice again. Roll out thrice. Apply lime juice at the other edge. Press the open sides and cut the extra dough. Put cuts on the roll.

(9) See that the bhakharwadis do not separate out. Fry in hot oil.

(10) Take enough oil for frying. Cut into pieces after 5 minutes.

Note : Do not cool too much or pieces would not be formed properly.

233. Ratlami Sev

Ingredients

(1) 250 grams chana flour (fine)

(2) 5 small pieces cinnamon powder and sieve

(3) 10 cloves powder and sieve

(4) 10 pepper corns powder and sieve

(5) $\frac{1}{2}$ tea spoon omum (ajawain) powder and sieve

(6) 1 table spoon red chilli powder

(7) 1 tea spoon white chilli powder

(8) A pinch asafoetida

(9) $1\frac{1}{2}$ tea spoon garam masala

(10) A pinch soda

(11) Black salt

(12) Oil   (13) Salt to taste

Method

(1) Add all masala to the flour and enough oil. Knead the dough. Take a small portion of dough and beat slightly.

(2) Place it on the frying spoon and press to make sev on the frying pan with hot oil. Fry the sev.

(3) If the sev is not crispy, add a little more soda and oil. Sprinkle black salt powder. Proportion of spices may vary according to the taste.

234. Batata Sev

Ingredients

(1) 250 grams potatoes

(2) 150 grams chana flour

(3) 1 tea spoon red chilli powder

(4) 8 pepper corns

(5) 1 tea spoon cinnamon-cloves powder

(6) A pinch asafoetida

(7) Oil   (8) Salt to taste

Method

(1) Boil, peel and grate potatoes.

(2) Add all ingredients except oil and knead the dough.

(3) Make sev and fry well.

235. Wheat Flour Chakali

Ingredients

(1) 200 grams wheat flour

(2) 2 tea spoons ginger-chilli paste

(3) 1 tea spoon sesame seeds

(4) $\frac{1}{4}$ cup curds

(5) Oil   (6) Salt to taste

Method

(1) Tie the wheat flour in a muslin cloth.

(2) Steam this in the pressure cooker.

Remove and break the lumps formed. Add all the other ingredients except oil.

(3) Put the chakali jali in the machine. Fill the machine with the dough. Make round chakali. Make 8 to 10 pieces and fry it in hot oil. The dough should hot be too hard.

236. Rice Flour Chakali

Ingredients

(1) 3 cups rice flour (2) 1 cup maida

(3) $\frac{1}{2}$ cup ghee

(4) 1 tea spoon red chilli powder

(5) $\frac{1}{2}$ tea spoon turmeric powder

(6) 1 tea spoon sesame seeds (powdered)

(7) Oil   (8) Salt to taste

Method

(1) Mix all ingredients and knead a soft dough. Put chakali jali in the machine.

(2) Fill the machine with the dough. Make round chakali. Make 8 to 10 pieces and fry in hot oil.

Variation

The chakali would be greenish in colour due to green chillies. Do not add red chilli powder.

237. Khasta Kachori (1)

[Makes 18 to 20 kachoris]

Ingredients

1. (1) 3 to 4 cinnamon pieces

(2) 3 to 4 cloves

(3) $1\frac{1}{2}$ table spoons fennel seeds

(4) $\frac{1}{2}$ table spoon cumin seeds

(5) $\frac{1}{2}$ table spoon sesame seeds

(6) 1 table spoon coarse chana flour (besan)

2. (1) $1\frac{1}{2}$ tea spoons red chilli powder

(2) $\frac{1}{2}$ tea spoon turmeric powder

(3) A pinch asafoetida

(4) 1 tea spoon garam masala

(5) $\frac{1}{4}$ tea spoon citric acid

(6) Salt to taste

3. (1) 250 grams maida

(2) 2 table spoons oil

(3) Salt to taste

Method

(1) Mix flour, salt and oil. Knead the dough like that used for making parathas.

(2) Roast chana flour and other ingredients of 1.

(3) Add all masalas of ingredients 2.

(4) Divide the dough into small portions. Roll out each portion into a small puri. Stuff 1 tea spoon of stuffing. Roll a little.

(5) Fry on a slow flame till very light pink.

(6) While serving add curds, sweet chutney, garlic chutney, chat masala, onions, sev, chopped coriander, sprouted mung and boiled potatoes (cut into pieces).

Note : The ingredients mentioned for serving are optional. Desired ingredients may be added while the others may be avoided.

238. Khasta Kachori (2)

[Makes 18 to 20 kachoris]

Ingredients

(1) 100 grams mung dal (2) Oil

(3) A pinch asafoetida

(4) 1 table spoon fennel seeds (powdered)

(5) $1\frac{1}{2}$ tea spoons red chilli powder

(6) 1 table spoon garam masala

(7) 1 tea spoon amchur powder or citric acid

(8) 250 grams maida

(9) 2 table spoons dalda ghee (hydro-genated fat)

(10) Salt to taste

Method

(1) Boil the mung dal till it is half done. Heat 1 table spoon of oil.

(2) Add asafoetida and fennel seeds, salt, red chilli powder, garam masala and amchur powder. Mix ghee and maida.

(3) Knead the dough like that made for making puri.

(4) Make 18 to 20 balls out of the dough. Roll thin and small puri. Stuff the cooled stuffing and close the kachori. Press lightly and roll a little.

(5) Fry till it is done for about 25 to 30 minutes on a low flame.

(6) Add curds, sweet chutney, garlic chutney, chat masala, chopped onions sev, coriander, sprouted mung and boiled potatoes (chopped).

Note : As mentioned on page 105 ingredients can be added as desired.

239. Khasta Kachori (3)

[Makes 20 to 22 kachoris]

Ingredients

(1) Stuffing masala of Khasta kachori as given in R. No. 237

(2) 2 potatoes   (3) 2 onions

(4) 1 tea spoon red chilli powder

(5) 2 tea spoons sugar

(6) 250 grams maida

(7) Oil   (8) Salt to taste

Method

(1) Prepare masala as that of khasta kachori. Boil, peel and mash potatoes.

(2) Add all masalas as desired.

(3) Mix flour, 2 table spoons oil and salt. Knead the dough. Divide the dough into small portions. Roll out each portion into small puri. Fill the stuffing and shape like kachori.

(4) Fry on a slow flame. While serving grate onions add salt, red chilli powder and sugar to this. Top the kachori with the topping while serving.

240. Dry Kachori

Ingredients

(1) $\frac{1}{2}$ cup chana flour (coarse)

(2) 1 cup chana flour (fine)   (3) oil

(4) 200 to 250 grams maida

(5) $1\frac{1}{2}$ tea spoon red chilli powder

(6) $\frac{1}{4}$ tea spoon turmeric powder

(7) 1 tea spoon dhanajeera powder

(8) 1 tea spoon sesame seeds

(9) 2 table spoons powdered sugar

(10) 1 table spoon fennel seeds

(11) $\frac{1}{2}$ tea spoon poppy seeds

(12) 6 small pieces of cinnamon

(13) 6 cloves   (14) 10 pepper corns

(15) $\frac{1}{2}$ tea spoon citric acids

(16) 1 tea spoon garam masala

(17) Salt to taste

Method

(1) Roast chana flour in a little oil. Add all masalas and other ingredients except maida and oil.

(2) Mix maida and oil. Knead the dough. Divide the dough into small portions.

(3) Roll each portion into small puri. Stuff the stuffing. Shape like kachori. Roll a little. Fry on a low flame.

241. Bajari Wada

Ingredients

(1) 2 cups bajari flour (coarse)

(2) $\frac{1}{2}$ cup wheat flour (fine)

(3) 1 table spoon red chilli powder

(4) $\frac{1}{4}$ tea spoon turmeric powder

(5) 1 tea spoon dhanajeera powder

(6) 2 table spoons jaggery

(7) 1 tea spoon garam masala

(8) $\frac{1}{2}$ cup sour curds

(9) 1 table spoon sesame seeds

(10) 1 tea spoon omum (ajawain)

(11) 10 cloves garlic

(12) 1 tea spoon coriander seeds

(13) Pickle oil   (14) Oil

(15) $\frac{1}{4}$ tea spoon soda

(16) A small piece of ginger

(17) 3 to 4 chillies   (18) Salt to taste

Method

(1) Mix both flours, add all masalas, ginger, chillies and garlic paste.

(2) Mix 2 table spoons oil, soda and a little water. Boil this mixture.

(3) Mix it with the flour. Knead the dough with luke-warm water. Take a small portion. Press like wada using a little water. Fry the wadas in hot oil.

242. Corn Wada

Ingredients

(1) 3 cups maida flour

(2) 1 cup wheat flour (fine)

(3) Oil

(4) 2 tea spoons red chilli powder

(5) $\frac{1}{2}$ tea spoon turmeric powder

(6) 2 tea spoons sesame seeds

(7) 10 cloves garlic (optional)

(8) 1 tea spoon garam masala

(9) 1 tea spoon dhanajeera powder

(10) 2 tea spoons methi masala

(11) 4 to 5 table spoons jaggery

(12) 1 tea spoon omum

(13) Curds as required

(14) Salt to taste

Method

(1) Mix both flours and masala. Knead the dough using sour curds. Do not add water.

(2) Keep aside for 2 hours knead well. Take a small portion of the dough. Make a wada by pressing.

(3) Use enough oil while pressing so that the dough does not stick. Fry in hot oil.

243. Lila Chiwada

Ingredients

(1) $\frac{1}{2}$ cup chana dal

(2) A pinch soda   (3) 5 potatoes

(4) 5 green chillies (fried)

(5) 2 tea spoons sesame seeds

(6) $\frac{1}{4}$ tea spoon citric acid

(7) 1 tea spoon sugar

(8) 2 tea spoons powdered sugar

(9) $\frac{1}{4}$ tea spoon turmeric powder

(10) Salt to taste

Method

(1) Soak chana dal for 6 hours. While soaking add a pinch of citric acid to it.

(2) Strain and spread the dal on a cloth. Peel and grate potatoes. Put the grated potatoes in water for sometime.

(3) Then strain and spread on a cloth. Fry chana dal and grated potatoes using sieve like frying spoon. Using rolling pin while frying potatoes.

(4) Mix all the remaining ingredients. Sprinkle it when chana dal and potatoes are half done.

244. Poha Chiwada

Ingredients

(1) 500 grams rice flakes

(2) $\frac{1}{2}$ cup groundnuts

(3) 10 to 12 cashewnuts

(4) 10 to 12 raisins

(5) A few curry leaves

(6) 7 to 8 green chillies

(7) 1 tea spoon red chilli powder

(8) 1 tea spoon turmeric powder

(9) 2 tea spoons powdered sugar

(10) 2 tea spoons sesame seeds

(11) 1 tea spoon fennel seeds

(12) 2 tea spoons sugar (granulated)

(13) $\frac{1}{2}$ tea spoon citric acid

(14) Oil   (15) Salt to taste

Method

(1) Fry the poha (rice flakes) using a sieve like frying spoon.

(2) Fry groundnuts, cashewnuts, raisins, curry leaves and green chillies. Add salt, turmeric powder, powdered sugar, sesame seeds, citric acid and fennel seeds. Mix properly.

(3) Add granulated sugar. Go on adding red chilli powder and turmeric powder to rice flakes while they are being fried so that the chiwada gets the right colour.

245. Roasted Poha Chiwada

Ingredients

(1) 500 grams nylon poha (or hajikhari poha)

(2) $\frac{1}{2}$ cup groundnuts

(3) $\frac{1}{2}$ cup roasted chana dal (daliya)

(4) Oil

(5) A few curry leaves

(6) 7 to 8 green chillies

(7) 2 tea spoons sesame seeds

(8) 1 tea spoon red chilli powder

(9) 1 tea spoon turmeric powder

(10) 3 table spoons sugar (powdered)

(11) Cashewnuts

(12) $\frac{1}{2}$ tea spoon citric acid

(13) 4 to 5 papad   (14) Salt to taste

Method

(1) Roast the rice flakes. Fry groundnuts, daliya and then add it in rice flakes.

(2) Heat 3 table spoons of oil for seasoning. Add curry leaves, chopped green chillies, sesame seeds, red chilli powder and turmeric powder. Add rice flakes, groundnuts and daliya.

(3) Add sugar, cashewnuts, raisins, citric acid, salt and roasted papad. Mix well.

Variation

(1) For making papad poha, fried or roasted papad may also be added.

(2) Garlic papad may also be added.

246. Raw Banana Chiwada

Ingredients

(1) 6 raw bananas

(2) $\frac{1}{2}$ tea spoon red chilli powder

(3) 4 green chillies

(4) 2 table spoons cashewnuts

(5) 1 table spoon raisins

(6) $\frac{1}{2}$ tea spoon lemon powder

(7) 2 tea spoons sesame seeds

(8) 1 table spoon sugar

(9) $\frac{1}{2}$ tea spoon poppy seeds

(10) Oil   (11) Salt to taste

Method

(1) Peel the raw bananas and grate them. Fry cashewnuts and raisins in the oil.

(2) Add all other ingredients as desired. Mix well.

247. Kharkhariya

Ingredients

(1) 6 raw bananas (2) Oil

(3) 2 tea spoons red chilli powder

(4) $\frac{1}{2}$ tea spoon turmeric powder

(5) 2 table spoons powdered sugar

(6) 1 tea spoon dhanajeera powder

(7) 2 tea spoons sesame seeds

(8) Salt to taste

Method

(1) Select thick, square shaped, fat bananas. Wash, peel and slice them. Fry the chips.

(2) Apply a little oil on the slicer. Place the slicer on the frying pan and slice the bananas directly a in hot oil.

(3) Heat a little oil in a pan. Add sesame seeds, a little red chilli powder and turmeric powder.

(4) Add the remaining masala. Add fried banana slices. Mix well.

Note : While making Kharkhariya for fasting avoid turmeric powder and dhanajeera powder.

248. Potato Chips

Ingredients

(1) 2 potatoes

(2) $\frac{1}{2}$ tea spoon turmeric powder

(3) Oil

(4) $\frac{1}{4}$ tea spoon pepper powder

(5) Salt to taste

Method

(1) Peel potatoes. Cut them into long strips. Add salt and turmeric powder to water.

(2) Soak the potato strips in this water. Remove and fry till light brown in colour. Sprinkle all masalas.

Note : For making chips for fast avoid using turmeric powder.

249. Spicy Bundi

Ingredients

(1) 250 grams chana flour

(2) 50 grams rice flour

(3) 1 tea spoon red chilli powder

(4) $\frac{1}{4}$ tea spoon turmeric powder

(5) Oil   (6) Salt to taste

Method

(1) Mix chana flour, rice flour and other ingredients and prepare a thin batter.

(2) Hold the bundi frying spoon a little above the frying pan.

(3) Pour a little batter on the frying spoon. Fry the bundi. Extra flour or water may be added to adjust the consistency of the batter.

(4) Wash the frying spoon each time after making the bundi. This would help to make nice bundis.

250. Spicy Groundnuts

Ingredients

(1) 250 grams salted groundnuts

(2) 2 table spoons oil

(3) $\frac{1}{2}$ tea spoon turmeric powder

(4) 2 tea spoons red chilli powder

(5) $\frac{1}{2}$ tea spoon pepper powder

(6) $\frac{1}{4}$ tea spoon black salt

(7) 2 table spoons powdered sugar

(8) $\frac{1}{4}$ tea spoon cinnamon-cloves powder

(9) 1 tea spoon amchur powder

(10) Salt to taste

Method

(1) Remove the skin of the groundnuts.

(2) Heat a little oil in a vessel. Add turmeric powder, red chilli powder and groundnuts. Add the remaining ingredients. Fry for a few minutes. Remove it from the flame.

251. Mung

Ingredients

(1) 250 grams mung

(2) $\frac{1}{2}$ tea spoon red chilli powder

(3) $\frac{1}{4}$ tea spoon turmeric powder

(4) A pinch asafoetida

(5) $\frac{1}{4}$ tea spoon black salt

(6) 2 tea spoons sugar (powdered)

(7) Salt to taste

Method

(1) Soak the mung for 6 to 8 hours. Then strain them.

(2) Fry the mung properly. Add the remaining ingredients. Mix well.

252. Dalmooth

Ingredients

(1) 250 grams black masoor

(2) 1 tea spoon black salt

(3) 1 tea spoon pepper

(4) 150 grams sev (fine)

(5) 50 grams coloured bundi

(6) Cashewnuts, raisins

(7) $\frac{1}{2}$ tea spoon cinnamon-cloves powder

(8) 1 tea spoon amchur powder

(9) Oil for frying   (10) Salt to taste

Method

(1) Soak the masoor for 6 to 8 hours.

(2) Strain and spread it on a cloth. Fry them in hot oil.

(3) Add all other ingredients. Mix well.

Note : Instead of amchur powder, $\frac{1}{2}$ tea spoon full of citric acid may also be used.

253. Chana Dal

Ingredients

(1) 250 grams chana dal

(2) A pinch soda   (3) Oil for frying

(4) 1 tea spoon red chilli powder

(5) $\frac{1}{2}$ tea spoon turmeric powder

(6) $\frac{1}{2}$ tea spoon citric acid

(7) $\frac{1}{2}$ onion (chopped finely)

(8) 2 table spoons finely chopped coriander leaves

(9) $\frac{1}{2}$ lime   (10) Salt to taste

Method

(1) Soak the dal for 8 hours. Strain and spread on a cloth.

(2) Fry it in hot oil. After each time let the oil get heated properly. Add a little soda while soaking the chana dal. Do not stir too much while frying.

(3) Add citric acid, turmeric powder and salt.

(4) While soaking the dal add a little soda to it. While frying the dal do not stir them constantly or it would not be crispy.

(5) While serving add chopped onions and lime juice. Decorate with chopped coriander leaves.

Variation

(1) Mung dal can also be made in the same way.

(2) **Mint chana dal :**

1. Wash and dry the mint leaves.
2. Roast them in a pan without oil. Cool it. Crush them and add $\frac{1}{2}$ tea spoon oil.
3. Add it to fried chana dal. Add all the masalas except turmeric powder.

254. Cheese Shakkarpara

Ingredients

(1) 6 table spoons maida

(2) 6 table spoons grated cheese

(3) 1 tea spoon baking powder

(4) 2 tea spoons pepper powder

(5) Ghee   (6) Salt to taste

Method

(1) Mix all ingredients except ghee. Knead a hard dough. Knead well till the dough is enough soft. Divide the dough into medium portions.

(2) Roll out each portion into a big roti. Cut the shakkarparas and fry them in ghee.

255. Shakkarpara

Ingredients

(1) 1 cup maida

(2) 2 table spoons butter

(3) $\frac{1}{2}$ cup powdered sugar

(4) $\frac{3}{4}$ cup grated fresh coconut

(5) 1 tea spoon cardamom powder

(6) 3 to 4 table spoons milk

(7) Ghee

(8) Salt to taste

Method

(1) Mix all ingredients except ghee. Knead a soft dough. Knead the dough using milk.

(2) Make a big roti and cut diamond shaped shakkarparas. Fry in ghee a few at a time.

256. Instant Wafers

Ingredients

(1) Potatoes (2) Oil (3) Salt to taste

Method

(1) Peel and slice potatoes. Soak the slices in water.

(2) Refrigerate them for 2 to 3 hours or soak in ice cold water and add ice cubes.

(3) Remove from water and spread on a cloth. Heat oil for frying.

(4) Add the slices and a little salt to oil. Fry on a low flame. Remove when wafers are crispy.

③ CORN DISHES

People prepare different snacks and sweet dishes from corn. For variation it is used instead of green peas. It is used in different forms. It is used whole (boiled), crushed or in various recipies it is boiled in milk.

257. Makai Chiwada
[Serves 3]
Ingredients

(1) 500 grams corn cobs
(2) 500 ml milk
(3) 2 table spoons oil
(4) 2 red chillies (whole)
(5) ½ tea spoon mustard seeds
(6) 1 tea spoon cinnamon-cloves (powder)
(7) A pinch asafoetida
(8) 1 tea spoon sesame seeds
(9) A pinch turmeric powder
(10) A small piece of ginger
(11) 4 to 5 finely chopped green chillies
(12) 1 lime   (13) 2 tea spoons sugar
(14) 1 tea spoon garam masala
(15) 4 table spoons coriander leaves
(16) 2 tea spoons desiccated coconuts
(17) Salt to taste

Method

(1) Grate the corn cobs. Add a little milk to it and boil in pressure cooker. Instead of pressure cooker, corn can be boiled in a vessel with 500 ml of milk.

(2) Heat a little oil in a vessel, add whole red chillies, mustard seeds, cinnamon, cloves, asafoetida and sesame seeds. Add a little turmeric powder and boiled corn. Fry for a few minutes.

(3) Add salt, ginger-chilli paste, lime juice and sugar. When it is thick enough remove it from the flame.

(4) Add garam masala, finely chopped coriander and grated coconut.

258. Halwa [Serves 6 to 7]
Ingredients

(1) 1 kg corn cobs   (2) 600 ml milk
(3) 1 table spoon ghee
(4) 100 grams sugar
(5) 1 tea spoon cardamom powder
(6) Yellow colour
(7) Essence   (8) A few almonds
(9) A few pistas   (10) A few raisins

Method

(1) Grate and boil corn in milk. Heat a little ghee in a pan. Add boiled corn and saute for few minutes. Add sugar, cardamom powder, colour and essence.

(2) When the mixture thickens remove it from flame. Decorate with almonds, pistas and raisins.

Note : Add enough milk for boiling corn.

259. Pattice
[Makes 18 to 20 pieces]
Ingredients

(1) 500 grams corn cobs
(2) ½ cup milk
(3) 400 grams potatoes
(4) 1 tea spoon cinnamon-cloves powder
(5) 1 tea spoon sugar
(6) ¼ tea spoon citric acid
(7) 1 tea spoon garam masala
(8) 1 tea spoon sesame seeds

(9) 6 to 7 green chillies

(10) A small piece of ginger

(11) 4 table spoons coconut

(12) A few raisins

(13) 4 table spoons finely chopped coriander

(14) 4 tea spoons bread crumbs

(15) 2 table spoons wheat flour (coarse)

(16) Rice flour

(17) Oil   (18) Salt to taste

Method

(1) Grate and boil corn in a pressure cooker with milk. Remove corn seeds from the corn cob and boil them.

(2) Heat a little oil in a vessel, add cinnamon and cloves powder. Add grated and boiled corn pulp.

(3) When the mixture thickens add grated potatoes and corn seeds. Mix properly.

(4) Remove it from the flame. Add all masalas, bread crumbs and wheat flour. Shape the mixture like pattice. Roll in flour. Fry in hot oil.

260. Roll
[Makes 18 to 20 rolls]
Ingredients

(1) 500 grams corn cobs

(2) ½ cup milk

(3) 400 grams potatoes

(4) 50 grams rice flakes

(5) Cashewnuts and raisins

(6) 2 table spoons bread crumbs

(7) 1 tea spoon cinnamon powder

(8) 1 table spoon arrow-root flour

(9) 2 table spoons ginger-chilli paste

(10) 1 lime   (11) 1 tea spoon sugar

(12) 50 grams vermicelli

(13) Oil   (14) Salt to taste

Method

(1) Grate the corn. Add ½ cup milk and boil it. Boil potatoes. Soak rice flakes.

(2) Mix all ingredients, except vermicelli.

(3) Make small rolls. Roll them in vermicelli and fry in hot oil.

261. Cutlets
[Makes 20 to 22 cutlets]
Ingredients

(1) 750 grams potatoes

(2) 1 table spoon ginger-chilli paste

(3) 1 lime

(4) 500 grams corn cobs

(5) ½ cup milk

(6) 2 table spoons desiccated coconut

(7) 1 tea spoon garam masala

(8) 50 grams coriander

(9) 2 table spoons sesame seeds

(10) 2 tea spoons sugar   (11) Oil

(12) 50 grams toast powder

(13) Salt to taste

Method

(1) Boil, peel and grate potatoes. Add salt, ½ table spoon green ginger-chilli paste and ½ lime juice to it. Cut corn cobs into half and boil in pressure cooker. Remove boiled corn seeds.

(2) Heat 2 table spoons oil in a pan. Saute the corn seeds. Add grated coconut, ½ lime juice, sesame seeds, ginger-chilli paste, garam masala, salt, chopped coriander. Divide the potato mixture into small portions.

(3) Take one portion press lightly on the palms. Fill in the corn stuffing. Shape like cutlet.

(4) Roll it in toast powder. Make cutlets of other mixture. Fry them till they are light pink in colour.

262. Wada, Gota
[Makes 18 to 20 pieces]

Ingredients

(1) 3 corn cobs

(2) 1 cup chana flour

(3) $\frac{1}{2}$ cup sour curds

(4) 1 tea spoon ginger-chilli paste

(5) $\frac{1}{4}$ tea spoon turmeric powder

(6) 3 table spoons coriander leaves (finely chopped)

(7) 2 table spoons coconut (grated) or desiccated coconut

(8) 2 tea spoons sugar

(9) Oil   (10) Salt to taste

Method

(1) Mix chana flour, grated corn and all the masalas to make the batter.

(2) Take a small portion of the batter and press lightly on the palms. Fry the wadas. For making gota add water to the batter and fry the gotas.

263. Dahiwada
[Makes 15 to 18 pieces]

Ingredients

(1) 500 grams corn cobs

(2) 50 grams wheat flour (coarse)

(3) 4 to 5 chillies (green)

(4) 1 table spoon sugar

(5) 1 table spoon amchur powder

(6) 1 tea spoon sesame seeds

(7) A pinch asafoetida

(8) A little curds

(9) Sweet chutney

(10) A little red chilli powder

(11) Oil   (12) Salt to taste

Method

(1) Grate corn. Add wheat flour, add all the masalas to it. Buttermilk may be added if required.

(2) Make wadas. Soak the wadas in hot water for some time. Press lightly to remove excess water. While serving add curds, sweet chutney, salt and red chilli powder.

264. Idli
[Makes 24 to 26 Idlis]

Ingredients

(1) 1 medium size corn cob or 300 grams corn cobs

(2) 1 cup milk   (3) Oil

(4) 1 tea spoon mustard seeds

(5) 1 tea spoon sesame seeds

(6) 1 tea spoon cinnamon-cloves powder

(7) 4 green chillies (paste)

(8) 1 lime

(9) 2 tea spoons sugar

(10) 1 tea spoon garam masala

(11) 2 tea spoons fresh coconut (grated)

(12) 500 grams idli flour

(13) Salt to taste

Method

(1) Boil grated corn with milk in a pressure cooker.

(2) Heat 2 table spoons oil in a pan. Add mustard seeds and sesame seeds. Add cinnamon-cloves powder, green chillies, boiled corn and all the masalas. Proceed as in R. No. 257. Make idli batter.

(3) Place some batter in the idli stand. Then put some corn mixture. Again place idli batter. Steam the idli.

Variation

(1) Corn mixture can be mixed in the idli batter and then steam the idlis in the idli stand. Serve with sambhar, curds or in curds chutney.

(2) Idlis can also be made by first putting the corn mixture in the stand and then pouring the idli batter over it.

265. Bhel

[Serves 5 to 6]

Ingredients

(1) 250 grams boiled potatoes

(2) 2 to 3 corn cobs

(3) 2 tomatoes (chopped)

(4) 2 onions   (5) Oil

(6) $\frac{1}{2}$ tea spoon garam masala

(7) $\frac{1}{4}$ tea spoon turmeric powder

(8) 1 tea spoon red chilli powder

(9) 1 table spoon green chillies (finely chopped)

(10) 250 grams green peas (boiled)

(11) 1 cup sev (fine)

(12) 4 table spoons finely chopped coriander leaves

(13) Chilli chutney (thin)

(14) Salt to taste

Method

(1) Remove corn seeds and boil or boil the corn cobs and then remove boiled corn seeds.

(2) Heat 1 table spoon oil in a vessel, add little garam masala and corn. Saute for few minutes. Add turmeric powder, red chilli powder and salt. Remove it from the flame.

(3) Heat 1 table spoon oil in another pan. Add red chillies and potatoes. Prepare stuffing as described above.

(4) Season green peas in the same way. Mix all the three mixtures. Place it in the serving bowl.

(5) Sprinkle sev, chopped coriander, tomatoes, onion rings and coriander chutney.

266. Handawa

[Serves 5 to 6]

Ingredients

(1) 400 grams rice

(2) 100 grams chana dal (Bengal gram dal)

(3) 100 grams tur dal

(4) 150 grams sour curds

(5) 400 grams corn cobs

(6) 1 table spoon ginger-chilli paste

(7) $\frac{1}{2}$ tea spoon turmeric powder

(8) 1 tea spoon red chilli powder

(9) 2 to 3 table spoons sugar

(10) Oil   (11) A pinch soda

(12) $\frac{1}{2}$ tea spoon mustard seeds

(13) A pinch asafoetida

(14) 1 tea spoon sesame seeds

(15) 1 tea spoon cinnamon and cloves powder

(16) Salt to taste

Method

(1) Wash rice, chana dal, tur dal and allow to dry them. Grind coarse.

(2) Add sour curds and make batter. Keep this aside for 4 to 6 hours. Boil corn seeds and crush them. Add these to the batter.

(3) Add ginger, chillies, turmeric powder, red chilli powder, salt and sugar. Heat $\frac{1}{4}$ cup oil and add soda to it. Add this to the batter.

(4) Heat 2 table spoons oil in a frying pan. Add mustard seeds, asafoetida, sesame seeds, cloves and cinnamon. Add the corn batter to it. Cover with a lid and allow it to cook.

(5) It can be also made in the handawa maker. Apply oil to the handawa maker. Pour the mixture in it. Cook it on high flame for 10 minutes and then on a low flame for 25 to 30 minutes.

4 (FASTING DISHES)

267. Rajgara Puri

[Serves 2 to 3]

Ingredients

(1) 250 grams rajgara flour

(2) Oil

(3) 1 potato (boiled, peeled and grated) or 1 ripe banana

(4) Salt to taste

Method

(1) Mix flour, salt, 1 tea spoon oil and potato.

(2) Knead the dough using luke-warm water.

(3) Make thick puris and fry in hot oil. Keep some flour aside for rolling puris.

268. Potato Vegetable (Suki Bhaji) [Serves 5]

Ingredients

(1) 500 grams potatoes

(2) Oil

(3) ½ tea spoon cumin seeds

(4) 1 tea spoon sesame seeds

(5) 3 to 4 green chillies

(6) ½ tea spoon cloves and cinnamon powder

(7) 50 grams groundnuts

(8) 2 table spoons desiccated coconut

(9) 1 lime

(10) 2 tea spoons sugar (11) Salt to taste

Method

(1) Boil, peel and cut potatoes into pieces. Heat 3 table spoons oil in a frying pan.

(2) Add cumin seeds, green chillies (chopped), cinnamon and cloves powder.

(3) Add cut potatoes, groundnuts, desiccated coconut, lime juice, sugar and salt. Fry for sometime.

Variation

Potato and sweet potato vegetable can be made in the same way. Also elephant foot can be used.

269. Moraiya [Serves 3 to 4]

Ingredients

(1) 125 grams moraiya (2) 2 potatoes

(3) 75 grams roasted groundnuts

(4) 2 table spoons oil

(5) ½ tea spoon cumin seeds

(6) 1 tea spoon cinnamon and cloves powder

(7) 2 red chillies

(8) ¼ tea spoon red chilli powder

(9) 2 tea spoons ginger-chilli paste

(10) 2 tea spoons sugar

(11) ½ cup curds   (12) Salt to taste

Method

(1) Wash moraiya. Add potatoes grated. Remove the skin of groundnuts and crush coarsely.

(2) Heat a little oil in a frying pan. Add cumin seeds, cinnamon and cloves powder and red chilli powder. Add some water.

(3) When the water starts boiling add moraiya, grated potatoes, ground-nuts, salt, ginger and green chillies.

(4) When moraiya gets cooked, add sugar and curds.

270. Sabudana Khichadi

[Serves 4]

Ingredients

(1) 125 grams sago
(2) 125 grams potatoes
(3) 125 grams groundnuts (roasted)
(4) 2 table spoons ghee
(5) 1 tea spoon cumin seeds
(6) $\frac{1}{2}$ tea spoon cloves-cinnamon powder
(7) 1 lime
(8) 2 table spoons sugar
(9) 3 table spoons grated coconut
(10) 1 tea spoon green chilli paste
(11) Salt to taste

Method

(1) Wash and strain the sago. Cut the potatoes into small pieces. Boil or fry them. Remove skin from groundnuts and grind coarsely.
(2) Heat the ghee in a frying pan. Add cumin seeds and sago. Mix well for a few minutes.
(3) Add potatoes, groundnuts and all the masalas. Mix well and remove from flame when sago is done.

271. Suran Khichadi

[Serves 5 to 6]

Ingredients

(1) 500 grams elephant foot
(2) 2 table spoons oil
(3) 1 tea spoon cumin seeds
(4) 1 tea spoon sesame seeds
(5) 1 tea spoon cinnamon and cloves powder
(6) 100 grams groundnuts
(7) 1 lime   (8) 2 tea spoons sugar
(9) 4 tea spoons grated coconut
(10) Salt to taste

Method

(1) Peel and grate elephant foot. Add salt and water to it. Keep aside for sometime. Then wash it for 3 to 4 times.
(2) Heat enough oil in a vessel. Add cumin seeds, cinnamon and cloves powder.
(3) Add elephant foot, groundnuts and cook on a low flame. When prepared, add lime juice and sugar.
(4) When khichadi become ready keep it in a vessel. Decorate with desiccated coconut.

272. Bhajiya [Serves 5 to 6]

Ingredients

(1) 200 grams shingoda flour
(2) 1 tea spoon red chilli powder
(3) 2 tea spoons sugar
(4) Potatoes   (5) Banana
(6) Mango   (7) Chillies
(8) Oil for frying   (9) Salt to taste

Method

(1) Cut potatoes, mango and banana into slices. Make batter of shingoda flour, salt, red chilli powder and sugar.
(2) Cut green chillies on one side and stuff in salt and sugar. Dip the slices in the batter.
(3) Fry the bhajiya in hot oil.

273. Sabudana Wada

[Serves 3 to 4]

Ingredients

(1) 2 cups sago
(2) 1 cup groundnuts
(3) 3 to 4 green chillies
(4) Raisins
(5) A small piece of ginger
(6) Curds

(7) 1 tea spoon cloves and cinnamon powder

(8) 2 tea spoons sugar

(9) Oil   (10) Salt to taste

Method

(1) Wash and strain the sago. Roast, peel and powder coarsely the groundnuts.

(2) Mix all ingredients and make small balls.

(3) Fry them in hot oil till they are crispy.

274. Batata Wada
[Makes 25 to 30 wadas]

Ingredients

(1) 500 grams potatoes

(2) 1 tea spoon red chilli powder

(3) $\frac{1}{2}$ lime

(4) 2 tea spoons sugar

(5) 100 grams shingoda flour

(6) 1 tea spoon cloves and cinnamon powder

(7) Oil   (8) Salt to taste

Method

(1) Boil, peel and grate potatoes. Add salt, red chilli powder, lime, sugar and cloves-cinnamon powder to it.

(2) Make a batter of shingoda flour, salt and red chilli powder. Make balls of potato stuffing. Dip the balls in the batter. Fry the balls in hot oil.

275. Sago Pattice [Serves 6]

Ingredients

(1) 250 grams sago

(2) 500 grams potatoes

(3) 2 tea spoons ginger-chilli paste

(4) 2 tea spoons sugar

(5) 1 lime

(6) 100 grams groundnuts

(7) 1 tea spoon cloves-cinnamon powder

(8) 50 grams rajgara or shingoda flour

(9) Salt to taste

Method

(1) Soak sago for 2 to 3 hours. Strain it to remove excess water.

(2) Boil potatoes. Add all masalas and other ingredients and sago. Make pattice.

(3) Some shingoda or rajgara flour may be added to make pattice crispy.

Variation

Pattice can be made by mixing sweet potato, elephant foot, potatoes and sago.

276. Suran [Serves 2 to 3]

Ingredients

(1) 250 grams elephant foot

(2) 1 tea spoon pepper

(3) $\frac{1}{2}$ lime

(4) 2 tea spoons powdered sugar

(5) Salt to taste

Method

(1) Cut the elephant foot into pieces. Boil them in enough water. Strain to remove excess water.

(2) Press lightly between palms to remove water. Fry them. Sprinkle salt, pepper, lime juice and sugar.

277. Kadhi [Serves 2]

Ingredients

(1) 2 cups sour buttermilk

(2) 3 table spoons shingoda or rajgara flour

(3) 1 tea spoon ginger-chilli paste

(4) 2 table spoons sugar

(5) 1 table spoon ghee

(6) 1 tea spoon cumin seeds

(7) 2 red chillies (whole)

(8) 1 tea spoon coconut

(9) Salt to taste

Method

(1) Beat buttermilk and flour together so that no lumps are formed.

(2) Add salt, ginger and chillies. Boil the mixture.

(3) Heat a little ghee in a vessel. Add cumin seeds and red chillies (whole). Add the seasoning to kadhi. Decorate with coconut. Serve hot.

278. Patara [Serves 6]

Ingredients

(1) 250 grams colocasia leaves

(2) 250 grams shingoda flour

(3) 1 tea spoon red chilli powder

(4) 2 tea spoons ginger-chilli paste

(5) 2 tea spoons sugar

(6) $\frac{1}{2}$ cup sour curds

(7) Oil

(8) 1 tea spoon clove and cinnamon powder

(9) 1 tea spoon cumin seeds

(10) 2 tea spoons sesame seeds

(11) 50 grams desiccated coconut

(12) Salt to taste

Method

(1) Sieve shingoda flour.

(2) Add salt, red chilli powder, ginger, chillies, sugar, curds, 1 table spoon oil, clove-cinnamon powder. Make a thick batter.

(3) Wash and wipe colocasia leaves. Remove the veins from the leaves. Apply the batter on the leaves and make rolls. Steam the rolls like muthiya.

(4) When it cools down, cut into pieces. Heat 4 table spoons oil in a frying pan. Add cumin seeds and sesame seeds. Add patara. Fry for sometime. Decorate with desiccated coconut. It can be served with seasoning added (without frying).

279. Banana Pakoda
[Makes 25 to 30 pieces]

Ingredients

(1) 5 ripe bananas

(2) Shingoda flour

(3) 1 tea spoon ginger-chilli paste

(4) 1 tea spoon cumin seeds (half crushed)

(5) Curds

(6) Oil   (7) Salt to taste

Method

(1) Peel and mash the bananas.

(2) Add all the other ingredients. Make batter with curds. Make pakodas from this batter.

(3) Fry in hot oil till it becomes light pink in colour.

280. Shingoda Sheera
[Serves 3 to 4]

Ingredients

(1) $\frac{1}{2}$ cup ghee

(2) 1 cup shingoda flour

(3) $\frac{3}{4}$ cup sugar

(4) 1 tea spoon cardamom powder

Method

(1) Heat $\frac{1}{2}$ cup ghee in a vessel. When it become hot, add 1 cup flour and roast it on a slow flame till it become light pink in colour.

(2) Add 1 cup hot water. Stir constantly.

(3) Add $\frac{3}{4}$ cup sugar and again stir constantly. When all the water is burnt, remove it from the flame. Sprinkle cardamom powder.

Variation

(1) Use milk instead of water to make Milk Sheera.

⑤ DEHYDRATED PRODUCTS

281. Potato Chips, Wafer

Ingredients

(1) Large potatoes
(2) A small piece of alum
(3) A little red chilli powder
(4) Powdered suger
(5) A little citric acid
(6) Salt to taste

Method

(1) Wash and peel the potatoes. Slice them or grate them with a thick grater. Soak the slices in water.

(2) Wash them 2 to 3 times. Take a big container. Fill half of the container with water. Boil it. Add salt and a small piece of alum. Mix properly.

(3) Rock salt may be used instead of ordinary salt. Separate the grated slices while adding them to the boiling water. When the slices are half cooked, remove and strain them.

(4) Add the remaining slices when the water boils again. Dry the slices in the sunshine. Store them in glass jar. While serving fry them in hot oil. Sprinkle red chilli powder, sugar and citric acid. (use the potato slicer for slicing potatoes).

282. Potato-Sabudana Sev, Chakali

Ingredients

(1) 250 grams sago

(2) Potato halwa can be made by boiling the potatoes.

(3) Rajgara flour can also be used instead of shingoda flour to make rajgara sheera.

(2) 5 kg potatoes
(3) White chilli powder
(4) A few cumin seeds
(5) Citric acid   (6) Salt to taste

Method

(1) In the morning soak the sago in water for 3 hours.

(2) Boil, peel and mash the potatoes. Strain the sago and crush it in the mixer.

(3) Mix the sago, salt, red chilli powder, cumin seeds powder, citric acid and mashed potatoes. Mix well.

(4) Make the sev with the sev making machine. Dry the sev in sun. Preserve in bottles.

(5) For the chakalies : 1 kg potatoes, 500 grams sago.

Soak the sago in water overnight. Mix sago and boiled, peeled and mashed the potatoes. Add all the masala as mentioned in the above recipe. Make the chakalies with the chakali machine. Dry in sun. Fry the sev and the chakalis in hot oil before serving.

Note : For potato-sabudana sev potatoes and sago can be also taken in equal amounts.

283. Sabudana Papadi, Sev

Ingredients

(1) Sago   (2) Rock salt
(3) A few cumin seeds (powdered)

(4) Red chilli powder

(5) Citric acid

Method

(1) Soak the sago at 6.00 pm in water. The water level should be $1\frac{1}{2}$ inch above the sago level.

(2) At 9.00 pm boil water in a vessel. For 1 bowl sago take a little less than $1\frac{1}{2}$ bowls of water.

(3) When the water starts boiling, add sago and stir properly. Cover it with a lid. Let the sago get cooked properly. The spoon should remain straight standing when placed in the centre.

(4) Do not soak sago for more than 3 hours. Remove it from the flame. Stir the mixture after 1 hour.

(5) If the mixture has more amount of water, then add some more sago (soaked in water). Keep the mixture aside overnight.

(6) If the mixture is still thin, add some boiled, peeled and grated potatoes. Potatoes would make the papadi whitish.

(7) In the morning add rock-salt, citric acid, cumin seeds (powdered), add red chilli powder. Make round papadies with a spoon on a plastic sheet. Sheets or make the sev with the machine. Dry in sunshine. Store in a jar. Fry in hot oil before serving.

284. Sabudana Kharavadi

Ingredients

(1) Sago

(2) Cumin seeds   (3) Salt to taste

Method

(1) Soak the sago in water, for 1 cup of sago take $2\frac{1}{2}$ cups of water. Boil the water. When the water starts boiling, add the sago to it.

(2) When the mixture thicken, add salt and cumin seeds. The sago should be cooked properly.

(3) A little water may be added, if required. Make round kharavadis with a table spoon on the plastic. Store in a glass bottle when dried well.

285. Sago Papad

Ingredients

(1) Sago   (2) Oil

(3) Food colour   (4) Salt to taste

Method

(1) Soak the sago in water overnight. The water level while soaking should not be above the sago level. Remove the excess water. In the morning, add in separate containers red, yellow and green colour to the soaked sago. Add salt to them. Mix properly.

(2) Apply a little oil to a lid. Place sago mixture into it. Spread properly. Avoid pouring too much or too little sago into the lid or the papad would not turn out to be good.

(3) In a big vessel place the sieve. Place the papads on the sieve or an idli stand.

(4) Place the papads on the plastic after 7 to 8 minutes. If the papads stick to the vessel, use a knife to remove them. When dried well, store in a glass bottle.

286. Sarewada

Ingredients

(1) 1 kg rice flour (coarse)

(2) 15 grams soda (kharo)

(3) Sago   (4) 20 grams salt

Method

(1) Measure 1 kg flour with a bowl. For 1 bowl of flour take a little less than 1 to $1\frac{1}{4}$ bowl of water. Boil the water.

(2) Add salt, soda a handful of sago to water.

(3) When the water starts boiling, add the flour. Stir properly. Add the cumin seeds and omum.

(4) Stir properly with one end of the rolling pin. Remove it from the flame.

(5) In a big vessel place a sieve as we place for muthiya. Cover the sieve with a muslin cloth. Make balls from the mixture. Place them on the sieve.

(6) When the mixture is cooked properly, remove it from the flame. Beat each ball very well. Divide the ball into small balls. Roll out each ball or press each ball in the machine. Dry the sarewadas on the plastic in the sunshine.

Note : (1) You can also first beat the dough properly and then keep it for steaming. Store in a jar with a tight lid. Fry in hot oil before serving.

(2) If the rice is new than less water is needed.

287. Potato Papad

Ingredients

(1) 250 grams sago
(2) $1\frac{1}{2}$ kg potatoes
(3) A little pepper powder
(4) A little red chilli powder
(5) A few cumin seeds
(6) Salt to taste

Method

1. (1) Soak the sago overnight in water. The water level should be a little above the sago level.

(2) The next morning boil the water in a bowl. When the water starts boiling, add the sago. Stir constantly. When the mixture becomes transperant, remove it from the flame.

(3) When it cools down sieve the mixture. For one bowl of sago, boil one bowl of water.

(4) Add boiled, peeled and grated potatoes to the mixture. Mix well. Add salt, red chilli powder and a little pepper powder.

(5) Fill the mixture in the machine for making sarewadas. Make papads and dry them on plastic. Store the papads in a tightly covered tin. Fry in hot oil before serving or roast on the flame and serve.

Method

2. (1) Wash and soak the sago. The water level should be a little above the sago level. Soak the sago overnight.

(2) The next morning apply a little oil to a plate. Place the sago in the greased dish. Steam them for 10 to 15 minutes.

(3) Mix warm boiled, peeled and grated potatoes to it. Pass the mixture through a sieve used for sieving flour. Add all the masalas and salt as mentioned above proceed as shown in the above recipe 1.

288. Chawla Dal Wadi

Ingredients

(1) 1 cup chawla dal (Cow's pea dal)
(2) 1 tea spoon ginger-chilli paste
(3) $\frac{1}{4}$ tea spoon asafoetida
(4) Salt to taste

Method

(1) Soak the chawla dal overnight in water. The next morning wash the dal properly and grind it in a mixture.

(2) Add salt. Mix properly. Take a small portion of dal paste in a plate.

(3) Add ginger-chilli paste and a little of asafoetida to it.

(4) Beat well till it is light and fluffy. Make small wadis (cubes) on plastic sheet. Repeat the same method for the remaining dal paste and make wadis.

(5) Dry in the sunshine. Store in a bottle. Do not add all the masalas at a time in the paste. Fry in hot oil before serving.

289. Poha Chakali

Ingredients

(1) 1 cup nylon poha (thin rice flakes)
(2) 1 tea spoon cumin seeds

(3) 4 to 5 green chillies (paste)
(4) Salt to taste

Method

(1) Wash and strain the rice flakes in a big vessel with holes. Place them in a plate. Add the remaining ingredients to the rice flakes. Mash very well.

(2) Make a dough. Put a small portion of the dough in the chakali machine.

(3) Make chakalis on a plastic sheet. Dry them in the sunshine.

(4) Store in a container with a tight lid. Fry in hot oil before serving.

6 PICKLES

290. Chhunda

Ingredients

(1) 1 kg raw mangoes
(2) 1 to $1\frac{1}{4}$ kg sugar
(3) 5 cinnamons, 15 cloves (powder)
(4) 1 tea spoon cumin seeds
(5) 2 table spoons red chilli powder
(6) 2 table spoons salt

Method

(1) Wash and peel raw mangoes. Grate them. Mix sugar. The proportion of sugar would depend upon the type of mangoes.

(2) For 1 kg of Rajapuri mangoes add 1 kg of sugar. For 1 kg of desi mangoes add $1\frac{1}{4}$ kg of sugar.

(3) Add salt to taste. Mix raw mangoes (grated), sugar, and salt in a stainless steel vessel. Tie a thin cloth over the vessel and keep in the sunshine.

(4) Keep in the sunshine for about 6 to 7 days.

(5) Mix everyday with one end of the rolling pin. Keep in sunshine till it attains consistency like sugar syrup.

(6) Add cinnamon and cloves powder, red chilli powder, half ground cumin seeds. Mix well.

(7) Keep in the sunshine for some more time. Then fill into glass jar when cool.

Note : Do not keep the mixture in the sunshine on the day when you add sugar to the grated mangoes. Keep the mixture in the sunshine the next day.

291. Vagharel Chhunda

Ingredients

(1) 1 kg raw mangoes
(2) 100 grams mustard oil
(3) 4 whole red chillies (dried)
(4) 1 tea spoon mustard seeds
(5) $1\frac{1}{2}$ tea spoons red chilli powder
(6) $\frac{1}{2}$ tea spoon turmeric powder
(7) $\frac{1}{4}$ tea spoon asafoetida

(8) 1 kg jaggery or sugar

(9) Salt to taste

Method

(1) Wash, peel and grate mangoes. Heat mustard oil in a vessel for seasoning. When it is hot, add whole red chillies, mustard seeds, red chilli powder, turmeric powder and asafoetida.

(2) Add grated mangoes and salt. Mix well for 10 minutes. Then add jaggery or sugar. The proportion of jaggery is equal to that of mangoes.

(3) When the mango is cooked and the syrup starts boiling, remove it from the flame. Keep the syrup little thin because it will thicken afterwards.

292. Vaghariya

Ingredients

(1) 1 kg raw mangoes

(2) 100 grams oil

(3) 4 whole red chillies (dried)

(4) 1 tea spoon mustard seeds

(5) $1\frac{1}{2}$ tea spoons red chilli powder

(6) $\frac{1}{4}$ tea spoon turmeric powder

(7) 1 kg sugar

(8) $1\frac{1}{4}$ tea spoon methi masala

(9) Asafoetida   (10) Salt to taste

Method

(1) Wash, peel and cut the mangoes into small pieces.

(2) Heat oil in a vessel. Add the whole red chillies, mustard seeds, a little red chilli powder, turmeric powder and asafoetida.

(3) Add the mango pieces. When the mango pieces are cooked, add salt and sugar.

(4) Remove the pickle from the flame when the syrup is still thin.

(5) Add the methi masala and additional red chilli powder.

Note : If all the red chilli powder is added in seasoning then it turns black.

293. Sunder Mango

Ingredients

(1) 1 kg raw mangoes

(2) A little turmeric powder

(3) 2 tea spoons oil

(4) 2 tea spoons methi (fenugreek seeds) dal

(5) 2 tea spoons red chilli powder

(6) Asafoetida

(7) 750 grams sugar   (8) Salt to taste

Method

(1) Wash, peel and cut the mangoes into small pieces. Mix turmeric powder and salt. Stir and leave for one day.

(2) The next day heat oil in a pan.

(3) Add methi dal, red chilli powder, additional turmeric powder and asafoetida. Mix well. Let it cool down. Mix $1\frac{1}{4}$ cup water in sugar and make the sugar syrup. Strain the water from the mango pieces.

(4) Spread the mango pieces on a cloth for 2 hours in shade. When the sugar syrup is ready, add the mango pieces to it. Stir properly.

Note : When the mango pieces are cooked well, add methi masala and additional salt (if required). Keep the sugar syrup thin enough as it would thicken afterwards. Take some cold water in a deep dish. Place the vessel of pickle in it. Stir at frequent intervals. Change the water for 2 to 3 times. This would help to keep the sugar syrup thin.

294. Boiled Pickle

Ingredients

(1) 1 kg raw mangoes

(2) Oil

(3) A pinch asafoetida

(4) 1 kg jaggery

(5) 2 tea spoons red chilli powder

(6) $\frac{1}{2}$ tea spoon turmeric powder

(7) 2 tea spoons fenugreek seed dal

(8) 2 tea spoons mustard seed dal

(9) 1 tea spoon mustard seeds

(10) Salt to taste

Method

(1) Wash, peel and cut the mangoes into small pieces. (For making pickle for a feast, do not peel the mangoes)

(2) Boil the mango pieces. Do not boil the mango pieces for long.

(3) Heat a little oil in a pan. Add asafoetida, jaggery and a little water. When it is thick enough (not too thick) add the mango pieces. Stir and cook for some more time.

(4) Test a drop of syrup, if it remains steady then the pickle is ready. Remove it from the flame.

(5) Add salt, red chilli powder, turmeric powder, fenugreek seeds dal and mustard seed dal.

(6) Add seasoning of hot oil, mustard seeds and red chilli powder. It gives good colour.

295. Khatiyu

Ingredients

(1) 1 kg raw mangoes

(2) 175 grams fenugreek seeds dal

(3) Red chilli powder

(4) Turmeric powder (5) Asafoetida

(6) Castor oil   (7) Mustard oil

(8) Salt to taste

Method

(1) Fill methi masala and fenugreek seeds dal in a cup. Use the same cup for

measuring 'desi' salt 1 cup, red chilli powder 1 cup. Add a little castor oil to the fenugreek seeds dal. Mix well.

(2) Add red chilli powder, turmeric powder, asafoetida, salt and warm mustard oil. Mix well. The proportion of salt and red chilli powder depends upon our own tastes.

(3) Wash and cut the mangoes into pieces. Remove the seeds. Mix the masala and the mango pieces properly. Fill in a jar.

(4) The next day pour mustard oil. The oil should be little above the pickle.

296. Sweet Pickle (1)

Ingredients

(1) 3 kg mangoes (Rajapuri)

(2) 1 tea spoon turmeric powder

(3) 100 grams fenugreek seeds dal (methi dal)

(4) 200 grams mustard seeds dal

(5) 3 table spoons red chilli powder

(6) $\frac{1}{2}$ tea spoon asafoetida

(7) 400 ml mustard oil

(8) 2 kg jaggery   (9) 1 kg sugar

(10) 250 grams dried dates

(11) Salt to taste

Method

(1) Wash and cut the mangoes into small pieces.

(2) Add salt and turmeric powder to it. Leave it aside for 2 days. Spread the mango pieces on a cloth for some time.

(3) In a plate place salt in the centre, then arrange mustard seeds dal, then arrange fenugreek seed dal, then red chilli powder, turmeric powder and asafoetida. Heat mustard oil. Add it to the masalas in the centre. Mix all the masalas well.

(4) Let it cool down. Then add jaggery, sugar and additional red chilli powder. Mix the mango pieces. Keep stirring daily for one week. Then fill the pickle a jar.

(5) Soak the dried dates in the water mixed with salt and turmeric water. When they are swollen, remove the seeds and chop them into long strips. Add them to the pickle.

297. Sweet Pickle (2)

Ingredients

(1) 1 kg Rajapuri mangoes
(2) Turmeric powder
(3) 100 grams dried dates
(4) 100 grams mustard seeds dal
(5) Red chilli powder
(6) 100 ml castor oil
(7) Asafoetida (8) 700 grams jaggery
(9) 100 ml sesame seed oil
(10) Salt to taste

Method

(1) Wash and cut the mangoes (without removing the skin) into small pieces. Add salt and turmeric powder. Mix very well for two-three times. Leave aside.

(2) If you have mixed mangoes, salt and turmeric powder today morning then remove the raw mango pieces from the vessel at 12.00 o'clock the next morning. Dry on the cloth.

(3) Clean the dates and soak them in the same water used for washing the mangoes. Stir them. When they are swollen, remove the seeds and cut into long strips. Add them to the pickle.

(4) Measure the fenugreek dal with a cup. For 1 cup dal take $\frac{1}{4}$ cup red chilli powder, a little less then $\frac{1}{4}$ cup

of salt. Heat castor oil till fumes are formed. Add fenugreek seeds dal and remove it from the flame.

(5) Roast it properly. Add asafoetida to the methi dal. Remove it in a dish and mix red chilli powder, salt, (additional) and a pinch of turmeric powder.

(6) Taste the masala. The proportion of the ingredients may be changed according to the taste. Add jaggery.

(7) Take sesame seeds oil in a big pan. Add raw mango pieces to it. Mix well. Add the masalas. Mix well again. Cover the vessel with a lid. Leave it in the vessel for one week. Stir everyday. Then fill the pickle in the jar.

Note : (1) Do not heat the vessel having sesame seeds oil.

(2) If the mango pieces are not yellow enough. Keep them in salt and turmeric mixture for 2 days.

298. Murabba

Ingredients

(1) 1 kg raw mangoes (2) $1\frac{1}{2}$ kg sugar
(3) Cinnamon and cloves
(4) A few strands safforon (dissolved)
(5) A little cardamom powder

Method

(1) Wash, peel and grate the mangoes. Add sugar and mix well.

(2) Keep in the sunshine the next day. Stir everyday. Keep in the sunshine for about 5 to 6 days. When the murabba is ready, add cloves, cinnamon, cardamom powder and safforon.

(3) If you do not want to keep in the sunshine mix sugar and grated mangoes. Heat the mixture.

(4) Stir constantly. When sugar syrup is ready, remove it from the flame. Add the remaining ingredients.

299. Green Chillies Pickle

Ingredients

(1) 1 kg green chillies
(2) 5 table spoons oil
(3) A few fenugreek seeds
(4) A few mustard seeds
(5) 200 grams mustard seed dal
(6) 4 limes   (7) Salt to taste

Method

(1) Wash and dry green chillies. Cut the chillies length wise. Put the chillies in a plastic sieve with large holes. Shake well to remove all the seeds from the chillies.

(2) Heat 5 large table spoons of oil. Place a steel tea strainer inside it. Add the fenugreek seeds inside the strainer. Roast it till it is light pink in colour. Remove the strainer. Then add mustard seeds and asafoetida to the same oil. Remove it from the flame.

(3) When the fenugreek seeds cool down, grind them into a fine powder. Measure the mustard seeds dal with a cup. Measure salt with the same cup. Measure salt little less than the mustard seed dal. Mix them well.

(4) Add powdered fenugreek seeds.

(5) Take a glass bowl or stainless steel bowl and first place this masala into it. Then add green chillies pieces.

(6) Pour lemon juice on it. Add the cooled mustard seeds seasoning. Do not stir or mix.

(7) Mix well the next day. Fill in glass bottles. This pickle remains good for 15 days without being put in the refrigerator. If stored in the refrigerator, it remains fresh for 1 year.

300. Red Kashmiri Chillies Chutney

Ingredients

(1) 1 kg red kashmiri chillies
(2) 1 kg sugar
(3) Cinnamon and cloves
(4) A little turmeric powder
(5) Salt to taste

Method

(1) Remove the stems and seeds from the chillies. Mix the chillies, salt and turmeric powder. Keep it aside for 5 to 6 hours. Strain them.

(2) Mix the chillies with sugar and grind them in the mixer. Additional salt may be added if required.

(3) Keep the vessel with the chilli mixture in the sunshine for 3 days. Add cinnamon-cloves powder.

301. Lemon Pickle

Ingredients

(1) 1 kg limes   (2) 1½ kg sugar
(3) Turmeric powder
(4) 1 table spoon red chilli powder
(5) Salt

Method

(1) Chop the lime into 4 pieces. Apply salt and turmeric powder to the lime pieces. Mix well. Keep it aside for 15 days (Till the lime skin softens). Keep on stirring everyday.

(2) Cut the lime into small pieces. Remove the seeds.

(3) Take sugar in a vessel and add water just enough to soak the sugar. Heat the syrup till it attains 2 strands (tar) consistency. Cool the sugar syrup. Add salt, fresh red chilli powder and lime pieces.

(4) Mix well and fill in bottles.

302. Vegetable Pickle

Ingredients

(1) 1 kg raw mangoes
(2) 250 grams lime
(3) 100 grams carrots
(4) 100 grams french beans
(5) 100 grams tendalis
(6) 100 grams green chillies
(7) 100 grams ginger
(8) 50 grams fresh turmeric
(9) 50 grams Ambahaldar (fresh white turmeric)
(10) 100 grams 'Kerda' fruits
(11) 100 grams Bedekar Masala or similar
(12) 50 grams mustard seeds dal
(13) Oil   (14) 100 grams desi salt

Method

(1) Wash all the vegetables, wipe them and spread them on a newspaper for 1 hour. Cut them into very small pieces.
(2) Take all the cut vegetables in a big vessel. Add salt and mix well. Keep it aside for 3 days. Stir it in the mornings and evenings everyday.
(3) When the vegetables are soft, add Bedekar (Achar) masala and mustard seeds dal. Mix thoroughly.
(4) Keep it aside for 2 to 3 days. Fill in the bottles.
(5) Add enough oil to cover the pickle and a little more.

303. Gunda Pickle

Ingredients

(1) 250 grams gundas
(2) 2 table spoons methi masala
(3) 100 grams oil
(4) 1 raw mango

Method

(1) Prepare the methi masala as in R. No. 295. Add a grated mango to the methi masala. Remove the seeds from gunda and fill in the methi masala.
(2) Heat a little oil and add the gundas. Cook till the gundas are soft. Cook on a low flame. This pickle remains fresh for about 10 days.
(3) If the pickle has to be stored for a longer time then fill it in a bottle. Add oil which is heated and then cooled. Add enough oil to cover the pickle.

304. Carrot Pickle

Ingredients

(1) 1 kg carrots
(2) 50 grams tamarind or amchur
(3) 50 grams mustard seed dal
(4) 250 grams sugar
(5) 250 grams oil
(6) 50 grams red chilli powder
(7) 50 grams green chillies (long strips)
(8) 50 grams ginger (long strips)
(9) 50 grams salt

Method

(1) Soak tamarind in water. Cut carrots into long strips. Tie the carrot strips in a cloth. Dip it in boiling water for 2 to 3 times.
(2) Spread the carrots on a piece of cloth for some time.
(3) In other dish, mix mustard seed dal, salt, sugar, oil, red chilli powder, ginger and chillies.
(4) Mash tamarind very well. Strain the mixture. Mix tamarind mixture, carrot strips and masala. Keep the pickle in the vessel for a day. Then fill in bottles next day.

305. Punjabi Pickle

Ingredients

(1) 1 kg raw desi mangoes (cut into small pieces)
(2) 100 grams green chillies (long strips)
(3) 125 grams carrots
(4) 125 grams ginger (cut into long strips)
(5) Turmeric (fresh)
(6) 700 grams lime (cut into four pieces)
(7) 200 grams mustard seeds dal
(8) 50 grams fenugreek seeds dal (methi dal)
(9) Red chilli powder
(10) $\frac{1}{2}$ tea spoon asafoetida
(11) $\frac{3}{4}$ tea spoon sodium benzoate
(12) Salt to taste

Method

(1) Chop ginger into long strips and yellow turmeric and white turmeric into round slices.

(2) Grind methi dal and mustard seed dal into very fine powder (flour like). Measure the dal flour in a vessel. Measure an equal quantity of salt and red chilli powder. Add asafoetida. Mix all ingredients thoroughly, except lime and Sodium Benzoate.

(3) Add lime juice of 4 limes. Next day add $\frac{3}{4}$ tea spoon of Sodium Benzoate. Mix well and fill in a jar.

Note : This pickle remains fresh for one month due to the preservative Sodium Benzoate.

(7) SOUTH INDIAN DISHES

306. Upama [Serves 2]

Ingredients

(1) 1 cup rawa
(2) 2 table spoons ghee
(3) 1 table spoon urad dal
(4) $\frac{1}{2}$ tea spoon mustard seeds
(5) 1 tea spoon sesame seeds
(6) 1 onion
(7) A few curry leaves
(8) 2 to 3 green chillies
(9) A pinch asafoetida   (10) 1 lime
(11) 1 tea spoon cloves and cinnamon powder
(12) 2 tea spoons sugar
(13) 1 ripe tomato
(14) 3 table spoons coriander leaves (finely chopped)
(15) Oil
(16) Salt to taste

Method

(1) Heat a little ghee in a vessel. Roast urad dal till light pink in colour.

(2) Add mustard seeds, sesame seeds, onions, curry leaves, green chillies and asafoetida. Saute for a few minutes. Add the rawa to it.

(3) Roast on a low flame like that for sheera till the rawa is light pink in colour. Add enough hot water. For 1 cup rawa, add 3 cups of water.

(4) When all the water evaporates, add salt, lime juice, cloves and cinnamon powder and sugar. Add tomatoes, finely chopped. Decorate with finely chopped coriander leaves can be added to the upama.

Variation

Various boiled and sauted vegetables like green peas, fresh beans, corn etc.

307. Onion Uttappa
[Makes 20 to 22 Uttappas]

Ingredients

(1) 1 cup urad dal   (2) 3 cups rawa

(3) $\frac{1}{2}$ cup curds   (4) Curry leaves

(5) $\frac{1}{2}$ tea spoon mustard seeds

(6) Oil

(7) 3 to 4 green chillies (finely chopped)

(8) 2 onions (cut into long strips)

(9) 2 tomatoes   (10) Salt to taste

Method

(1) Soak the dal for 3 to 4 hours. Grind the dal. Add rawa and salt. Add the curds while grinding the dal. It would help in fermentation.

(2) Heat 2 table spoons oil in a pan. Add mustard seeds, green chillies, curry leaves and onions.

(3) Saute till the onions are brown in colour. Add this to the batter. Mix very well. Spread one spoon of the batter on the non-stick griddle (non-stick tava). Sprinkle finely chopped ripe tomatoes. Cover the uttappa with a deep vessel. Serve hot with coconut and coriander chutney.

Variation

1. Add crushed dosa masala to idli or dosa batter. Make thick uttappa from the batter. Sprinkle finely chopped tomatoes, onions, capsicum and coriander leaves. When one side is properly roasted turn it upside-down and roast the other side.

2. (1) Soak 1 cup rawa in $\frac{1}{2}$ cup curds for half an hour.

   (2) Add ginger, chillies, coriander, $\frac{1}{2}$ lime juice, 1 onion (finely chopped), 1 tomato (chopped), 1 capsicum (finely chopped) and salt to taste.

(3) Make uttappas on a non stick griddle.

(4) The batter can be applied to bread slices cut into two triangles. Then roast them on a frying pan.

308. Idli [Makes 36 Idlis]

Ingredients

(1) 3 cups rice   (2) 1 cup urad dal

(3) $\frac{1}{2}$ cup curds   (4) 1 tea spoon soda

(5) 2 table spoons oil

(6) Salt to taste

Method

(1) For making idlis using flour, make the batter in the morning and make idlis in the evening. Mix idli flour, luke warm water, curds and salt. Mix very well. Keep aside for fermentation.

(2) For idlis using rice and urad dal, wash and soak them separately for overnight. Grind rice and dal separately. Urad dal should be ground to a very fine paste. Rice can be ground coarsely. Then mix the paste very well. Keep overnight.

(3) While making idlis by either method mix a little oil, water and soda. Heat the mixture. Add this mixture to the idli batter. Add more water if required.

(4) Apply a little oil to the idli moulds. Fill the batter in the moulds with a spoon and steam for 8 to 10 minutes.

(5) Serve hot idlis with chutney and sambhar.

309. Rawa Idli
[Makes 16 to 18 Idlis]

Ingredients

(1) 1 cup urad dal   (2) 2 cups rawa

(3) 1 cup sour curds

(4) A pinch soda-bi-carb

(5) 1 table spoon oil   (6) Salt to taste

Method

(1) Soak the urad dal for 4 to 5 hours. Then drain and grind to a very fine paste.

(2) Heat a little oil in a vessel. Roast rawa till it is light pink in colour. Cool it and add curds to it. Soak it in curds for sometime.

(3) Add urad dal paste, salt and soda to the rawa. Mix very well. Cover it with a lid and keep aside for 5 to 6 hours to allow it to ferment.

(4) Boil water in an idli not or pressure cooker and steam the idlis until they are soft. Serve with chutney and sambhar.

310. Vegetable Rawa Idli

[Makes 10 Idlis]

Ingredients

(1) 1 cup rawa

(2) 1 cup sour curds

(3) 1 tea spoon fruit salt

(4) $\frac{1}{4}$ cup cabbage (grated)

(5) $\frac{1}{2}$ carrot (grated)

(6) 2 table spoons finely chopped coriander

(7) Salt to taste

Method

(1) Roast the rawa on the griddle. Mix curds and fruit salt to the rawa. Add enough water and salt to the batter. Keep it aside for half an hour.

(2) Mix all vegetables to the idli batter. Steam the idlis until they are soft.

Note : (1) Serve them hot with chutney and sambhar.

(2) If you don't want to add vegetables, than rawa idli is also made by this method.

Variation

Idlis can be also made without adding vegetables.

311. Chutney for Idli

Ingredients

(1) 1 fresh coconut (grated)

(2) 1 lime

(3) 2 tea spoons sugar

(4) 3 to 4 green chillies

(5) $\frac{1}{2}$ cup curds

(6) 1 tea spoon oil

(7) $\frac{1}{2}$ tea spoon mustard seeds

(8) A pinch asafoetida

(9) A few curry leaves

(10) Salt to taste

Method

(1) Mix coconut, salt, lime juice, sugar, green chillies and grind them in the mixer.

(2) Then add a little curds to the chutney.

(3) Heat 1 tea spoon oil in a vessel for seasoning. Add mustard seeds, asafoetida and curry leaves. Add this to the chutney.

Variation

(1) For chutney using desiccated coconut. Roast and grind urad dal. Mix desiccated coconut, salt, lime, sugar, green chillies and curds to it. Add seasoning as described above.

(2) Chutney can be also made from roasted chana dal (daliya), ground-nuts and urad dal. Mix all ingredients and grind.

(3) Idli can also serve with coriander chutney.

312. Sambhar [Serves 6 to 8]

Ingredients

(1) 2 cups tuver dal

(2) 2 onions
(grated or cut into small pieces)
(3) 2 table spoons amchur powder or a little tamarind
(4) 1 table spoon dhana jeera powder
(5) Oil
(6) 1 tea spoon mustard seeds
(7) 2 tea spoons red chilli powder
(8) $\frac{1}{2}$ tea spoon turmeric powder
(9) 1 boiled potato
(10) 4 whole chillies
(11) 1 tea spoon cumin seeds
(12) Curry leaves
(13) $\frac{1}{4}$ tea spoon asafoetida
(14) 1 table spoon jaggery
(15) 1 tea spoon garam masala
(16) 2 tea spoons M.T.R. masala
(17) 1 tea spoon ginger-chilli paste
(18) 4 table spoons coriander leaves (finely chopped)
(19) Salt to taste

Method

(1) Boil the dal and onions in the pressure cooker. Beat the boiled dal well.
(2) Add all the masalas. Heat 1 tea spoon oil in a pan. Add $\frac{1}{2}$ tea spoon mustard seeds, $\frac{1}{2}$ tea spoon red chilli powder and $\frac{1}{4}$ tea spoon turmeric powder. Add the potato pieces. Let it get cooked well.
(3) Heat oil for seasoning. Add whole red chillies, $\frac{1}{2}$ tea spoon mustard seeds, cumin seeds, curry leaves, $1\frac{1}{2}$ tea spoons red chilli powder, $\frac{1}{4}$ tea spoon turmeric powder and asafoetida. Add seasoning, garam masala and 2 tea spoons M.T.R. sambhar masala. Decorate with chopped coriander leaves. Serve hot with uttappa, wada, idli or dosa and chutney.

313. Masala Dosa [Serves 6 to 8]

Ingredients

(1) $3\frac{1}{2}$ cups rice
(2) $1\frac{1}{2}$ cups urad dal
(3) 100 grams green peas
(4) 1 kg potatoes (boiled)
(5) 500 grams onions (cut lengthwise)
(6) Oil
(7) 1 tea spoon mustard seeds
(8) 10 to 12 green chillies (chopped finely)
(9) A few curry leaves
(10) $1\frac{1}{2}$ tea spoons turmeric powder
(11) 2 lime
(12) 2 tea spoons sugar
(13) 1 tea spoon garam masala
(14) A few coriander leaves
(15) $\frac{1}{2}$ tea spoon cumin seeds
(16) Salt to taste

Method

(1) Wash and soak rice and urad dal in water overnight.
(2) Next morning, grind them to a fine paste. Mix well, add salt and keep aside. (In summer do not add salt. Make the dosas in the evening.) Soak the dry green peas in the morning. Cut the potatoes length wise.
(3) Heat enough oil in a vessel. Add cumin seeds, green chillies, curry leaves, turmeric powder and onions. Saute for few minutes. Add green peas and potatoes.
(4) While frying onions add little salt that is just enough for onions. Then add the additional salt, sugar and lime juice. Sprinkle finely chopped coriander.
(5) Heat a griddle or a non-stick fry pan. Grind the flour into a fine powder. Add salt and cumin seeds to the dosa batter.

(6) Spread a little oil or ghee all over it. Then spread the batter with a serving spoon or a katori.

(7) Pour a little oil or ghee all round the dosa. Mix $\frac{1}{2}$ tea spoon oil and water in a katori.

(8) After making each dosa, dip a cloth in this oil and water mixture. Wipe the griddle with the cloth. Fill the masala (potatoes and peas) in the centre.

Serve hot and crispy dosa with chutney and sambhar.

Note : You can soak the dal and rice early in the morning, grind it in the afternoon and make the dosas at night for dinner.

Variation

Dosa Roll : Make rolls of the masala. Dip them in the dosa batter and fry them till golden brown in colour.

314. White Dhokala (Idada)

[Serves 8]

Ingredients

(1) 3 cups rice

(2) 1 cup urad dal

(3) 2 table spoons curds

(4) 2 table spoons oil

(5) 1 tea spoon soda

(6) Red chilli powder and pepper powder to taste

(7) Salt to taste

Method

(1) Wash the rice and urad dal and spread them on a piece of cloth. Dry them in sunlight and grind them into a fine flour. For making dhokalas in the evening, soak the flour in the morning.

(2) Add salt to the batter 2 hours before making dhokala. A little curds may be added for good fermentation. In winters add the salt in the mornings.

(3) Take some batter and add a little oil and soda and beat very well. Keep the batter thin. Pour the batter in a dish. Steam the thali like idlis or muthiyas.

(4) Pepper powder or red chilli powder can be sprinkled on top if desired.

(5) Cut into medium sized pieces as serve hot.

315. Rawa Dhokala [Serves 2]

Ingredients

(1) 1 cup rawa

(2) $\frac{1}{2}$ cup curds

(3) $\frac{1}{2}$ tea spoon soda

(4) A pinch asafoetida

(5) 1 table spoon oil

(6) $\frac{1}{2}$ tea spoon mustard seeds

(7) 1 tea spoon sesame seeds

(8) A few curry leaves

(9) 3 green chillies

(10) 2 table spoons grated coconut

(11) 3 table spoons coriander leaves (finely chopped)

(12) Salt to taste

Method

(1) Mix rawa, salt, soda and asafoetida. Make a batter using enough water. Make dhokalas immediately.

(2) Heat 1 table spoon oil for seasoning. Add mustard seeds, sesame seeds, curry leaves and green chillies (finely chopped) to the oil when the dhokalas are done pour the seasoning over it.

(3) Decorate with grated coconut and finely chopped coriander.

Note : If the dhokalas are not soft enough, a little more soda may be added.

316. Tricolour Dhokala
[Serves 5 to 6]

Ingredients

(1) 250 grams dhokala flour

(2) Curds

(3) 250 grams besan (fine chana flour)

(4) Coriander chutney

(5) Sweet chutney (6) Oil

(7) 1 tea spoon soda

(8) 1 tea spoon mustard seeds

(9) 1 tea spoon sesame seeds

(10) 4 table spoons finely chopped coriander leaves

(11) Salt to taste

Method

(1) For making dhokalas in the evening, make the batter in the morning. Mix flour and little curds with enough amount of water to prepare the batter.

(2) Mix chana flour and curds. Make batter in an other vessel.

(3) Prepare coriander and sweet chutneys. Add 1 table spoon chana flour to the coriander chutney.

(4) Do not make the chutney too thin.

(5) In the evening, take 2 table spoons warm oil in a cup. Add a little soda to it. Mix very well. Add this to both the batter. Add salt to it.

(6) Pour the dhokala batter (white) in a greased thali. Steam the dhokala batter (white) in a greased thali. Steam the dhokalas. Make thick dhokalas.

(7) When they are half done spread the green chutney all over the dhokala. Pour the khaman batter (yellow) on it. Cover with a lid and steam them. When the dhokalas are done remove it from the flame and put cut marks on them. Pour the seasoning on it. Serve the pieces with sweet chutney.

Note : (1) For dry dhokala flour use 3 cups rice and 1 cup urad dal.

(2) Tricoloured dhokalas can be also made by preparing white and khaman dhokalas separately. Then when done remove the dhokala thali and spread the coriander chutney over it. Place the khaman layer over it. Press lightly. Pour the seasoning on it. Cut into small pieces serve with sweet chutney.

317. Medu Vada
[Makes 50 to 60 pieces]

Ingredients

(1) 3 cups urad dal (2) 1 cup rice

(3) Oil   (4) Salt to taste

Method

(1) Soak the urad dal for 6 hours. Grind this to a fine paste in a mixer.

(2) Add salt and mix very well. Heat oil in a kadai. Apply a little water on your fingers. Take lemon size balls of this dough, flatten them a little, make a hole in the middle and deep fry them in oil, till they turn golden brown. Vada's can be also made in the vada maker. Serve hot with sambhar.

Note : (1) 2 table spoons ginger-chilli paste and 4 table spoons chopped coriander leaves can be also added to the wada batter.

(2) If the vadas are not enough soft and a little soda to the batter.

318. Vada Sambhar (1)
[Makes 15 to 20 Vadas]

Ingredients

(1) 250 grams masala for batata wada

(2) 100 grams idli batter

(3) Sambhar   (4) Oil

Method

(1) Make balls of the batata wada masala.

(2) Dip them in the idli batter and deep fry them. Serve them hot with sambhar (with onions added).

319. Vada Sambhar (2)
[Makes 40 to 50 Vadas]

Ingredients

(1) 4 cups chana dal

(2) 1 cup urad dal

(3) 200 grams cabbage (grated)

(4) 3 onions (grated)

(5) 2 tea spoons ginger-chilli paste

(6) Oil   (7) Salt to taste

Method

(1) Soak both the dals separately for 8 to 10 hours.

(2) Grind them into a fine paste. Add all the vegetables and other ingredients.

(3) Keep the batter thick. Make vadas like medu vada or make them in the vada maker.

Note : Serve hot with sambhar, coconut chutney and coriander chutney.

320. Dhokala [Serves 5 to 6]

Ingredients

(1) 2 cups mung dal

(2) 1 cup urad dal

(3) 2 tea spoons ginger-chilli paste

(4) 2 table spoons oil

(5) $\frac{1}{2}$ tea spoon mustard seeds

(6) 1 tea spoon sesame seeds

(7) Salt to taste

Method

(1) Soak both the dals for 4 to 6 hours. Grind them into a fine paste.

(2) Keep it overnight for fermentation. Add salt and ginger-chilli paste. Make thick dhokalas.

(3) Heat a little oil for seasoning. Add mustard seeds and sesame seeds. Add the seasoning to the dhokalas.

(4) Serve hot.

321. Vegetable Dhokala
[Serves 8 to 10]

Ingredients

(1) 1 cup rice   (2) 1 cup urad dal

(3) 1 cup chana dal

(4) 1 cup mung dal

(5) A small piece of ginger

(6) 8 to 10 chillies   (7) 8 cloves garlic

(8) 100 grams green peas

(9) 100 grams carrots

(10) 100 grams french beans

(11) Oil

(12) 1 tea spoon mustard seeds

(13) 1 tea spoon sesame seeds

(14) 4 table spoons coriander leaves (finely chopped)

(15) Salt to taste

Method

(1) Soak rice and all the dals for 5 to 6 hours in water. Add ginger, chilli and garlic paste and salt to it.

(2) Heat 1 table spoon oil in a pan. Add all the vegetables. Saute for sometime. Add a little water. When cooked add them to the batter.

(3) Add 1 table spoon oil to the batter. Steam the dhokalas. Make thick dhokalas.

(4) Heat 3 to 4 table spoons oil for seasoning. Add mustard and sesame seeds to it. Pour the seasoning over the dhokalas.

(5) Serve hot.

322. Groundnut Chutney

Ingredients

(1) 100 grams groundnuts (roasted)

(2) 6 cloves garlic

(3) A small piece of ginger

(4) 4 green chillies

(5) 4 table spoons oil

(6) A few mustard seeds

(7) 1 tea spoon urad dal

(8) A few curry leaves

(9) 4 table spoons coriander leaves

(10) Salt to taste

Method

(1) Mix all ingredients and grind into a fine paste.

(2) Heat 4 table spoons oil for seasoning in a vessel. Add mustard seeds, urad dal and curry leaves. Add the seasoning to the chutney. Mix well.

323. Damani Dhokala

[Serves 10 to 12]

Ingredients

(1) 3 cups rice

(2) 1 cup urad dal

(3) 250 grams curds

(4) 100 grams green peas

(5) 100 grams french beans
(cut into small pieces)

(6) 100 grams carrots
(cut into small pieces)

(7) 1 pomegranate

(8) 1 tea spoon soda

(9) 1 tea spoon citric acid

(10) $\frac{1}{2}$ cup oil

(11) Green chutney (12) Salt to taste

Method

(1) Grind rice and urad dal to a coarse flour. Add curds to it. Add enough water and make the batter.

(2) Keep the batter aside for 4 hours. Add boiled vegetables, pomegranate seeds, salt, soda, citric acid and oil to it.

(3) Make idlis in biscuit moulds. Serve hot with green chutney.

324. Idli Bonda

[Serves 3 to 4]

Ingredients

(1) 500 grams jeerasar rice flour

(2) 250 grams urad dal

(3) 250 grams curds

(4) 1 tea spoon soda

(5) 1 tea spoon citric acid

(6) Green chutney

(7) 100 grams rice flour

(8) Tomato sauce

(9) Oil   (10) Salt to taste

Method

(1) Mix rice flour and urad dal. Grind into a coarse flour. Add curds and make a thin batter. Keep aside for a few hours for fermentation.

(2) While making the idlis add salt, soda and citric acid to the batter.

(3) Steam idlis in katoris. Divide each idli into two horizontally. Apply green chutney to it. Again between the two pieces.

(4) Prepare a thin batter of rice flour and salt.

(5) Dip the idli in this batter and fry them in hot oil till golden brown in colour.

8 — NAN, PARATHA, ROTI

325. Butter Nan [Makes 15 nan]

Ingredients

(1) 4 cups maida

(2) 1 tea spoon baking powder

(3) $\frac{1}{4}$ cup milk

(4) 2 table spoons curds

(5) 1 tea spoon sugar

(6) 1 tea spoon dry yeast + $\frac{3}{4}$ cup luke warm water

(7) 2 tea spoons melted ghee

(8) Butter

(9) Salt to taste

Method

(1) Sieve maida, baking powder and salt.

(2) Heat milk and add sugar and yeast to it. Dissolve them and add the mixture to the flour. Knead a hard dough.

(3) Mix curds with the dough and knead well again. Add ghee and knead again. Knead well till the dough is soft. Keep the dough under a wet cloth for 4 to 5 hours.

(4) Divide the dough into small balls (a little bigger than a lime). Apply a little ghee to the balls. Cover the balls with wet cloth for 15 to 20 minutes.

(5) Apply a little ghee to the rolling pin. Roll out nans in the shape of triangles. Apply a little water on one side of the nan. Paste the nan on the hot griddle. After a few seconds, place the griddle upside down on the gas.

(6) When the nan is roasted apply butter. Serve hot.

Note : After rolling the nan, you can also sprinkle a few kalonji seeds on it and roll again slightly to press them.

326. Misi Roti [Serves 3 to 4]

Ingredients

(1) 2 cups spinach (finally chopped)

(2) A pinch asafoetida

(3) A pinch turmeric powder

(4) 1 cup maida

(5) 1 cup wheat flour

(6) 1 cup chana flour

(7) $\frac{1}{4}$ cup methi leaves (finely chopped)

(8) $\frac{1}{4}$ cup suva bhaji (finely chopped)

(9) $\frac{1}{4}$ cup coriander leaves (finely chopped)

(10) A small piece of ginger

(11) 5 green chillies

(12) 1 onion (finely chopped)

(13) Butter

(14) Salt to taste

Method

(1) Put the spinach in boiling hot water for 2 minutes. Strain, cool and grind to a fine paste.

(2) Add asafoetida, salt and turmeric powder to the spinach paste.

(3) Mix all the three flours, enough ghee, salt, all other green leafy vegetables, spinach paste, ginger-chilli paste and onions.

(4) Knead the dough. Make it a little softer than the paratha dough. Roll out as rotis (a little thinner than parathas). Roast it on the griddle. Apply butter. Serve hot.

Note : It can be also roasted on the griddle like *thepalas* using a little oil or ghee.

327. Hari Puri Kulcha
[Makes 20 to 25 Kulchas]
Ingredients

(1) 100 grams fresh beans (crushed coarsely)

(2) 1 tea spoon sesame seeds

(3) ½ tea spoon mustard seeds

(4) 1 tea spoon ginger-chilli paste

(5) ½ tea spoon citric acid

(6) 2 tea spoons sugar

(7) 1 tea spoon garam masala

(8) 4 table spoons coriander leaves

(9) 3 table spoons grated coconut

(10) 250 grams spinach

(11) 2½ cups wheat flour

(12) Oil   (13) Salt to taste

Method

(1) Heat a little oil in a pan. Add sesame seeds and mustard seeds. Add the fresh beans. Saute for a few minutes.

(2) Add salt and masalas, like that for kachori. Add finely chopped coriander leaves and grated coconut (desiccated coconut). Do not add cashewnuts and raisins.

(3) Wash and boil the spinach leaves for 2 minutes. Cool and strain them. Blenderise in the mixer to make a fine paste.

(4) Mix wheat flour, salt, oil, spinach paste and kachori masala. Knead the dough like puri. Divide the dough into big balls. Roll out each ball into thick and large puris. Fry the puris in hot oil.

Note : Serve hot only.

328. Palak Puri-Green Puri
[Makes 35 to 40 Puris]
Ingredients

(1) 200 grams spinach

(2) 2 table spoons green chilli paste

(3) 2 cups wheat flour

(4) 2 table spoons ghee

(5) Oil   (6) Salt to taste

Method

(1) Wash and boil the spinach leaves for 2 minutes. Add a little salt to the water. Cool and blenderise it to a fine paste.

(2) Add 2 to 3 green chillies to the spinach while blendersing.

(3) Add salt and ghee in flour.

(4) Knead the dough using this spinach paste. Add water only if it is required. Knead a hard dough.

(5) Divide the dough into small balls. Roll out each ball into a small puri. Fry the puris in hot oil.

Note : 2 table spoons of rawa can be added to the dough if desired.

329. Paneer Chilla
[Makes 12 to 15 pieces]
Ingredients

(1) 1 cup mung dal (with skin)

(2) 2 medium sized ginger piece (grated)

(3) 7 to 8 green chillies

(4) 3 table spoons coriander leaves (finely chopped)

(5) 2 onions (grated)

(6) 4 cloves garlic (7) Paneer (grated)

(8) Sweet chutney (9) Salt to taste

Method

(1) Soak the mung dal for 2 hours. Grind it into a coarse paste. Add ginger, chillies, coriander, salt and grated onions.

(2) Heat a griddle. Drop a spoonful of the mixture and spread lightly. Sprinkle finely chopped green chillies, ginger and paneer. Add oil on all side of the pudla. Press lightly.

(3) While serving place the side of the chilla having paneer on the top side. Apply coriander, garlic and sweet chutney (optional). Serve immediately.

* **Green chutney :** Mix ginger, chillies, coriander leaves, fresh or desiccated coconut, salt, sugar and lime juice. Grind all the ingredients in the mixer to make a fine paste.

* **Garlic chutney :** Mix garlic, salt and red chilli powder. Blenderise to make garlic chutney.

330. Stuffed Potato Paratha
[Serve 6 to 7]
Ingredients

(1) 500 grams potatoes
(2) 2 tea spoons ginger-chilli paste
(3) 4 table spoons coriander leaves
(4) $\frac{1}{2}$ tea spoon citric acid
(5) 2 tea spoons sugar
(6) 1 tea spoon garam masala
(7) 250 grams onions
(8) Rice flour
(9) 200 grams wheat flour
(10) Oil   (11) Salt to taste

Method

(1) Boil, peel and grate potatoes. Add all the masalas. Grate the onions. Press lightly between the palms to remove excess water. Add grated onions to the mashed potatoes. Mix well. Mix flour, salt and oil.

(2) Knead the dough a little harder then the chapati dough. Divide the dough into small balls.

(3) Roll out each ball a little. Place a little stuffing in the centre. Bring the edges together and make a ball again. Roll it again into a thick roti. Roast on a griddle using oil. Serve hot.

331. Fresh Green Beans Paratha
[Serves 3]
Ingredients

(1) 250 grams fresh beans
(2) 2 potatoes
(3) 2 tea spoons ginger-chilli paste
(4) $\frac{1}{4}$ cup coriander leaves (finely chopped)
(5) 4 table spoons coconut (grated)
(6) 1 tea spoon garam masala
(7) 1 lime
(8.) 2 tea spoons sugar
(9) 1 tea spoon sesame seeds
(10) 125 grams wheat flour
(11) Oil   (12) Salt to taste

Method

(1) Grind the fresh beans coarsely. Saute them in a little oil. Add all masalas, like kachori masala. Boil, peel and grate the potatoes. Mix the potatoes with kachori masala.

(2) Mix wheat flour, salt and oil. Knead the dough. Divide the dough into small balls. Roll out each ball lightly. Place a little stuffing mixture in the centre. Bring the edges together. Make a ball again. Roll out into a thick roti. Roast on the griddle using oil. Serve hot.

332. Raddish Paratha – Muli Ke Parathe [Serves 3 to 4]
Ingredients

(1) 200 grams raddish leaves
(2) 1 raddish (approximately 200 grams)
(3) 100 grams potatoes
(4) 4 green chillies
(5) $\frac{1}{2}$ tea spoon turmeric powder
(6) 1 lime
(7) 1 tea spoon garam masala

(8) 1 tea spoon sugar

(9) 200 to 250 grams wheat flour

(10) Oil

(11) Salt to taste

Method

(1) Chop the raddish leaves finely. Grate the raddish.

(2) Boil, peel and grate the potatoes. Mix it with raddish leaves.

(3) Add salt, green chillies, turmeric powder, lime juice, garam masala and sugar.

(4) Mix flour, salt and oil. Knead a soft dough. Divide the dough into small balls. Roll out a ball slightly. Place the stuffing in the centre. Bring the edge together and make into a ball again. Roll it out into a thick roti. Roast the roti on the griddle using oil.

333. Palak Paratha

[Makes 8 to 10 Parathas]

Ingredients

(1) 1 cup spinach

(2) 1 onion (finely chopped)

(3) 2 cups wheat flour

(4) 1 tea spoon ginger-chilli paste

(5) 4 table spoons coriander leaves

(6) Oil

(7) Salt to taste

Method

(1) Chop the spinach leaves. Boil, cool and blenderise to make a fine paste. Saute onions in very little oil for few minutes.

(2) Mix spinach paste, onions, ginger-chilli paste, coriander leaves, red chilli powder, salt, 1 table spoon oil and wheat flour. Knead the dough like that needed for paratha. The water used for boiling spinach may be used for kneading the dough.

(3) Divide the dough into big balls. Roll out each ball into a thick roti or paratha. Roast on a griddle using a little oil. Serve hot with curds.

Variation

Desiccated coconut and powdered groundnuts may be also added to the parathas.

Note : Instead of onion 1 boiled potato can be also added.

334. Gobhi-Ke-Parathe

[Seves 3]

Ingredients

(1) 250 grams cauliflower

(2) 125 grams wheat flour

(3) Oil

(4) $\frac{1}{2}$ tea spoon mustard seeds

(5) 1 tea spoon sesame seeds

(6) 1 tea spoon ginger-chilli paste

(7) $\frac{1}{2}$ cup coriander leaves (finely chopped)

(8) A lime   (9) 2 tea spoons sugar

(10) 1 tea spoon garam masala

(11) 2 potatoes (12) Salt to taste

Method

(1) Grate the cauliflower. Heat a little oil in a vessel. Add mustard seeds and sesame seeds for seasoning. Add grated cauliflower. Saute for a few minutes. Add salt and all the masalas.

(2) Boil, peel and grate potatoes. Mix the potatoes with cauliflower.

(3) Mix flour, salt and oil. Knead a soft dough. Divide the dough into small balls. Roll out a ball lightly. Place the stuffing in the centre. Bring the edges together and make a ball again. Roll it into a thick roti or paratha. Roast the paratha on the griddle using oil. Serve hot.

Variation

(1) Carrots, potatoes-onions parathas

(2) Potato, cabbage, onion parathas

(3) Potato and green peas parathas can be made by the same method

335. Chana Flour Pudla

[Serves 5 to 6]

Ingredients

(1) 250 grams chana flour (fine)

(2) 2 tea spoons chilli paste

(3) A pinch asafoetida

(4) 100 grams methi leaves (finely chopped)

(5) 1 tea spoon ginger paste

(6) 2 onions (grated)

(7) 6 cloves garlic (paste)

(8) 4 table spoons finely chopped coriander leaves

(9) $\frac{1}{2}$ cup curds

(10) Oil   (11) Salt to taste

Method

(1) Mix all ingredients. Heat the griddle.

(2) Drop a spoonful on the mixture on the griddle. Spread a little with a serving spoon.

(3) Roast on both sides using enough oil.

336. Corn Chanki

[Serves 6 to 7]

Ingredients

(1) 3 cups maize flour

(2) A little less then 1 cup wheat flour

(3) 250 grams bottlegourd (dudhi)

(4) 1 tea spoon chilli paste

(5) $\frac{1}{2}$ tea spoon turmeric powder

(6) 2 table spoons jaggery

(7) 1 tea spoon omum

(8) Oil   (9) Curds

(10) 1 tea spoon garlic (paste)

(11) Salt to taste

Method

(1) Mix maize flour, wheat flour, grated dudhi, oil, salt and all masalas.

(2) Knead a hard dough. Keep the dough aside for 2 hours.

(3) Divide the dough into small balls. Roll out each ball into small chanki (small thick roti). Roll out putting plastic sheets on the sides. Fry all chankis. Serve with curds chutney. For chutney mix curds, salt and red chilli powder.

337. Bajara Roti (Dhebra)

[Serves 4 to 5]

Ingredients

(1) 50 grams wheat flour

(2) 250 grams bajari flour

(3) Oil

(4) 1 tea spoon red chilli powder

(5) $\frac{1}{2}$ tea spoon turmeric powder

(6) 2 table spoons jaggery

(7) 1 table spoon sesame seeds

(8) $\frac{1}{2}$ tea spoon omum

(9) 1 cup curds

(10) 8 cloves garlic (paste)

(11) Pickle oil   (12) 4 chillis (paste)

(13) A small piece of ginger

(14) A pinch asafoetida

(15) Salt to taste

Method

(1) Mix all ingredients and 2 table spoons oil. Knead the dough.

(2) Divide the dough into small balls. Roll out each ball into a thick roti or dhebra. Roast on the griddle using oil.

338. Methi Roti (Dhebra)

[Serves 5 to 6]

Ingredients

(1) Add the other masalas in the same way as for bajari dhebra

(2) 250 grams methi bhaji

(3) $\frac{1}{2}$ cup finely chopped coriander leaves

(4) 50 grams garlic

(5) 2 table spoons sesame seeds

Method

(1) Mix all ingredients and knead a dough.

(2) Divide the dough into small balls.

(3) Roll out each ball into a thick roti or dhebra. Roast the roti on the griddle using oil.

339. Coriander Roti (Dhebra)

[Serves 5 to 6]

Method

The same as methi dhebra. Only instead of methi leaves and 250 grams of coriander leaves.

Note : 50 grams of bajari flour can be also added.

340. Dudhi Roti (Dhebra)

[Serves 5 to 6]

Ingredients

(1) 500 grams grated bottlegourd (dudhi)

(2) 500 grams wheat flour

(3) Curds

(4) Sugar or jaggery

(5) Turmeric powder

(6) 50 grams garlic

(7) Green chillies (paste)

(8) A few coriander leaves (finely chopped)

(9) Salt to taste

Method

(1) Mix all ingredients.

(2) Make dhebras like methi dhebras.

Note : The quantity of the wheat flour depends upon the quality of bottlegourd. If it is soft and fresh, more flour is required.

341. Cow's Peas Leaves (Choli) Paratha [Serves 3]

Ingredients

(1) 250 grams cow's peas leaves

(2) Oil

(3) $\frac{1}{2}$ tea spoon mustard seeds

(4) 1 tea spoon sesame seeds

(5) 2 potatoes

(6) 2 tea spoons ginger-chilli paste

(7) $\frac{1}{2}$ tea spoon citric acid

(8) 2 tea spoons sugar

(9) 1 tea spoon garam masala

(10) 4 table spoons coriander leaves

(11) 150 grams wheat flour

(12) Salt to taste

Method

(1) Chop the choli leaves. Blenderise them to make a fine paste. Heat a little oil in a vessel. Add mustard seeds, and sesame seeds. Add the choli paste. Saute for a few minutes.

(2) Boil, peel and grate potatoes. Add them to the choli paste. Add all the masalas. Remove it from the flame.

(3) Mix flour, salt and oil. Knead the dough like that kneaded for roti. Divide the dough into small balls. Fill the stuffing, close the edges roll out the parathas. Roast the paratha on griddle using oil.

342. Beet Root Puri [Serves 2]

Ingredients

(1) 100 grams wheat flour

(2) 100 grams beet root
(peeled and blenderised)

(3) Oil   (4) Salt to taste

Method

(1) Mix all ingredients and knead the dough. Divide the dough into small balls.

(2) Roll out each ball into a thick puri. Fry them in hot oil.

9 INDIAN VEGETABLES

343. Undhiya [Serves 5 to 7]

Ingredients

(1) 500 grams potatoes

(2) 500 grams sweet potato

(3) 150 grams yam   (4) Oil

(5) 100 grams chana flour (coarse)

(6) 2 table spoons wheat flour (coarse)

(7) 1 tea spoon red chilli powder

(8) 1 tea spoon turmeric powder

(9) 2 table spoons dhana jeera powder

(10) 1 table spoon sugar (powdered)

(11) 150 grams methi leaves

(12) 150 grams small brinjals (surati ravaiya)

(13) 25 grams ginger

(14) 100 grams green chillies

(15) 1 big bunch of coriander leaves

(16) 2 table spoons sugar

(17) $\frac{1}{2}$ tea spoon soda

(18) 1 tea spoon garam masala

(19) 2 tea spoons sesame seeds

(20) $\frac{1}{4}$ tea spoon asafoetida

(21) $\frac{1}{2}$ coconut (with water)

(22) 75 grams garlic

(23) 4 whole red chillies

(24) 1 tea spoon omum

(25) 500 grams papadi (beans)

(26) 150 grams papadi (without beans)

(27) 350 grams tuver (fresh beans)

(28) Salt to taste

Method

(1) Wash and peel the potatoes, sweet potatoes and yam. Wipe them and cut into medium size pieces. Fry them in hot oil.

(2) Chop the methi leaves finely. Wash and strain them. Apply a little salt to the methi leaves. Keep aside for a few minutes. Press the methi leaves to remove the excess water.

(3) Mix wheat flour, coarse chana flour, salt, red chilli powder, turmeric powder, dhana jeera powder, powdered sugar, oil and methi leaves.

(4) Mix well. Knead the dough. Make a hard dough. Divide the dough into small balls and make muthiyas. Deep fry the muthiya.

(5) Wash brinjal and put 2 cuts on the top side. The pieces must not be separated. Mix ginger-chilli paste, finely chopped coriander leaves, sugar, salt, dhana jeera powder, a little soda, garam masala and sesame seeds. Stuff this masalas in the brinjal.

(6) Crushed fresh beans also can be added in the masala for stuffing. Heat a little oil in a kadhai. Add the brinjal and let it get cooked.

(7) Mix finely chopped coriander leaves, ginger-chilli paste, sesame seeds, grated coconut, garlic paste, sugar, salt and dhana jeera powder.

(8) Heat enough oil in a kadhai. Add whole red chillies (dried), omum, red chilli powder, turmeric powder and asafoetida. Add papadi, val and fresh beans.

(9) Add a little salt and citric acid (dissolved in water). Cover it with a lid. Cook it till it becomes soft. They may also be cooked in the pressure cooker for one whistle.

(10) Mix the fried potatoes, sweet potatoes and yam pieces with the mixed coriander coconut masala. Then add brinjal and muthiyas to it. Mix very well. Add the fresh beans. When the beans are cooked well add the remaining masala. Mix again. Decorate with finely chopped coriander leaves and grated coconut.

Note : The quantity of green chillies depends upon own's taste.

344. Ravaiya with Green Beans [Serves 5 to 7]

Ingredients

(1) 200 grams fresh beans (washed and crushed)

(2) 8 to 10 green chillies (paste)

(3) 1 big bunch of coriander leaves (finely chopped)

(4) 50 grams grated coconut

(5) 4 tea spoons sugar

(6) 2 tea spoons garam masala

(7) 4 table spoons dhana jeera powder

(8) Oil

(9) $\frac{1}{2}$ tea spoon mustard seeds

(10) 1 tea spoon sesame seeds

(11) $\frac{1}{2}$ tea spoon red chilli powder

(12) $\frac{1}{4}$ tea spoon turmeric powder

(13) A pinch asafoetida

(14) $\frac{1}{4}$ tea spoon soda

(15) 250 grams brinjal (ravaiya)

(16) 4 big potatoes (peeled and cut into long pieces)

(17) 3 capsicums (cut into long strips)

(18) 1 lime   (19) Salt to taste

Method

(1) Mix all the masalas in coriander leaves. Wash and make cuts in the ravaiya from the top. Do not separate the pieces.

(2) Fill the masala in the ravaiya.

(3) Heat enough oil in a kadhai. Add sesame seeds, mustard seeds, red chilli powder, a little turmeric powder, asafoetida and citric acid. Add a little water. When the water starts boiling add all vegetables. Add the additional masala.

(4) Cook on a low flame. When the vegetables are cooked, add a little lime juice.

345. Bhindi Ravaiya [Serves 6]

Ingredients

(1) 500 grams bhindi (lady's fingers)

(2) Oil

(3) 1 tea spoon cumin seeds

(4) A pinch asafoetida

(5) 2 tea spoons ginger-chilli paste

(6) 50 grams grated coconut

(7) 100 grams coriander leaves

(8) 1 lime

(9) 2 tea spoons garam masala

(10) Salt to taste

Method

(1) Wash and wipe the lady's fingers. Place a cut lengthwise. Fry them in hot oil on a high flame.

(2) Heat a little oil in a vessel. Add cumin seeds, asafoetida, ginger, chillies, grated coconut, salt, coriander leaves and lime. Add the fried lady's fingers. Mix well. Remove it from the flame.

346. Stuffed Bhindi [Serves 4]

Ingredients

(1) 250 grams lady's fingers

(2) 150 grams chana flour

(3) 2 tea spoons red chilli powder

(4) 1 tea spoon turmeric powder

(5) 3 tea spoons dhana jeera powder

(6) 1 tea spoon garam masala

(7) 3 tea spoons sugar

(8) A lime

(9) Oil

(10) 1 tea spoon cumin seeds

(11) 2 table spoons coriander leaves

(12) Salt to taste

Method

(1) Wash the lady's fingers. Put a cut lengthwise.

(2) Mix chana flour (besan) and all the masalas. Mix well. Stuff this masala in the lady's fingers.

(3) Heat enough oil in kadhai. Add the cumin seeds and stuffed lady's fingers. Cover with a lid. Add the additional masala. When it is cooked remove it from the flame. Decorate with finely chopped coriander leaves.

347. Onion-Papad Vegetable [Serves 2]

Ingredients

(1) 4 papads

(2) 2 table spoons oil

(3) ½ tea spoon cumin seeds

(4) A pinch asafoetida

(5) 100 grams spring onions

(6) 1 tea spoon dhana jeera powder

(7) 1 tea spoon red chilli powder

(8) ½ tea spoon turmeric powder

(9) Salt to taste

Method

(1) Cut the papads into medium size pieces. Heat oil in a vessel. Add cumin seeds. Add the papad pieces.

(2) Add 1 cup water and finely chopped spring onions along with the leaves. Cook for 5 to 7 minutes.

(3) Add salt, dhana jeera powder, red chilli powder and turmeric powder.

Note : Instead of spring onions, plain onions may also be added.

348. Methi-Papad Vegetable [Serves 4]

Ingredients

(1) 100 grams methi leaves

(2) 2 table spoons oil

(3) ½ tea spoon turmeric powder

(4) 1 tea spoon red chilli powder

(5) 3 table spoons jaggery

(6) 3 to 4 papads

(7) 1 tea spoon dhana jeera powder

(8) 1 tea spoon garam masala

(9) ½ lime

(10) Salt to taste

Method

(1) Chop the methi leaves. Soak them in water for a few minutes. Then boil the methi leaves for a few minutes.

(2) Heat a little oil in a vessel. Add turmeric powder, red chilli powder and boiled methi. Add water.

(3) The water in which the methi leaves were boiled may also be added.

When the water starts boiling, add the papad pieces. Add dhana jeera powder, garam masala, lime juice or amchur powder and remove it from the flame.

349. Turia-Patara Vegetable

[Serves 4]

Ingredients

(1) 150 grams colacasia leaves for patara (boiled)

(2) 150 grams turia

(3) 2 table spoons oil

(4) 1 tea spoon cumin seeds

(5) A pinch asafoetida

(6) $\frac{1}{2}$ tea spoon turmeric powder

(7) 1 tea spoon red chilli powder

(8) 1 tea spoon dhana jeera powder

(9) 1 tea spoon garam masala

(10) 1 tea spoon sugar

(11) 1 lime

(12) 3 table spoons finely chopped coriander leaves

(13) 100 grams spinach

(14) Salt to taste

Method

(1) Make boiled pataras as described in R. No. 129.

(2) Peel off the turia and cut it into small pieces.

(3) Heat a little oil in a vessel. Add cumin seeds, asafoetida, red chilli powder, turmeric powder and turia pieces. Add a little water and salt.

(4) When the turia are cooked, add pieces of boiled pataras. Add all the masalas. Keep some gravy in the vegetables. Instead of water, spinach paste may be also added. Decorate with chopped coriander leaves.

Note : You can also prepare Dudhi-Patara Vegetable in the same way.

350. Onion-Potato Vegetable

[Serves 5]

Ingredients

(1) 250 grams potatoes

(2) 300 grams onions

(3) 3 table spoons oil

(4) $\frac{1}{2}$ tea spoon mustard seeds

(5) A pinch asafoetida

(6) 2 tea spoons red chilli powder

(7) 1 lime

(8) 1 tea spoon dhana jeera powder

(9) Salt to taste

Method

(1) Boil and peel the potatoes. Cut them lengthwise. Chop the onions lengthwise.

(2) Heat oil in a vessel. Add mustard seeds, asafoetida, red chilli powder and onions.

(3) When the onions are brown in colour, add potatoes, salt, lime juice, dhana jeera powder and red chilli powder. Decorate with finely chopped coriander leaves. Serve hot.

351. Cluster Beans (Guvar)

Vegetable [Serves 2 to 3]

Ingredients

(1) 250 grams cluster beans (Guvar)

(2) 2 table spoons oil

(3) 1 onion

(4) $\frac{1}{2}$ tea spoon cumin seeds

(5) $\frac{1}{2}$ cup curds

(6) 1 tea spoon red chilli powder

(7) $\frac{1}{2}$ tea spoon turmeric powder

(8) 1 tea spoon dhana jeera powder

(9) 1 tea spoon sugar

(10) 2 table spoons coriander leaves

(11) Salt to taste

Method

(1) Heat oil in a kadhai. Add cumin seeds and very finely chopped onions. Fry it till the onions are brown in colour.

(2) Mix curds with salt, red chilli powder, turmeric powder, dhana jeera powder and very little water.

(3) Add this curds mixture to the onions. Saute for a few minutes. Cut guvar into medium sized pieces. Boil them. Add them to the onions. Add a little sugar (optional). Remove it from the flame. When the guvar is cooked, sprinkle chopped coriander leaves on it. Serve hot.

352. Grated Raw Papaya
[Serves 4]

Ingredients

(1) 400 grams raw papaya

(2) 1 lime

(3) 2 table spoons oil

(4) $\frac{1}{2}$ tea spoon mustard seeds

(5) 3 to 4 green chillies (cut lengthwise)

(6) A pinch asafoetida

(7) Salt to taste

Method

(1) Peel and grate raw papaya. Apply salt and keep aside for a few minutes. Press lightly to remove the excess water from it. Add additional salt (if required) and lime juice.

(2) Heat a little oil. Add mustard seeds, asafoetida and green chillies. Add the seasoning to the papaya. Mix well.

353. Brinjal-Potato Vegetable
[Serves 5 to 6]

Ingredients

(1) 3 brinjals

(2) 2 potatoes

(3) 3 table spoons oil

(4) $\frac{1}{2}$ tea spoon mustard seeds

(5) $\frac{1}{2}$ tea spoon cumin seeds

(6) A pinch asafoetida

(7) 100 grams chana flour

(8) 1 tea spoon red chilli powder

(9) $\frac{1}{2}$ tea spoon turmeric powder

(10) 1 tea spoon dhana jeera powder

(11) 1 tea spoon garam masala

(12) 1 tea spoon sugar

(13) 6 cloves garlic (paste)

(14) 50 grams groundnuts

(15) Salt to taste

Method

(1) Heat oil in a vessel. Add mustard seeds, cumin seeds and asafoetida to prepare the seasoning. Add brinjals and potatoes cut into pieces. Add salt and little water and cook until they are done.

(2) Mix chana flour and all masalas. Add little oil to it. Mix well and add to the vegetables. Add garlic paste.

(3) The vegetable should have a thick gravy. Lastly, add groundnut powder. Serve hot.

354. Baigan Bharta [Serves 4]

Ingredients

(1) 250 grams large brinjal (bhutta)

(2) 2 table spoons oil

(3) 2 tea spoons ghee

(4) 1 tea spoon cumin seeds

(5) A pinch asafoetida

(6) $\frac{1}{4}$ tea spoon turmeric powder

(7) 1 tea spoon red chilli powder

(8) 200 grams onions

(9) 10 cloves garlic

(10) 100 grams tomatoes   (11) 1 lime

(12) 1 table spoon ginger-chilli paste

(13) 1 tea spoon garam masala

(14) 1 tea spoon finely chopped coriander leaves

(15) Salt to taste

Method

(1) Apply a little oil to the brinjal. Put it directly on the gas flame. Roast it. Keep on turning it at frequent intervals. When the brinjal is roasted properly, remove it from the flame. Peel and mash it well.

(2) Heat a little oil or ghee in a kadhai. Add asafoetida, turmeric powder, red chilli powder, spiring onions (finely chopped) and garlic (finely chopped). Saute for a few minutes.

(3) Add tomatoes (finely chopped) and mashed brinjal, salt, lime juice, ginger chilli paste and garam masala. Fry for a few minutes. Decorate it with chopped coriander. Serve hot.

355. Potato Vegetable with Thick Gravy [Serves 3]

Ingredients

(1) 250 grams potatoes

(2) 2 table spoons oil

(3) $\frac{1}{2}$ tea spoon mustard seeds

(4) A pinch asafoetida

(5) $\frac{1}{2}$ tea spoon turmeric powder

(6) 1 tea spoon red chilli powder

(7) 2 tea spoons dhana jeera powder

(8) 1 tea spoon garam masala

(9) 2 table spoons jaggery

(10) 1 tea spoon amchur powder

(11) Salt to taste

Method

(1) Cut the potatoes into small pieces with or without peeling as desired.

(2) Heat oil in a vessel for seasoning. Add mustard seeds, asafoetida, $\frac{1}{2}$ tea spoon red chilli powder and $\frac{1}{4}$ tea spoon turmeric powder. Add the potatoes (pieces). Add salt and water. Cook it till the potatoes are done.

(3) Mix $\frac{1}{2}$ tea spoon red chilli powder, $\frac{1}{4}$ tea spoon turmeric powder, dhana jeera powder, garam masala, jaggery, amchur powder and a little water in a cup. Mix well. Add this mixture to the potatoes when they are cooked.

(4) Boil it till the gravy thickens. Remove it from the flame. Sprinkle chopped coriander leaves on top.

356. Palak-Mung Dal Vegetable [Serves 3]

Ingredients

(1) $\frac{1}{2}$ cup mung dal

(2) 1 bunch spinach

(3) 2 table spoons oil

(4) $\frac{1}{2}$ tea spoon cumin seeds

(5) A pinch asafoetida

(6) $\frac{1}{2}$ tea spoon turmeric powder

(7) 1 tea spoon red chilli powder

(8) 2 tomatoes

(9) 1 tea spoon sugar

(10) 1 tea spoon garam masala

(11) Salt to taste

Method

(1) Soak the mung dal in water for one hour. Chop the spinach very finely and wash them well.

(2) Heat a little oil for seasoning in a pan. Add cumin seeds, asafoetida, turmeric powder, red chilli powder and mung dal.

(3) Then add spinach, salt, finely chopped tomatoes, sugar and garam masala. Heat till done.

357. Mung Dal-Tandalja Vegetable [Serves 3]

Instead of spinach take same quantity of tandalja leaves. The other ingredients and method remain the same as in R. No. 356.

358. Gunda Ravaiya [Serves 2]

Ingredients

(1) 200 grams yellow gundas

(2) 100 grams chana flour

(3) 1 tea spoon red chilli powder

(4) $\frac{1}{2}$ tea spoon turmeric powder

(5) 1 tea spoon garam masala

(6) 2 tea spoons sugar

(7) Oil   (8) Salt to taste

Method

(1) Wash and remove the seeds from the gundas. Mix all the other ingredients.

(2) Stuff the masala in gundas. Heat oil in a kadhai.

(3) Add the gundas. Let them cook until they become soft.

Note : (1) Gundas can also be boiled in the pressure cooker and than added.

(2) Instead of yellow gundas, green variety of gundas can also be used.

359. Sev-Tomato Vegetable [Serves 3 to 4]

Ingredients

(1) 250 grams red tomatoes

(2) 2 table spoons oil

(3) $\frac{1}{2}$ tea spoon cumin seeds

(4) $\frac{1}{2}$ tea spoon mustard seeds

(5) 1 tea spoon red chilli powder

(6) 1 table spoon jaggery

(7) $\frac{1}{2}$ tea spoon turmeric powder

(8) 1 tea spoon dhana jeera powder

(9) 1 tea spoon garam masala

(10) 100 grams thick sev

(11) Salt to taste

Method

(1) Chop the tomatoes into big pieces.

(2) Heat the oil for seasoning. Add cumin seeds, mustard seeds, tomatoes, salt, chilli powder, jaggery, turmeric powder, dhana jeera powder, garam masala and a little water.

(3) When it starts boiling, add sev. Let it simmer for a few minutes. Remove it from the flame.

360. Potato-Methi Vegetable [Serves 4 to 5]

Ingredients

(1) 250 grams potatoes

(2) 2 table spoons oil

(3) $\frac{1}{2}$ tea spoon mustard seeds

(4) A pinch asafoetida

(5) 1 tea spoon ginger-chilli paste

(6) $\frac{1}{2}$ tea spoon turmeric powder

(7) 1 tea spoon dhana jeera powder

(8) Jaggery as desired

(9) 250 grams methi leaves

(10) 1 tea spoon garam masala

(11) 1 lime   (12) Salt to taste

Method

(1) Peel and cut the potatoes into small pieces.

(2) Heat oil in a vessel. Add mustard seeds, asafoetida and potatoes for seasoning. Add the ginger-chilli paste, salt, red chilli powder, turmeric powder, dhana jeera powder and jaggery.

(3) Chop the methi leaves very finely. Wash and add to potatoes. When cooked, add garam masala and lime juice.

361. Panchratna Karela

[Serves 4 to 5]

Ingredients

(1) 250 grams karelas

(2) 2 raw bananas (3) Oil

(4) 50 grams groundnuts

(5) 50 grams cashewnuts

(6) 50 grams currants

(7) 50 grams black currants

(8) 25 grams sesame seeds

(9) $\frac{1}{2}$ tea spoon turmeric powder

(10) 2 tea spoons dhana jeera powder

(11) 50 grams powdered sugar

(12) 25 grams desiccated coconut

(13) 1 tea spoon garam masala

(14) 1 tea spoon ginger-chilli paste

(15) 1 tea spoon red chilli powder

(16) Salt to taste

Method

(1) Peel and cut the karela into pieces lengthwise. Add salt to them and rub well. Keep aside for some time. Peel the bananas and cut them into pieces lengthwise.

(2) Fry the karela and banana pieces. Soak the groundnuts in water.

(3) Heat oil in a vessel. Add cashewnuts, raisins, groundnuts, black currants, sesame seeds, turmeric powder, dhana jeera powder, powdered sugar, desiccated coconut, garam masala, salt, ginger-chilli paste and red chilli powder. Mix well.

(4) Mix the fried karela and banana pieces well.

362. Ratalu-Fresh Beans (Val)

Vegetable [Serves 5 to 6]

Ingredients

(1) 250 grams val (fresh beans)

(2) 500 grams yam

(3) 3 table spoons oil

(4) 1 tea spoon omum

(5) A pinch of asafoetida

(6) 2 tea spoons chilli paste

(7) $\frac{1}{4}$ tea spoon turmeric powder

(8) 2 limes (9) 4 tea spoons sugar

(10) 200 grams finely chopped coriander leaves

(11) 50 grams desiccated coconut

(12) 2 tea spoons dhana jeera powder

(13) 1 tea spoon garam masala

(14) Salt to taste

Method

(1) Boil the fresh beans (val). Peel the ratalu (yam) and cut into small pieces. Fry the ratalu pieces.

(2) Heat oil in a vessel. Add ginger-chilli paste, turmeric powder, lime juice, sugar, coriander leaves, salt, desiccated coconut, dhana jeera powder, garam masala, boiled val and fried ratalu pieces.

(3) Mix well. Let it simmer for 5 minutes. Remove it from the flame. Decorate with finely chopped coriander leaves before serving.

363. Green Potato Chips

Vegetable [Serves 4 to 5]

Ingredients

(1) 500 grams potatoes

(2) 250 grams spinach

(3) 25 grams fresh garlic (paste)

(4) Oil

(5) $\frac{1}{2}$ tea spoon cumin seeds

(6) A pinch asafoetida

(7) 1 tea spoon ginger-chilli paste

(8) $\frac{1}{2}$ tea spoon turmeric powder

(9) 1 table spoon dhana jeera powder

(10) 50 grams coriander leaves

(11) 1 lemon   (12) Salt to taste

Method

(1) Peel and cut the potatoes lengthwise into long chips. Fry the potato chips.

(2) Chop the spinach finely and wash it well. Heat oil in a kadhai for seasoning.

(3) Add cumin seeds, ginger-chilli paste and asafoetida. Fry for 2 to 3 seconds. Add spinach, salt, turmeric powder, dhana jeera powder and lime juice. Cook for a few minutes. Then add potato chips. Mix well. Decorate with finely chopped coriander leaves.

364. Bhindi with Capsicum [Serves 5]

Ingredients

(1) 300 grams lady's fingers

(2) 300 grams capsicum

(3) Oil

(4) $\frac{1}{2}$ tea spoon cumin seeds

(5) A pinch asafoetida

(6) 1 tea spoon ginger-chilli paste

(7) $\frac{1}{4}$ tea spoon turmeric powder

(8) 2 table spoons dhana jeera powder

(9) 50 grams desiccated coconut

(10) 200 grams coriander leaves

(11) Salt to taste

Method

(1) Cut the lady's fingers and capsicum lengthwise. Fry them on high flame. Heat a little oil for seasoning. Add cumin seeds and asafoetida.

(2) Add turmeric powder, dhana jeera powder and fry for a few minutes.

(3) Add finely chopped tomatoes, salt, red chilli powder and grated coconut. Lastly, add lady's fingers and capsicum. Let it simmer for a few minutes on low flame. Remove it

from the flame. Decorate with finely chopped coriander leaves.

365. Lady's Fingers with Tomatoes [Serves 4 to 5]

Ingredients

(1) 300 grams lady's fingers   (2) Oil

(3) $\frac{1}{2}$ tea spoon cumin seeds

(4) A pinch asafoetida

(5) $\frac{1}{4}$ tea spoon turmeric powder

(6) 3 table spoons dhana jeera powder

(7) 50 grams desiccated coconut

(8) 300 grams finely chopped tomatoes

(9) 1 tea spoon red chilli powder

(10) 100 grams coriander leaves

(11) Salt to taste

Method

(1) Cut the lady's fingers into long strips and fry them. Heat the oil in a vessel. Add the cumin seeds and asafoetida. Fry for 2 to 3 seconds.

(2) Add the turmeric powder and dhana jeera powder. Fry again for 2 to 3 seconds.

(3) Add desiccated coconut, tomatoes, salt, red chilli powder and lady's fingers. Fry for a few minutes. Garnish with chopped coriander.

366. Mung Dal [Serves 4]

Ingredients

(1) 1 cup mung dal

(2) 2 table spoons oil

(3) 1 tea spoon cumin seeds

(4) A pinch asafoetida

(5) 1 tea spoon red chilli powder

(6) 1 tea spoon ginger-chilli paste

(7) 2 tea spoons sugar

(8) $\frac{1}{2}$ tea spoon turmeric powder

(9) 8 cloves garlic

(10) 2 table spoons coriander leaves

(11) Salt to taste

Method

(1) Wash and soak the mung dal for at least 2 hours. Heat oil in a kadhai. Add cumin seeds and asafoetida. Add the soaked mung dal and water enough to cover the dal.

(2) Add red chilli powder, turmeric powder, ginger-chilli paste and sugar.

(3) Garlic paste also may be added (optional). The dal should remain whole after cooking. It should have some amount of gravy. Decorate with chopped coriander.

367. Chana Dal [Serves 4]

Ingredients

(1) 1 cup chana dal

(2) 2 table spoons oil

(3) $\frac{1}{2}$ tea spoon mustard seeds

(4) A pinch asafoetida

(5) $\frac{1}{4}$ tea spoon turmeric powder

(6) $\frac{1}{2}$ tea spoon ginger-chilli paste

(7) 1 tea spoon red chilli powder

(8) 1 table spoon jaggery

(9) Salt to taste

Method

(1) Wash and soak the chana dal for at least 2 hours.

(2) Heat oil in a vessel for seasoning. Add mustard seeds, asafoetida, turmeric powder and chillies. Add the soaked chana dal with enough water. Add salt, red chilli powder and jaggery. The dal should have some gravy.

Variation

(1) Boiled bottle gourd or pumpkin pieces, can also be added to it.

(2) For making punjabi bottle gourd-chana dal vegetable make gravy of onions, garlic and tomatoes.

368. Val Dal [Serves 4]

Ingredients

(1) 1 cup val dal

(2) 2 table spoons oil

(3) 1 tea spoon omum

(4) A pinch asafoetida

(5) $\frac{1}{2}$ tea spoon turmeric powder

(6) 1 tea spoon red chilli powder

(7) A pinch soda

(8) 2 tea spoons sugar

(9) Salt to taste

Method

(1) Soak the val dal overnight in water. Heat oil for seasoning in a kadhai. Add omum, asafoetida, turmeric powder, red chilli powder and dal. Add enough water to it. Add a little soda. Mix well. Let it simmer for a few minutes.

(2) Add sugar and salt. Cook it on a low flame. Do not stir too frequently or the dal will break.

Note : Garlic paste may be added if desired. Additional warm water may be added if necessary.

369. Urad dal [Serves 4]

Ingredients

(1) 1 cup urad dal

(2) 1 tea spoon ginger-chilli paste

(3) 1 lime   (4) 2 tea spoons sugar

(5) 1 table spoon ghee

(6) $\frac{1}{2}$ tea spoon cumin seeds

(7) A pinch asafoetida

(8) 4 table spoons finely chopped coriander leaves for garnishing

(9) Salt to taste

Method

(1) Boil enough amount of water in a vessel. Add washed dal to boiling water. Remove the dirt layer that is formed at the top while boiling.

(2) When the dal is cooked, add salt, ginger-chilli paste, lime juice and sugar. Do not over cook the dal or it will be sticky.

(3) Add the seasoning of ghee, cumin seeds and asafoetida to the dal. Decorate with the finely chopped coriander leaves. Serve hot.

 PUNJABI DISHES

Points to Remember :

1. This basic Punjabi recipes include parathas, nans, vegetables, pulavs and dals.

2. Pumpkin is used for thickening the gravy. It is peeled, grated and then used in various recipes. Pumpkin does not have any taste of its own. For people who do not eat onions can substitute onions with pumpkin, bottle gourd or cabbage. These vegetables can be grated or blenderised.

3. While preparing Punjabi vegetables, pulav or biriyani, make use of dalda ghee (hydrogenated fat). While serving, add a little amount of pure ghee to the dish. People who do not like dalda ghee, may mix pure ghee and oil for preparing the recipe. Avoid using only pure ghee or butter as it gives a burnt taste to the recipe when heated a little excessively.

4. Always dissolve the corn flour in cold water before using. This would prevent lump formation. Instead of corn flour, mawa (grated) can be also used. It would help in thickening the gravy.

5. Boil water with a little salt and citric acid. Add the chopped spinach to the boiling water. Boil for two minutes. Remove it from the flame. Strain the spinach. Pour cold water on the boiled spinach. Blend in a liquidiser. This would retain the colour of the spinach.

6. **Tomato puree :** Heat water in a pan. Add tomatoes to it. Boil for about two minutes. Remove it from the flame. Peel the tomatoes and cut them into large pieces. Blend in liquidiser.

7. **Vegetable Stock :** $\frac{1}{2}$ cup potatoes, $\frac{1}{2}$ cup carrots, $\frac{1}{2}$ cup bottle gourd, $\frac{1}{2}$ cup cabbage, $\frac{1}{2}$ cup onions, $\frac{1}{2}$ cup spinach leaves (chopped).

   Method : Cut all the vegetable into small pieces. Heat 3 cups of water in a vessel. Add all the vegetables to it. Boil the vegetables on a high flame for 10 minutes. Remove it from the flame. Keep it aside for 1 to $1\frac{1}{2}$ hours. Covered with a lid. Strain the vegetables. The vegetable stock is ready. The vegetables can be used to make mixed vegetables.

8. **Vegetable Stock Cube :** Two varieties of stocks are available in the market – the vegetable stock and the non-vegetable stock so better choose carefully. Add one cube in 2 cups of water. Boil the mixture. Cool it and use it for various recipes.

9. **Boiled Vegetables :** Take 1 cup water in a pan. Add a pinch of salt, a pinch of soda and 4 tea spoons of sugar to the water. Add french beans and cauliflower to it. Boil on a high flame for 5 minutes. Then add green peas and carrots. Cook for another 4 minutes. Do not cover the pan with the lid. Strain all vegetables. Cool them before

use. Adding salt would enhance its taste. Soda would keep the colour bright and sugar would give the vegetables natural sweetness.

10. **How to make rice for various recipes :** Wash and soak basmati rice for 2 hours. Boil 5 cups of water. Strain the rice and add it to boiling water. When the rice is 95 % cooked, drain out the water. Pour 4 to 5 glasses of ice-cold water on it. This would stop further cooking and each grain remains separate. Place the rice in a pan. Add 2 tea spoons of pure ghee to the cooked rice and mix very well.

11. **Punjabi Curds :** Take 500 ml of milk. Keep about 2 table spoons of milk. Dissolve 1 tea spoon of corn flour in 2 table spoons of milk that is kept aside. When the milk starts boiling, add the corn flour to it. Remove it from the flame when the milk thickens a little. Cool the milk till it is luke warm. Add 1 tea spoon of curds to it. Mix well, cover it with a lid and keep it aside to set. When the curds is fully set, keep it in the refrigerator.

12. **Pink Onions :** Select very small onions. Peel them. In a bowl take $\frac{1}{2}$ cup vinegar, a little salt and a little grated beetroot. Soak the onions in this mixture for 2 to 3 hours. Remove it from vinegar before serving.

13. **White Sauce :** Heat about 2 table spoons of ghee. Add $\frac{1}{2}$ cup of maida. Cook for 2 minutes without browing while stirring throughout. Gradually add 1 cup of milk and $\frac{1}{2}$ cup of water. Mix until well blended. Stir constantly until the sauce thickens. Add salt and pepper. Mix well.

370. Chhole, Puri [Serves 5]

Ingredients

(1) 250 grams kabuli chana (chhole)

(2) $\frac{1}{2}$ tea spoon soda

(3) 2 table spoons chana dal

(4) 1 tea spoon tea leaves

(5) 5 to 6 kokams

(6) 3 onions   (7) 8 cloves garlic

(8) 2 tomatoes   (9) 2 pieces cinnamon

(10) 8 to 10 cloves

(11) 15 to 20 pepper corns

(12) 4 big cardamom or 6 small cardamom

(13) 1 table spoon anardana (powdered)

(14) 3 table spoons magatari seeds

(15) 3 table spoons desiccated coconut

(16) 1 tea spoon garam masala

(17) 1 tea spoon red chilli powder

(18) $\frac{1}{2}$ tea spoon turmeric powder

(19) 1 tea spoon dhana jeera powder

(20) 1 table spoon chole masala

(21) A small piece of ginger

(22) 5 green chillies (paste)

(23) 2 table spoons ghee

(24) 1 table spoon oil + oil for frying

(25) 3 table spoons coriander leaves (finely chopped)

(26) Salt to taste

Method for making Chhole

(1) Soak the chhole (kabuli chana) for 6 to 7 hours. Add a little soda and boil the chole in a pressure cooker. While boiling add a little chana dal to it.

(2) Tie the tea leaves and kokams in a small piece of cloth. Add this potali to the chana while boiling them. Crush onions, tomatoes and garlic separately to a paste. Soak the magatari seeds in water for few minutes. Crush them into a paste.

(3) Mix cinnamon, cloves, magatari paste, desiccated coconut, garam masala, salt, red chilli powder, dhana jeera powder, chhole masala, ginger-chilli paste and dried chilli paste in a bowl. Add a little water to it. Soak these masalas for half an hour.

(4) Heat the ghee and oil and fry the onions, garlic and tomato paste until light pink in colour.

(5) When the ghee separates, add the soaked masala. Fry again for 3 to 4 minutes. Add crushed tomatoes and fry for few minutes.

(6) Remove the tea potali from the chhole. Add chole and cook for few minutes.

(7) Garnish with chopped coriander.

Method for making Puri

Take 250 grams maida, 2 table spoons wheat flour, salt, 2 table spoons oil and 1 table spoon curds. Mix all ingredients and knead a soft dough. Divide the dough into medium sized balls. Roll out each ball into a thick puri. Fry them in hot oil.

For Serving : Chop the onions into long slices. Chop 10 green chillies lengthwise and fry them. Add salt to the onions and chillies.

Method for making Bhatura

(1) Take the same ingredients as used for puri. Knead a hard dough. Divide the dough into medium sized balls.

(2) Roll out each ball into a thick puri. Cut the puri from both sides to have an oval puri. Fry the puris in hot oil.

Oval   Half moon shape

371. Aloo Matar – Matar Paneer [Serves 5 to 6]

Ingredients

(1) 200 grams potatoes

(2) 400 grams green peas

(3) 2 onions (finely chopped or crushed)

(4) 4 almonds

(5) 3 small pieces of cinnamon

(6) 5 cloves

(7) 1 table spoon khus khus

(8) 1 table spoon coriander seeds

(9) 10 pepper corns (10) 6 cardamoms

(11) 3 table spoons oil

(12) 1 table spoon ghee

(13) 150 grams tomatoes

(14) 1 tea spoon garam masala

(15) 1 tea spoon red chilli powder

(16) $\frac{1}{2}$ cup chopped coriander

(17) 200 grams paneer

(18) Salt to taste

Method

(1) Peel the potatoes and cut them into square cubes. Fry the potatoes.

(2) Mix almonds, cinnamon, cloves, khus khus, coriander seeds and pepper. Grind all these ingredients to a fine paste.

(3) Heat a little oil and ghee. Fry the onions for 2 to 3 minutes.

(4) Add the tomato gravy to it. Fry for 2 minutes. When the mixture starts boiling, add the dry fruit paste and the other masalas. Fry again for 2 to 3 minutes.

(5) Add green peas, potatoes and a little water. Add salt.

(6) Cook for a few more minutes till the gravy is thick enough. Remove it from the flame. Garnish with chopped coriander.

372. Dum Aloo [Serves 4 to 5]

Ingredients

(1) $1\frac{1}{2}$ cups red gravy according to R. No. 373

(2) 200 grams medium potatoes

(3) Oil

(4) $\frac{1}{4}$ tea spoon turmeric powder

(5) 2 table spoons cream

(6) Salt to taste

Method

(1) Peel the potatoes and prick them. Soak them in water with salt and turmeric powder for half an hour. Deep fry in ghee until they are cooked. Big potatoes can be cut with the cutter into small round shaped pieces.

(2) Mix them to the red gravy. Add cream and garnish with finely chopped coriander leaves.

373. Red Gravy [Makes 3 cups]

Ingredients

(1) 2 table spoons oil

(2) 20 grams ginger

(3) 5 red kashmiri chillies (dried)

(4) 10 garlic cloves

(5) 3 small pieces of cinnamon

(6) 3 cloves

(7) $\frac{1}{4}$ tea spoon coriander seeds

(8) 100 grams onions (paste)

(9) 2 tea spoons garam masala

(10) 1 tea spoon dhana jeera powder

(11) $\frac{1}{4}$ tea spoon turmeric powder

(12) 50 grams butter

(13) 100 grams cashewnuts, magatari seeds, khus khus (paste)

(14) 100 grams tomato ketchup

(15) A few drops of edible red colour

(16) 1 tea spoon salt

Method

(1) Mix ginger, chillies, garlic, cinnamon, cloves and cumin seeds. Grind all these into a fine paste. Heat 2 table spoons of oil.

(2) Fry this paste for 5 minutes. Add the onion paste and fry again for 2 minutes. Add the remaining

masalas and fry again for a few minutes till the masala is brown in colour.

(3) Add 50 grams of butter. Mix cashewnuts, khus khus and magatari seeds and grind them to a fine paste. Fry the paste for 2 to 3 minutes. Add tomato ketchup and water. Cook for another 10 minutes. If the colour is less, than add a few drops of edible red colour.

Variation

For preparing light yellow coloured gravy :

(1) Substitute red kashmiri chillies with 1 tea spoon regular chilli powder.

(2) Add $\frac{1}{2}$ tea spoon turmeric powder.

(3) Avoid red colour.

Note : (1) If poppy seeds cannot be graind to a live paste, soak it in water and crush it the next morning to à fine paste.

(2) Soak the red kashmiri chillies in water for half an hour and then grind it to a fine paste. It would give red colour.

374. White Gravy [Makes 4 cups]

Ingredients

(1) 2 table spoons oil

(2) A small piece of ginger

(3) 2 green chillies (4) 10 garlic cloves

(5) 3 small pieces of cinnamon

(6) 3 cloves

(7) $\frac{1}{4}$ tea spoon coriander seeds

(8) 1 tea spoon cumin seeds

(9) 2 to 3 onions (paste)

(10) 1 tea spoon dhana jeera powder

(11) $\frac{1}{4}$ tea spoon turmeric powder

(12) 1 tea spoon red chilli powder

(13) 1 tea spoon garam masala

(14) 1 piece tomato gravy

(15) 100 grams cashewnuts, magatari seeds and khus khus paste

(16) 1 tea spoon butter

(17) 1 cup water   (18) $\frac{1}{4}$ cup milk

(19) 3 table spoons mawa

(20) 3 table spoons fresh cream

(21) 1 tea spoon salt

Method

(1) Mix ginger, chillies, garlic, cinnamon, cloves and cumin seeds. Grind all these ingredients to a fine paste.

(2) Heat oil in a kadhai. Fry the paste for 5 minutes. Add onion paste. Fry again for few minutes. Add salt, dhana jeera powder, turmeric powder, red chilli powder and garam masala. Cook on a low flame till it becomes brown.

(3) Add the freshly pureed tomatoes. Cook till dry and oil separates. Add cashewnuts, magatari seeds and khus khus paste. Fry for another 4 to 5 minutes till oil separates. Add butter and enough water.

(4) Add milk when the mixture starts boiling. Stir constantly so that the milk does not curdle. If the milk curdles then beat the gravy well with the hand mixer. Simmer on low flame. Add mawa and fresh cream. Mix well. Remove it from the flame.

375. Navratna Curry

[Serves 5 to 6]

Ingredients

(1) 50 grams paneer   (2) Ghee

(3) 10 cashewnuts

(4) 50 grams potatoes

(5) $\frac{1}{2}$ cup coconut (grated)

(6) 1 tea spoon roasted chana dal (daliya)

(7) A small piece of ginger

(8) 2 green chillies

(9) 4 table spoons coriander leaves (finely chopped)

(10) 1 table spoon dhana jeera powder

(11) 8 to 10 mint leaves

(12) $\frac{1}{2}$ table spoon khus khus

(13) 1 tea spoon cumin seeds

(14) Oil   (15) 2 onions (paste)

(16) 7 to 8 cloves garlic (paste)

(17) 150 grams tomatoes

(18) 50 grams cauliflower

(19) 50 grams french beans

(20) 50 grams carrots

(21) 50 grams green peas

(22) 50 grams capsicum

(23) 3 slices of pineapple + 3 table spoons sugar

(24) 1 apple   (25) 2 chikoos

(26) 25 grams cherries   (27) 1 cup milk

(28) 1 table spoon corn flour

(29) A little butter

(30) 10 raisins   (31) 5 almonds

(32) $\frac{1}{2}$ cup pineapple syrup

(33) $\frac{1}{2}$ cup cream   (34) Salt to taste

Method

(1) Cut the paneer into small square pieces and deep fry in ghee. Soak the fried paneer pieces in water for some time. Cut the potatoes into cubes. Fry cashewnuts and potato cubes.

(2) Mix desiccated coconut, daliya, ginger, green chillies, coriander leaves, dhana jeera powder, mint leaves, khus khus and cumin seeds and grind them into a fine paste.

(3) Heat 4 table spoons oil in kadhai. Fry the paste for at least 4 to 5 minutes.

(4) Add the onion paste. Fry again for 3 to 4 minutes.

(5) Boil the tomatoes in water for 5 minutes. Remove the skin and grind into a fine paste.

(6) Boil all the vegetables except capsicum.

(7) Chop the pineapple into small pieces. Add a little sugar and enough water to it. Cook it in the pressure cooker for one whistle. If you have enough time, mix the pineapple pieces with sugar and keep it aside for one day. Sugar syrup will be formed by itself. Add mixed boiled vegetables to the gravy. Mix the corn flour in $\frac{1}{2}$ tea cup of water and add it to the gravy.

(8) Add fruits and dry fruits to the gravy. Boil for 10 minutes. Add salt, sugar and pineapple syrup. Remove it from the flame. Add fresh cream while serving.

Note : The main nine ingredients in the navratna curry are potatoes, paneer, green peas, carrots, apples, pineapples, cashewnuts, raisins and capsicum.

376. Khoya Kaju [Serves 4 to 5]

Ingredients

(1) 2 cups white gravy according to R. No. 374

(2) 100 grams cashewnuts

(3) Ghee

(4) 1 cup cream

Method

(1) Heat the ghee. Fry the cashewnuts in ghee till they become golden brown in colour.

(2) Add them to the white gravy. Beat the cream well. While serving add more cream. Serve hot.

377. Khoya Makhana [Serves 5 to 6]

Ingredients

(1) 50 grams mawa

(2) 3 table spoons ghee

(3) 50 grams makhana   (4) Oil

(5) 2 onions (grated)

(6) 100 grams cashewnuts

(7) 1 cup tomato puree

(8) A big piece of ginger (paste)

(9) 2 tea spoons garam masala

(10) 5 green chillies (paste)

(11) 1 table spoon dhana jeera powder

(12) 1 cup curds

(13) $\frac{1}{2}$ cup finely chopped coriander leaves

(14) Salt to taste

Method

(1) Roast the khoya in ghee on low flame for 5 minutes. Deep fry the makhana very lightly in oil.

(2) Heat 3 table spoons ghee in a vessel and fry the onions for at least 5 minutes. Add cashewnuts and fry them till they are pink in colour.

(3) Add the tomato puree. Fry again for 5 minutes. Add khoya, all masalas and coriander leaves.

(4) Add curds and 1 cup of water. Boil for 10 minutes. Add the makhana just before serving. Garnish with chopped coriander leaves. Serve hot.

378. Vegetable Jaipuri [Serves 5 to 6]

Ingredients

(1) 2 carrots (peeled and cut into small pieces)

(2) 250 grams cabbage (thin shreds)

(3) 2 potatoes (boiled and cut into small pieces)

(4) 100 grams green peas (boiled)

(5) 2 table spoons ghee

(6) 3 tomatoes

(7) 3 green chillies

(8) $\frac{1}{2}$ tea spoon sugar

(9) $\frac{1}{2}$ tea spoon red chilli powder

(10) $\frac{1}{2}$ cup finely chopped coriander leaves

(11) Salt to taste

To be ground into a paste

(1) 2 table spoons desiccated coconut

(2) 1 tea spoon coriander seeds

(3) $\frac{1}{4}$ table spoon turmeric powder

(4) 1 onion   (5) 5 cloves garlic

Dry Masala

(1) 5 pieces of cinnamon

(2) 5 cloves

(3) 7 pepper corns

(4) $\frac{1}{2}$ tea spoon cumin seeds

Method

(1) Heat ghee in a kadhai and fry the paste for at least 3 to 4 minutes.

(2) Add cabbage and sprinkle a little water. Cover with a lid and cook it for a few minutes.

(3) Add potatoes, green peas, carrots, pieces of tomatoes and all dry masalas. Mix well and fry for 3 to 4 minutes.

(4) Sprinkle a little water on it.

(5) Add salt, sugar, green chillies (pieces) and red chilli powder. Boil for about 2 minutes. Remove it from the flame. Serve hot. Decorate with chopped coriander leaves.

(6) Add 1 tea spoon of ghee before serving.

379. Vegetable Singapuri
[Serves 3 to 4]

Ingredients

(1) 100 grams green peas

(2) 200 grams cauliflower (cut into large pieces)

(3) 50 grams potatoes (cut into pieces)

(4) 50 grams carrots (cut into long strips)

(5) A pinch of soda

(6) 2 table spoons ghee

(7) 2 table spoons grated cheese

(8) Salt to taste

Any other vegetables other than this can also be used.

To be ground into paste

(1) 25 grams cashewnuts

(2) 1 small piece of ginger

(3) 2 onions   (4) 6 cloves garlic

(5) 4 table spoons tomato sauce

(6) 1 table spoon chilli sauce

(7) 6 kashmiri red chillies (dried)

(8) $\frac{1}{2}$ table spoon coriander seeds

(9) 1 tea spoon cumin seeds

(10) 4 cardamom pods

(11) 2 small pieces of cinnamon

(12) 4 cloves (Roast cinnamon, clove, cardamom, coriander seeds and cumin seeds before grinding into a paste)

(13) 50 grams mawa

(14) 50 grams cream   (15) Salt to taste

Method

(1) Chop all the vegetables into small pieces. Apply a little soda and salt to the vegetables. Steam all vegetables.

(2) Heat the ghee in a vessel and fry the paste for at least 4 to 5 minutes till the ghee separates. Add mixed boiled vegetables and salt.

(3) Add enough milk or water to make a thick gravy. Boil for a few minutes till the gravy thickens. Remove it from the flame. Garnish with grated cheese. Serve hot.

Note : Do not add mawa and cream while making the paste. But add the mawa and cream to the paste. First add the mawa and mix it well. Then add the cream and mix well.

380. Kashmiri Fruit Kofta Curry

[Serves 5 to 6]

Ingredients for the koftas

(1) 100 grams potatoes

(2) 100 grams yam or sweet potatoes

(3) 1 medium sized beetroot

(4) 1 table spoon corn flour

(5) Oil

(6) Salt to taste

Ingredients for the filling

(1) 2 slices pineapple

(2) A small apple

(3) 25 grams mawa

(4) 2 green chillies

(5) 4 to 6 cashewnuts

(6) Salt to taste

To be ground into paste

(1) 1 tea spoon coriander seeds

(2) 1 tea spoon cumin seeds

(3) 4 cardamom pods

(4) 3 small pieces of cinnamon

(5) 3 cloves

(6) 1 table spoon cashewnuts

(7) 3 green chillies

(8) A small piece of ginger

(9) $\frac{1}{4}$ cup mint leaves

(10) $\frac{1}{4}$ cup coriander leaves

(11) 1 onion

Roast the dry masala. Add a little water to it. Then add it to the remaining ingredients and grind to a paste.

Ingredients for the gravy

(1) 200 grams tomatoes

(2) 100 grams green peas

(3) $\frac{1}{2}$ cup curds

(4) 2 table spoons ghee

(5) 1 cup water

(6) 1 tea spoon corn flour

(7) 2 tea spoons sugar

(8) 2 table spoons fresh cream or malai

(9) Salt to taste

Method

To prepare the koftas :

(1) Boil, peel and mash the potatoes, yam and beetroot.

(2) Add salt and corn flour. Mix well.

(3) Chop the pineapple and apple into small pieces. Mix them with the potato mixture. Make small balls out of it. To prepare the filling mix cashewnuts, salt and red chilli powder. Flatten each ball of the potato mixture. Put 1 tea spoon of the kaju filling. Form a ball again. Deep fry 2 to 3 koftas at a time in medium hot oil keep aside.

For the curry :

(1) Boil the tomatoes for a few minutes. Skin the tomatoes. Crush them in a liquidiser. Apply salt and a little soda to the green peas. Steam them.

(2) Heat the ghee in a vessel and fry the paste for a few minutes. Add the tomato soup.

(3) Mix curds and corn flour. Add that to the gravy.

(4) Boil for 2 to 3 minutes. Then add enough water, salt, sugar, green peas and the left over filling (if any). Boil for 10 minutes. Pour the hot gravy on the koftas. Add the cream. Serve hot.

381. Cheese Rogan Josh

[Serves 4]

Ingredients

(1) $1\frac{1}{2}$ cups red gravy according to R. No. 373

(2) 100 grams potatoes

(3) $\frac{1}{2}$ cup green peas

(4) 50 grams french beans

(5) 100 grams carrots

(6) 1 cube cheese

(7) $\frac{1}{4}$ cup malai or fresh cream

(8) Oil   (9) Salt to taste

Method

(1) Peel the potatoes and cut them into small pieces. Deep fry in ghee or oil until they are cooked. Cut the french beans and carrots into small pieces. Boil them along with green peas.

(2) Mix the vegetables with the red gravy according to R. No. 373. Boil for 2 to 3 minutes. Add $\frac{1}{4}$ cup cream. Sprinkle 1 cube of cheese (grated). Serve hot.

382. Mix Vegetable Curry

[Serves 4]

(1) Method and Ingredients are the same as those given for cheese rogan josh in R. No. 381.

(2) Only do not add cheese and cream.

383. Vegetable Makkhanwala

[Serves 3 to 4]

Ingredients

(1) 2 table spoons maida

(2) 2 table spoons ghee

(3) $\frac{1}{2}$ cup milk

(4) 1 tea spoon pepper powder

(5) 2 small onions

(6) 2 tomatoes

(7) 2 table spoons oil or ghee

(8) 1 tea spoon red chilli powder

(9) 1 tea spoon garam masala

(10) $\frac{1}{2}$ potato

(11) 50 grams green peas

(12) 50 grams carrots

(13) 100 grams french beans

(14) 1 tea spoon sugar

(15) $\frac{1}{2}$ cup tomato ketchup

(16) Salt to taste

Method

For the white sauce :

(1) Heat 2 to 3 table spoons of ghee, add 2 table spoons maida and cook for a few minutes.

(2) Go on stirring so that it does not become brown. Then go on pouring milk. First put just enough milk to make a paste. Then add the remaining milk.

(3) Stir constantly. If lumps are formed stir it with a hand mixer. When it thickens, add pepper and sugar. Thus white sauce will be prepared. Crush onions and tomatoes.

(4) Heat the ghee and fry the onion paste for a few minutes. Add the tomato paste, red chilli powder and garam masala. Fry again for 2 to 3 minutes. Add the white sauce. Stir constantly. Skin the potatoes and cut into small pieces. Deep fry them in ghee till they are done.

(5) Cut all the other vegetables into small pieces and boil them. Boil the green peas. Add all vegetables to the gravy.

(6) Add salt and $\frac{1}{2}$ cup of tomato ketchup. Boil well for a few minutes. Serve hot.

384. Vegetable Kolhapuri

[Serves 5 to 7]

Ingredients

(1) 100 grams green peas

(2) 100 grams carrots

(3) 50 grams french beans

(4) 150 grams cauliflower

(5) A pinch of soda

(6) 4 tea spoons sugar

(7) 250 grams onions

(8) 150 grams pumpkin

(9) 3 table spoons ghee

(10) 3 bay leaves

(11) 4 red chillies (dried)

(12) $\frac{1}{2}$ cup tomato puree

(13) 2 cinnamon   (14) 5 cloves

(15) 5 pepper corns

(16) 2 cardamom pods

(17) $\frac{1}{4}$ tea spoon cumin seeds

(18) $\frac{1}{4}$ tea spoon fennel seeds

(19) $\frac{1}{4}$ tea spoon coriander seeds

(20) 1 table spoon garam masala

(21) $\frac{1}{4}$ cup curds   (22) 50 grams mawa

(23) $\frac{1}{2}$ cup white sauce

(24) 1 table spoon red chilli powder

(25) $\frac{1}{2}$ cup chopped coriander leaves

(26) $\frac{1}{2}$ tea spoon white vineger

(27) Salt to taste

Method

(1) Cut carrots, french beans and cauliflower into small pieces.

(2) Add green peas and 2 cups of water to the vegetables. Add a pinch of soda, 1 tea spoon salt and 4 table spoons sugar to it. Boil the vegetables on high flame. Strain the vegetables.

(3) Chop 50 grams onions finely and cut 200 grams of onions into long slices. Heat the oil in a vessel and fry the onions till they becomes light brown in colour. Cool them and grind into a fine paste. Peel the pumpkin and grind it into a fine paste.

(4) Heat the ghee in a vessel. Add the bay leaves, whole red chillies and finely chopped onions. Fry for 5 minutes.

(5) Add the pumpkin paste and fry for another 5 minutes. Add the tomato puree. Fry again for 5 minutes. Add 1 cup of water.

(6) Add the powdered masala, garam masala, curds, mawa, white sauce and $\frac{1}{2}$ cup of water. Boil for 5 minutes.

(7) Remove the bay leaves. Add all the vegetables, salt, red chilli powder, coriander leaves and vinegar. Add enough amount of water so that the gravy is neither too thin nor too thick. Add enough water. Boil for a few minutes. Serve hot.

385. Sarson Da Saag
[Serves 3 to 4]
Ingredients

(1) 250 grams sarson leaves (mustard leaves)

(2) 150 grams spinach

(3) 50 grams carrots

(4) $\frac{1}{2}$ cup corn seeds

(5) 100 grams tomatoes

(6) 3 tea spoons corn flour

(7) 4 green chillies

(8) 1 tea spoon cumin seeds

(9) A pinch asafoetida

(10) 5 cloves garlic (finely chopped)

(11) 100 grams finely chopped onions

(12) 3 table spoons ghee

(13) $\frac{1}{2}$ cup finely chopped coriander leaves

(14) 1 tea spoon sugar

(15) 2 table spoons butter

(16) Salt to taste

Method

(1) Chop the sarson leaves and spinach finely. Boil them for 2 minutes. Cool and grind them into a fine paste.

(2) Grate the carrots. Boil the corn seeds till they are half done and crush them. Chop the tomatoes into small pieces. Dissolve the corn flour in $\frac{1}{2}$ cup of water. Mix into the spinach paste.

(3) Heat the ghee in a vessel and fry the cumin seeds and asafoetida for 1 minute. Add garlic, onions and carrots. Fry again for 2 to 3 minutes.

(4) Add corn seeds, green chillies, coriander, tomatoes, salt and sugar. Mix well and fry for 5 minutes. Add the bhaji paste.

(5) Boil it for 5 minutes. Add butter. Serve hot.

386. Rajma [Serves 4 to 6]

Ingredients

(1) 150 grams rajma (kidney beans)

(2) $1\frac{1}{2}$ cups red gravy according to R. No. 373

Method

(1) Soak the rajma for 5 to 6 hours in water. Boil them. Mash all the rajma except a few beans.

(2) Prepare the red gravy as given in R. No. 373. Add the rajma. Boil for 2 to 3 minutes. Rajma can also be used for topping.

387. Rajasthani Bataki [Serves 4 to 5]

Ingredients

(1) 250 grams medium sized potatoes

(2) 25 grams garlic cloves (paste)

(3) 4 whole red chillies (dried – reshampatti)

(4) $\frac{1}{2}$ table spoon coriander seeds

(5) A small piece of cinnamon

(6) 5 cloves

(7) 2 bay leaves

(8) 2 table spoons ghee

(9) $\frac{1}{2}$ tea spoon cumin seeds

(10) A pinch asafoetida

(11) 1 tea spoon ginger-chilli paste

(12) 250 grams fresh curds

(13) $\frac{1}{2}$ fresh coconut

(14) 1 tea spoon dhana jeera powder

(15) Salt to taste

Method

(1) Boil and peel the small potatoes. Cut them into 2 pieces each.

(2) Mix red chilli powder, coriander seeds, cinnamon, cloves and bay leaves (tamal patra). Soak all these ingredients in a little water. Grind them to a fine paste.

(3) Heat the ghee and fry cumin seeds and asafoetida for 1 minutes. Add garlic paste and fry again.

(4) Add the paste, ginger, chillies, dhana jeera powder, curds, salt and desiccated coconut. Fry for 2 to 3 minutes. Add the potatoes. Fry again for 2 to 3 minutes. Serve hot.

388. Paneer Tikka [Makes 15 tikkas]

Ingredients

(1) 200 grams paneer

(2) 100 grams capsicum

(3) 100 grams onions

(4) 2 tomatoes

(5) $1\frac{1}{4}$ cups coriander leaves

(6) 1 large piece of ginger (paste)

(7) 6 cloves garlic (paste)

(8) A few drops of edible food colour (red)

(9) 1 tea spoon white vinegar

(10) 1 tea spoon red chilli powder

(11) 2 tea spoons corn flour

(12) 1 tea spoon garam masala

(13) 1 tea spoon turmeric powder

(14) 1 tea spoon pepper powder

(15) A little black salt

(16) 2 tea spoons shaljeera

(17) 1 cup curds

(18) 6 table spoons butter

(19) A little chat masala

(20) 1 lime

(21) Salt to taste

Method

(1) Cut the paneer and capsicum into 2 inches square pieces. Cut the onions into 2 inches pieces and then separates. Soak the tomatoes in chilled water for some time. Cut the tomatoes and keep it aside into 3 inch square pieces. Remove the pulp from the tomatoes.

(2) **Marinade :** Mix curds and all the masalas except butter. Mix well. Mix capsicum, tomatoes, paneer and onions to it. Keep aside the marinated paneer, capsicum, tomatoes and onions for atleast 1½ to 2 hours. Arrange tightly one piece of paneer, capsicum, tomato and onion on the skewers. Brush generously with butter.

(3) If there is place on the skewers then arrange another line of vegetables and paneer.

(4) Bake for 10 minutes at 200° C. Remove from the oven. Attach a tooth pick to each piece. Arrange them in a serving dish.

(5) Serve really hot, after sprinking the tikkas with some lemon juice and chat masala. Pineapple pieces can also be used.

389. Paneer Tikka Masala

[Serves 3 to 4]

Ingredients

(1) 100 + 50 grams paneer

(2) 150 grams onions

(3) 5 cloves garlic (paste)

(4) 3 table spoons ghee

(5) 50 grams tomato ketchup

(6) 150 grams tomatoes

(7) 1 table spoon khus khus

(8) ½ table spoon magatari seeds

(9) 2 pieces javantri (mace)

(10) ½ tea spoon fennel seeds

(11) 1 table spoon coriander seeds

(12) A little nag kesar

(13) 2 tamal patras (bay leaves)

(14) A small piece of ginger

(15) 50 grams white mawa

(16) Salt to taste

Method

(1) Take 100 grams of paneer. Cut the paneer into triangular pieces. Deep fry them in ghee. Soak them in water after frying.

(2) Grind onions and garlic into a paste.

(3) Heat the ghee in a vessel. Fry the paste for 3 to 4 minutes. Add tomato paste and ketchup. Add the other masalas, after grinding them into a paste.

(4) Add ginger (grated), mawa, 50 grams paneer (grated) and fried paneer pieces.

(5) Add enough water. Boil for 10 minutes. The tikkas will be red in colour. Serve hot.

390. Paneer Pasanda

[Serves 5 to 6]

Ingredients

(1) 200 grams paneer

(2) 2 tomatoes

(3) 3 onions   (4) Oil

(5) 100 grams magatari seeds

(6) ½ cup finely chopped coriander leaves

(7) ½ tea spoon red chilli powder

(8) $\frac{1}{2}$ tea spoon turmeric powder

(9) 1 tea spoon garam masala

(10) 10 grams ginger

(11) 5 cloves garlic

(12) A pinch ajinomoto

(13) 2 table spoons cream or malai

(14) $\frac{1}{4}$ tea spoon nutmeg powder

(15) Salt to taste

Method

(1) Cut the paneer into $1\frac{1}{2}$ inches squares. Deep fry in oil till they are golden brown in colour. Soak the fried paneer pieces into water.

(2) Grind onions and tomatoes into a paste.

(3) Heat 2 table spoons oil in a vessel. Fry the onion paste for 2 to 3 minutes. Add magatari seeds and chopped coriander leaves. Add red chilli powder, turmeric powder, garam masala, ginger-garlic paste, salt and ajinomoto. Fry for 2 minutes.

(4) Add the tomato paste and 1 glass of water. Boil the gravy. When it boils, add fresh cream or malai and paneer pieces.

(5) Sprinkle a little nutmeg powder while serving.

391. Paneer Bhurjee
[Serves 4 to 5]

Ingredients and Method

(1) Boil milk. Add lime juice to the boiling milk slowly. For 1 litre of milk add juice of 1 lime.

(2) Stir slowly. When the milk curdles, strain it through a muslin cloth.

(3) Wash the paneer with fresh water. Put the paneer in the muslin cloth. Place it on the rolling board. Press it by putting some heavy weight on it. Keep aside for some time.

(4) For preparing paneer bhurjee make the same gravy as that used for paneer pasanda. Add 150 to 200 grams grated paneer to it. Boil for 10 minutes. Serve hot with parathas.

392. Paneer Makhani
[Serves 5 to 6]
Ingredients

(1) 200 grams paneer   (2) Oil

(3) 8 almonds
(boil, peel and grind to a fine paste)

(4) $1\frac{1}{2}$ cups coconut milk

(5) 2 table spoons ghee

(6) 3 onions (paste)

(7) 2 green chillies

(8) 50 grams mawa

(9) 1 tea spoon curry powder

(10) 1 tea spoon garam masala

(11) 1 tea spoon dhana jeera powder

(12) 6 cashewnuts

(13) 10 raisins

(14) $\frac{1}{4}$ tea spoon turmeric powder

(15) Juice of $\frac{1}{2}$ lime

(16) 2 table spoons butter

(17) 2 table spoons finely chopped coriander leaves

(18) 2 table spoons cream

(19) Salt to taste

To be ground into a paste (Add a little water while grinding the paste) :

(1) 4 cloves garlic

(2) 4 whole red chillies (dried)

(3) 1 table spoon cumin seeds

(4) $1\frac{1}{2}$ table spoons desiccated coconut

(5) $\frac{1}{2}$ table spoon khus khus (poppy seeds)

(6) $\frac{1}{2}$ table spoon coriander seeds

(7) 6 cloves

(8) 1 tea spoon turmeric powder

(9) 3 cardamom pods

(10) 2 pieces of cinnamon

(11) 5 pepper corns

Method

(1) Cut the paneer into long pieces and deep fry in ghee.

(2) Soak the fried paneer pieces in water.

(3) Grate a fresh coconut, add $\frac{1}{2}$ cup of hot water to it.

(4) Grind it to a fine paste in the mixer. Strain the mixture to obtain coconut milk. Press well. Again add $\frac{1}{2}$ cup of warm water to the left over grated coconut. Grind it again in the mixer. Strain again.

(5) Add the almond paste to this coconut milk. Heat the ghee in a vessel. Fry the onions and green chillies (paste) till pink in colour. Add the paste and fry again for 5 to 6 minutes.

(6) When the ghee separates, add the grated mawa, coconut milk with the almond paste, salt and paneer pieces.

(7) Boil for 5 minutes. Add curry masala, dhana jeera powder, cashewnuts, raisins, a little turmeric powder and lime juice. Remove it from the flame. Add the butter or ghee for seasoning. Add cream.

(8) Garnish with finely chopped coriander leaves. Serve hot.

393. Palak Paneer [Serves 4]

Ingredients

(1) 250 grams spinach

(2) A pinch of soda

(3) A small piece of ginger (paste)

(4) 4 green chillies (paste)

(5) 3 onions (paste)

(6) 2 table spoons ghee

(7) 6 cloves garlic (paste)

(8) 100 grams coriander

(9) 1 tea spoon garam masala

(10) 100 grams paneer

(11) 3 table spoons curds or cream (beat the curds well) (optional)

(12) Salt to taste

Method

(1) Chop the spinach. Boil water with a pinch of soda and salt. Add the chopped spinach to the boiling water and keep it in boiling water for 2 minutes. Remove it from the flame. Strain the spinach. Put it in ice cold water for some time. Strain it and keep aside.

(2) Mix spinach, ginger and chillies and grind it in the liquidiser into a fine paste.

(3) Heat the ghee in a kadhai and fry the onion paste for a few minutes. Add the garlic paste, salt, coriander leaves paste, a little garam masala and the spinach paste. Boil for few minutes. Cut the paneer into small pieces and fry them in ghee. Soak the fried paneer pieces in water for some time so that they would become soft. Add the paneer pieces to the gravy. Boil for 1 to 2 minutes. Remove the mixture from the flame. Lime juice may be added if desired. Serve hot.

Note : Addition of curds or cream is optional. Add paneer to the gravy and remove it from the flame.

394. Corn, Capsicum, Peas, Paneer [Serves 4 to 6]

Ingredients

(1) 2 cups white gravy according to R. No. 374

(2) 250 grams corn seeds

(3) 200 grams green peas

(4) 100 grams paneer

(5) Ghee or oil

(6) 100 grams capsicum

(7) Salt to taste

Method

(1) Prepare the white gravy as given in R. No. 374. Boil the corn seeds and green peas.

(2) Cut the paneer into small square pieces and fry them in ghee. Soak the fried paneer pieces in water.

(3) Chop the capsicum into small pieces.

(4) Boil the white gravy. Add all the other ingredients and boil for a few minutes. Remove it from the flame. Serve hot.

395. Green Bataki

[Serves 3 to 4]

Ingredients

(1) 250 grams potatoes

(2) Oil

(3) 250 grams spinach

(4) 25 grams fresh garlic

(5) 1 table spoon ghee

(6) $\frac{1}{2}$ tea spoon cumin seeds

(7) A pinch asafoetida

(8) A small piece of ginger

(9) 4 to 5 green chillies

(10) 4 table spoons finely chopped coriander leaves

(11) $\frac{1}{2}$ tea spoon turmeric powder

(12) 1 tea spoon dhana jeera powder

(13) 1 tea spoon garam masala

(14) Salt to taste

Method

(1) Skin the potatoes, half boil them and then deep fry them in ghee until they are cooked.

(2) Chop, wash and then grind the spinach into a fine paste. Chop and grind green fresh garlic to a fine paste.

(3) Heat 1 table spoon oil and 1 table spoon ghee. Now fry the cumin seeds and asafoetida for 1 minute. Add spinach and garlic paste. Fry for 1 minute.

(4) Add salt and ginger-chilli paste. Fry again for few seconds.

(5) Add 1 tea spoon turmeric powder, dhana jeera powder and garam masala. When it starts boiling, add the fried potatoes. Boil for 5 to 6 minutes. Garnish with finely chopped coriander leaves. Serve hot.

396. Malai Kofta

[Serves 4 to 6]

Ingredients

(1) 250 grams potatoes

(2) 1 tea spoon green chillies (paste)

(3) 1 table spoon corn flour

(4) 1 table spoon arrowroot flour or toast powder

(5) 100 grams paneer

(6) 15 almonds   (7) 15 pistas

(8) A few strands of kesar (9) Oil

(10) 2 cups white gravy according to R. No. 374

(11) 2 table spoons malai or mawa

(12) 2 to 3 tea spoons cream

(13) Salt to taste

Method

(1) Boil the potatoes, peel and mash them. Add salt, green chillies, corn flour and arrowroot flour or toast powder to the mashed potatoes. Mix well and keep aside.

(2) For the filling, grate the paneer and knead it well to make it very smooth. Add almonds, pistas, kesar and salt to it. Mix well.

(3) Flatten each ball of potato mixture. Put 1 tea spoon of the paneer filling in each ball. Form a ball again. Deep fry 2 to 3 koftas at a time in medium hot oil. Keep aside.

(4) Prepare the white gravy according to R. No. 374. Add additional malai or mawa to it. While serving boil the gravy. Add the koftas. Keep on a low flame for half a minute. Serve immediately, after sprinking it with cream and chopped coriander leaves.

Variation

Instead of the white gravy, red gravy can also be used for the koftas.

397. Paneer Kofta

[Serves 4]

Method

(1) Grate 100 grams paneer and knead well. Add green chillies and salt to it. Mix well. Make small balls. Deep fry 2 to 3 koftas at a time in medium hot oil. Keep aside.

(2) Prepare the red gravy according to R. No. 373. While serving boil the gravy. Add the koftas. Keep on a low flame for half a minute. Serve immediately. Garnish with finely chopped coriander leaves.

(3) If the koftas crack, then a little corn flour or arrow root flour may be also added.

398. Dudhi Kofta Curry

[Serves 4 to 5]

Ingredients

(1) 250 grams dudhi (bottlegourd)
(2) 3 potatoes
(3) 1 tea spoon red chilli powder
(4) $\frac{1}{2}$ tea spoon turmeric powder
(5) 1 tea spoon dry pani puri masala

(6) 1 tea spoon garam masala
(7) 1 to $1\frac{1}{2}$ cups wheat flour (coarse)
(8) 2 to 3 table spoons malai or cream
(9) Oil
(10) $1\frac{1}{2}$ cups red gravy according to R. No. 373
(11) Salt to taste

Method

(1) Chop the dudhi into big pieces and boil them in the pressure cooker. Peel the potatoes. Grate the potatoes and dudhi.

(2) Add salt, pani puri masala, garam masala, turmeric powder and wheat flour to it. Add enough malai to it.

(3) Keep the dough soft. Left over rice (cooked) can also be added to this. Make small balls. Deep fry 2 to 3 koftas at a time in medium hot oil. Keep aside. Prepare the red gravy as shown in R. No. 373. While serving boil the gravy.

(4) Add the koftas. Keep on a low flame for half a minute. Serve immediately. Garnish with finely chopped coriander leaves.

399. Kofta Noorjahani

[Serves 3 to 4]

Ingredients

(1) 250 grams potatoes
(2) 50 grams paneer
(3) 1 tea spoon corn flour
(4) A small piece of ginger (paste)
(5) $\frac{1}{2}$ tea spoon green chillies
(6) $\frac{1}{2}$ carrot
(7) 2 table spoons cashewnuts (soaked and ground into a paste)
(8) Oil   (9) 2 onions
(10) 6 cloves garlic
(11) $\frac{1}{2}$ tea spoon turmeric powder

(12) 1 tea spoon red chilli powder

(13) 1 tea spoon garam masala

(14) Salt to taste

Method

To prepare the koftas :

(1) Mix grated paneer, boiled and grated potatoes, corn flour, ginger, chillies and salt. Mix well. Make small balls for the filling.

(2) Mix grated carrots and kaju paste. Flatten each ball of the paneer, potato mixture, put 1 tea spoon of the carrot filling. Form a ball again. Roll each ball in corn flour. Deep fry 2 to 3 koftas at a time in medium hot oil. Keep aside.

To prepare the Gravy :

(1) Heat 2 table spoons ghee in a heavy bottomed kadhai and fry the onion paste till the onions turn light brown and the ghee separates.

(2) Add ginger-garlic paste, turmeric powder, red chilli powder and enough water. Boil for 10 minutes.

(3) Add salt and garam masala. To serve boil the gravy. Add the koftas. Keep on a low flame for half a minute. Serve immediately. Garnish with finely chopped coriander leaves before serving.

400. Palak Kofta [Serves 4]

Ingredients

(1) 250 grams spinach

(2) 4 tea spoons maida

(3) 4 table spoons corn flour

(4) 100 grams paneer

(5) 4 green chillies

(6) 3 table spoons finely chopped coriander leaves

(7) 2 table spoons desiccated coconut

(8) 2 table spoons groundnuts powder

(9) $\frac{1}{2}$ lime   (10) 2 tea spoons sugar

(11) Oil   (12) Malai

(13) $1\frac{1}{2}$ cups red gravy according to R. No. 373

(14) Salt to taste

Method

(1) To prepare the koftas, chop the spinach finely. Boil it for 2 to 3 minutes. Strain and cool it.

(2) Add a little maida, corn flour, salt, 1 tea spoon oil and some malai to the spinach. Mix well. Make small balls.

(3) For the filling, mix grated paneer, salt, green chillies, coriander leaves, desiccated coconut, groundnuts powder, sugar and lime juice. Mix well.

(4) Flatten each ball of the spinach mixture, put 1 tea spoon of the paneer filling. Form a ball again. Deep fry 2 to 3 koftas at a time in medium hot oil. Keep aside. If the koftas are harder then add more amount of malai to the spinach mixture. If the koftas start breaking, while frying, add a little maida or corn flour.

(5) Prepare the red gravy as shown in R. No. 373. To serve, boil the gravy. Add the koftas. Keep on low flame for half a minute. Serve immediately.

401. Nargisi Kofta
[Serves 4 to 6]

Ingredients

(1) 300 grams potatoes

(2) 200 grams green peas

(3) 6 green chillies

(4) 4 cardamom pods (powdered)

(5) 4 table spoons corn flour

(6) 200 grams paneer

(7) 3 table spoons milk powder

(8) $\frac{1}{4}$ tea spoon baking powder

(9) 1 tea spoon powdered sugar

(10) Oil

(11) 4 onions

(12) $2\frac{1}{2}$ cups milk

(13) 2 table spoons ghee

(14) 3 bay leaves

(15) A pinch of soda

(16) 2 tea spoons red chilli powder

(17) $\frac{1}{4}$ tea spoon turmeric powder

(18) 1 tea spoon garam masala

(19) 1 cup cream   (20) Salt to taste

To be ground into a powder
Dry Masala :

(1) 4 tea spoons khus khus (poppy seeds)

(2) 4 cardamom pods

(3) 4 pieces of mace (javantri)

(4) $\frac{1}{2}$ tea spoon shahjeera

Other masala to be ground into a paste :

(1) 2 cloves garlic

(2) 6 cashewnuts

(3) 3 tea spoons desiccated coconut

(4) 3 tomatoes (cut into pieces)

(5) A small piece of ginger

Method

(1) Mix boiled, peeled and grated potatoes, crushed green peas, green chillies, cardamom powder, corn flour, grated paneer, milk powder, salt, baking powder and powdered sugar.

(2) Mix well.

(3) Make small balls. Deep fry 2 to 3 koftas at a time in medium hot oil. Keep aside. If the koftas start breaking more amount of corn flour can be added.

(4) Cut the onions into thin long slices. Deep fry them till they become golden brown in colour.

(5) When they cools down, add $\frac{1}{2}$ cup of milk and grind the onions to a fine paste. Add masala no. 1 and 2 to the onion paste. Mix well.

(6) Heat the ghee in a vessel and fry the bay leaves for 2 minutes. Add the onion paste and fry for another 4 to 5 minutes.

(7) Add a pinch of soda, remaining milk, red chilli powder, turmeric powder and 1 cup of water. Stir constantly.

(8) When the gravy starts boiling, add salt and garam masala.

(9) Add cream and remove it from the flame. While serving, boil the gravy. Add the koftas. Keep on low flame for 5 minutes. Serve immediately.

402. Mougalai Cabbage-Cauliflower [Serves 4 to 5]

Ingredients

(1) 250 grams cabbage

(2) 250 grams cauliflower

(3) 150 grams green peas

(4) 6 cloves garlic

(5) 2 onions

(6) 250 grams tomatoes

(7) 2 table spoons ghee

(8) 2 table spoons oil

(9) A pinch asafoetida

(10) $\frac{1}{2}$ tea spoon turmeric powder

(11) 2 table spoons sugar

(12) Salt to taste

To be ground into a paste :

(1) 2 table spoons coriander seeds

(2) 1 table spoon cumin seeds

(3) 8 pepper corns

(4) 2 small pieces of cinnamon

(5) 5 cloves

(6) $\frac{1}{4}$ cup groundnuts or kaju or $\frac{1}{2}$ cup magatari seeds

(7) 1 tea spoon sesame seeds

(8) A small piece of ginger

(9) 5 to 6 cardamom pods

(10) 5 to 6 green chillies

Method

(1) Chop the cauliflower and cabbage into big pieces. Boil enough water. Add a pinch of soda, salt, 4 table spoons sugar, cauliflower and cabbage pieces. Boil them. Boil the green peas. Grind the onions and garlic to a fine paste. Boil and peel the tomatoes. Grind them into a fine paste.

(2) Heat the ghee in a vessel for seasoning.

(3) Add a pinch of asafoetida, turmeric powder, onion-garlic paste and the masala paste. Heat for 8 to 10 minutes till the ghee separates. Add the tomato pulp, salt and sugar. Fry again for 3 to 4 minutes.

(4) Add boiled vegetables. Simmer on a low flame for 4 to 5 minutes. Add chopped coriander leaves and serve. The proportion of sugar and red chilli powder may vary according to the tastes.

403. Garden Surprise

[Serves 4 to 5]

Ingredients

(1) 50 grams french beans

(2) 100 grams small potatoes

(3) 100 grams green peas

(4) 100 grams small onions

(5) 50 grams carrots

(6) Mougalai cabbage-cauliflower gravy

(7) A pinch of soda

(8) 5 tea spoons sugar

(9) Salt to taste

Method

(1) Boil enough water. Add a pinch of soda, 1 tea spoon salt and 5 tea spoons sugar.

(2) Add the french beans (finely chopped), potatoes and green peas. Cook till the vegetables are boiled. Steam the onion slices and carrots (cut into long strips). Put them in a sieve on the same vessel.

(3) After boiling, cool them. Prepare the mougalai gravy as described in R. No. 402. Mix all the vegetables to it. If it is too spicy, cream, malai or curds can be added.

(4) To colour the onions soak them in vinegar. Add a few drops of edible red colour and salt to it.

404. Masala Masoor

[Serves 4 to 6]

Ingredients

(1) 1 cup whole masoor

(2) 200 grams small onions

(3) 4 table spoons ghee

(4) 2 onions sliced

(5) 100 grams tomatoes

To be ground into a paste :

(1) 4 red chillies (dried)

(2) 7 to 8 cloves garlic

(3) 1 tea spoon cumin seeds

(4) A small piece of ginger

(5) 4 table spoons finely chopped coriander leaves

(6) Salt to taste

Method

(1) Wash the masoor. Add 2 cups of water and onions. Boil it in a pressure cooker.

(2) Heat the ghee in a kadhai. Add the sliced onions and fry them for a few minutes.

(3) Add the paste and fry again for 5 minutes.

(4) Add the masoor and the tomato pulp. Cover it with a lid. Let it simmer on a low flame for 15 minutes. Decorate with finely chopped coriander leaves. Serve hot.

405. Butter Matar Paneer
[Serves 3 to 4]

Ingredients

(1) 100 grams paneer
(2) 100 grams green peas
(3) 20 grams khus khus
(4) 50 grams magatari seeds
(5) 2 table spoons ghee
(6) 1 table spoon oil
(7) $\frac{1}{2}$ tea spoon cumin seeds
(8) A pinch asafoetida
(9) 1 tea spoon ginger-chilli paste
(10) 100 grams onions
(11) 10 cloves garlic
(12) 250 grams tomatoes
(13) 1 tea spoon turmeric powder
(14) A small desiccated coconut
(15) 2 tea spoons garam masala
(16) 30 grams butter
(17) Salt to taste

Method

(1) Cut the paneer into long pieces and deep fry in ghee. Soak the fried paneer pieces in water.

(2) Boil the green peas in water with a little salt added to it. Soak the khus khus and magatari seeds in water for 1 hour. Strain to remove the water. Grind it into a fine paste.

(3) Heat ghee, oil and fry the cumin seeds, and asafoetida for 1 minute. Add ginger-chilli paste and onion-garlic paste. Fry for 4 to 5 minutes.

(4) Add the khus khus paste, turmeric powder, desiccated coconut, garam masala and salt. Fry it till the ghee separates.

(5) Add butter, green peas and paneer pieces. Let it simmer on a low flame for 5 minutes. Remove it from the flame. Serve hot.

406. Stuffed Tomatoes In Gravy
[Serves 5]

Ingredients

(1) 500 grams long, hard tomatoes of equal size
(2) 1 table spoon butter
(3) 2 table spoons cashewnuts
(4) 2 tea spoons ginger-chilli paste
(5) 3 medium sized boiled potatoes
(6) Sugar to taste
(7) 1 tea spoon garam masala
(8) Salt to taste

For the gravy :

(1) 1 table spoon butter
(2) Tomato paste (pulp scooped from the tomatoes and ground into a paste)
(3) 50 grams tomatoes (paste)
(4) 2 table spoons sugar
(5) Salt to taste

To be ground into a paste :

(1) 3 kashmiri red chillies
(2) 1 tea spoon cumin seeds
(3) 1 table spoon coriander seeds
(4) 1 piece cinnamon
(5) 3 cloves
(6) 2 medium sized onions
(7) 1 piece ginger
(8) 4 cloves garlic

Roast all the dry masalas. Add onion, ginger, garlic and a little water to it and ground into a paste.

Method

Fry the tomatoes lightly on a medium flame. Skin the tomatoes. Cut the tomatoes into two. Scoop out the centres. Grind the centres in the mixer. Keep it aside for the gravy.

For the filling in the tomatoes

(1) Melt the butter and add the cashewnuts in a vessel. Fry for 1 minute. Add ginger-chilli paste, boiled, peeled and grated potatoes, salt, sugar and garam masala.

(2) Mix well and cook for a few minutes. Stuff the tomatoes with the filling.

For the gravy

(1) Melt the butter. Add the grounded masala and fry for 2 minutes. Add the tomato pulp, salt and sugar. Boil it for 2 minutes. Remove it from the flame.

(2) Arrange the tomatoes on a greased aluminium baking dish. Pour the boiling gravy on top. Bake in a hot oven to 180° C for 20 minutes. Serve hot.

Note : Instead of baking, it can be also cooked on a non-stick pan. Covered with a lid.

407. Vegetable Pulav [Serves 5]

Ingredients

(1) 1 cup uncooked basmati rice
(2) $\frac{1}{2}$ lime   (3) Oil
(4) 100 grams potatoes
(5) 100 grams french beans
(6) 100 grams carrots
(7) 100 grams green peas
(8) 2 table spoons ghee
(9) 1 tea spoon cumin seeds
(10) 4 pieces cinnamon
(11) 6 cloves
(12) 4 green chillies
(13) A small piece of ginger
(14) $\frac{1}{4}$ tea spoon turmeric powder
(15) 10 kajus   (16) 15 raisins
(17) 1 tea spoon garam masala
(18) Salt to taste

Method

(1) Soak the rice in water for at least 2 to 3 hours.

(2) Boil the rice in water with a little lime juice and 1 tea spoon of oil. When the rice is half cooked drain the water. Each grain of the cooked rice should be separate.

(3) Cut the vegetables into small pieces and boil them.

(4) Heat 1 table spoon oil in a vessel and fry the cumin seeds, cloves and cinnamon for 1 minute. Add the green chillies, ginger, turmeric powder, potatoes, green peas, french beans and carrots. Fry them for 2 minutes.

(5) Add salt, cashewnuts, raisins and garam masala. Add the half cooked rice. Mix carefully (The rice grain should not break).

(6) For making different layers, take a large glass serving bowl. Spread half of the rice, then spread half of the vegetables, next spread a further half of the rice and finally spread the remaining vegetables.

(7) Decorate with finely chopped coriander leaves and fresh coconut (grated). Serve hot.

408. Vegetable Biryani
[Serves 4 to 5]

Ingredients

(1) 50 grams cabbage
(2) 50 grams carrots
(3) 25 grams french beans

(4) 50 grams green peas

(5) 50 grams cauliflower

(6) $\frac{1}{2}$ cup red gravy according to R. No. 373

(7) 1 cup uncooked rice

(8) 1 tea spoon red chilli powder

(9) $\frac{1}{2}$ tea spoon turmeric powder

(10) 1 tea spoon garam masala

(11) 6 cashewnuts   (12) 4 almonds

(13) 15 grams groundnuts

(14) 4 strands of kesar

(15) 2 table spoons finely chopped coriander leaves

(16) 2 table spoons ghee

(17) Salt to taste

Method

Chop and boil the vegetables. Prepare the red gravy according to R. No. 373. Boil the red gravy. Add the boiled vegetables to it. Keep it aside. Boil the rice. Each grain of the cooked rice should be separate. Add red chilli powder, turmeric powder and garam masala to it. Take a large bowl. Make four layers by spreading half of the rice, then spreading half of the vegetables, next spreading the remaining half of the rice and finally spreading the remaining vegetables. Garnish with kajus, almonds, groundnuts, a few strands of kesar and chopped coriander leaves.

409. Shahi Biryani
[Serves 4 to 5]

Ingredients

(1) 1 cup uncooked rice

(2) $\frac{1}{2}$ cup red gravy according to R. No. 373

(3) 10 cashewnuts (4) 15 raisins

(5) 6 almonds   (6) 10 groundnuts

(7) A few strands of kesar

(8) Salt to taste

Method

(1) Boil the rice. Each grain of the cooked rice should be separate. Prepare a red gravy according to R. No. 373. Add less amount of water. Add more amount of masalas.

(2) Mix the rice and the red gravy. Decorate with cashewnuts, raisins, almonds, groundnuts and kesar strands.

410. Green Pulav
[Serves 4 to 5]

Ingredients

(1) 1 cup basmati rice (cooked separately)

(2) 2 table spoons ghee

(3) 1 table spoon oil

(4) $\frac{1}{2}$ tea spoon cumin seeds

(5) 2 capsicum cut into thin, long strips

(6) 4 table spoons green chutney

(7) 100 grams french beans cut into small pieces and boiled

(8) 100 grams green peas boiled in salt and water

(9) 1 tea spoon garam masala

(10) 10 cashewnuts

(11) 15 raisins

(12) 250 grams spinach boiled and ground into a fine paste

(13) Salt to taste

Method

(1) Heat the ghee and oil in a kadhai and fry the cumin seeds for 1 minute.

(2) Add the capsicum and salt. Fry for 2 to 3 minutes. Add the green chutney.

(3) Add the remaining ingredients.

(4) Mix well very carefully. Cashewnuts and raisins are optional.

(5) To make it greener, you can also add boiled and crushed spinach.

411. Black Dal [Serves 6]

Ingredients

(1) 100 grams masoor

(2) 100 grams rajma

(3) 2 table spoons ghee

(4) 2 onions   (5) 6 cloves garlic

(6) 4 tomatoes (grated)

(7) 2 tea spoons garam masala

(8) Salt to taste

Method

(1) Soak the masoor and rajma in water for 6 to 7 hours. Boil them.

(2) Heat the ghee in a vessel. Add onion and garlic paste to it. Fry for 5 minutes. Add the tomatoes. Prepare the red gravy by this method. Boil the gravy. Add the boiled pulses, salt and garam masala. Let it simmer for 5 to 10 minutes. Garnish with chopped coriander leaves. Serve hot.

412. Dal Fry [Serves 5 to 6]

Ingredients

(1) 1 cup tuver dal

(2) $\frac{1}{2}$ cup chana dal

(3) $\frac{1}{2}$ cup masoor dal

(4) $\frac{1}{2}$ cup mung dal

(5) $1\frac{1}{4}$ cup urad dal

(6) 2 table spoons ghee or butter

(7) A pinch asafoetida

(8) 1 tea spoon cumin seeds

(9) 4 finely chopped onions

(10) 10 cloves garlic

(11) 5 green chillies

(12) 4 tomatoes

(13) 1 tea spoon red chilli powder

(14) 1 tea spoon dhana jeera powder

(15) 1 tea spoon garam masala

(16) 1 tea spoon cloves cinnamon powder

(17) A small piece of ginger

(18) 50 grams butter (for the topping)

(19) Salt to taste

Method

(1) Wash and boil the dals in a pressure cooker. Do not stir the dals after they are cooled.

(2) Heat the ghee or butter in a vessel and fry cumin seeds and asafoetida for 1 minute. Add finely chopped onions. Fry them for 2 to 3 minutes.

(3) Add ginger, chilli, garlic paste and again fry for 2 minutes.

(4) Add the tomato pulp. Fry for 2 to 3 minutes.

(5) Add the dals, salt, red chilli powder, dhana jeera powder, garam masala and cloves cinnamon powder. Simmer for 5 minutes. Add a little butter. Remove it from the flame. Garnish with chopped coriander leaves. Serve hot.

413. Dhansak [Serves 3 to 4]

Ingredients

(1) 2 table spoons mung dal

(2) 2 table spoons chana dal

(3) 1 table spoon val dal

(4) 4 table spoons tuver dal

(5) 2 table spoons masoor dal

(6) 1 potato

(7) 100 grams pumpkin

(8) 1 small brinjal

(9) 1 small piece of dudhi (bottlegourd)

(10) 50 grams sweet potatoes

(11) 1 cup methi leaves (fenugreek leaves)

(12) 2 table spoons mint leaves

(13) 50 grams tomatoes   (14) 2 onions

(15) 2 table spoons ghee

(16) 5 cloves garlic

(17) 2 pieces cinnamon   (18) 3 cloves

(19) 2 cardamoms pods

(20) 5 pepper corns

(21) 1 tea spoon cumin seeds

(22) 1 tea spoon dhana jeera powder

(23) 1 tea spoon desiccated coconut

(24) A small piece of ginger

(25) 5 green chillies

(26) $\frac{1}{2}$ tea spoon turmeric powder

(27) 4 tea spoons chopped coriander leaves

(28) 1 lime

(29) 1 tea spoons garam masala

(30) Salt to taste

Method

(1) Boil all dals, onions and vegetables together. Mash them well.

(2) Heat 2 table spoons of ghee.

(3) Add $\frac{1}{2}$ grated onion, garlic paste, cinnamon, cloves, cardamom, pepper and all the masalas. Fry for 2 to 3 minutes.

(4) Add the chillies (paste), turmeric powder, ginger (paste), coriander leaves (finely chopped), all dals and vegetables.

(5) Add enough water, salt, lime juice and garam masala.

(6) Let it simmer for 5 minutes. Remove it from the flame.

414. Jeera Rice [Serves 4]

Ingredients

(1) 1 cup uncooked basmati rice

(2) 2 table spoons ghee

(3) 2 tea spoons cumin seeds

(4) 1 onion (long slices)

(5) 1 tea spoon garam masala

(6) 10 to 12 cashewnuts

(7) 15 raisins

(8) 2 table spoons finely chopped coriander leaves

(9) Salt to taste

Method

(1) Soak the rice in water for 2 hours. Boil the rice in water. Each grain of the cooked rice should be separate. Heat the ghee, oil and fry the cumin seeds for 1 minute. Fry the onion slices for 2 minutes.

(2) Add rice, salt and garam masala. Mix well. Deep fry cashewnuts and raisins. Decorate with cashewnuts, raisins and finely chopped coriander leaves.

415. Pulav [Serves 4 to 6]

Ingredients

(1) 1 potato   (2) 100 grams carrots

(3) 1 cup uncooked rice

(4) 100 grams green peas

(5) 2 table spoons ghee

(6) 1 table spoon oil

(7) 1 tea spoon cinnamon-cloves powder

(8) 2 onions   (9) 10 cashewnuts

(10) 15 raisins   (11) 1 tomato

(12) 1 tea spoon garam masala

(13) $\frac{1}{4}$ tea spoon turmeric powder

(14) $\frac{1}{2}$ tea spoon red chilli powder

(15) 2 tea spoons coriander leaves

(16) $\frac{1}{2}$ lime   (17) Salt to taste

Method

(1) Cut the potatoes and carrots into small pieces. Soak the rice in water for 2 hours.

(2) Boil enough water. Add the soaked rice, potatoes and carrots.

(3) When the rice and vegetables are cooked, strain them. Keep it aside to cool for 1 hour. Each grain of the cooked rice should be separate.

(4) Heat the ghee, fry the cloves and cinnamon for 1 minute. Add finely chopped onions and fry for 3 to 4 minutes.

(5) Add cashewnuts, raisins, finely chopped tomatoes, garam masala, turmeric powder, red chilli powder, finely chopped coriander leaves and lime juice. Fry for 2 to 3 minutes. A little citric acid can be used instead of lime juice. Add the cooked rice and vegetable. Mix well very lightly so that the rice grains does not break.

416. Chhole Pulav
[Serves 5 to 6]

Ingredients

(1) 150 grams boiled kabuli chana
(2) 1 table spoon oil
(3) 1 table spoon ghee
(4) 1 tea spoon cumin seeds
(5) 2 bay leaves
(6) A few curry leaves
(7) 1 onion
(8) 1 tomato
(9) 1 tea spoon red chilli powder
(10) A pinch of asafoetida
(11) $\frac{1}{2}$ tea spoon turmeric powder
(12) 1 tea spoon garam masala
(13) 1 cup uncooked rice
(14) Salt to taste

Method

(1) Soak the chhole for overnight in water. Boil them with a pinch of soda.

(2) Heat the ghee and fry the cumin seeds for a few seconds. Add the bay leaves, curry leaves and finely chopped onions. Fry for 2 to 3 minutes.

(3) Add finely chopped tomatoes. Fry for 2 to 3 minutes. Add red chilli powder,

asafoetida, turmeric powder and garam masala. Add the boiled chana and mix well.

(4) Soak the rice in water for 2 hours. Boil the rice. Each grain of the cooked rice should be separate. Mix the rice with the chhole. Garnish with finely chopped coriander leaves.

417. Kaju Curry [Serves 4 to 5]

Ingredients

(1) 125 grams cashewnuts pieces (soaked)
(2) 150 grams onions
(3) 25 grams garlic (paste)
(4) 50 grams poppy seeds (khus khus)
(5) 80 grams magatari seeds (Soak for 1 hour and grind into a paste)
(6) 3 table spoons dalda ghee
(7) $\frac{1}{2}$ tea spoon cumin seeds
(8) A pinch asafoetida
(9) 1 tea spoon red chilli powder
(10) 1 tea spoon turmeric powder
(11) 100 grams tomato sauce
(12) 25 grams garam masala
(13) Salt to taste

Method

(1) Cut the onions into big pieces and boil them. Grind the onions into a fine paste.

(2) Heat the ghee (dalda) in a vessel and fry cumin seeds for 1 minute.

(3) Add the onion, garlic and ginger (paste), green chillies (paste), red chilli powder and turmeric powder. Fry for 4 to 5 minutes.

(4) Add salt, tomato sauce and garam masala. Fry again for a few minutes till the ghee separates. Add the cashewnuts and mix well.

Variation

Kaju Mattar Kofta : Add 100 grams of green peas to the kaju curry to prepare kaju mattar kofta.

418. Punjabi Cauliflower

[Serves 3 to 4]

Ingredients

(1) 250 grams cauliflower (2) Oil

(3) 150 grams tomatoes (paste)

(4) 100 grams onions (paste)

(5) 4 to 6 cloves garlic (paste)

(6) 1 table spoon ghee

(7) A pinch asafoetida

(8) A small piece of ginger

(9) 4 green chillies

(10) $\frac{1}{4}$ tea spoon turmeric powder

(11) 1 tea spoon red chilli powder

(12) 1 tea spoon garam masala

(13) 1 tea spoon dhana jeera powder

(14) Salt to taste

Method

(1) Cut the cauliflower into big pieces and wash them properly. Heat the oil in a vessel. Fry the cauliflower pieces.

(2) Heat 1 table spoon oil and ghee in a vessel. Add a pinch of asafoetida. Add ginger, chillies, garlic, onion (paste and grated) and tomatoes. Fry for 2 to 3 minutes.

(3) Add turmeric powder, red chilli powder, salt, dhana jeera powder, garam masala and cauliflower.

(4) Let it simmer on low flame for 5 minutes. Remove it from the flame.

419. Sindhi Cauliflower

[Serves 4 to 6]

Ingredients

(1) 500 grams cauliflower

(2) $1\frac{1}{2}$ cups mint leaves

(3) 7 cloves garlic

(4) A small piece of ginger

(5) 8 green chillies

(6) 2 cups coriander leaves (chopped)

(7) 2 tea spoons coriander seeds

(8) 1 tea spoon cumin seeds

(9) 6 table spoons oil

(10) A pinch asafoetida

(11) 3 tea spoons chat masala

(12) $\frac{1}{2}$ tea spoon turmeric powder

(13) $\frac{1}{4}$ cup tomato puree

(14) 2 table spoons ghee

(15) Salt to taste

Method

(1) Mix mint leaves, ginger, chillies, coriander leaves, coriander seeds and cumin seeds. Grind them in the mixer into a fine paste.

(2) Heat the ghee in a vessel. Add asafoetida, chat masala — the paste, turmeric powder and the tomato puree to it. Fry for 5 minutes.

(3) Cut the caulifower into big pieces. Add 1 cup water to it and boil it on a low flame. Stir at frequent intervals.

(4) Do not over cook the cauliflower. When the cauliflower is cooked, add the ghee and remove it from the flame.

420. Punjabi Corn Paneer

[Serves 4 to 6]

Ingredients

(1) 200 grams paneer

(2) 25 grams khus khus

(3) 50 grams magatari seeds

(4) Oil

(5) 2 table spoons dalda ghee

(6) $\frac{1}{2}$ tea spoon cumin seeds

(7) A pinch asafoetida

(8) 1 tea spoon ginger-chilli paste

(9) 1 tea spoon turmeric powder

(10) 1 tea spoon garam masala

(11) 100 grams onions (paste)

(12) 10 cloves garlic (paste)

(13) 100 grams tomato sauce

(14) 1 tea spoon red chilli powder

(15) 100 grams corn seeds

(16) Salt to taste

Method

(1) Cut the paneer into long pieces and deep fry them in ghee. Soak them in water.

(2) Soak the poppy seeds and magatari seeds in water for 1 hour. Then grind them into a paste.

(3) Heat 1 table spoon ghee in a vessel and fry the cumin seeds and asafoetida for 1 minute. Add the ginger-chilli paste, turmeric powder, garam masala, onion and garlic paste. Fry for 4 to 5 minutes.

(4) Add the tomato sauce, poppy seeds and magatari seeds paste, red chilli powder and salt. Fry again for 4 to 5 minutes.

(5) Add the boiled corn seeds and the paneer pieces. Let it simmer on a low flame for 5 minutes. Remove it from the flame.

Variation

Punjabi Corn French Beans :
Instead of paneer add 150 grams of french beans. Cut the beans into big pieces and boil them. Rest of the recipe remains the same.

421. Baby Corn Capsicum Red Masala [Serves 4 to 5]

To be ground into a paste

(1) 2 onions paste

(2) 10 cloves garlic paste

(3) 250 grams tomatoes grated and strained

(4) 2 capsicums cut into long strips

(5) 100 grams baby corn (boiled and cut into slices)

(6) 2 table spoons ghee

(7) 1 table spoon oil

(8) 1 tea spoon red chilli powder

(9) $\frac{1}{2}$ tea spoon turmeric powder

(10) 1 tea spoon dhana jeera powder

(11) 1 tea spoon garam masala

(12) 1 tea spoon sugar

(13) 1 tomato cut into long strips

(14) Salt to taste

Ingredients

(1) 1 tea spoon cumin seeds

(2) 2 pieces of cinnamon and 3 cloves

(3) 5 pepper corns

(4) 1 table spoon coriander seeds

(5) 5 cashewnuts

(6) 25 grams magatari seeds

(7) 1 table spoon sesame seeds

(8) A little water

Method

(1) Heat the ghee in a vessel. Add the masala paste and fry for 2 to 3 minutes.

(2) Add the onion-garlic paste. Fry for 4 to 5 minutes.

(3) Add the tomato puree, salt, red chilli powder turmeric powder, dhana jeera powder, garam masala, sugar, tomato and capsicum. Fry again for 4 to 5 minutes.

(4) Add the baby corn slices. Let it simmer for 5 minutes. Serve hot.

Points to Remember :

1. The basic cooking vessel for the chinese dishes is the wok, which is essentially a cone shaped vessel with a rounded bottom. In chinese cooking the food is cooked evenly at fast heat. Most of the dishes are served very hot.

2. To parboil vegetables like green peas, baby corn and cauliflower. Put plenty of water to boil. Add the vegetables and cook them for 5 minutes until they are crunchy. To maintain the colour of the vegetables do not cover them while boiling. Boil the corn seeds in the pressure cooker. Dry onions can be used instead of spring onions.

3. For various recipes heat the oil and stir fry onions, garlic and ginger paste. Then add the vegetables and fry for a few minutes. Lastly, add the noodles or rice as mentioned in the recipe.

4. Chinese cooking includes the use of red chilli sauce, green chilli sauce, soya sauce, Ajinomoto, white pepper powder, tomato ketchup, white vinegar and brown vinegar.

5. The vegetables that are used in various recipes should be roughly of even size.

6. **Chinese Vegetable Stock :**

   100 grams cabbage roughly chopped into big pieces.

   50 grams onions

   50 grams carrots

   25 grams capsicum

   50 grams french beans

   A small piece of ginger

   A few coriander leaves

   2 cloves garlic

   ### Method

   Chop all the vegetables into small pieces. Boil 3 cups of water. Add all the ingredients when the water starts boiling. Boil for 10 minutes on a medium to low flame. Remove it from the flame. Cover it with a lid and keep aside for 30 minutes. Drain out the water. The water is known as the vegetable stock. Add various masalas to the vegetables and you can prepare mixed vegetable. Use the stock as required.

7. Dissolve the required quantity of corn flour in water or milk. Be sure to stir the mixture well so that lumps are not formed as the cornflour tends to stick to the bottom of the vessel.

8. A few drops of edible red colour can be added to the vegetables. Red chilli oil can also be prepared. Take $\frac{1}{2}$ cup oil and 10 to 12 red chillies. Break the red chillies into large pieces. Heat the oil on a high flame and add the chillies. Immediately switch off the gas. Cover it and allow it to stand for 2 hours. Strain and use as required.

9. The use of mashroom in various recipes is optional.

10. **How to cook noodles :** Break the noodles into fairly small pieces. Put plenty of water to boil. When the water starts boiling, add the noodles. Cook on a high flame. When the noodles are cooked, remove them from the flame and immediately strain and then wash under cold running water. Add 2 tea spoons of oil and mix well. This prevents the noodles from sticking.

    Fried noodles : Boil the noodles. Apply a little oil and corn flour to them. Spread the noodles on a clean piece of cloth and allow to dry for atleast 2 hours. Heat the oil in a wok or a frying pan over a medium flame. Fry small quantities of noodles at a time in the hot oil until it becomes golden brown. Remove the noodles from the oil and drain thoroughly before stirring. Repeat with the remaining noodles.

11. **To cook the rice :** The rice should be of thick variety. Basmati rice should not be used because its flavour would suppress the flavour of vegetables. Soak 1 cup of uncooked rice for 1 hour. Heat 5 cups of water. When the water starts boiling, add the rice. Do not over cook the rice. Add 2 table spoons of refined oil. When the rice is cooked, drain the water add place the rice under cold running water. This will help the grain to separate. For the preparation of Chinese recipes, the rice should be cooked well in advance. At least two to three hours before hand.

12. **Chillies in Vinegar :** Cut the chillies and add to the white vinegar. Soak them in vinegar for 2 hours. Use as required.

422. Sweet And Sour Vegetable Soup [Serves 6 to 8]

Ingredients

(1) 50 grams onions chopped into large pieces

(2) 50 grams capsicum (big pieces)

(3) 2 table spoons oil

(4) 100 grams carrots (big pieces)

(5) 50 grams cauliflower (big pieces)

(6) 50 grams cabbage (big pieces)

(7) A pinch ajinomoto

(8) $\frac{1}{2}$ tea spoon white pepper powder

(9) 1 tea spoon vinegar

(10) 100 grams tomato ketchup

(11) 20 grams sugar

(12) 3 table spoons corn flour

(13) Salt to taste

Method

(1) Heat about 2 table spoons of oil. Add the onions and capsicum pieces. Fry for few minutes.

(2) Boil the carrots, cauliflower and cabbage.

(3) Add them to the onions and capsicum.

(4) Add enough water, salt, ajinomoto, white pepper powder, vinegar, tomato ketchup and sugar. Cook for 2 minutes.

(5) Mix the corn flour in a little water and add to the soup. Boil for 1 minute, while stirring continuously. Serve hot.

423. Hot and Sour Soup

[Serves 6 to 8]

Ingredients

(1) 1 spring onion chopped finely with the greens

(2) A small piece of crushed ginger

(3) 2 tea spoons oil

(4) 50 grams finely chopped carrots

(5) Finely chopped 5 french beans

(6) 50 grams cauliflower small florets

(7) 50 grams shredded cabbage

(8) 2 cups water

(9) 25 grams red chilli sauce

(10) 10 grams soya sauce

(11) 1 tea spoon vinegar

(12) 20 grams finely chopped capsicums

(13) 30 grams finely chopped tomatoes

(14) For the stock water $\frac{1}{2}$ carrot, 1 small potato, 50 grams bottlegourd

(15) 1 table spoon corn flour

(16) 4 cloves (powdered)

(17) 2 cardamom pods (powdered)

(18) 2 bay leaves   (19) 1 lime

(20) 2 table spoons finely chopped coriander leaves

(21) Salt to taste

Method

(1) Heat 1 tea spoon oil in a wok on a high flame. Add the onions and ginger. Fry for 2 to 3 minutes on a low flame.

(2) Add a little more oil and carrots, french beans, cauliflower and cabbage.

(3) Add 2 cups of water. Boil the mixture. When it starts boiling add all the sauces, capsicum, tomatoes and the stock.

(4) For the stock – Boil $\frac{1}{2}$ carrot, 1 potato and a small piece of bottlegourd. Crush these in the blenderiser. Strain and add to the soup mixture.

(5) Add salt, lime juice, clove, cardamom and bay leaves. Remove the bay leaves while serving. Cook for 2 minutes. Top with chopped coriander leaves. Serve hot with chillies in vinegar, soya sauce and chilli sauce.

424. Sweet Corn Soup
[Serves 5 to 6]

Ingredients

(1) 5 large fresh corncobs
(2) 3 tea spoons sugar
(3) 3 to 4 tea spoons soya sauce
(4) A pinch ajinomoto
(5) 1 table spoon green chilli sauce
(6) 1 tea spoon corn flour
(7) 4 cups water
(8) Salt to taste

Method

(1) Grate 3 corncobs. Boil the remaining 2 corncobs in the pressure cooker and take out whole cornseeds from them.

(2) Add salt, sugar, ajinomoto, soya sauce and chilli sauce. Mix the corn flour in 2 tea cups of cold water and

add to the cooked corn mixture. Boil for at least 30 minutes. Serve hot with chillies in vinegar and soya sauce.

Variation

Finely chopped french beans, carrots, capsicums, tomatoes and cheese may be added to the soup.

Chilli Vinegar : 8 table spoons vinegar, 4 green chillies (chopped finely), $\frac{1}{2}$ tea spoon salt. Mix all the ingredients and boil the mixture for 1 minute on a low flame.

425. Spring Roll
[Makes 25 to 30 Rolls]

Ingredients

For the covering :

(1) 1 cup maida
(2) 1 table spoon rawa
(3) $\frac{1}{4}$ tea spoon baking powder
(4) 1 table spoon oil
(5) Cold water   (6) Salt to taste

For the stuffing :

(1) 50 grams french beans
(2) 50 grams carrots
(3) 50 grams cabbage
(4) 50 grams capsicums
(5) 3 table spoons oil + oil for frying
(6) $\frac{1}{4}$ tea spoon ajinomoto
(7) $\frac{1}{2}$ cup sprouted mung
(8) 1 tea spoon chilli sauce
(9) 1 tea spoon soya sauce
(10) 1 tea spoon red chilli powder
(11) Salt to taste

Method

(1) Sieve the flour with salt and baking powder added to it. Add the rawa to the maida. Add the oil and enough water to form a semi-soft dough. Knead the dough. Leave for about 10 minutes.

(2) For the stuffing, cut the vegetables (except beans sprouts) into long thin strips. Soak them in cold water for 2 hours.

(3) Heat the oil thoroughly in a vessel and add ajinomoto powder, capsicum, french beans and mung. Cook on a high flame. Cover the vessel with a lid. Cook for 10 minutes. Add cabbage and carrots. Cook for 2 minutes. Add salt.

(4) Remove it from the flame when all the water evaporates. Add chilli sauce, soya sauce and red chilli powder.

(5) Knead the dough well. Divide the dough into 10 small balls. Roll out each ball into chapatties. Spread the stuffing on one end and roll up. Seal the edges with a little water. Sprinkle a little maida on it.

(6) Deep fry in hot oil. Cut into $1\frac{1}{2}$ pieces when hot.

(7) Serve hot with chilli sauce. The rolls can be half fried and kept aside. Refry them while serving.

Note : The rolls should be fried immediately because if they are kept for some time they will crack.

426. Chinese Samosa
[Makes 25 to 30 Samosas]

Ingredients

(1) 50 grams spaghetti (break into small pieces)

(2) 3 table spoons oil

(3) 100 grams shredded cabbage

(4) 50 grams sliced capsicums

(5) 50 grams french beans, cut into long strips

(6) 50 grams carrots, cut into long strips

(7) $\frac{1}{2}$ cup sprouted mung

(8) 1 tea spoon chilli sauce

(9) 1 tea spoon soya sauce

(10) 1 tea spoon red chilli powder

(11) 1 cup maida   (12) $\frac{1}{2}$ lime

(13) $\frac{1}{4}$ tea spoon baking powder

(14) Oil for frying

(15) A pinch ajinomoto (16) Salt to taste

Method

(1) Heat plenty of water. When it starts boiling, add the spaghetti. Add 1 table spoon of refined oil while the spaghetti is being cooked. When the spaghetti is cooked, remove it from the fire and immediately strain in a colander (or a large soup strainer) under cold running water. This helps the spaghetti to separate. Add 2 tea spoons of oil so that the spaghetti does not stick with one another (use after 1 hour).

(2) Heat the oil on a high flame in a wok. Add the vegetables, salt and ajino-moto and stir fry over a high flame till the vegetables are half done. Add the chilli sauce, spaghetti, soya sauce, and red chilli powder. Mix well.

(3) For the outer covering, mix maida, oil, salt, lime juice and baking powder. Add enough water to form a semi-soft dough. Knead the dough. Divide the dough into small balls. Roll out each ball into a puri. Put the stuffing in the centre of the puri.

(4) Roll up like a bundle (potali). You can also shape like regular Punjabi samosas or ghugharas and seal the edges. Deep fry in hot oil.

Variation

(1) **Chinese Ghughara :** Shape like regular ghugharas (kanan)

(2) **Wontons :** If you shape them like spring they are called wontons.

427. Vegetable Manchurian
[Serves 5 to 6]

Ingredients for Manchurian

(1) 150 grams grated carrots

(2) 150 grams finely chopped or grated cabbage

(3) 50 grams finely chopped capsicum

(4) 1 finely chopped green chilli

(5) 200 grams maida

(6) 50 grams corn flour

(7) 1 tea spoon pepper powder

(8) Oil

(9) A pinch ajinomoto

(10) Salt to taste

Ingredients for the Gravy (Sauce)

(1) 10 grams ginger

(2) 5 grams green chillies

(3) 10 grams garlic

(4) 1 table spoon oil

(5) A pinch ajinomoto

(6) 1 tea spoon soya sauce

(7) 1 table spoon chilli sauce

(8) 2 table spoons tomato ketchup

(9) 1 tea spoon pepper powder

(10) 3 table spoons corn flour

(11) Salt to taste

Method for the Manchurian

(1) Mix the cabbage, carrots, salt, capsicum, green chillies, pepper, a little oil, ajinomoto, maida and corn flour. Mix well.

(2) Shape spoonfuls of the mixture into small balls. If you find it difficult to form balls, sprinkle a little water. Deep fry in hot oil until they are golden brown.

Method for the Gravy

(1) Heat the oil in a wok or a frying pan on a high flame. Add garlic, green chillies and ginger and stir. Fry on a high flame for a few seconds. Add 2 glasses of water. Mix well the corn flour with $\frac{1}{4}$ cup of water.

(2) Add 2 table spoons corn flour mixture, soya sauce, chilli sauce, ajinomoto and a little tomato ketchup and cook for few minutes. Just before serving put the balls in the gravy and cook for few minutes. Serve hot.

428. Frankee [Serves 6 to 8]

Ingredients

For the covering :

(1) 250 grams (2 cups) maida

(2) $\frac{1}{2}$ tea spoon yeast

(3) $\frac{1}{2}$ tea spoon sugar

(4) 2 table spoons oil

(5) 100 grams wheat flour

(6) $\frac{1}{2}$ tea spoon soda

(7) 1 table spoon curds

(8) 1 tea spoon salt

For the stuffing :

(1) 500 grams potatoes

(2) 3 onions (finely chopped)

(3) 2 tomatoes

(4) 8 to 10 cloves garlic (finely chopped)

(5) 1 capsicum (finely chopped)

(6) 1 tea spoon red chilli powder

(7) 1 tea spoon green chilli paste

(8) $\frac{1}{2}$ lime

(9) 2 tea spoons sugar

(10) 1 tea spoon garam masala

(11) 3 slices bread

(12) Cabbage (shredded)

(13) Carrots (long strips)

(14) Onions (slices)

(15) 3 tea spoons chilli sauce

(16) Spicy coriander chutney

(17) Dates chutney

(18) $\frac{1}{4}$ tea spoon soya sauce

(19) Salt to taste

Method

For the covering :

(1) Mix yeast, sugar, 1 table spoon maida and luke warm water. Cover it with a lid. Keep aside for few minutes. Mix maida, yeast, salt and enough water to form a semi-soft dough. Knead the dough. Leave for about 2 to 3 hours.

(2) Instead of yeast, curds can be used. Mix curds, citric acid, sugar, maida and enough water to form a hard dough.

(3) Knead the dough. Leave for about 2 to 3 hours. Nan and pizza base can be also made from this dough.

(4) Divide the dough into medium sized balls. Roll out each ball into a chapatti. Roast on the griddle on both sides. Do not roast them too much.

(5) Keep the rotis covered in a napkin.

For the stuffing :

(1) Boil, peel and grate the potatoes. Add onions, capsicum, tomatoes and garlic. Make a stuffing like batatawada masala.

(2) Soak the bread slices in water for a few minutes. Remove and squeeze them. Mash them very well. Mix them well with the potato mixture.

(3) Shape the stuffing like long rolls. Rub them in maida. Deep fry in hot oil.

To serve

(1) Heat the griddle. Add 1 tea spoon of oil on the griddle and place the rolls on it. Roast the roll till they are properly hot. Shift them on the edges of the griddle. Roast each roti on both the sides for some time. Remove the roti from the flame.

(2) Place it in a serving dish. Place the roll on it. Apply coriander chutney and dates chutney on it. Sprinkle finely chopped onions and chat masala on it. Roll the roti like a roll and serve hot.

Frankee can be served in various ways :

(1) If you don't want to fry the rolls, then the roll can be roasted on the griddle in a little oil. Then roast the roti on both the sides and place the roll inside the roti.

(2) Shallow fry the rolls on the griddle. Also roast the roti on the griddle. Place the roll on the roti and sprinkle finely chopped cabbage, onions, carrots (cut into long strips), chilli sauce, soya sauce and a little chat masala. Mix a little amchur powder to the chat masala.

429. Fried Rice [Serves 5]

Ingredients

(1) 500 grams uncooked rice

(2) Oil

(3) A pinch citric acid

(4) 100 grams fresh beans

(5) 100 grams carrots

(6) 3 spring onions

(7) A little ajinomoto

(8) 1 capsicum

(9) 1 tea spoon soya sauce

(10) $\frac{1}{2}$ tea spoon pepper powder

(11) 1 tea spoon vinegar

(12) Salt to taste

Method

(1) Soak the rice for 2 hours. Put plenty of water for boiling. Add the rice when the water starts boiling.

(2) Add a little oil and salt to it while the rice is being cooked. Remove it from the flame when the rice is par-boiled.

Cut all the vegetables into small pieces. Chop the leaves of the spring onions. Again put plenty of water for boiling. Add the finely chopped french beans. Add a little soda and salt to the water while boiling. Drain the water after the french beans are cooked.

(3) Heat the oil thoroughly in a vessel and add the vegetables and ajinomoto. Cook on a high flame for 3 to 4 minutes.

(4) Add salt, soya sauce, white pepper powder, vinegar and the rice. Mix very well and cook for 2 minutes. Sprinkle some finely chopped spring onions. Serve hot with chillies in vinegar and chilli sauce.

430. American Chopsey
[Serves 5]
Ingredients

(1) 50 grams onions (finely chopped)

(2) 3 spring onions (with leaves) (finely chopped)

(3) 2 (50 grams) capsicum (finely chopped)

(4) Oil

(5) 300 grams cabbage (shredded)

(6) 100 grams carrots (long strips)

(7) 50 grams french beans (finely chopped)

(8) 2 pinch ajinomoto

(9) 300 ml water

(10) 200 grams tomato ketchup

(11) 25 grams sugar (2 table spoons)

(12) 1 tea spoon pepper powder

(13) 100 grams fresh tomatoes

(14) 3 table spoons corn flour

(15) 1 lime

(16) 1 tea spoon vinegar

(17) Salt to taste

Method

(1) Heat 1 table spoon oil thoroughly in a vessel and add the onions, spring onions and capsicum and cook on a high flame for 5 minutes.

(2) Add cabbage, carrots, french beans, salt and ajinomoto. Cook again for a few minutes.

(3) Add 300 ml of water to it.

(4) For the sauce mix 1 finely chopped spring onion, tomato ketchup, sugar, salt, pepper powder and ajinomoto. Place all the ingredients of the sauce in a vessel and mix well and put it to boil.

(5) Add the prepared sauce and fresh tomatoes cut into big pieces (sprouted mung and boiled noodles may be also added) to the vegetables.

(6) Mix well. Dissolve well 3 table spoons of corn flour in water. Add it to the prepared mixture.

(7) Go on cooking and stirring until the sauce is thick. Remove it from the flame and add lime juice and vinegar.

Ingredients for the topping noodles

(1) 2 cups maida

(2) 2 table spoons oil

(3) A pinch baking powder

(4) Oil for frying

(5) 1 tea spoon salt

Method for the topping noodles

(1) Mix all the ingredients and knead a hard dough with cold water. Divide the dough into small balls. Roll out each ball into thin rotis.

(2) Cut the rotis into long; narrow, strips. Let them dry for some time. Deep fry them.

Note : Serve hot and topped with the fried noodles.

431. Vegetable Hakka Noodles
[Serves 5 to 6]

Ingredients

For the stir fried vegetables :

(1) 100 grams capsicum (long strips)
(2) 100 grams onions (slices or rings)
(3) 5 tea spoons oil
(4) 200 grams cabbage (shredded)
(5) 50 grams french beans (finely chopped)
(6) 100 grams carrots (long strips)
(7) 100 grams noodles
(8) $\frac{1}{2}$ tea spoon white pepper powder
(9) A pinch ajinomoto
(10) 2 tea spoons soya sauce
(11) Salt to taste

Method

(1) Chop the capsicum into long strip.
(2) Chop the onions into long slices.
(3) Heat 2 tea spoons oil in a wok or frying pan on a high flame.
(4) Add the cabbage, capsicums, onions, french beans, carrots and ajinomoto. Cook on a high flame for 2 minutes.
(5) Add the noodles, pepper powder, soya sauce and salt.
(6) Mix well and cook for 1 minute. Serve hot.

Method for Boiling the Noodles

Boil the noodles with a little oil in the water. Drain all the water when they are cooked. Pour cold water on the noodles. Add 2 tea spoons oil to it. This would prevent the noodles from sticking to each other.

432. Schezuan Sauce

Ingredients

(1) 8 red chillies whole
(2) 4 cloves garlic (finely chopped)
(3) 4 table spoons oil
(4) 3 cloves garlic
(5) $\frac{1}{2}$ tea spoon ginger (finely chopped)
(6) 1 capsicum (finely chopped)
(7) 8 french beans (finely chopped)
(8) 2 onions (finely chopped)
(9) 250 grams tomatoes (finely chopped)
(10) A pinch ajinomoto
(11) 3 table spoons white vinegar
(12) 1 table spoon corn flour (dissolved well in water)
(13) 2 table spoons sugar
(14) A few drops of edible red colour
(15) Salt to taste

Method

(1) Boil $\frac{1}{2}$ cup of water. Add the red chillies and garlic to it. Cook for a few minutes. Cool it. Grind into a smooth paste in a liquidiser using a little water.
(2) Heat 4 table spoons oil in a wok or a frying pan and fry the garlic, ginger, capsicum, french beans and onions. Fry for 2 minutes.
(3) Add the tomatoes, chilli-garlic paste and ajinomoto.
(4) Mix well and cook for 2 minutes. Add vinegar and the corn flour mixture.
(5) Boil for 3 minutes while stirring through out. Add a few drops of edible red colour and remove it from the flame when it thickens like tomato ketchup. Use as required.

Note : This sauce can be preserved in the fridge for a long time.

433. Schezuan Noodles
[Serves 2]

Prepare the hakka noodles as per the R. No. 431. Also prepare the schezuan sauce as per the R. No. 432. Mix 100 grams of the hakka noodles and 2 cups of the schezuan sauce.

434. Paneer Chilli Fry

[Serves 4 to 5]

Ingredients

(1) 250 grams paneer (2) Oil

(3) Ginger, cut into long strips

(4) 6 cloves garlic

(5) 4 green chillies cut into strips

(6) 2 onions (finely chopped)

(7) 2 capsicums (finely chopped)

(8) 2 tea spoons chilli sauce

(9) 2 tea spoons tomato sauce

(10) 1 tea spoon pepper powder

(11) A pinch ajinomoto

(12) 1 tea spoon soya sauce

(13) 200 grams maida

(14) 50 grams corn flour

(15) 1 tea spoon salt

Method

(1) Heat 3 table spoons oil and fry the green chillies and ginger for 2 to 3 minutes.

(2) Add onions and capsicum. Stir fry for 3 to 4 minutes.

(3) Add the chilli sauce, tomato sauce, pepper powder, ajinomoto, salt, $\frac{1}{2}$ cup water and soya sauce. Boil for a few minutes.

(4) Grate the paneer. Mix paneer, maida, corn flour and salt.

(5) Add enough water to make a batter like that made for pakodas. Drop a spoonful of the batter in hot oil and fry the pakodas.

Note : If the pakodas are not soft then a little malai or oil can be added. Deep fry the pakodas till golden brown. Add the pakodas to the boiling gravy. Boil for 4 to 5 minutes.

435. Vegetable Chow Chow

[Serves 4]

Ingredients

(1) 100 grams cucumber

(2) 100 grams cabbage

(3) 100 grams cauliflower

(4) 200 grams french beans

(5) 2 spring onions (6) 2 capsicums

(7) 2 carrots (8) 3 onions

(9) 2 table spoons oil

(10) 2 pinches ajinomoto powder

(11) 2 table spoons corn flour, dissolved in water

(12) 1 table spoon vinegar

(13) 1 table spoon chilli sauce

(14) 2 table spoons soya sauce

(15) Salt to taste

Method

(1) Cut all the vegetables into long thin strips.

(2) Heat the oil thoroughly in a vessel and add the vegetables, salt and ajinomoto powder. Cook on a high flame for 5 to 7 minutes.

(3) When the vegetables are par-boiled, add the corn flour mixture. Add 2 cups of water and boil it.

(4) When the sauce is thick, add vinegar, chilli sauce and soya sauce. Cook for 2 to 3 minutes on a low flame. Remove it from the flame. If the sauce has become too thick, add a little water and salt while re-heating it.

Serve hot with chillies in vinegar and chilli sauce.

Note : (1) Instead of cucumber, 100 grams noodles can be added.

(2) 100 grams sprouted mung may also be added.

436. Chinese Corn Pakoda

[Serves 5 to 6]

Ingredients

(1) 500 grams corn

(2) $\frac{1}{2}$ cup milk

(3) 1 table spoon corn flour

(4) $\frac{1}{2}$ tea spoon pepper powder

(5) 1 tea spoon soya sauce

(6) 1 tea spoon chilli sauce

(7) 50 grams onions (finely chopped)

(8) 50 grams capsicum (finely chopped)

(9) $\frac{1}{4}$ cup maida

(10) Sandwhich bread

(11) Oil   (12) Salt to taste

Method

(1) Take out the corn seeds from the corncobs and boil them. Dissolve the corn flour in cold milk and prepare the white sauce.

(2) Add the corn seeds, salt, pepper, soya sauce, chilli sauce, onions and capsicum to the white sauce.

(3) Mix maida and salt. Add enough water to it to make the batter.

(4) Remove the edges from the bread slices and cut them into square pieces. Put a little amount of the corn stuffing on the bread slice. Dip the side with the stuffing in the maida batter. Deep fry the pakodas in hot oil.

(5) If the stuffing is soft, then apply a little rawa or toast powder above the stuffing and then dip in the batter.

Variation

Cut the bread slices into triangles. Put a little amount of the stuffing on the slices. Sprinkle toast powder on it. Sprinkle grated cheese and bake the toast in the oven. Serve hot.

12 MEXICAN DISHES

Points to Remember :

1. In Mexican dishes tortilla is used very frequently. It is a roti made by mixing corn flour and maida or wheat flour.

2. White and red kidney beans are commonly used in the Mexican recipes.

3. The Mexican dishes are very spicy in taste. They call chillies as 'pepper'.

4. Light lemon yellow coloured corncobs are called 'American Corn'. The corncobs are boiled for 5 minutes in hot water. These corn seeds are sweeter in taste than the regular whitish corn. The regular corn can be used instead of this 'American Corn.'

5. Led hot sauce is widely used in the Mexican dishes.

6. The majority of the Mexican dishes are baked in the oven. Bake the dishes just before serving them. Serve them hot.

437. Tacos [Serves 4 to 5]

Ingredients

For the outer covering (Tacos) :

(1) $\frac{3}{4}$ cup yellow maize flour (makai-ka-atta)

(2) $\frac{1}{2}$ cup maida

(3) Oil

(4) Salt to taste

For the stuffing :

(1) 100 grams kidney beans of any variety (rajma)

(2) $\frac{1}{4}$ tea spoon soda

(3) 1 table spoon ghee

(4) 1 onion (finely chopped)

(5) 2 spring onions (finely chopped)

(6) 1 tea spoon garlic paste

(7) 2 table spoons tomato gravy

(8) 1 tea spoon red chilli powder

(9) 1 table spoon butter

(10) 1 table spoon cheese

(11) 1 tea spoon chilli sauce (red)

(12) Salt to taste

For the topping :

(1) Finely chopped cabbage

(2) Finely chopped spring onions

(3) Grated cheese

Method

For the tacos :

(1) Mix the flour. Add 2 table spoons oil and salt and make a semi soft dough by adding water.

(2) Roll out thin puris with the help of plain flour. Prick lightly with a fork.

(3) Deep fry in hot oil on both sides and then bend into a 'U' shape while hot. Cool and store the tacos in an air-tight tin.

For the stuffing :

(1) Soak the beans overnight. Add a little salt and soda and cook the beans in a pressure cooker. Drain the beans and mash them a little.

(2) Grind some of the rajmas to a paste.

(3) Heat the ghee in a vessel and fry the onions, garlic and the spring onions for 2 minutes. Add the beans, tomato ketchup or tomato gravy, red chilli powder, salt, butter, cheese and chilli sauce. Remove it from the flame when it thickens a little.

To Serve :

(1) In the fold of each taco, fill 2 tea spoons of the stuffing.

(2) Fill with the chopped vegetables. Sprinkle grated cheese on the top and serve the tacos.

438. Mexican Cutlet
[Serves 4 to 5]
Ingredients

(1) 250 grams potatoes

(2) 1 table spoon corn flour

(3) $\frac{1}{2}$ lime juice

(4) Salt to taste

For the stuffing :

(1) 100 grams kidney beans or baked beans tin

(2) $\frac{1}{4}$ tea spoon soda

(3) Oil

(4) 1 finely chopped onion

(5) 1 tea spoon vinegar

(6) $\frac{1}{2}$ tea spoon pepper powder

(7) 1 tea spoon red chilli powder

(8) 2 table spoons tomato ketchup

(9) Green chutney of coriander and mint leaves

(10) Salt to taste

Method

(1) Boil, peel and grate the potatoes. Mix corn flour, salt and lime juice to it. Mix well. Divide the mixture into medium sized balls.

(2) Heat 2 table spoons oil in a vessel. Fry the onions for a few minutes. Add the boiled rajma or baked beans and all the masalas. Mix well. Cook till the mixture thickens.

(3) Take a small ball of the potato mixture press it lightly and give it an oblong shape. Apply a little chutney on it. Place one tea spoon of beans. Place another ball of the potato mixture with the chutney applied. Press lightly.

(4) Heat a little oil on the griddle and roast the cutlets on it. Roast them on both the sides. Serve hot.

Variation

Boil, peel and grate the potatoes. Add slightly mashed rajma and all the masalas to it. Add finely chopped onions and mix well. Roll in vermicilli and then fry till they are golden brown. Serve hot.

439. Enchiladas
[Serves 5 to 6]
Ingredients
For the rotis :
(1) 1 cup corn flour (makai-ka-atta)
(2) $\frac{1}{2}$ cup maida
(3) 2 tea spoons oil
(4) Salt to taste

For the stuffing :
(1) 4 table spoons oil
(2) $\frac{1}{2}$ table spoon omum
(3) 2 finely chopped onions
(4) 3 finely chopped capsicums
(5) $1\frac{1}{2}$ tin baked beans or 1 cup white rajma (boiled)
(6) 1 tea spoon red chilli powder
(7) 1 cup grated cheese
(8) 1 cup paneer
(9) Salt to taste

For the gravy :
(1) 2 table spoons oil
(2) A few omum seeds
(3) 5 cloves garlic
(4) 250 grams onions
(5) 2 table spoons cream
(6) 2 table spoons tomato ketchup
(7) 2 capsicums
(8) 1 kg tomato pulp
(9) 1 tea spoon red chilli powder
(10) $\frac{1}{2}$ lime juice
(11) 1 table spoon maida
(12) 1 tea spoon chilli sauce
(13) Salt to taste

For Serving :
(1) 1 cube cheese
(2) Cabbage

Method

For the dough :
Mix the flours. Add the oil and salt and make a soft dough by adding water. Divide the dough into small balls. Roll out each ball into a thin roti. Roast the rotis on the hot griddle. Roast on both the sides. Do not roast them too long.

For the stuffing :
(1) Heat 4 table spoons of oil in a frying pan. Add omum, onions and capsicums. Fry for few minutes.
(2) Add the beans or rajma. Add salt and chilli powder. Mix well and cook for 3 to 4 minutes till it thickens a little. When the mixture is cool, add cheese and paneer. Mix well.

For the gravy :
(1) Heat the oil in a vessel. Add omum, garlic, onions, cream, tomato ketchup and capsicum. Fry for about 4 to 5 minutes.
(2) Add the tomato pulp and all the masalas.
(3) Grease a baking dish. Place a roti. Fill the stuffing mixture in the centre. Sprinkle grated cheese on it. Roll it from both the sides. Place the roll in the baking dish. Pour the gravy and sprinkle the cheese over it. While serving decorate with shredded cabbage. Bake in an oven for 15 to 20 minutes.

Variation

Instead of rajma, saute the mixed vegetables in butter. Add white sauce, soya sauce, salt and pepper.

440. American Mint Burger
[Makes 6 Burgers]

Ingredients

For the pattice :

(1) 500 grams potatoes (cabbage optional)
(2) 1 tea spoon cloves cinnamon powder
(3) $\frac{1}{2}$ tea spoon pepper powder
(4) $\frac{1}{4}$ tea spoon cardamom powder
(5) 4 tea spoons chilli paste
(6) $\frac{1}{2}$ tea spoon ginger paste
(7) $\frac{1}{2}$ lime juice or amchur powder as per taste
(8) Sugar to taste
(9) $\frac{1}{4}$ cup arrowroot flour
(10) Oil for roasting
(11) Salt to taste

For the stuffing :

(1) 6 burger buns
(2) 100 grams butter
(3) $\frac{1}{2}$ cup tomato ketchup
(4) 2 onions
(5) $\frac{1}{2}$ cup mint chutney
(6) 1 tomato
(7) 1 cucumber
(8) $\frac{1}{2}$ cup grated cheese

Method

(1) Boil, peel and grate the potatoes. Mix all the masalas to it. Divide the potato mixture into 6 balls. Roll the balls in arrowroot flour. Cut the bun from the centre into two.
(2) Apply butter. Roast one side on a hot griddle. Apply tomato ketchup to the other side of the bun.
(3) Place finely chopped onions on it. Place the pattice. Apply mint chutney to the top part of the bun. Place sliced tomatoes and cucumber on the pattice.
(4) Sprinkle grated cheese. Place the top side of the bun. Serve with potato wafers or chips.

441. Basic Red Hot Sauce
[Makes 3 cups]

Ingredients

(1) 6 dry red chillies
(2) 4 green chillies, long strips
(3) 3 onions paste
(4) 2 table spoons oil
(5) 5 cloves garlic paste
(6) 1 cup tomato puree
(7) 1 table spoon corn flour, dissolved in a little water
(8) $\frac{1}{2}$ cup water
(9) 2 table spoons sugar
(10) 1 tea spoon cumin seeds
(11) 1 tea spoon omum (12) Salt to taste

Method

(1) Soak the chillies in $\frac{1}{2}$ tea cup of hot water for 10 minutes. Grind them to a fine paste.
(2) Heat the oil in a vessel and fry the onion-garlic paste, red chilli paste and green chillies.
(3) Fry for few minutes.
(4) Add the tomato puree, corn flour mixture, sugar, salt and omum. Go on stirring it continuously. Boil till the mixture thickens like a sauce. Cool and use as required.

Note : If you are using readymade tomato sauce, then add 2 tea spoons red chilli powder, $\frac{1}{2}$ tea spoon omum and a little water to chilli tomato ketchup.

442. Nachoz [Serves 5 to 6]

Ingredients

(1) 1 cup corn flour (makai-ka-atta)

(2) $\frac{1}{2}$ cup maida

(3) 3 table spoons oil

(4) $\frac{1}{4}$ tea spoon turmeric powder

(5) $\frac{1}{4}$ tea spoon omum powder

(6) 1 tea spoon red chilli powder

(7) $\frac{1}{2}$ tea spoon black salt powder

(8) Salt to taste

Method

(1) Mix the flour. Add the oil, salt, turmeric powder and omum. Make a semisoft dough by adding water. Keep it aside for sometime. Divide the dough into small balls.

(2) Roll out each ball into a thin round puri about 5" in diameter. Prick lightly with a fork. Keep it on a paper for drying for some time.

(3) Divide the puris into 4 equal triangulars. Deep fry in oil very lightly. Delicious Nachoz are ready.

(4) Sprinkle a little salt, red chilli powder and black salt powder before serving.

Note : Nachoz can be preserved in an air tight container for 10 to 15 days.

443. Nachoz with White Cheese Salsa [Serves 6 to 7]

Ingredients

(1) 1 cup milk

(2) 1 table spoon corn flour

(3) $\frac{1}{2}$ tea spoon pepper powder

(4) 1 cup grated cheese

(5) 1 table spoon butter

(6) Nachoz according to R. No. 442

(7) 2 to 3 onions (rings)

(8) 3 capsicums thin rings

(9) 4 cubes cheese   (10) Salt to taste

Method

(1) Dissolve the corn flour in 1 cup of milk. Boil the corn mixture with constant stirring.

(2) Add $\frac{1}{2}$ tea spoon pepper powder, salt grated cheese and butter. Mix well. Remove it from the flame.

(3) Place the prepared nachoz in a greased baking dish. Arrange the onion and capsicum rings over it. Pour the white sauce over it. Sprinkle grated cheese all over it. Bake in an oven at 150° C for 15 minutes.

444. Nachoz with Red Salsa [Serves 5 to 6]

Ingredients

(1) $\frac{1}{2}$ cup carrot

(2) $\frac{1}{2}$ cup cucumber

(3) 1 onion

(4) 50 grams pumpkin

(5) $\frac{1}{2}$ cup finely chopped coriander leaves

(6) 1 tea spoon oil

(7) $\frac{1}{2}$ cup tomato ketchup

(8) 3 tea spoons red chilli powder

(9) 3 tea spoons vinegar

(10) $\frac{1}{2}$ tea spoon omum

(11) $\frac{1}{2}$ tea spoon cumin seeds powder

(12) 4 cloves garlic

(13) 2 tea spoons tobasco sauce

(14) A few drops of edible red colour

(15) Nachoz   (16) Salt to taste

For the tobasco sauce :

(1) $\frac{1}{2}$ cup tomato ketchup

(2) $\frac{1}{2}$ cup white vinegar

(3) $\frac{1}{2}$ cup sugar

(4) 1 tea spoon corn flour

(5) 1 tea spoon chilli sauce

(6) $\frac{1}{4}$ cup water

(7) 2 table spoons worcestershire sauce

Method

(1) Grate the carrots, cucumber, onion and pumpkin. Squeeze them lightly to remove the water.

(2) Mix finely chopped coriander leaves. Mix 1 tea spoon oil to the mixture.

(3) Mix ½ cup tomato ketchup, red chilli powder, vinegar, omum, cumin powder, garlic paste, salt, tobasco sauce and few drops of edible red colour.

(4) Mix these ingredients well. Add the mixture to the vegetables to prepare hot red salsa.

Note : Serve Nachoz with Hot Red Salsa.

For the Tobasco Sauce :

(1) Dissolve the corn flour in water. Mix all the remaining ingredients to it. Boil the mixture for 10 minutes. Cool it and fill the sauce in the bottle.

(2) Use as required. Store it in the refrigerator. It can be used in various Italian dishes, Thai foods, and Mexican dishes.

445. Tortilla Soup

[Serves 5 to 6]

Ingredients

(1) 50 grams paneer (grated)

(2) 1 cheese cube (grated)

(3) 500 grams tomatoes

(4) 2 table spoons butter

(5) 1 grated onion   (6) 1 cup water

(7) 2 tea spoons corn flour

(8) 2 table spoons American or regular corn

(9) ½ vegetable stock cube

(10) ½ tea spoon sugar

(11) 6 tea spoons fresh cream

(12) 1 cup Nachoz powdered

(13) Salt to taste

Method

(1) Boil the tomatoes in water for 10 minutes. Strain all the water.

(2) Take off the skin when cool. Crush them in the blenderiser and pass through a sieve. Heat the butter in a vessel.

(3) Add onions and fry for a few minutes. Add tomato puree and ½ cup of water. Dissolve the corn flour in ½ cup of water.

(4) Add it to the tomato mixture. Stir constantly. Boil the mixture for 5 minutes.

(5) Add corn, paneer, stock cube, sugar and salt. Boil the soup for few minutes.

(6) Mix 1 tea spoon fresh cream, grated cheese and Nachoz powder in the serving bowl. Serve the soup hot.

Note : Instead of Nachoz powder, cornchips or bhel puri's puris also can be powdered and used.

446. Kidney Beans Roll

[Serves 5 to 6]

Ingredients

For the rolls :

(1) 1½ cups rajma

(2) 3 table spoons oil

(3) 2 onions (finely chopped)

(4) 4 cloves garlic (finely chopped)

(5) 2 tomatoes, cut into small pieces

(6) 2 tea spoons red chilli powder

(7) 1 tea spoon pepper powder

(8) 1 tea spoon corn flour

(9) Salt to taste

For the Pan Cake :

(1) 1 cup corn flour

(2) 1 cup wheat flour

(3) 1 tea spoon oil

(4) ½ cup milk   (5) Salt to taste

Method

(1) Soak the kidney beans for 6 to 8 hours.

(2) Heat the oil in a vessel. Add the onions and fry for a few minutes. Add garlic and tomato pieces.

(3) Add red chilli powder, pepper powder, salt and the kidney beans. Mix well. Add 1 cup of water and boil in the pressure cooker. When boiled properly crush the rajma mixture in the blenderiser along with water.

(4) Heat 2 table spoons of oil in a vessel. Add the kidney beans mixture. Stir constantly.

(5) Dissolve the corn flour in water. Add it to the rajma mixture. When the mixture is thick enough, remove it from the flame. Divide the mixture into small balls and make rolls.

(6) Mix the flours. Add the oil, salt and milk. Make the batter using enough water.

(7) Heat a non-stick frying pan. Pour a little batter and spread the batter with a spoon to form an oval shaped, thick pan cake. Cook on both the sides till crisp.

(8) Cool them and cut into long strips. Put each roll in each strip and roll it like khandavi. Seal the edge with a tooth-pick.

447. Falafal [Serves 5 to 6]

Ingredients

For the rotis :

(1) 1 cup corn flour (makai-ka-atta)

(2) ½ cup maida

(3) ½ tea spoon ghee

(4) Salt to taste

For the Bhajiyas :

(1) 150 grams mung dal

(2) ½ table spoon red chilli powder

(3) 4 green chillies (4) Oil

(5) A small piece of ginger

(6) 2 table spoons chopped coriander leaves

(7) A pinch soda   (8) 1 onion

(9) ½ tea spoon coriander seeds

(10) ½ tea spoon pepper powder

(11) Oil for frying

(12) Salt to taste

For White Sauce :

(1) ½ cup fresh curds

(2) 1 table spoon sesame seeds

(3) ½ tea spoon mustard powder

(4) ½ table spoon white pepper powder

(5) 2 table spoons white vinegar

(6) 1 table spoon oil   (7) Salt to taste

For Red Sauce :

(1) ½ cup tomato sauce

(2) 5 cloves garlic paste

(3) 3 tea spoons red chilli powder

(4) Salt to taste

For the Salad :

(1) 50 grams finely chopped cucumber

(2) 50 grams finely chopped cabbage

(3) 50 grams finely chopped tomatoes

(4) 2 finely chopped onions

(5) Pepper powder

(6) Salt to taste

Method

For the rotis :

(1) Mix the flour. Add the ghee and salt and make a soft dough by adding water. Divide the dough into small balls. Roll out each ball into thin rotis.

(2) Roast them on the griddle like phulkas (thin rotis).

For the Bhajiyas :

(1) Soak the mung dal or chana dal in water for 5 to 6 hours. Grind it in the mixer into a coarse paste.

(2) Add all the masalas, ginger-chilli paste, pepper powder and coriander. Fry big and crispy bhajiyas.

For the White Sauce :

(1) Tie the curds into a muslin cloth. Hang it for half an hour.

(2) Roast the sesame seeds and crush them coarsely. Add all the ingredients to the thick curds. Mix well.

For the Red Sauce :

Mix all the ingredients well.

For the Salad :

Mix all the vegetables with pepper powder and salt.

How to Proceed :

(1) Separate the two sides of the phulka. Place 2 to 3 bhajiyas in the centre of the phulka.

(2) Pour the white and the red sauce on it.

(3) Arrange the salad over it. Serve immediately.

Variation

(1) Instead of rotis, burger buns can also be used. Cut the bun from the centre. Remove the bread portion from the centre to make the bun hollow from the centre. Roast the bun in little butter. Arrange the ingredients and serve immediately.

(2) Instead of the red sauce, hot tomato sauce can also be used.

(3) Pizza can also be used. Slice the pizza bread into two. Place the cut part on the top side. Scoop it from the centre. Fill in the stuffing and serve immediately.

448. Chilli Bean Soup

[Serves 5 to 6]

Ingredients

(1) 500 grams tomatoes
(2) 2 tea spoons oil
(3) 2 spring onions (finely chopped)
(4) 1 capsicum (finely chopped)
(5) 1 onion (finely chopped)
(6) $\frac{1}{2}$ small tin (100 grams) baked beans
(7) $\frac{1}{4}$ tea spoon red chilli powder
(8) A pinch omum
(9) 2 tea spoons sugar
(10) Grated cheese
(11) Salt to taste

Method

(1) Cut the tomatoes into big pieces, add 3 cups of water and cook. When cooked, take out the soup by passing through a sieve.

(2) Heat the oil in a vessel and add the onions, capsicums and the spring onions and fry for few minutes. Add the tomato soup and boil for few minutes.

(3) Add the baked beans, salt, omum and sugar. Cook for few minutes. Serve hot with grated cheese.

449. Chilli Railnose

[Serves 3 to 4]

Ingredients

(1) 100 grams paneer
(2) 1 onion   (3) 6 capsicums
(4) $\frac{1}{2}$ cup maida   (5) $\frac{1}{2}$ cup water
(6) 1 tea spoon baking powder
(7) Oil for frying
(8) 1 cup Hot Mexican Sauce according to R. No. 441
(9) Cheese   (10) Salt to taste

Method

(1) Grate the paneer with a thick grater or cut the paneer and onions finely.

(2) Mix well and add salt.

(3) Cut off the tops of the chillies and scoop out the centres. Put in boiling water for 2 minutes. Drain the chillies. Stuff the chillies with the paneer mixture.

(4) Mix maida, salt, baking powder and water and make the batter.

(5) Dip the chillies into the batter and deep fry in hot oil. While serving, pour the hot sauce and grated cheese over it. Bake it in hot oven for 10 minutes or let it simmer on a non-stick pan on low flame for 10 minutes.

450. Mexican Stuffed Capsicum

[Serves 3 to 4]

Ingredients

(1) 200 grams potatoes

(2) 150 grams boiled green peas

(3) $\frac{1}{2}$ cup spaghetti boiled

(4) 6 capsicums

(5) 1 tea spoon ginger-chilli paste

(6) 6 tooth picks

(7) Salt to taste

For the Gravy :

(1) 1 table spoon butter

(2) 1 onion (finely chopped)

(3) 1 table spoon maida

(4) 500 grams tomatoes

(5) 1 table spoon sugar

(6) 1 tea spoon red chilli powder

(7) Salt to taste

Method

(1) Boil, peel and grate the potatoes.

(2) Cut off the tops of the capsicums and scoop out the centres. Put in boiling water for 5 minutes. Drain the chillies. Keep them in the refrigerator upside down for sometime.

(3) Mix grated potatoes, green peas, spaghetti, salt, ginger and chillies. Stuff this stuffing in the capsicums. Cover with the capsicum tops. Place a tooth pick at the top.

For the gravy :

(1) Heat the butter in a vessel. Add finely chopped onions. Fry it for few minutes. Add the maida and stir fry for few minutes.

(2) Soak the tomatoes in boiling water for 5 minutes. Remove the skin from the tomatoes and blenderise them. Add this pulp to the onions. Add all the masalas. Boil the mixture for 15 minutes.

(3) Arrange the capsicums in a baking dish and pour the hot gravy over it. Bake it in a hot oven for 15 minutes or let it simmer on low flame for 10 minutes in a non-stick pan. Serve hot.

451. Mexican Hot Chocolate

[Serves 4]

Ingredients

(1) 1 table spoon cocoa powder

(2) $\frac{1}{2}$ tea spoon cinnamon powder

(3) 1 table spoon sugar

(4) 4 cups milk

(5) 4 drops vanilla essence

(6) 100 grams fresh cream

Method

(1) Mix the cocoa, sugar and cinnamon powder in a small bowl.

(2) Heat 1 cup of the milk in a vessel. When it starts boiling, add the cocoa mixture and beat until the mixture is very smooth.

(3) Add the rest of the milk and heat on a low flame. Add vanilla essence and fresh cream to the mixture. Beat with a hand mixer till it is frothy, just before serving.

452. Toastados [Serves 5 to 6]

Ingredients

(1) $1\frac{1}{4}$ cups corn flour (makai-ka-atta)
(2) $\frac{1}{2}$ cup maida
(3) 4 table spoons oil
(4) $\frac{1}{2}$ tea spoon omum
(5) Salt to taste

For the stuffing :

(1) 1 cup red rajma (or baked beans)
(2) 2 table spoons oil
(3) 1 finely chopped onion
(4) 1 boiled potato
(5) $\frac{1}{2}$ cup boiled mixed vegetables (french beans, carrots)
(6) 1 tea spoon red chilli powder
(7) 2 tea spoons sugar
(8) 1 tea spoon vinegar
(9) 1 table spoon butter
(10) Salt to taste

For the topping :

(1) Cabbage   (2) Carrots
(3) Cheese (grated)
(4) Onions (finely chopped)

Method

(1) Soak the kidney beans in water for 6 hours. Cook the beans in a pressure cooker.
(2) Mix the flours. Add salt and oil and make a soft dough by adding water. Divide the dough into small balls. Roll out each ball into thin rounds like puri. Prick lightly with a fork. Deep fry in hot oil on both sides.

(3) Heat the oil in a vessel and fry the onions for a short time. Add the beans, potatoes and other vegetables. Cook it for some time till all the water evaporates.
(4) Put a little stuffing on the puri. Sprinkle chopped vegetables over it. Sprinkle grated cheese and serve.

Variation

Roll out the dough into big puris. Apply a little oil to the small katoris or moulds. Press the puri over a mould or katori. Deep fry in hot oil. Toastadas can be also made in this way.

453. Mexican Rice [Serves 4]

Ingredients

(1) 1 cup uncooked rice
(2) $\frac{1}{4}$ cup rajma
(3) 6 cloves garlic paste
(4) 1 tomato (finely chopped)
(5) 3 table spoons ghee
(6) 10 to 12 pepper corns
(7) 2 onions (long strips or slices)
(8) 1 tea spoon red chilli powder
(9) 1 table spoon vinegar
(10) $\frac{1}{2}$ cup carrots (grated)
(11) 1 capsicum (long strips)
(12) A pinch ajinomoto
(13) 1 table spoon chilli sauce
(14) 1 tea spoon soya sauce
(15) Salt to taste

Method

(1) Soak the beans for 2 hours. Cook the beans in pressure cooker. Drain it.
(2) Heat the ghee in a vessel and fry the onions, pepper and the garlic paste. Fry for 5 minutes.
(3) Add the rice and fry for 2 minutes. Add just enough hot water to cook

the rice. Cook on a low flame for some time.

(4) Add red chilli powder, salt, vinegar and the beans. Cook again for a few minutes.

(5) In a broad vessel, heat the ghee and

fry the sliced onions, carrots, capsicum and ajinomoto. Fry again for 2 minutes.

(6) Add the rice and mix well.

(7) Decorate with finely chopped tomatoes and serve hot.

(13) BURMESE DISHES

454. Khowsuey [Serves 4 to 6]

Ingredients

For mint chutney :

(1) $\frac{1}{4}$ cup mint leaves

(2) $\frac{1}{2}$ cup coriander leaves

(3) A small piece of ginger

(4) 10 green chillies

(5) $\frac{1}{2}$ lime juice

(6) $\frac{1}{2}$ cup water   (7) Salt to taste

Mix all the ingredients and ground them into a fine paste.

For vegetable curry :

(1) 100 grams cauliflower

(2) 100 grams carrots

(3) 1 tomato

(4) 2 onions

(5) 2 potatoes

(6) 25 grams french beans

(7) $\frac{1}{4}$ cup ghee

(8) A pinch soda

(9) $1\frac{1}{2}$ tea spoons ginger-chilli paste

(10) 5 cloves garlic paste

(11) $\frac{1}{2}$ cup coconut milk

(12) 1 table spoon corn flour

(13) 2 table spoons roasted chana dal powder (daliya powder)

(14) 1 cup C shaped macaroni

(15) 1 tea spoon soya sauce

(16) 100 grams potato wafers (dehydrated with holes)

(17) Wheat flour strips

(18) Salt to taste

Method

For the strips :

(1) Mix 1 cup flour, oil and salt and knead a hard dough by adding water.

(2) Roll out thin and big rounds. Cut them into long strips. Cut the strips into 2" pieces. Deep fry in hot oil.

For coconut milk : Grate $\frac{1}{2}$ coconut and add 1 to $1\frac{1}{2}$ cups of hot water. Blend in a liquidiser and strain.

(1) Boil the macaroni with 1 tea spoon of oil.

(2) Wash under running water. Drain the water. Spread the macaroni in a plate and add 1 tea spoon of oil.

(3) Cut the vegetables into small pieces.

(4) Heat the ghee in a vessel and fry the french beans. Add the onions and fry again for few minutes.

(5) Add the other vegetables, a pinch of soda and salt. Fry for 10 minutes. Add 1 to $1\frac{1}{2}$ cups of water and cook it for some time.

(6) When the vegetables are cooked, add the ginger-chilli paste, garlic paste, tomatoes and coconut milk. Mix well. Dissolve the corn flour in a little water.

(7) When the mixture starts boiling add the corn flour and daliya powder. Remove it from the flame when the mixture is thick enough.

How to serve :

(1) Place the macaroni in a large serving dish. Place the vegetables on it. Place the fried strips above it.

(2) Sprinkle mint chutney, soya sauce and lastly some macaroni over it. Serve with potato wafers.

455. Burmese Budijaw (Bhajiyas) [Serves 3 to 4]

Ingredients

For the budijaw :

(1) 100 grams maida

(2) $\frac{1}{4}$ tea spoon pepper powder

(3) 1 tea spoon garam masala

(4) 2 table spoons oil + oil for frying

(5) 1 tea spoon red chilli powder

(6) 250 grams bottlegourd (dudhi)

(7) Salt to taste

To be ground into a paste :

(1) 2 onions (paste)

(2) 1 tea spoon ginger-chilli paste

For the chutney :

(1) 3 table spoons tomato ketchup

(2) 10 cloves garlic

(3) $\frac{1}{2}$ lime

(4) A little red chilli powder

(5) Salt to taste

Method

For the budijaw :

(1) Mix the flour, salt, red chilli powder, pepper powder, garam masala, ginger,

chillies, onions, red chilli powder and oil. Add enough water to make a batter.

(2) Peel the bottlegourd and cut into fingers. Dip the dudhi fingers into the batter and deep fry in oil until crisp. (The fingers take a long time to fry.)

(3) Mix all the chutney ingredients and grind to a fine paste. Serve hot budijaw with the chutney.

456. Burmese Pyajo (Koftas) [Serves 4 to 5]

Ingredients

For the Koftas :

(1) 100 grams chana dal

(2) 1 tea spoon green chilli paste

(3) 1 onion

(4) Oil

(5) Salt to taste

For the curry :

(1) $\frac{1}{2}$ coconut

(2) 2 table spoons ghee

(3) 3 cinnamon sticks

(4) 3 cloves

(5) 2 potatoes (boiled)

(6) 1 tea spoon red chilli powder

(7) 2 table spoons maida

(8) 1 table spoon curds

(9) 3 table spoons powdered gram dal (daliya)

(10) 1 cup boiled gram (chana)

(11) 1 cup crushed wafers

(12) 2 onions (finely chopped)

(13) Garlic chutney

(14) Dates chutney

(15) 2 tea spoons garam masala

(16) Salt to taste

Method

For the Koftas :

(1) Soak the dal overnight. Drain the water in the morning. Add the green chillies and grind the dal coarsely.

(2) Add salt and sliced onions. Shape like koftas. Deep fry in hot oil.

For the curry :

(1) Grate the coconut. Add hot water and blend in a liquidiser strain. Again add hot water to the remaining pulp. Blend and strain it again.

(2) Heat some ghee in a vessel. Fry cloves and cinnamon. Cut the potatoes into cubes.

(3) Mix the potatoes, coconut milk, salt, red chilli powder, maida and daliya powder. Boil for atleast 20 to 25 minutes on a low flame. Keep stirring constantly.

How to serve :

(1) Put the koftas at the bottom in a big serving dish. Pour the curry on them. Sprinkle crushed wafers, boiled grams and onions.

(2) Serve the chutney and garam masala separately.

457. Burmese Bhel with Curry

[Serves 4 to 5]

Ingredients

(1) 150 grams green peas

(2) Oil

(3) 1 tea spoon cloves and cinnamon powder

(4) 2 tea spoons sugar

(5) 1 lime juice

(6) 1 tea spoon ginger-chilli paste

(7) 100 grams cabbage (shredded)

(8) 2 tomatoes (small pieces)

(9) 1 pomegranate

(10) 25 bhel puris (rolled thin and not puffed)

(11) $\frac{1}{2}$ fresh coconut

(12) 2 tea spoons ghee

(13) A few curry leaves

(14) $\frac{1}{2}$ cup carrots (grated)

(15) $\frac{1}{2}$ tea spoon pepper powder

(16) 1 cup noodles

(17) 50 grams fine sev

(18) 1 cup finely chopped coriander leaves

(19) A little chat masala

(20) Salt to taste

Method

(1) Grind the green peas coarsely. Heat 2 table spoons of oil in a vessel. Add the cloves cinnamon powder and the peas. Fry for some time.

(2) Add salt, 1 tea spoon sugar, $\frac{1}{2}$ lime juice, ginger and chillies.

(3) Break the puris into small pieces.

(4) Grate the coconut. Add hot water to it. Blend in a liquidiser and strain.

(5) Heat a little ghee in a vessel. Add the curry leaves and coconut milk. Let it boil. Add enough water, salt and 1 tea spoon sugar. Boil again till it is thick enough.

(6) Mix the cabbage, carrots, salt, pepper powder and $\frac{1}{2}$ lime juice.

(7) Boil the noodles with 2 tea spoons of oil. When boiled, wash them under running water. Place the noodles in a dish and add 1 tea spoon of oil. Mix well.

How to serve :

(1) First place the noodles in a bowl. Sprinkle a little salt and pepper powder on it. Spread the peas stuffing over it.

(2) Then spread the carrots, cabbage and tomatoes on it. Arrange the puris over it.

(3) Decorate with pomegranate seeds, sev and coriander leaves.

Sprinkle a little chat masala over it. Serve immediately with the curry.

458. Burmese Rice
[Serves 4 to 5]
Ingredients

(1) 1 cup uncooked rice

(2) 25 grams french beans

(3) 1 carrot

(4) 50 grams cauliflower

(5) 1 capsicum

(6) 2 onions

(7) 50 grams green peas

(8) 1 tea spoon white vinegar

(9) $\frac{1}{4}$ cup oil

(10) 2 tea spoons sugar

(11) 3 cinnamon sticks

(12) 3 cloves

(13) 1 tea spoon chilli sauce

(14) 4 table spoons tomato ketchup

(15) Salt to taste

To be ground into a paste :

(1) 4 green chillies

(2) A small piece of ginger

(3) 1 tea spoon cumin seeds

(4) 2 sticks cinnamon

(5) 2 cloves

(6) $\frac{1}{2}$ tea spoon red chilli powder

Method

(1) Cut the onions and capsicums into long strips.

(2) Chop all the other vegetables into small pieces. Steam all the vegetables.

(3) Add the vinegar to the paste and mix well. Add the capsicum and allow to marinate in the paste for some time. Soak the rice for 2 hours.

(4) Boil the water and add the uncooked, soaked rice to it. Add a little salt to the rice (Do not over cook). Strain the rice in a sieve and wash under running water. Spread the rice on a big plate.

(5) Heat 2 table spoons of oil in a vessel. Add sugar to it when hot. When the sugar melts, add the cinnamon and cloves and fry for few seconds.

(6) Heat the remaining oil in a vessel and fry the onions until they are golden in colour. Remove them from the flame.

(7) Add the capsicum, $\frac{1}{2}$ tea spoon chilli sauce, salt, 3 table spoons tomato ketchup and boiled vegetables. Mix both the mixture.

(8) Add 1 table spoon tomato ketchup, $\frac{1}{2}$ tea spoon chilli sauce and salt in rice.

(9) On a non-stick pan, spread the rice and the vegetables in alternate layers so that there are 3 to 4 layers. Cover and cook on a low flame for 15 minutes or bake in a hot oven at 230° C for 20 minutes.

Points to remember :

1. Thai foods are very easy to make.

2. Thai cusine includes the use of rice and various herbs like green tea leaves, tulsi, ginger, green chillies, coriander leaves and mint leaves.

3. In thai cooking coriander is used along with the stems and the roots. So the roots should be soaked in water for some time and then washed thoroughly before use.

4. Green tea leaves are known as 'Lemon Grass.' They are used for taste and aroma. They are tied up into a bunch and then added to the recipe. When the recipe is done, the bunch is removed off.

5. 'Broccoli' is a green coloured cauliflower. But regular cauliflower can be also used.

6. 'Capsicum' is called 'peppers'. Various varieties of capsicums are available and used in the recipes like yellow and red capsicums. If they are not available, then green capsicums can be used.

7. Small corn cobs are known as baby corn. They are boiled in water for 5 to 7 minutes before use.

8. In India button mushrooms are available. They are of two varieties, frozen and fresh. Frozen mushrooms are soaked in water for 25 minutes and then boiled in hot water for 5 to 7 minutes. Usually Gujaratis do not eat mushrooms. The use of mushrooms is optional.

9. 'Tofu' is a product made from soya beans. Instead of Tofu, regular paneer can be used.

10. 'Lemon Rind' means lemon peels. Peel the yellow skin of a lemon with a sharp knife. It is used for its aroma and for decoration.

11. Seasoning cube is used instead of the vegetable stock. Mix 1 cube in 3 cups of water. The cube has salt added to it. So little less salt is added to the recipes.

12. 'Pumpkin' is 'Kaddu.'

13. **Coconut Cream :** Grate the coconut. Add 1 cup of hot water and let it stand for 25 to 30 minutes. Strain it and refrigerate it for some time. The mixture would thicken like cream.

Add 2 cups of hot water to the left over coconut and blenderise it. Strain it. Again add hot water to the left over coconut and repeat the process.

Instead of coconut cream, coconut milk can be made. For that, grate the coconut and add 3 cups of hot water. Blenderise and strain. Repeat the same process for 2 to 3 times to get coconut milk.

14. To reduce the cooking time, the basic 2 to 3 curries in the Thai cusine can be pre-prepared and kept ready in advance. These curries can be used with noodles, vermicilli, rice or any of the vegetables to prepare various recipes. The red curry paste, green curry paste and vegetable stock can be prepared and stored, for using them as and when required.

459. Red Curry Paste

[Make ½ cup]

Ingredients

(1) 10 red whole chillies

(2) 1 onion (3) 6 cloves garlic

(4) 4" piece of ginger

(5) 2 sticks lemon grass (green tea leaves)

(6) 5 sticks coriander leaves

(7) 1 table spoon coriander seeds

(8) 2 table spoons cumin seeds powder

(9) $\frac{1}{2}$ tea spoon pepper powder

(10) $\frac{1}{4}$ cup water

(11) Salt to taste

Method

(1) Soak the red chillies in water for 15 minutes. Drain the water.

(2) Grind all the ingredients together. Store in a bottle.

(3) The curry paste would remain fresh for 2 months in the freezing chamber of the refrigerator.

460. Green Curry Paste

[Makes $\frac{1}{2}$ cup or 8 table spoons]

Ingredients

(1) 1 onion (chopped finely)

(2) 2" piece of ginger (chopped finely)

(3) 6 cloves garlic (chopped finely)

(4) Peels of 1 lemon (chopped finely)

(5) 10 green chillies

(6) $1\frac{1}{2}$ cups coriander leaves

(7) 1 table spoon coriander seeds

(8) 1 tea spoon cumin seeds powder

(9) 2 stems lemon grass (green tea leaves)

(10) $\frac{1}{2}$ tea spoon pepper powder

(11) $\frac{1}{4}$ cup water

(12) Salt to taste

Method

(1) Mix all the ingredients. Grind the ingredients together. Store in a bottle.

(2) The curry paste would remain fresh for 2 months in the freezing chamber of the refrigerator.

461. Vegetable Stock

[Makes 2 to $2\frac{1}{2}$ cups]

Ingredients

(1) $\frac{1}{2}$ cup onion (finely chopped)

(2) 1 stick celery (finely chopped)

(3) 2 carrots (grated)

(4) 2 sticks coriander leaves (with the roots)

(5) 3 sticks china grass

(6) $\frac{1}{2}$ table spoon pepper corns

Method

(1) Wash the coriander root thoroughly.

(2) Boil 3 cups of water. Add all the ingredients and boil them. When the mixture starts boiling, cover the vessel with a lid and cook on a low flame for 15 minutes.

(3) When it is cool, strain the mixture. This water is used as the vegetable stock.

For Boiled Noodles :

(1) Boil 1 litre of water. Add 1 tea spoon of oil to it. When the water starts boiling add the noodles. Cook on a high flame.

(2) When the noodles are cooked, remove them from the flame and immediately strain and then wash under cold running water. Spread the noodles in a dish and add 1 tea spoon oil to it. This prevents the noodles from sticking.

(3) Macaroni, spaghetti or paste is boiled in the same manner.

For Paneer :

(1) Boil 1 litre of milk. When the milk starts boiling, slowly add the juice of one lemon. Stir constantly when the milk curdles and the whey separates, remove it from the flame. Strain it through a muslin cloth. If the whey does not separate out properly, add more lime juice till the milk curdles properly.

(2) Wash the paneer with water. Place the paneer in a muslin cloth and press it with some weight. Keep it like that for some time till all the excess water drains out.

(3) Paneer can be also made in the paneer maker.

462. Thai Green Curry

[Serves 4 to 5]

Ingredients

(1) 4 table spoons green curry paste according to R. No. 460

(2) $\frac{1}{2}$ cup button mushrooms (cut into pieces – optional)

(3) $\frac{1}{4}$ cup green peas

(4) $\frac{1}{2}$ cup cauliflower (cut into pieces)

(5) $\frac{1}{2}$ capsicum (cut into square pieces)

(6) $\frac{1}{2}$ cup baby corn (cut into small pieces)

(7) $\frac{1}{2}$ cup paneer (cut into cubes – readymade or homemade)

(8) 1 table spoon oil

(9) $1\frac{1}{2}$ cups coconut milk

(10) 1 tea spoon sugar

(11) Salt to taste

Method

(1) Boil the mushrooms, peas, cauli-flower, capsicum and baby corn. Fry the paneer cubes.

(2) Heat a little oil in a vessel.

(3) Add the green curry paste and cook for 2 minutes.

(4) Add coconut milk and all the other ingredients. Boil for few minutes. Serve hot with rice.

Note : (1) Any other vegetables can be used.

(2) 1 cup = 16 table spoons

463. Thai Red Curry

[Serves 3 to 4]

Ingredients

(1) 4 table spoons red curry paste

(2) 1 table spoon corn flour (dissolved in a little water)

(3) 1 cup coconut milk

(4) 1 table spoon oil

(5) $\frac{1}{4}$ tea spoon soya sauce

(6) 10 to 12 tulsi leaves (chopped finely)

(7) $\frac{1}{4}$ cup baby corn (cut into long slices)

(8) 1 brinjal (sliced)

(9) $\frac{1}{2}$ cup cauliflower (cut into small pieces)

(10) $\frac{1}{4}$ cup mushrooms (sliced – optional)

(11) Salt to taste

Method

(1) Mix corn flour and coconut milk.

(2) Heat the oil in a vessel. Add the red curry paste. Cook for 5 minutes.

(3) Add the coconut milk, soya sauce, tulsi leaves and all the vegetables.

(4) Boil for 10 to 15 minutes. When the vegetables are cooked add salt.

(5) Boil till the curry is thick enough. Serve hot with noodles or rice.

Note : (1) Any other vegetable can be also used.

(2) 1 cup = 16 table spoons

464. Vegetables In Roasted Curry [Serves 2 to 3]

Ingredients

(1) 1 tea spoon oil

(2) 1 small onion (finely chopped)

(3) 1 small piece of ginger (paste)

(4) 6 green chillies (paste)

(5) $\frac{1}{2}$ tea spoon red chilli powder

(6) 100 grams mixed vegetables (cauliflower, potatoes, carrtos – cut into small pieces)

(7) $\frac{1}{2}$ cup water

(8) 1 table spoon corn flour (dissolved in water)

(9) 1 table spoon red curry paste

(10) Salt to taste

Method

(1) Heat the oil in a vessel. Add the onions, ginger, chillies and fry for few minutes.

(2) Add red chilli powder and all vegetables. Add $\frac{1}{2}$ cup of water. Cook till the vegetables are done.

(3) Add the corn flour and the red curry paste. Remove it from the flame when the curry is thick enough.

465. Thai Pumpkin Soup [Serves 5 to 6]

Ingredients

(1) 1 table spoon oil

(2) 1 onion (finely chopped)

(3) 1 table spoon red curry paste

(4) $1\frac{1}{2}$ cups red pumpkin (peeled and cut into small pieces)

(5) 1 cup coconut milk

(6) $\frac{1}{2}$ seasoning cube (vegetarian)

(7) 2 table spoons coriander leaves (chopped finely)

(8) Salt to taste

Method

(1) Heat the oil in a vessel. Add onions and fry for 5 minutes. Add the red curry paste and fry again for 4 minutes.

(2) Add pumpkin, coconut milk, seasoning cube and 2 cups of water. Cover the vessel with a lid and cook for 15 to 20 minutes.

(3) When the pumpkin is cooked (avoid over cooking), keep half the curry aside. Cook the remaining puree for some more time till it is thick enough.

(4) Mix bottle the purees. Add salt and coriander leaves.

Note : For making a thick soup, boil all the puree. For making thin soup, remove half of it and boil the remaining half till thick. Mix both to have a thin soup.

466. Sago Soup [Serves 4]

Ingredients

(1) 1 seasoning cube (vegetarian)

(2) 4 cups water

(3) 2 tea spoons sago

(4) 1 small onion (long thin slices)

(5) 1 carrot (cut into long thin strips)

(6) $\frac{1}{4}$ tea spoon pepper powder

(7) 1 tea spoon lime juice

(8) 1 tea spoon soya sauce

(9) $\frac{1}{2}$ tea spoon sugar

(10) Salt to taste

For serving :

(1) Thin onion rings

(2) 1 tea spoon finely chopped coriander

Method

(1) Mix 4 cups of water, 1 seasoning cube and sago. Boil for few minutes until the sago is fully cooked.

(2) Add the onions and carrots. Boil again for 5 minutes.

(3) Add salt, pepper powder, lime juice and sugar.

(4) When the soup thickens, decorate with onion rings and sprinkle finely chopped coriander leaves. Serve hot.

Note : Instead of water and seasoning cube mixture, 4 cups of vegetable stock can also be used. Seasoning cube already has some amount of salt, so reduce the amount of salt to be put in the soup.

467. White Baby Corn Soup

[Serves 4]

Ingredients

(1) 1 seasoning cube (vegetarian)

(2) 2 spring onions (finely chopped)

(3) $\frac{1}{2}$ tea spoon sugar

(4) 1 table spoon soya sauce

(5) $\frac{1}{2}$ tea spoon white pepper powder

(6) 1 cup tofu (paneer)
       (cut into small cubes)

(7) 1 tea spoon coriander (finely chopped)

(8) Salt to taste

Method

(1) Boil 4 cups of water and 1 seasoning cube. Add the spring onions, sugar, soya sauce, pepper powder and salt to taste. Boil the mixture for 5 minutes.

(2) Just before serving add the paneer cubes and boil for 2 minutes. Garnish with chopped coriander leaves. Serve hot.

Note : Instead of water and seasoning cube mixture, 4 cups of vegetable stock can also be used. Seasoning cube already has some amount of salt, so reduce the amount of salt to be put in the soup.

468. Hot and Sweet Dip

[Makes 1 cup]

Ingredients

(1) 2 table spoons vinegar

(2) $\frac{3}{4}$ cup sugar

(3) 1 cup water

(4) 1 table spoon red chilli flakes

(5) 1 table spoon salt

Method

(1) Mix vinegar, sugar and water. Boil the mixture until a thick syrup is formed.

(2) Cool the syrup slightly and add red chilli powder and salt.

(3) Keep the mixture aside for 5 hours. Reheat the mixture while serving.

Note : The proportion of vinegar and red chilli powder can be alternated according to one's taste.

469. Fried Bean Curd with Hot and Sweet Dip

[Serves 3 to 4]

Ingredients

(1) 4 cups tofu (paneer)

(2) Hot and sweet dip according to R. No. 468

(3) Oil

Method

(1) Cut the paneer into small triangles. Fry them in hot oil untill they become golden brown. Soak the paneer triangles in water for some time.

(2) Drain the water. Add them to the hot and sweet dip while serving.

Note : Paneer can be cut into various shapes as one desires.

470. Crispy Vegetables

[Serves 4]

Ingredients

(1) 400 grams mixed vegetables (capsicum, carrots, cauliflower)

(2) 1 cup maida   (3) $\frac{1}{2}$ cup corn flour

(4) 1 tea spoon sesame seeds

(5) $\frac{1}{4}$ tea spoon pepper powder

(6) Oil

(7) Salt to taste

Method

(1) Mix the flours, salt, sesame seeds, pepper powder and enough water to make a thick batter. Cut the vegetables into various shapes.

(2) Soak the vegetables in water for some time.

(3) Drain the water. Dip the vegetables in the batter and deep fry them on a low flame till they are golden brown in colour. Serve hot.

471. Crispy Fried Beans Sandwich [Serves 5 to 6]

Ingredients

(1) 1 cup mung dal

(2) 6 cloves garlic

(3) $\frac{1}{2}$ tea spoon coriander seeds

(4) A small piece of ginger

(5) $\frac{1}{2}$ tea spoon pepper powder

(6) 5 green chillies

(7) 1 tea spoon soya sauce

(8) 1 bread slice

(9) Oil   (10) 4 onions

(11) Red chilli sauce or Thai red curry paste

(12) Salt to taste

Method

(1) Soak the mung dal for 1 hour. Wash and grind it into a paste. Add salt, garlic, coriander seeds, ginger, pepper, green chillies, soya sauce and a little water to make a thick paste. Add it to the mung dal paste and mix well.

(2) Cut 4 bread slices into small pieces. Place the stuffing on the bread slice. Press well.

(3) Fry them in hot oil with the stuffing side dipped in oil. Fry till they are golden brown in colour. When they are slightly cooled, cut into 2 triangular pieces.

(4) On one triangular piece place the onions, then the red curry paste or red chilli sauce. Place the other piece above it. Serve immediately wrapped in a paper napkin.

472. Sweet Corn Cake

[Serves 5 to 6]

Ingredients

(1) 2 cups fresh corn seeds

(2) 2 table spoons red curry paste

(3) 1 table spoon soya sauce

(4) 5 table spoons rice flour

(5) Oil   (6) Salt to taste

Method

(1) Crush the corn seeds slightly in the mixer. Add the red curry paste, salt, soya sauce and rice flour to it. Mix well.

(2) Apply a little oil to your palms and roll out the mixture into small pattices. Deep fry in hot oil. Serve hot with the Dip.

473. Green Rice [Serves 4 to 5]

Ingredients

(1) 1 cup basmati rice (uncooked)

(2) 2 table spoons oil

(3) 2 cups coconut milk

(4) 1 bay leaf

(5) 3 table spoons coriander leaves (finely chopped)

(6) 2 table spoons fresh mint leaves (finely chopped)

(7) 2 green chillies (paste)

(8) Salt to taste

Method

(1) Wash and soak the rice for 2 hours. Heat the oil in a vessel. Drain the water from the rice and add them to the hot oil. Roast the rice for 5 to 7 minutes on a low flame.

(2) Add the coconut milk, bay leaf and salt.

(3) Cover the vessel with a lid and cook on a low flame. When the rice is cooked well, remove the bay leaf. Garnish with finely chopped coriander leaves, mint leaves and green chillies.

474. Thai Fried Rice

[Serves 4 to 5]

Ingredients

(1) 1½ cups basmati rice (boiled)

(2) 1 table spoon oil

(3) 3 to 4 baby corn (thin slices)

(4) 1 small capsicum (thin slices)

(5) 1 table spoon red curry paste or green curry paste

(6) 2 red or green chillies paste

(7) 3 spring onions (finely chopped)

(8) 1 table spoon soya sauce

(9) Pepper to taste

(10) Salt to taste

Method

(1) Heat the oil in a vessel. Add the baby corn, and the capsicum. Fry for 3 to 5 minutes.

(2) If you want to make green coloured rice add the green curry paste and green chilli.

(3) While making red rice add the red curry paste and red chilli powder.

(4) Add spring onions, rice, soya sauce, salt and pepper. Serve hot.

Note : The proportion of the green and the red curry paste depends upon one's taste.

475. Thai Fried Noodles

[Serves 5 to 6]

Ingredients

(1) 3 cups vermicelli (boiled)

(2) 4 table spoons oil

(3) 2 cloves garlic (paste)

(4) 1 cup paneer (cut into cubes and fried)

(5) 4 spring onions (finely chopped)

(6) 1 cup sprouted mung

(7) 2 table spoons roasted groundnuts (chopped into small pieces)

(8) 1 tea spoon red chilli powder

(9) 2 table spoons soya sauce

(10) 1 table spoon lime juice

(11) 3 tea spoons sugar

(12) Salt to taste

For serving :

(1) Small pieces of 2 table spoons roasted ground nuts

(2) 1 table spoon finely chopped onion

(3) 1 lemon rind

Method

(1) Heat the oil in a vessel. Add garlic and fry for 1 minute. Add the fried paneer, spring onions, sprouted mung, roasted groundnuts, vermicelli, salt, red chilli powder, soya sauce and sugar.

(2) Mix well. Garnish with onions and chopped coriander leaves. Sprinkle groundnut pieces. Serve hot with lemon, cut into small pieces.

Note : Prepare the dish just before serving as it cannot be reheated.

476. Puff [Makes 8 puffs]

Ingredients

(1) 250 grams maida

(2) 3 table spoons oil + oil for frying

(3) 2 table spoons malai (cream)

(4) 3 table spoons ghee

(5) 300 grams potatoes

(6) 50 grams green peas

(7) 1 tea spoon ginger-chilli paste

(8) 1 tea spoon red chilli powder

(9) 4 table spoons coriander leaves

(10) $\frac{1}{4}$ tea spoon turmeric powder

(11) 2 tea spoons garam masala

(12) 1 lime   (13) 1 table spoon sugar

(14) Garlic   (15) Salt to taste

Method

(1) Mix maida, salt, more amount of oil and a little cream.

(2) Knead a puri like dough.

(3) Make a paste by mixing maida and ghee.

(4) Mix well to make a smooth paste. Boil potatoes and green peas and mix all the masalas. Add the garlic chutney or garlic paste.

(5) Divide the dough into 3 big balls.

(6) Roll out each ball into a thick roti. Divide the roti into half (6 parts).

(7) Apply the prepared maida paste on one roti. Place the other roti over it and apply the paste on it. Place the third roti over it.

(8) Spread the prepared masala over it and give shape like dosa. Spread the masala on its half portion and put the layer of roti on it. Press its ends.

(9) Cut it into three portions again, press its ends.

(10) Fry them on a low flame. Puffs baked in the oven.

(11) Serve the puffs with coriander chutney and tomato ketchup.

Variation

Spread coriander chutney over the puff. Add finely chopped onions over it. Spread tomato ketchup over it. Sprinkle grated cheese on it. Bake it in hot oven for 5 minutes. Serve hot.

477. Pizza [Makes 4]

Various recipes for the dough

Ingredients 1

(1) 2 cups maida

(2) 3 to 4 table spoons ghee

(3) 1 tea spoon soda

(4) $\frac{1}{2}$ tea spoon a little citric acid

(5) Salt to taste

Method 1

(1) Add ghee to the maida. Mix the other ingredients and knead a semi soft dough using luke warm water. Allow the dough to rest for 4 to 6 hours in the sun or any warm place.

(2) Prepare a thick roti and put it on a non-stick pan. Cover with a lid and roast it on both the sides.

Ingredients 2

(1) 2 cups maida

(2) $\frac{3}{4}$ cup warm water

(3) 1 tea spoon sugar

(4) $1\frac{1}{2}$ to 2 tea spoons fresh or dry yeast

(5) 3 table spoons oil or ghee

(6) Salt to taste

Method 2

(1) Dissolve the sugar in a bowl of luke warm water. Then add the yeast to it.

(2) Cover the vessel with a lid. Keep aside for 10 minutes. When the yeast dissolves in the water, add oil to it.

(3) Mix the flour, salt, yeast and add enough warm water to make a soft dough.

(4) Apply a little oil to the palms. Knead the dough for 5 to 10 minutes.

(5) Cover the dough and allow it to rest in the sun or a warm place for 4 to 6 hours. When the dough is almost double in size, knead it again. Divide the dough into medium size balls.

(6) Press flat with the help of a flat surface e.g. a dish, using enough maida if required. Apply a little oil and sprinkle grated cheese. Cover with a lid and bake in a hot oven.

Ingredients 3

(1) 2 cups maida

(2) 2 tea spoons baking powder

(3) A little curds   (4) Salt to taste

Method 3

(1) Mix all the ingredients and make a soft dough by adding water. Knead well.

(2) Allow it to rest for 7 to 8 hours. Divide the dough into medium size balls.

(3) Press flat with the help of a flat surface e.g. a dish. Cover with a lid and bake in a hot oven.

Ingredients 4

(1) 200 grams maida

(2) 1 tea spoon baking powder

(3) 3 table spoons ghee

(4) $\frac{3}{4}$ cup milk   (5) Salt to taste

Method 4

(1) Sieve the maida and baking powder. Mix all the ingredients and make a soft dough.

(2) Allow it to rest in a warm place.

(3) Divide the dough into medium size balls. Press flat with the flat surface e.g. a dish. Place in a greased baking dish. Bake in a hot oven.

Ingredients 5

(1) $\frac{3}{4}$ cup curds

(2) 1 tea spoon soda

(3) 1 tea spoon sugar

(4) 2 cups maida   (5) Salt to taste

Method 5

Same as method 4.

Note : (1) Substitute fresh yeast by using a mixture of $\frac{1}{2}$ tea spoon soda, $\frac{1}{2}$ cup sour curds, $\frac{1}{2}$ tea spoon sugar, $\frac{1}{2}$ tea spoon salt. Mix all ingredients and keep aside for 5 minutes.

(2) Then use it for kneading the dough. Allow the dough to rest for 2 hours.

(3) If you like soft pizzas, add curds in the dough.

(4) If you like hard pizza then add less curds or avoid curds. Instead use citric acid.

(5) Pizza's can be also made by adding enough ghee to the maida. Add salt and a pinch of soda. Allow the dough to rest for 3 hours.

Variation

Quick Pizza :

(1) Substitute the pizza base by the regular bread slices are used. Remove the crust from the bread slices.

(2) Apply a little butter and toast the bread slice till it becomes, light brown in colour. Spread a little gravy, finely chopped onions and capsicum slices. Sprinkle grated cheese. Serve immediately.

478. Pizza Gravy
[Makes gravy for 4 pizzas]

Ingredients

(1) 500 grams tomatoes

(2) 2 table spoons oil

(3) A pinch omum

(4) 1 onion (finely chopped)

(5) 5 cloves garlic (paste)

(6) $\frac{1}{2}$ tea spoon sugar

(7) $\frac{1}{2}$ tea spoon red chilli powder

(8) 1 tea spoon corn flour   or
       1 table spoon maida

(9) 2 table spoons grated cheese

(10) Salt to taste

Method 1

(1) Boil the tomatoes for few minutes. When cool, grind them. Make a thick soup by passing through a sieve.

(2) Heat the oil in a vessel, add the omum and onions. Fry for few minutes. Add the remaining ingredients.

(3) Dissolve the corn flour in a little tomato soup. Add it to the gravy. Cook the gravy till it is thick.

Method 2

(1) Chop 1 onion, $\frac{1}{2}$ tomato and 2 cloves of garlic.

(2) Heat a little ghee in a vessel. Add the onions and fry for few seconds. Add garlic and tomatoes and fry again for few minutes. Add the sauce and salt. Boil for few minutes.

Method 3

(1) Crush onions, tomatoes, garlic, ginger and green chillies together. Heat some oil in a vessel. Fry the paste for few minutes.

(2) Add salt, red chilli powder, sugar, cloves cinnamon powder, pepper powder and garam masala. Add

enough amount of grated cheese to the mixture. Boil till the mixture thickens.

Method 4

(1) Prepare the tomato filling.

(2) Add boiled vegetables to it. (finely chopped cauliflower, carrots, potatoes, french beans, green peas etc.), or you can place the vegetables on the pizza base and then pour the tomato filling over it.

For Serving :

(1) You can roast the pizza on the griddle or a non-stick pan. Cover it with a deep dish. Roast the pizza until it is light brown from the base.

(2) Turn the base upside down and spread the gravy or tomato ketchup over it.

(3) Arrange the capsicum rings and finely chopped onions over it.

(4) Sprinkle grated cheese and roast again on a low flame for few minutes. Sprinkle more grated cheese while serving. Cut into pieces and serve hot.

Note : (1) You can prepare pizza without the oven by the above method. Pizza base can be prepared in advance.

(2) While serving, just reheat the pizza base and spread the gravy over it. Arrange the capsicums and finely chopped onions over it. Sprinkle grated cheese before serving.

479. Italian Tomato Vermicelli Soup [Serves 5]

Ingredients

(1) $\frac{1}{4}$ cup vermicelli
       (broken into small pieces)

(2) 2 table spoons butter

(3) $\frac{1}{4}$ cup onions (grated)

(4) 1 table spoon coriander leaves (finely chopped)

(5) 150 grams tomatoes (boiled, peeled and crushed)

(6) 3 cups hot water

(7) 1 cheese cube (grated)

(8) $\frac{1}{2}$ tea spoon pepper powder

(9) A pinch omum

(10) $\frac{1}{2}$ tea spoon tobasco sauce

(11) Salt to taste

Method

(1) Heat 1 table spoon of butter in vessel. Add the vermicelli and roast it on a low flame for 5 minutes. Remove it in a dish when it is roasted.

(2) Heat 1 table spoon of butter in the same vessel, add onions and fry for 4 minutes.

(3) Add coriander leaves, tomato puree, hot water, $\frac{1}{2}$ cheese cube (grated), salt, pepper powder, omum and the roasted vermicelli.

(4) Boil for 10 to 12 minutes. Stir constantly.

(5) Add $\frac{1}{2}$ tea spoon of tobasco sauce. Sprinkle grated cheese and serve hot.

480. Cheese Macaroni
[Serves 3 to 4]

Ingredients

(1) 1 cup macaroni (boiled)

(2) 2 table spoons ghee

(3) 2 table spoons maida

(4) 2 cups milk

(5) $\frac{1}{2}$ tea spoon pepper powder

(6) 1 tea spoon sugar

(7) 1 capsicum (optional)

(8) A little rawa

(9) 1 to 2 cheese cubes

(10) Tomato ketchup   (11) Salt to taste

Method

(1) In plenty of water add the macaroni and a little salt. Cook in a pressure cooker upto 4 whistles.

(2) Heat a little ghee in a vessel. Add the maida and roast it for a few minutes. Add the milk slowly and stir constantly.

(3) Prepare the white sauce. Add salt, pepper powder and sugar to the sauce. Wash the macaroni in running water. Add the macaroni to the white sauce.

(4) Add the chopped capsicums. Boil the mixture for few minutes. Pour the mixture in a greased baking dish. Sprinkle a little rawa and grated cheese over it.

(5) Bake in a hot oven for few minutes.

(6) While serving, add tomato ketchup and sprinkle grated cheese to it.

Variation

Boiled vegetables can also be added. To make vegetable macaroni, steam the vegetables like french beans, carrots and green peas.

481. Spaghetti [Serves 3 to 4]

Ingredients

(1) 1 cup spaghetti (boiled)

(2) 1 tea spoon oil

(3) 2 cups white sauce (4) Cheese

(5) Tomato ketchup   (6) Salt to taste

Method

(1) Heat plenty of water in a vessel. When the water starts boiling add a little salt and the spaghetti to it. Add a little oil to it.

(2) When it is half cooked, drain into a colander and wash under running water. Add a little oil to keep the spaghetti separate.

(3) Mix the spaghetti with the white sauce. Cook it till it is thick enough. Sprinkle grated cheese and tomato ketchup over it. Serve hot.

482. Cheese Spaghetti *OR* Macaroni with Pineapple

[Serves 5 to 6]

Ingredients

(1) 1 cup pineapple pieces
(2) 4 table spoons sugar
(3) 2 cups white sauce
(4) $\frac{1}{2}$ tea spoon pepper powder
(5) 1 cup boiled spaghetti or macaroni
(6) Cheese
(7) Tomato sauce
(8) 1 capsicum
(9) 2 tomatoes
(10) Salt to taste

Method

(1) Chop the pineapple into small pieces. Add the sugar and cook in the pressure cooker upto 1 whistle.

(2) Prepare the white sauce.

(3) Add salt, pepper powder, pineapple along with the syrup and macaroni or spaghetti to the white sauce.

(4) Boil it for a few minutes. Remove it from the flame.

(5) Serve hot with grated cheese and tomato sauce. It can also be baked in a hot oven.

Note : You can also arrange capsicum and tomato rings on it and sprinkle grated cheese.

483. Baked Vegetables

[Serves 4 to 5]

Ingredients

(1) 4 potatoes
(2) 4 slices pineapple
(3) 100 grams carrots
(4) 100 grams french beans
(5) 100 grams green peas
(6) 2 cups white sauce
(7) $\frac{1}{2}$ tea spoon pepper powder
(8) 1 table spoon sugar
(9) 1 table spoon ghee
(10) 1 table spoon maida
(11) 2 cubes cheese   (12) A little rawa
(13) Tomato ketchup (14) Salt to taste

Method

(1) Chop the potatoes and pineapple into small square pieces. Chop the carrots and french beans finely. Boil all the vegetables including green peas and pineapple. Drain in a colander.

(2) Prepare the white sauce by mixing $\frac{1}{2}$ cup maida, $1\frac{1}{4}$ cups cold milk and a little water. Boil the mixture till it is thick enough. Add salt, pineapple and pepper powder to it.

(3) Mix vegetables, sugar and salt.

(4) Grease and dust a baking dish. Spread grated cheese at the base. Then pour the mixture over it.

(5) Sprinkle grated cheese and rawa over it. Bake it on a high flame for 10 minutes and then on a low flame. Remove it from the flame when the upper layer becomes crispy and the lower layer starts sticking. It can also be baked in a hot oven.

Note : (1) You may substitute rawa by 2 or 3 marie or glucose biscuits (powdered). It would make the layer more crispy.

(2) Fill the lower dish of the handwa maker with sand.

(3) 1 cup boiled spaghetti may be added.

484. Mixed Baked Dish

[Serves 4 to 5]

Ingredients

(1) 4 slices pineapple

(2) 200 grams mixed vegetables (potatoes, french beans, carrots, green peas)

(3) 2 cups white sauce

(4) 100 grams macaroni

(5) 100 grams spaghetti

(6) 1 tea spoon sugar　(7) Salt to taste

Method

(1) Boil all ingredients except white sauce.

(2) Mix the vegetables with the white sauce. Add salt and sugar. This dish requires less sugar.

(3) Bake as that given for R. No. 483.

485. Baked Dish

Ingredients

For the gravy :

(1) 150 grams maida

(2) 700 ml milk　(3) 200 grams butter

(4) A little pepper powder

(5) Salt to taste

Method

(1) Heat the butter in a vessel. Roast the maida in it for few minutes.

(2) Add the milk slowly while constant stirring. Add salt and pepper powder. Instead of butter, ghee also may be used.

(3) The gravy for baked dish is prepared in this manner.

(4) Various other ingredients can be added to make various baked dishes like corn, cabbage, spinach.

(5) Paneer, small samosas, small kachoris, potatoes, yam, carrots, french beans, cauliflower or kidney beans can be also added.

(6) For preparing white gravy baked dish, add the vegetables into white gravy.

(7) For preparing red gravy baked dish, add the tomato ketchup to the white gravy.

(8) For preparing green coloured baked dish add spinach paste to the white gravy.

(9) Prepare white, red or green gravy by the method mentioned above. For preparing paneer baked dish, make any one of the gravy of your choice.

Variation

For corn baked dish, mix boiled corn with this gravy.

486. Stuffed Toast

[Serves 4 to 5]

Ingredients

(1) 150 grams paneer

(2) 1 big onion　　(3) 2 capsicums

(4) 2 table spoons butter

(5) $\frac{1}{2}$ cup tomato ketchup

(6) 2 table spoons chilli sauce

(7) $\frac{1}{4}$ tea spoon red chilli powder

(8) 1 big packet sandwich bread

(9) Cheese　　　(10) Salt to taste

Method

(1) Chop the paneer, onion and capsicums finely.

(2) Heat the butter in a vessel. Add the onions and fry for few minutes.

(3) Add the capsicums, paneer, tomato

ketchup, chilli sauce, red chilli powder and salt. Mix well.

(4) Toast the bread slices and cut them into small rounds with the help of a katori.

(5) Apply butter to it, spread the mixture, and cheese over one slice. Cover with other buttered toast.

(6) Toast the sandwiches in a toaster or by cooking on a griddle until they are crisp and brown on either side.

Note : Bake the sandwich in a hot oven for 10 minutes before serving. Serve hot.

(16) BISCUITS

487. Coconut Biscuits

Ingredients

(1) 1 cup ghee
(2) 1 tea spoon baking powder
(3) $2\frac{1}{2}$ cups maida (4) $\frac{1}{2}$ cup rawa
(5) 1 cup desiccated coconut
(6) 1 tea spoon nutmeg powder
(7) 1 tea spoon cardamom powder
(8) $1\frac{1}{4}$ cups powdered sugar (sieved)

Method

(1) Cream the ghee very well until light and creamy. Add 1 tea spoon baking powder and all other ingredients.

(2) Add a little milk and mix well. A little milk makes them soft.

(3) Shape the biscuits into small rounds. Arrange them on a well greased baking tin.

(4) Bake in a hot oven for 15 to 20 minutes at 180° C or 350° F. Cool the biscuits.

Note : (1) Do not add a lot of milk or the biscuits would become hard.

(2) The proportion of desiccated coconut can be increased if desired.

488. Kaju Biscuits

Ingredients

Substitute desiccated coconut with

$\frac{1}{2}$ cup of cashewnut powder. Rest of the ingredients are same as that given for R. No. 487.

Method

As per coconut biscuits.

Variation

Chocolate Biscuits : Substitute desiccated coconut with sufficient quantity of cocoa powder.

489. Cocoa Coil Biscuits

Ingredients

(1) 125 grams butter
(2) 1 cup sugar
(3) A little less than $\frac{1}{2}$ cup milk
(4) $\frac{1}{2}$ tea spcon soda
(5) 250 grams maida
(6) 3 tea spoons cocoa powder

Method

(1) Cream the butter, sugar, soda and milk very well until light and creamy.

(2) Sieve the flour and add to the cream mixture.

(3) Divide the mixture into two equal parts. Add sieved cocoa powder to one portion. Mix and knead well. Divide the dough into equal small balls. Roll out each dough of both the colours.

(4) Place both the rotis with cocoa on the another roti. Roll up like a swiss roll. Cut into thick slices. Press by hand.

(5) Roll them lightly. Arrange the biscuits in a greased baking tin. Bake the biscuits in a moderately hot oven for few minutes until done.

490. Badam Biscuits

Ingredients

(1) 4 table spoons butter

(2) $\frac{1}{2}$ cup powdered sugar

(3) $\frac{1}{3}$ cup (50 grams) icing sugar

(4) 2 to 3 drops almond or vanilla essence

(5) $\frac{1}{2}$ cup maida

(6) $\frac{1}{4}$ tea spoon baking powder

(7) 8 table spoons almond powder ($\frac{1}{2}$ cup)

(8) 2 table spoons milk

(9) A few almond pieces and glazed cherries for decoration.

Method

(1) Cream the butter very well until it is light and creamy. Add sugar and cream again.

(2) Sieve the flour and baking powder together. Mix the almond powder to the flour.

(3) Mix the cream mixture. Add just enough milk to make a soft dough. Divide the dough into small balls. Press them and roll very lightly.

(4) Grease a baking tin and arrange the biscuits leaving a little space between them.

(5) Top with almonds and small slices of glazed cherries. Refrigerate the tray for half an hour.

(6) Bake the biscuits in a hot oven at 180° C (350° F) for 15 to 20 minutes.

(7) When the biscuits become light pink at the base, remove the baking tin from the oven. Cool the biscuits on the tray and then remove. Store in an air tight container.

491. Cashew-Choco Biscuits

Ingredients

(1) 100 grams butter

(2) 100 grams powdered sugar

(3) 2 to 3 drops almond or vanilla essence

(4) 100 grams maida

(5) $1\frac{1}{2}$ table spoons cocoa powder

(6) 100 grams cashewnut powder

Method

(1) Cream the butter very well. Add the sugar and cream well again.

(2) Sieve the flour and cocoa powder together. Add the cashewnut powder to it and mix well.

(3) Mix the cream mixture.

(4) Refrigerate the mixture for half an hour. Divide the mixture into big balls. Roll out each ball into a big and thick roti. Cut with a round biscuit cutter. In every alternate biscuit, make a hole in the centre.

(5) Grease and dust a baking tin.

(6) Arrange the biscuits on it and bake in a moderate oven at 350° F (180° C) for 15 to 20 minutes. Remove it when they become light pink coloured at the base. Cool the biscuits.

(7) Make pairs of one biscuits with hole and the other without the hole.

For the butter icing :

(1) Cream 1 table spoon soft butter until it is soft and white.

(2) Worn in 6 to 7 table spoons sieved icing sugar, with 2 drops of vanilla essence and colouring as required.

(3) If the icing is very soft add more amount of icing sugar and if it is too thick then add a little more butter to it. The icing should be very smooth so that it can spread properly.

(4) Sandwich the biscuits with vanilla butter icing.

492. Walnut Biscuits

Ingredients

(1) 8 table spoons butter
(2) $\frac{1}{2}$ cup powdered sugar
(3) 2 to 3 drops vanilla essence
(4) 2 cups maida
(5) $\frac{1}{4}$ tea spoon soda
(6) 1 tea spoon cocoa powder
(7) 4 table spoons walnut powder

Method

(1) Cream the butter and sugar very well till the mixture is light and creamy.
(2) Sieve the flour, soda and cocoa powder together. Mix the walnut powder to it.
(3) Mix the cream mixture. Add just enough milk to make a soft dough. Divide the dough into two balls.
(4) Roll out each ball into a thin roti in between two plastics.
(5) Cut with a round biscuit cutter.
(6) Grease a baking tin and arrange the biscuits on it. Refrigerate the tray for half an hour.
(7) Bake the biscuits in a hot oven at 180° C or 350° F for 15 to 20 minutes. Cool the biscuits and store in a air tight container.

493. Peanut Biscuits

Ingredients

(1) 150 grams maida
(2) A pinch soda
(3) $\frac{1}{4}$ tea spoon pepper powder
(4) 80 grams butter
(5) 75 grams grated cheese
(6) $\frac{1}{2}$ tea spoon maid mustard (powdered mustard dal) (optional)
(7) 5 table spoons salted peanuts (powdered coarsely)
(8) $\frac{1}{2}$ tea spoon salt

Method

(1) Sieve the flour, salt, soda and pepper powder together.
(2) Add the butter, cheese, mustard powder and 50 grams of peanut powder (remove the skin).
(3) Add just enough cold water to make a soft dough. Divide the dough into big balls. Roll out each ball into a thick and big roti. Brush the roti with milk. Sprinkle the remaining peanut powder over it and press lightly.
(4) Cut the roti into long strips and place them in a greased baking dish. Bake in a hot oven at 180° C or 350° F for 15 to 20 minutes.
(5) Cool them and store in an air tight container.

494. Butter Biscuits

Ingredients

(1) 250 grams butter
(2) 6 table spoons powdered sugar
(3) $\frac{1}{2}$ tea spoon vanilla essence
(4) 250 grams maida
(5) 1 cup cashewnut pieces or walnut pieces
(6) A little icing sugar

Method

(1) Cream the butter.
(2) Add the sugar and cream again very well till the mixture is light and creamy. Add the vanilla essence. Sieve the flour and add the walnut or cashewnut powder to it. Add the cream mixture and make a soft dough.
(3) Divide the dough into small balls. Place the ball in a greased baking dish. Refrigerate the tray for half an hour.

(4) Then bake the biscuits in a hot oven at 180° C or 350° F for 15 to 20 minutes.

(5) Remove the biscuits and roll in icing sugar when they are still hot.

495. Chocolate Bits Biscuits

Ingredients

(1) 120 grams (8 table spoons) butter

(2) $\frac{3}{4}$ cup sugar   (3) $1\frac{1}{4}$ cups maida

(4) $\frac{3}{4}$ tea spoon baking powder

(5) A pinch soda

(6) 2 to 3 drops vanilla essence

(7) 240 grams cooking chocolate

(8) $\frac{1}{4}$ tea spoon salt

Method

(1) Cream the butter. Add the sugar and cream well again till light and creamy.

(2) Sieve the flour, baking powder, soda and salt together. Mix a little vanilla essence and 2 tea spoons of water to the creamed butter.

(3) Mix the flour mixture. Add the chocolate pieces. Add just enough water to make a semi-liquid batter.

(4) Place 1 tea spoon of the batter in a greased baking dish. Leaving enough distance between the biscuits. Bake the biscuits in a hot oven at 180° C or 350° F for 15 to 20 minutes.

Chocolate topping :

(1) For chocolate topping on any biscuit with chocolate melt the chocolate in a double boiler. Cool it a little.

(2) Spread the melted chocolate on top of the biscuits with a spoon.

496. Kesar Nankhatai

Ingredients

(1) 50 grams ghee

(2) 50 grams powdered sugar

(3) $\frac{1}{2}$ tea spoon cardamom powder

(4) A pinch nutmeg powder

(5) 1 tea spoon milk

(6) 2 pinches saffron (dissolved in milk)

(7) 1 tea spoon curds

(8) A pinch soda

(9) 50 grams maida   (10) 50 grams rawa

Method

(1) Cream the ghee well. Add sugar and cream again very well until the mixture is light and creamy.

(2) Add cardamom powder, nutmeg powder, saffron, curds and soda-bi-carb and mix well.

(3) Sieve the flour and rawa together. Add the flour mixture to the cream mixture and knead well. Form into small rounds.

(4) Arrange on a greased baking tin and bake in a moderately hot. Oven at 180° C or 350° F for 25 to 30 minutes.

(5) Cool and store in air tight containers.

497. Aneri Special Mixed Fruit Toffee (Chocolate)

Ingredients

(1) 2 apples   (2) 2 chikoos

(3) 200 grams pineapple (i.e. 300 grams fruit pulp)

(4) 3 tea spoons glucose powder

(5) 3 tea spoons sugar

(6) 3 tea spoons butter or ghee

(7) 3 tea spoons cocoa powder

(8) 3 tea spoons drinking chocolate

(9) Milkmaid

(10) A few drops edible colour

(11) A few drops essence as desired

Method

(1) Wash the fruits well. Cut fruits like apples and pineapple into small pieces and boil them for 15 to 20 minutes.

(2) Take water just enough to cover the fruits. Stir constantly.

(3) For soft fruits like chikoo, mash them to make a pulp. Mix all the fruit pulps and cook until the pulp is reduced upto $\frac{1}{3}$ of the quantity.

(4) Then add glucose powder, sugar and butter of ghee. Lower the flame and add cocoa powder and chocolate powder.

(5) When the mixture is thick enough add a little milkmaid to it and cook for sometime. (Substitute milkmaid by 6 table spoons milk and 3 table spoons sugar. Boil it till the mixture is thick. Cool and use.)

(6) Add the desired colour (dissolved in a little milk). Remove the mixture from the flame. Cool a little and add the essence.

(7) Grease a dish with butter. Spread the mixture in the dish. Shape the toffees as desired.

Note : (1) If the mixture is very soft, add more milk powder. Walnut pieces also may be added. Place the toffees in colourful toffee papers.

(2) Any seasonal fruits can be used.

498. Non-Cooked Chocolate

Ingredients

(1) 4 table spoons icing sugar

(2) 4 table spoons milk powder

(3) 4 table spoons drinking chocolate

(4) 2 table spoons walnut powder

(5) 1 tea spoon cocoa powder

(6) 1 tea spoon milk

Method

(1) Mix all the ingredients. Add just enough cold water to make a soft dough. Apply a little ghee to your hands and divide the dough into small balls. Shape them into small rounds by hand or place them in greased chocolate moulds.

(2) Cashew, almonds or peanut pieces can be stuffed in between.

Note : If the chocolate is very soft, add more milk powder or icing sugar as required.

(17) CAKES, ICING

499. Chocolate Cake
[Makes 6 pieces]

Ingredients

(1) 24 Parle Glucose Biscuits (Marie)

(2) 2 to 3 tea spoons coffee

(3) $\frac{1}{2}$ cup fresh cream

(4) A little drinking chocolate

(5) 100 grams icing sugar

(6) 100 grams margarine (butter)

(7) Any jam (pineapple, mixed fruit, strawberry, etc.)

(8) 4 walnuts or a few cashewnuts and cherries

For the cream mixture : Strain 2 table spoons cream to remove any left over milk. Sieve 1 table spoon icing sugar and 2 table spoons drinking chocolate, for 2 to 3 times. Mix it to the cream and beat well.

For the butter mixture : 4 table spoons butter or margarine, 3 table spoons drinking chocolate powder and 5 table spoons icing sugar. Mix all the ingredients well.

Method

(1) Boil half cup of water, add 2 tea spoons of coffee and switch off the gas. Strain and cool it. Grease the serving dish.

(2) Dip the biscuits into the coffee untill they lose their crispness. Place 6 softened biscuits near each other.

(3) Spread half of the cream mixture over 6 biscuits.

(4) Repeat the layers of biscuits softened in water with coffee added.

(5) Spread a layer of jam over it.

(6) Again place a layer of softened biscuits.

(7) Spread the remaining half of the cream mixture over it.

(8) Again place a layer of softened biscuits.

(9) Spread the butter mixture all over the biscuits. Decorate with walnuts.

This cake has 6 layers of biscuits. You can make the cake of 1, 2, 3, 4, 5, 7 layers also and of different shapes.

Note : If you like your cake to be sweet then use glucose biscuits otherwise use marie biscuits. Refrigerate this cake for atleast 1 hour before serving. Store this cake in the fridge.

500. Black Forest Cake (1)
[Makes 25 to 30 pieces]

Ingredients

(1) 200 grams butter (homemade or outer)

(2) 250 to 300 grams powdered sugar

(3) 225 grams maida

(4) 200 grams milk powder

(5) 1 level tea spoon soda

(6) 1 level tea spoon baking powder

(7) 2 table spoons drinking chocolate

(8) 6 to 8 table spoons cocoa powder

(9) 350 ml Thumps Up or Coke or Pepsi

Method

(1) Beat the butter well. Add the sugar and beat well again until the mixture is light and creamy.

(2) Sieve the flour, milk powder, drinking chocolate, soda, baking powder and cocoa together twice.

(3) Go on adding the flour mixture to the creamed butter, 1 spoon at a time. Go on mixing well. Do this until the mixture becomes harder. Then add all the remaining flour mixture together and mix very well with hand.

(4) Add 350 ml of Thumps Up and mix well, so that no lumps are formed.

(5) Grease and dust a baking tin of the handava cooker. Fill the lower vessel with sand. Heat the sand by heating the vessel for few minutes.

(6) Then pour the cake mixture into the baking tin and cook it on a high flame for 5 to 10 minutes.

(7) Then cook it on a low flame for another 20 minutes. When the cake leaves the sides of the tin, it is said to be 'done.' Remove the cake from the flame. Cool the cake for 20 minutes.

(8) Then turn the tin upside down and remove the cake. Divide the cake into 2 parts horizontally. Place the frosting on the lower part. Put the other part on the top and press well.

(9) Decorate the cake with the frosting on all sides. Proceed for icing on the top.

Note : (1) You can bake the cake in oven at 100° C for 25 to 30 minutes.

(2) If you want dark coloured cake then add more amount of cocoa powder.

501. Black Forest Cake (2)
[Makes 20 to 25 pieces]

Ingredients

(1) $2\frac{1}{4}$ cups maida

(2) 1 tea spoon baking powder

(3) 1 tea spoon soda-bi-carb

(4) $\frac{1}{4}$ tea spoon salt

(5) 350 grams $1\frac{2}{3}$ cups $(1 + \frac{1}{3} + \frac{1}{3})$ fine sugar granules (Do not use powdered sugar)

(6) $\frac{2}{3}$ cup cocoa powder (6 table spoons)

(7) 2 eggs

(8) 2 packets butter (700 grams)

(9) $1\frac{1}{4}$ cups water

(10) $\frac{1}{4}$ tea spoon vanilla essence

Method

(1) Sieve the flour, baking powder, soda-bi-carb and salt together twice.

(2) In a vessel, mix sugar, cocoa powder, eggs, butter, water and vanilla essence together. Additional water may be added if required.

(3) Beat the ingredients very well till light and fluffy. Add the flour mixture and beat well again.

(4) Grease and dust the baking tin.

(5) Pour the cake mixture into the prepared tin. Bake in a hot oven at 100° C for 15 to 20 minutes.

(6) Cool the cake and divide horizontally into two parts. Place the frosting on the lower layer. Put the other part on the top and press well.

For the butter icing :

(1) For frosting in R. N. 500 & 501, mix 100 grams sieved icing sugar in 50 grams butter.

(2) For making chocolate butter icing add cocoa to the butter icing. For glazed icing sprinkle sugar water.

502. Frosting, Icing

(1) Frosting and icing are made with butter, milk or water and icing sugar. Frosting is an excellent coating over the cakes.

(2) It can be either white or coloured.

(3) Frosting should be like a paste that can be easily spread with a knife.

(4) After doing the frosting keep it aside for sometime so that the icing sugar would set. The design on this frosting is called icing.

(5) If the frosting has dried up too much the icing would not stick properly to it. A little warm water can be applied on the frosting.

(6) Icing can be placed in a plastic cone and sealed with a thread and stored for a longer period of time in the fridge. White using remove it from the fridge one hour before and then a little warm water to the cone and mix well.

Ingredients

1. Glaze frosting :

(1) 120 grams icing sugar

(2) 2 tea spoons hot water

(3) $\frac{1}{2}$ tea spoon lime juice

(4) Mix all the ingredients very well. If the mixture is thin, add additional amount of sugar and if the mixture is too thick, add additional amount of warm water.

2. (1) 2 table spoons water

(2) $\frac{1}{4}$ cup sugar

(3) 1 table spoon cocoa

(4) 3 table spoons corn flour (dissolved in water)

(5) Mix all the ingredients together and heat them for a few minutes. Remove it from the flame and add 2 to 3 table spoons of ghee or butter to it.

503. Whipped Cream Frosting

Ingredients

(1) $\frac{3}{4}$ tea spoon gelatine

(2) 1 table spoon water

(3) 250 grams cream or soft butter

(4) 4 table spoons icing sugar

(5) 1 drop vanilla essence

Method

(1) Mix the gelatine in a little water and soak it for 5 minutes.

(2) Heat on a low flame for 2 minutes until it dissolves completely. Refrigerate the cream. Mix the gelatine solution and cream.

(3) Refrigerate it for 1 hour. Beat the cream well. Add the sugar and mix well. When it is thick enough add the essence. Spread the cream on the cake with a cone or knife.

Note : Instead of vanilla, cocoa can also be added.

504. Chocolate Butter Icing

Ingredients

(1) 1 table spoon butter

(2) 6 to 8 table spoons icing sugar

(3) 2 table spoons cocoa powder

Method

(1) Cream all the ingredients together.

(2) To make a firmer icing additional icing sugar may be added or if it is too thick, additional butter can be added. It is filled in a cone for piping.

505. Icing

Ingredients

(1) A little pure ghee, butter or dalda ghee

(2) 4 to 5 table spoons icing sugar

(3) A little milk

(4) 2 to 3 drops water

Method

(1) Mix all the ingredients and knead into a soft dough.

(2) This dough can be used to make flowers, leaves, steam, etc. It can be softened and filled into the piping bag for piping out floweres etc.

(3) Gems, jintan, grated chocolate, cherries, tuti-fruiti, dry fruits or various fresh fruits can also be used for decoration.

(4) To colour the icing add a few drops of edible colour to the basic icing.

(5) You can make pan out of green coloured icing. White coloured icing can be used for writing a name or a message on chocolate frosting. It looks very nice.

506. Chocolate Pudding

[Serves 7 to 8]

Ingredients

(1) 1 litre milk

(2) 5 table spoons drinking chocolate

(3) $2\frac{1}{2}$ table spoons cocoa powder

(4) 2 table spoons custard powder

(5) 1 table spoon coffee powder

(6) 5 table spoons sugar

(7) 25 grams cashewnuts powder, walnut powder

(8) 3 table spoons gelatine

(9) 200 grams marie biscuits

Method

(1) Sieve all the powders separately. Boil the milk with sugar. Dissolve the custard powder in a little cold milk.

(2) When the milk starts boiling, add the custard powder to it. Stir constantly. Add drinking chocolate, cocoa powder and coffee one by one. Add kaju and walnut powder.

(3) Boil $\frac{1}{2}$ cup of water and add the gelatine to it. Boil the gelatine mixture for a few minutes. Add this gelatine mixture to the boiling milk mixture. Remove it from the flame.

(4) Add 100 grams marie biscuit powder.

(5) Divide the remaining biscuits into 2 pieces. Place pieces of marie biscuits in a serving bowl. Pour a few spoons full of the prepared mixture over it.

(6) Again place pieces of marie biscuits over it and pour the prepared mixture over it.

(7) Place the serving bowl in the deep fridge for setting. When the pudding is partially set, sprinkle cashewnuts

and walnut powder over it. Again put it in the freezer.

Note : (1) Do not place the bowl in the freezer for a long time as the glass bowl might break. After some time place the serving bowl in the lower compartment of the refrigerator.

(2) Cut the pudding into pieces and serve.

507. Fruit Pudding

[Serves 7 to 8]

Ingredients

(1) 125 grams strawberry jelly

(2) 2 tea spoons sugar

(3) 200 to 250 grams fruit cake

(4) 1 banana

(5) 1 small apple

(6) 150 grams grapes

(7) 1 orange (chikoo or other seasonal fruits may also be added)

(8) 1 cup cream

Method

(1) Take 250 ml of water. Boil 125 ml of water out of that. When the water starts boiling, add 2 tea spoons of sugar to it. When it starts boiling, remove it from the flame.

(2) Add the jelly powder to it. Stir constantly until the jelly crystals dissolve. Add the remaining 125 ml of water to it. Pour the jelly into the mould and put to set in the refrigerator.

(3) It would set completely within $1\frac{1}{2}$ to 2 hours.

(4) Place a little powdered cake in the serving dish. Cover the cake powder with small pieces of fruits.

(5) Cut the jelly into small pieces. Place the jelly pieces on the fruits.

(6) Mix a little milk, sugar and cream together. Beat them well until it is thick. Pour this beaten cream over the jelly layer. Again arrange the fruits on the cream. Cover the cream with the cake. Again cover the cake with the beaten cream.

(7) Decorate with cherries, grapes and apple cut into long slices. Serve it chilled. In this pudding the proportion of any ingredients may be changed if desired (depending on the availability of fruit).

Note : The quantity of water to be added is different for every company. So the quantity of water should be added as written on the packet.

508. Mango Pudding
[Serves 4]
Ingredients

(1) 1 cup mango pulp
(alphanso or payari)

(2) $1\frac{1}{2}$ tea spoons gelatine

(3) 200 grams cream

(4) 5 to 6 table spoons powdered sugar

(5) $\frac{1}{2}$ tea spoon orange essence

(6) 1 tea spoon lime juice

Method

(1) Dissolve the gelatine in 4 table spoons of hot water. If it starts getting thick then it can be reheated, or place the bowl in a container of hot water.

(2) Place the cream in a bowl with ice. Add sugar to the cream and beat well with a hand mixer.

(3) Remove the cream container from the ice container and add the mango pulp and lime juice.

(4) Add the gelatine and mix well. When set, decorate with mango pieces and tuti fruiti. Serve chilled.

509. Orange Pudding
[Serves 5 to 7]
Ingredients

(1) 125 grams orange jelly

(2) 200 to 250 grams vanilla ice cream

(3) 3 oranges (pieces)

Method

(1) Prepare the orange jelly by dissolving the jelly crystals in hot water and place the refrigerator for setting.

(2) Add vanilla ice cream and orange pieces to the partially set jelly.

(3) Set in the refrigerator unmould while serving.

510. Kasata Pudding
[Serves 4 to 6]
Ingredients

(1) 4 cups milk

(2) $2\frac{1}{2}$ table spoons sugar

(3) 4 table spoons custard powder

(4) 2 cups cream   (5) 4 to 6 toast

(6) Red coloured gems

Method

(1) Mix the milk with $1\frac{1}{4}$ table spoons sugar and boil.

(2) Mix the custard powder in a little cold water to a smooth paste. When the milk starts boiling, add the custard powder gradually. Cook for 1 minute. Cool the sauce.

(3) Mix the cream with sugar (powdered) and beat well.

(4) Place the toast at the base in a serving bowl. Cover the toast with the custard sauce. Pour the sweetened cream over it. Refrigerate for some time.

(5) Decorate with gems. Place in the lower compartment of the fridge and refrigerate for some time. Cut into pieces and serve.

511. Topping, Monaco Dip

Ingredients

(1) 2 cups maska (curds out of which water is drained), paneer, cheese

(2) 2 table spoons fresh cream

(3) 1 finely chopped onion

(4) 1 finely chopped capsicum

(5) Few green chillies

(6) A little pepper powder

(7) 1 packet monaco biscuits

(8) Salt to taste

Method

1. (1) Tie the fresh curds in a muslin cloth and keep aside for some time.

   (2) Add capsicums, onions and cream to it. Add salt and pepper to taste.

   (3) Cool for some time in the refrigerator.

   (4) While serving, place the mixture in the centre and arrange the monaco biscuits around it. Paneer and cheese may be also added.

2. Tie the curds and drain all the water. Add grated cucumber to it. Place this topping on the monaco biscuits and serve.

3. Mix finely chopped onions, tomatoes, chat masala and grated cheese. Apply a little coriander chutney to the monaco biscuits and place the topping over it.

4. Red gravy with rajma or tacos stuffing mixture can be placed on the monaco biscuits. Sprinkle a little grated cheese on it.

5. White gravy with boiled corn seeds can be placed on monaco biscuits.

6. Rajma and corn seeds in gravy can be placed over monaco biscuits. Sprinkle grated cheese over it.

7. Spread some pizza gravy on the biscuits and garnish with grated cheese.

8. **For pizzas or bread slices :**
   Spread some pizza gravy on the pizza base or bread slices. Place some corn in white gravy topping on it.

19 MASALAS

512. Garam Masala

Ingredients

(1) 40 grams cinnamon
(2) 40 grams cloves
(3) 100 grams dagada phool
(4) 100 grams badiya
(5) 100 grams bay leaves
(6) 600 grams coriander seeds

   Roast them before mixing with other ingredients

(7) 100 grams shahjeera
(8) 40 grams cardamom
(9) 80 grams nagkesar
(10) 200 grams cumin seeds
(11) 50 grams mace (javantri)
(12) 2 nutmeg

Method

(1) Mix all the ingredients and grind into a fine powder.
(2) Mix 250 grams red chilli powder, 50 grams turmeric powder, 50 grams khus khus (powder) and 100 grams magatari seeds (powder).

513. Masala for Tea

Ingredients

(1) 100 grams dry ginger
(2) 50 grams pepper
(3) 50 grams cinnamon
(4) 25 grams cardamom
(5) 1 nutmeg
(6) A little javantri (mace)

Method

Grind all the ingredients into a fine powder and mix them well.

514. Methi Masala

Ingredients

(1) Methi seeds (fenugreek seeds)
(2) Red chilli powder
(3) Turmeric powder
(4) Asafoetida   (5) Oil
(6) Mustard seed dal   (7) Salt

Method

(1) Roast the methi seeds. Cool them a little. Grind them into a very coarse powder or you can also use readymade methi dal. Roast the Salt.
(2) Mix 1 cup methi dal, little less than 1 cup salt, 1 cup red chilli powder, a little turmeric powder and a little asafoetida.
(3) Mix oil, castor oil or mustard oil. Mix well.

515. Masala for Buttermilk, Limewater, Sugarcane Juice

Ingredients

(1) 1 tea spoon black salt powder
(2) 2 table spoons roasted cumin seeds powder
(3) $\frac{1}{2}$ table spoon pepper powder
(4) $\frac{1}{2}$ table spoon cumin seed powder (raw)
(5) $\frac{1}{4}$ tea spoon asafoetida
(6) 5 table spoons salt

Method

Mix all the ingredients and sieve them together.

516. Chat Masala

Ingredients

(1) 50 grams amchur powder

(2) 30 grams cumin seeds powder (raw)

(3) 20 grams pepper powder

(4) 1 tea spoon asafoetida

(5) 2 tea spoons black salt powder

(6) Salt to taste

Method

Mix all the ingredients well.

517. Punjabi Masala

Ingredients

(1) 100 grams coriander seeds

(2) 25 grams cumin seeds

(3) 50 grams sesame seeds

(4) 50 grams magatari seeds

(5) 2 grams cinnamon

(6) 5 grams cloves

(7) 10 grams pepper corns

(8) 20 grams poppy seeds

(9) 20 grams red chilli powder

(10) 2 table spoons oil

Method

(1) Roast, grind and sieve the coriander seeds and cumin seeds. Roast and grind magatari seeds and sesame seeds (do not sieve).

(2) Grind cloves, cinnamon and pepper into a fine powder. Sieve them.

(3) Mix all the ingredients well. Heat oil and cool it slightly. Mix it well with all the ingredients.

518. Thandai Masala

Ingredients

(1) 100 grams cardamom

(2) 100 grams sugar

(3) 400 grams fennel seeds

(4) 100 grams magatari seeds

(5) 125 grams white pepper corns

(6) 100 grams poppy seeds

(7) 100 grams almonds

Method

Grind all the ingredients separately. Mix them. While using, add 1 tea spoon for 1 cup of milk.

Note : Other optional ingredients that may be added as under :

(1) 50 grams kesar strands

(2) 20 grams lindipiper

(3) 40 grams rose petals

(4) 5 grams cumin seeds

(5) 5 grams cloves

(6) A little gulkand

Grind all the ingredients separately and mix them well.

519. Fresh Punjabi Masala

Ingredients

(1) 2 table spoons coriander seeds

(2) 1 table spoon cumin seeds

(3) 8 pepper corns

(4) 2 cinnamon sticks, 5 cloves

(5) 2 table spoons cashewnuts or groundnuts or magatari seeds

(6) $\frac{1}{2}$ cup sesame seeds

(7) 5 to 6 cardamoms

(8) A small piece of ginger

(9) 6 to 7 green chillies

Method

(1) Mix all the ingredients and grind it into a fine paste.

(2) This masala is used for various Punjabi Dishes like ragada pattice, sev usal, chhole tikkiya, etc. to make them delicious.

20 (CHUTNEY, RAITA)

520. Coriander Chutney

Ingredients

(1) 1 cup finely chopped coriander leaves

(2) 6 cloves finely chopped garlic

(3) Salt to taste

(4) 1 tea spoon sesame seeds

(5) 2 tea spoons desiccated coconut

(6) 1 tea spoon groundnuts

(7) 3 tea spoons sugar

(8) 1 lime

(9) 4 green chillies

(10) A small piece of ginger

(11) 1 tea spoon cumin seeds

Method

(1) Grind the cumin seeds, sesame seeds, desiccated coconut and groundnuts partially.

(2) Then add all the ingredients and grind into a fine paste.

521. Mint Chutney

Ingredients

(1) 1 cup coriander chutney according to R. No. 520

(2) ½ cup mint leaves

(3) A small piece of ginger

(4) 2 green chillies

(5) 1 lime

(6) Salt to taste

Method

(1) Mix all the ingredients and grind into a fine paste.

(2) While using this green chutney for bhel, add 1 cup of water to it.

522. Khajur-Amchur Chutney

(Dried Mango)

Ingredients

(1) 250 grams khajur

(2) 250 grams amchur powder

(3) 250 grams jaggery

(4) A little red chilli powder

(5) 1 tea spoon oil

(6) A little dhana jeera powder

(7) 1 tea spoon cumin seed powder (roasted)

(8) Salt to taste

Method

(1) Remove the seeds from the khajur. Mix amchur powder, jaggery, red chilli powder and oil. Boil the mixture until the dates are soft.

(2) Blenderise the mixture into a fine paste. Pass it through a sieve and add salt and cumin seeds powder. Boil the paste again for a few minutes.

Dates Chutney for Bhel

Ingredients

(1) 250 grams dates

(2) 3 to 4 pieces dry mango

(3) 1 cup jaggery

(4) 2 lemons   (5) Salt to taste

Method

(1) Wash the dates and dry mango.

(2) Add jaggery and 2 glasses of water to it. Cook in the pressure cooker.

(3) When it cools down, remove the seeds from the dates.

(4) Blenderise the mixture into a fine paste and pass it through a sieve. Add lemon juice and salt to it.

523. Garlic Chutney

Ingredients

(1) 25 cloves garlic (paste)
(2) 4 tea spoons oil
(3) 3 tea spoons red chilli powder
(4) A small piece of jaggery
(5) 1 tea spoon cumin seeds powder
(6) $\frac{1}{2}$ tea spoon salt

Method

Mix garlic paste, cumin seeds powder, salt, red chilli powder, oil and jaggery.

Garlic chutney for Bhel :

(1) Crush the garlic and add salt, red chilli powder and half cup of water to it.
(2) Blenderise it again.

524. Groundnuts-Daliyas (Roasted) Chutney

Ingredients

(1) 100 grams groundnuts
(2) 100 grams daliya
(3) 50 grams sesame seeds
(4) 2 table spoons oil
(5) 2 tea spoons red chilli powder
(6) $\frac{1}{2}$ tea spoon turmeric powder
(7) 1 tea spoon citric acid
(8) 1 tea spoon powdered sugar
(9) Salt to taste

Method

(1) Roast and peel the groundnuts. Crush them coarsely. Roast the daliya and crush them. Roast the sesame seeds.
(2) Heat the oil in a vessel. Add 1 tea spoon red chilli powder and turmeric powder. Then add groundnuts, daliya, sesame seeds and salt.

(3) Remove it from the flame and add citric acid, powdered sugar and 1 tea spoon red chilli powder.

Note : Additional amount of sesame seeds may be added if desired.

525. Sandwich Chutney

Ingredients

(1) 2 cups spinach
(boiled for 5 minutes in water)
(2) 10 green chillies
(3) 1 tea spoon white vinegar
(4) 2 potatoes
(boiled and cut into pieces)
(5) Salt to taste

Method

Mix all the ingredients and blenderise into a fine paste.

526. Cucumber Raita

Ingredients

(1) 250 grams cucumber
(2) Salt to taste
(3) 1 tea spoon mustard seed dal
(4) 500 ml curds
(5) 2 tea spoons sugar
(6) Finely chopped coriander leaves for decoration

Method

(1) Grate the tender cucumber with the skin. Squeeze the grated cucumber lightly.
(2) In monsoons apply a little ghee to the grated and squeezed cucumber so that it does not leave water.
(3) Remove the whey from the curds by straining it through a muslin cloth.
(4) Beat the curds and add cucumber, mustard seed dal, sugar and salt. Always prepare the raita 1 hour before serving so that the mustard dal would get formented.

Variation

Pomegranate-cucumber raita : Add pomegranate seeds to the cucumber raita.

527. Banana Raita

Ingredients

(1) 2 bananas   (2) Salt to taste
(3) 1 tea spoon cumin seeds (powdered)
(4) 250 ml curds
(5) A small piece of ginger
(6) Few green chillies
(7) 1 tea spoon sugar
(8) Few coriander leaves

Method

(1) Chop the bananas into small pieces.
(2) Strain the curds by passing it through a muslin cloth. Mix all ingredients. Garnish with finely chopped coriander leaves.

528. Carrot Raita

Ingredients

(1) 250 grams carrots (2) 250 ml curds
(3) $\frac{1}{2}$ tea spoon ginger-chillies (paste)
(4) 1 tea spoon oil
(5) $\frac{1}{2}$ tea spoon mustard seeds
(6) A pinch asafoetida
(7) 1 tea spoon sugar
(8) 2 table spoons finely chopped coriander leaves
(9) Salt to taste

Method

(1) Boil 250 grams carrots. Peel them and remove the centre white portion and grate the carrots.
(2) Mix curds, carrots, ginger, chillies and salt.
(3) Heat the oil in a vessel and add mustard seeds and asafoetida for seasoning. Add sugar. Mix well. Garnish with finely chopped coriander leaves.

529. Pumpkin Raita

Ingredients

(1) 50 ml curds
(2) A small piece of ginger
(3) Salt to taste
(4) Few green chillies
(5) 1 tea spoon cumin seeds (powdered)
(6) 2 tea spoons sugar
(7) 250 grams pumpkin

Method

Peel, boil and mash the pumpkin. Strain the curds through a muslin cloth. Mix pumpkin and other ingredients. Garnish with finely chopped coriander.

530. Tomato Raita [Serves 4]

Ingredients

(1) 100 grams tomatoes (chopped finely)
(2) 250 ml curds
(3) 1 tea spoon cumin seeds (powdered)
(4) 2 tea spoons sugar
(5) 2 table spoons coriander leaves
(6) Salt to taste

Method

(1) Mix all the ingredients.
(2) Garnish with finely chopped coriander leaves.

531. Rayan Raita [Serves 3 to 4]

Ingredients

(1) 150 grams rayans (yellow berries)
(2) 250 ml curds
(3) 2 tea spoons sugar
(4) 1 tea spoon cumin seeds powder
(5) Salt to taste

Method

(1) Beat the curds well.
(2) Soak the rayans in water for some time. Remove the seeds from it.
(3) Mix all the ingredients.

532. Dried Dates Raita

[Serves 4 to 5]

Ingredients

(1) 100 grams dried dates

(2) 250 ml fresh curds

(3) 1 tea spoon cumin seeds powder

(4) 1 tea spoon sugar   (5) Salt to taste

Method

(1) Soak the dates for 4 hours.

(2) Chop them into small pieces. Mix all the ingredients.

533. Bundi Raita [Serves 4]

Ingredients

(1) 100 grams spicy bundi

(2) 200 ml curds

(3) A little khajur chutney

(4) 2 table spoons coriander leaves (chopped finely)

(5) 2 green chillies (chopped finely)

(6) Salt to taste

Method

(1) Beat the curds well. Add salt to it.

(2) Pour the curds over the bundi. Add the khajur chutney.

(3) Garnish with finely chopped coriander leaves and green chillies.

534. Darabari Raita

[Serves 4 to 5]

Ingredients

(1) 250 ml fresh curds

(2) 1 chiku   (3) $\frac{1}{2}$ banana

(4) 1 orange   (5) $\frac{1}{2}$ alfanso mango

(6) Few pieces of papaya

(7) 1 tea spoon cumin seeds powder

(8) 2 tea spoons sugar (9) Salt to taste

Method

(1) Tie the curds in a muslin cloth and keep it aside for some time.

(2) Chop all the fruits into small pieces. Mix them with the curds. Orange juice may be also added to give colour to the raita.

(3) Mix the other ingredients.

535. Pineapple Raita

[Serves 4 to 5]

Ingredients

(1) 4 slices of pineapple

(2) 250 ml fresh curds

(3) 2 tea spoons sugar

(4) $\frac{1}{2}$ tea spoon ginger-chilli (paste)

(5) 2 table spoons coriander leaves

(6) Salt to taste

Method

(1) Tie the curds in a muslin cloth and keep it aside for some time.

(2) Mix all the ingredients and garnish with green chillies and finely chopped coriander leaves.

(3) Chill it before serving.

536. Vegetable Raita

[Serves 4 to 5]

Ingredients

(1) 250 grams mixed vegetables (boiled) (Potatoes, peas, carrots, cauliflower, pumpkin, bottlegourd, capsicum, cucumber, etc.)

(2) 250 ml fresh curds

(3) 2 tea spoons sugar

(4) $\frac{1}{2}$ tea spoon ginger-chilli paste

(5) Coriander leaves

(6) A little cream (beaten slightly)

(7) Salt to taste

Method

(1) Mix all the ingredients.

(2) Beat the cream and curds slightly. Garnish with chopped coriander leaves.

21 SALADS

537. Cucumber Salad

[Serves 5 to 6]

Ingredients

(1) 250 grams cucumber

(2) 2 table spoons sugar

(3) 50 grams daliya

(4) 50 grams groundnuts
(coarsely ground)

(5) 5 green chillies (paste)

(6) $\frac{1}{2}$ tea spoon citric acid

(7) 2 table spoons sesame seeds

(8) 50 grams coriander leaves

(9) 100 grams desiccated coconut

(10) 1 pomegranate

(11) Salt to taste

Method

(1) Wash and chop the cucumber in chop-n-churn. Add salt and sugar to it. Keep it aside for some time. Squeeze it lightly.

(2) Mix all the ingredients.

(3) Garnish with finely chopped coriander leaves. Pomegranate seeds may be added if desired.

538. Guava-Tomato Salad

[Serves 4]

Ingredients

(1) 1 guava   (2) 2 tomatoes

(3) 1 tea spoon cumin seeds powder

(4) 1 tea spoon sugar

(5) Salt to taste

(6) Finely chopped coriander leaves

Method

(1) Chop the guava and tomatoes into small pieces. Mix all the ingredients.

(2) Garnish with finely chopped coriander leaves.

539. Onion-Tomato Salad

[Serves 2]

Ingredients

(1) 1 onion   (2) 2 tomatoes

(3) 1 tea spoon dhana jeera powder

(4) 1 tea spoon cumin seeds powder

(5) 1 tea spoon sugar

(6) $\frac{1}{2}$ tea spoon chat masala

(7) Salt to taste

(8) Finely chopped coriander leaves

Method

(1) Chop the onion and tomatoes into small pieces. Mix all the ingredients.

(2) Garnish with chopped coriander leaves.

540. Onion, Cabbage, Cucumber, Carrot, Tomato Salad

Ingredients and Method

Chop all the vegetables into small pieces. Add salt and chat masala to it. Mix well.

541. Paneer Salad

[Serves 4 to 5]

Ingredients

(1) 200 grams paneer pieces

(2) 100 grams cucumber
(cut into small pieces)

(3) 2 tea spoons desiccated coconut

(4) 1 tea spoon pepper powder

(5) 2 tea spoons groundnut powder

(6) Few coriander leaves

(7) Salt to taste

Method

Mix all the ingredients and garnish with finely chopped coriander leaves.

542. Sprouted Mung, Cucumber, Pomegranate Salad
[Serves 5 to 6]
Ingredients

(1) 100 grams sprouted mung

(2) 100 grams cucumber (peeled and chopped into small pieces)

(3) 100 grams capsicum (cut into small pieces)

(4) 1 red pomegranate

(5) Finely chopped coriander leaves

Method

(1) Mix all ingredients, sprinkle a little chat masala and mix well.

(2) Garnish with finely chopped coriander leaves.

543. Decorative Mixed Salad

Ingredients

(1) Cabbage (grated)

(2) Tomatoes (small pieces)

(3) Cucumber (grated)

(4) Carrots (grated)   (5) Grapes

(6) Beetroot (boiled and cut 1 slice. Grate the remaining)

(7) Apple (cut into small pieces)

(8) Desiccated coconut

(9) Groundnut powder

(10) Cumin seeds (powdered)

(11) Ginger-chilli paste

For the masala :

(1) Desiccated coconut

(2) Groundnut powder

(3) Sugar and cumin seeds

(4) A little citric acid

(5) Garam masala

(6) Salt to taste

Method

(1) Add salt to the cabbage and keep it aside for some time. Squeeze it lightly to remove the water.

(2) Mix the masala with the salad ingredients except beetroot, grapes, apple, tomatoes and a little desiccated coconut.

(3) Spread the salad in a serving dish. Cover the four parts of the dish with beetroot. Colour half of the desiccated coconut with edible yellow colour and leave the remaining half white.

(4) Place the beetroot slice in the centre of the dish.

(5) Place 4 cuts on the tomatoes and place it on the beetroot slice.

(6) Cover two parts with white desiccated coconut and two parts with yellow coloured desiccated coconut. Place the fruit pieces at the edge.

544. Pulses Salad

Ingredients

(1) Sprouted pulses (mung, muth, rajma, chana, etc.)

(2) Chat masala

(3) Lime juice   (4) Salt to taste

Method

(1) Sprout all pulses. Boil the rajma. Mix salt and chat masala. Add the lime juice.

(2) Decorate with chopped corriander leaves.

545. Fruit Dish

Ingredients

(1) Pineapples   (2) Cherries

(3) Grapes   (4) Apples

(5) Chiku   (6) Black grapes

(7) Pomegranate (8) Mango

(9) A little fruit masala

Method

Chop all fruits in square or equal size and arrange them nicely in a serving dish. Sprinkle a little chat masala over it. Take all fruits as required.

546. Plain Salad

Ingredients

(1) Cucumber   (2) Tomatoes

(3) Onions   (4) Capsicum

(5) Carrots   (6) Beetroots

(7) Cabbage   (8) Coriander leaves

(9) Spinach leaves

(10) Boiled potatoes

(11) Lime

(12) A little chat masala

Method

(1) Chop various vegetables into various shapes and sizes. Arrange them in various shapes.

(2) Add salt, chat masala and lime juice to them.

(3) Add the masala lastly otherwise the vegetables would become soggy. Decorate with finely chopped coriander leaves.

547. Apple-Cucumber Salad

[Serves 4 to 5]

Ingredients

(1) 1 cucumber

(2) 2 small apples

(3) 1 tea spoon pepper powder

(4) $\frac{1}{2}$ lime juice

(5) 100 grams cream

(6) Few mint leaves (finely chopped)

(7) Salt to taste

Method

(1) Cut the cucumber into thin slices. Peel and remove the hard core and slice the apples.

(2) Mix cucumber and apples and add the lemon juice, salt and pepper. Mix well.

(3) Add cream and pour the salad in the serving bowl. Sprinkle finely chopped mint leaves.

548. Russian Salad

[Serves 5 to 6]

Ingredients

(1) $1\frac{1}{2}$ cups fresh curds

(2) 1 small apple

(3) 50 grams pineapple

(4) $\frac{1}{4}$ cup pomegranate seeds

(5) 50 grams grapes

(6) 50 grams cherries

(7) 1 small cucumber

(8) 50 grams cabbage (shredded)

(9) 1 tea spoon pepper powder

(10) 2 tea spoons powdered sugar

(11) Salt to taste

Method

(1) Tie the curds in a thin muslin cloth and keep aside for some time.

(2) Add small pieces of apples, pineapple, pomegranate and cherries. Add grapes, grated cucumber (remove the water by squeezing lightly) and cabbage (soaked in ice cold water for some time before adding).

(3) Add salt, pepper and sugar. Cool in the refrigerator. Serve chilled.

549. Jelly Salad [Serves 4 to 5]

Ingredients

(1) 100 grams jelly powder

(2) 200 ml water

(3) Few drops edible colour

(4) Sugar (5) Apples

(6) Pineapple (7) Cherries

(8) Grapes

Method

(1) Dissolve the jelly crystals in 100 ml of hot water and add the remaining cold water.

(2) Prepare jelly of 2 to 3 different colours and set them in separate moulds.

(3) Add sugar to the jelly mixture. Add finely chopped fruits as desired. Set it in the freezer compartment of the refrigerator.

(4) When it is set, cut the jelly into small pieces. While serving, mix the jellies of different colours or you can serve a single coloured jelly with only one fruit.

(22) SOUPS

550. Tomato Soup

[Serves 5 to 6]

Ingredients

(1) 700 grams tomatoes

(2) 2 table spoons butter

(3) 2 onions

(4) 2 cloves garlic

(5) 1 potato

(6) $\frac{1}{2}$ tea spoon cinnamon powder, a few cloves, cardamom and pepper powder

(7) 3 tea spoons sugar

(8) 1 tea spoon red chilli powder

(9) 2 table spoons grated cheese

(10) Fried small bread crumbs

(11) $\frac{1}{2}$ cup cream

For the white sauce :

(1) $\frac{1}{2}$ cup milk

(2) 1 tea spoon corn flour

(3) 1 tea spoon butter

(4) $\frac{1}{2}$ tea spoon pepper powder

(5) Salt to taste

Method

(1) Dissolve the corn flour in cold milk. Mix 1 tea spoon butter, salt and pepper powder to the milk corn flour mixture. Heat the mixture with constant stirring until it thickens.

(2) Heat a little butter and add the onions and garlic to it. Fry for a few minutes. Add the tomato and potato pieces.

(3) Add 2 cups of water and cook in the pressure cooker for 2 whistles. Cool and pass the mixture through a sieve. Add all the masalas and boil the mixture for a few minutes.

(4) Add the prepared white sauce. Remove it from the flame.

(5) Sprinkle grated cheese on top. Serve hot with bread crumbs and little cream on top.

551. Minestrone Soup

[Serves 6 to 7]

Ingredients

(1) 2 table spoons butter

(2) 2 finely chopped onions

(3) 2 cloves garlic

(4) 1 carrot   (5) 1 capsicum

(6) $\frac{1}{2}$ cup green peas (boiled)

(7) 1 cup cabbage (finely chopped)

(8) 700 grams tomatoes

(9) 1 table spoon corn flour

(10) $\frac{1}{4}$ cup baked beans

(11) $\frac{1}{2}$ cup macaroni (boiled)

(12) $\frac{1}{2}$ tea spoon powdered cinnamon, cloves, cardamom and pepper

(13) 3 tea spoons sugar

(14) 1 tea spoon red chilli powder

(15) $\frac{1}{2}$ cup white sauce

(16) 1 tea spoon ajinomoto

(17) 4 cups water

(18) $\frac{1}{2}$ cup grated cheese

(19) Salt to taste

Method

(1) Heat the butter in a vessel and stir. Fry the onions for 2 to 3 minutes. Add the garlic paste and fry again for few seconds.

(2) Add all the vegetables, salt and pepper and 2 cups of water. Cook until all the vegetables are tender. Do not over cook the vegetables.

(3) Chop the tomatoes into small pieces and mix them with remaining 2 cups of water. Cook them. Blend the mixture in a liquidizer and strain.

(4) Add the tomato soup to the cooked vegetables. Dissolve the corn flour in a little cold water. Add it to the soup.

(5) Add the beans, macaroni and all the remaining ingredients to the soup. Boil the soup till the cheese melts.

(6) Garnished with grated cheese while serving.

552. Spinach Soup
[Serves 5 to 6]
Ingredients

(1) 500 grams spinach

(2) 2 onions

(3) 6 cloves garlic

(4) A pinch soda

(5) $1\frac{1}{2}$ tea spoons sugar

(6) 150 grams green peas

(7) 2 table spoons corn flour

(8) A little pepper powder

(9) A little nutmeg powder

(10) 4 table spoons malai

(11) Fried bread pieces for serving

(12) Salt to taste

Method

(1) Boil 3 glasses of water. Chop the spinach and onions finely. When the water starts boiling add the spinach, onions, garlic, a pinch of soda, sugar, green peas and salt. Boil for 5 minutes without the lid on.

(2) Cool the mixture and blend it in a liquidizer and strain. Dissolve the corn flour in 1 cup water and add it to the soup.

(3) Boil the soup for a few minutes. Add salt and sugar.

(4) While serving add pepper and nutmeg powder. Serve hot with fresh cream and bread crumbs.

Note : (1) Cabbage, capsicums, carrots can be partially boiled with a little soda and added to the soup.

(2) Boiled green peas may also be added to the soup.

553. Guava, Tomato, Potato Soup [Serves 4 to 5]

Ingredients

(1) 3 potatoes   (2) 3 guavas

(3) 4 red tomatoes

(4) 3 table spoons oil or ghee

(5) 1 tea spoon cumin seeds and fenugreek seeds

(6) 6 cloves garlic

(7) 4 green chillies (paste)

(8) A small piece of ginger (paste)

(9) 250 ml curds

(10) 3 table spoons chana flour

(11) 3 table spoons sugar

(12) 1 tea spoon red chilli powder

(13) 4 table spoons coriander leaves (finely chopped)

(14) Salt to taste

Method

(1) Cut the guavas, potatoes and vegetables into small pieces.

(2) Heat the oil or ghee in a vessel. Add the cumin seeds and fry for a few seconds for seasoning. Add garlic paste and potatoes. Add enough water and cook until the potatoes are soft.

(3) Add the guava pieces, green chillies, salt and tomatoes. Mix the curds and chana flour and beat well. Mix the curds mixture to the soup.

(4) Add sugar, red chilli powder and boil for a few minutes. Garnish with chopped coriander leaves. Serve hot.

554. Dapaka Kadhi [Serves 5 to 6]

Ingredients

(1) 1 cup curds

(2) $\frac{1}{2}$ cup chana flour

(3) 1 tea spoon red chilli powder

(4) $\frac{1}{4}$ tea spoon turmeric powder

(5) 2 table spoons oil

(6) $\frac{1}{4}$ tea spoon fenugreek seeds

(7) 2 red chillies (whole)

(8) 2 onions

(9) 2 potatoes

(10) 4 green chillies

(11) $\frac{1}{2}$ tea spoon baking powder

(12) Oil for frying   (13) Salt to taste

Method

For the kadhi :

(1) Mix curds, 2 table spoons flour, water, salt, red chilli powder and turmeric powder.

(2) Mix well so that no lumps are formed.

(3) Heat the oil in a vessel and add fenugreek seeds and whole red chillies. Fry for few seconds and when the seasoning is ready add the curds mixture. Add pakodas to the kadhi.

For the Pakodas : Cut the onions and potatoes into small pieces. Add salt, the remaining chana flour, red chilli powder, turmeric powder, baking powder and a little water. Heat the oil in a vessel for frying and deep fry the pakodas.

Variation

Navratna Kadhi : Add different coloured bundis to the plain kadhi.

555. Corn Soup [Serves 4 to 5]

Ingredients

(1) $1\frac{1}{2}$ cups grated corn

(2) $\frac{1}{4}$ cup corn seeds

(3) $1\frac{1}{2}$ to 2 cups water

(4) 2 to 3 table spoons butter

(5) 2 table spoons maida

(6) 2 cups milk

(7)   2 table spoons sugar

(8) $\frac{1}{4}$ tea spoon pepper powder

(9) $\frac{1}{4}$ cup cream or malai

(10)   Salt to taste

Method

(1)   Grate the corn. Add $1\frac{1}{2}$ cups of water to it. While add $\frac{1}{2}$ cup of water to the corn seeds and cook in a pressure cooker.

(2)   Cool a little and blend the grated corn in a liquidiser and strain.

(3)   Add the corn seeds to it along with the water. Mix well.

(4)   Heat the butter in a vessel and add the maida to it. Mix well. Go on adding gradually the milk with constant stirring.

(5)   Add the corn paste to the prepared white sauce.

(6)   Add sugar, salt and pepper powder.

(7)   Serve hot with a topping of fresh cream.

556. Corn and Tomato Soup

[Serves 6 to 7]

Ingredients

(1)   3 corncobs

(2)   1 table spoon sugar

(3)   Tomato soup (according to R. No. 550)

(4)   A little pepper powder

(5) $\frac{1}{2}$ cup cream

Method

(1)   Take out whole corns from the corn-cobs with a knife. Add 1 cup water and cook in a pressure cooker. Add sugar to it.

(2)   Add the corn seeds to the prepared tomato soup and boil on a slow flame for 10 minutes.

(3)   While serving sprinkle a little pepper powder. Mix well. Serve hot with the topping of fresh cream.

557. Cheese Fruit Sticks

Ingredients

(1)   Black grapes

(2)   Little less than $\frac{1}{2}$ " cheese pieces (square)

(3)   Grapes

(4)   Salt and pepper powder taste

(5)   Pineapple pieces

(6)   Cucumber slices

Method

(1)   Chop the raisins horizontally into 2 pieces. Sprinkle salt and pepper on all the ingredients except the cheese and grapes.

(2)   Fix the grapes on the tooth picks then the black grapes, then the cheese cubes, followed by a piece of pineapple and lastly a slice of cucumber.

(3)   Arrange them in a flat plate, in a standing position. They can also be fixed in the apples and served. If you serve fixed in the apples avoid using cucumber slice.

558. Paneer Vegetable Sticks

Ingredients

(1) $\frac{1}{2}$ " piece of paneer

(2)   Ghee for frying the paneer

(3)   A little pepper powder

(4)   Tomatoes (small slices)

(5)   Onions (small slices)

(6)   Few coriander leaves

(7)   Few green chillies cut into round pieces

(8)   Salt to taste

Method

(1) Deep fry the paneer pieces in ghee until golden brown. Sprinkle salt and paneer. Arrange the tomato slices in a flat dish.

(2) Place an onion slices over it. Place the paneer cube on it. Garnish with green chillies and coriander leaves. Fix a toothpick on it.

(23) SQUASH, JELLY, JAMS, KETCHUP, JUICE

559. Black Grapes Squash

Ingredients

(1) $1\frac{1}{2}$ kg black grapes
(2) 600 grams sugar
(3) A pinch ($1\frac{1}{2}$ gram) sodium benzoate
(4) 2 tea spoons citric acid

Method

(1) Blenderise the black grapes in the mixer to obtain the pulp. Prepare the sugar syrup with sugar and water and cool it.

(2) Add the fruit pulp. Add the sodium benzoate and citric acid. Pour into a dry, sterilized bottle. Close the bottle.

560. Orange Squash

Ingredients

(1) Orange   (2) Sugar
(3) Citric acid
(4) Few drops edible orange colour
(5) Potassium-meta-bi-sulphite

Method

(1) Select medium sized, fresh, fully riped, firm and slightly heavy oranges.

(2) Extract the juice and strain it.

(3) Calculate double the amount of sugar as that of juice and keep aside. Add water to the sugar as much quantity as that of the juice. Measure the

amount of preservative, for every one kilogram of the total quantity of water, sugar and the juice, add 5 grams of the preservative. Heat the above mixture.

(4) Remove it from the flame when the sugar dissolves. Strain the mixture through a muslin cloth and cool it.

(5) Add the strained fruit juice in the cooled prepared syrup.

(6) Dissolve the edible colour in a few drops of water and add it to the squash. Lastly add potassium-meta-bi-sulphite. For every kilogram of the total quantity add $\frac{3}{4}$ gram of it. Add the preservative Potassium-meta-bi-sulphite dissolved in small quantity of water.

(7) Pour the squash in a dry sterilized bottle.

561. Chocolate Orange Jelly

Ingredients

(1) 100 grams orange jelly
(2) 4 table spoons water
(3) $\frac{3}{4}$ cup milk
(4) 2 tea spoons grated chocolate

Method

(1) Mix the jelly crystals with water and boil it until the jelly crystals dissolve. Pour the jelly mixture in the mould, and keep in the refrigerator until it cools (do not let it set).

(2) Gradually go on adding milk with constant stirring.

(3) Pour the mixture in the mould and keep in refrigerator until it sets. Unmould it while serving. Sprinkle grated chocolate on top of it.

562. Apple Jam

Ingredients

(1) Apples   (2) 1 banana
(3) Sugar   (4) Citric acid

Method

(1) Select fully riped and fresh fruits. Wash the fruits thoroughly with water to remove the dirt and dust present on the surface. Chop the fruit into small and uniform pieces. Add the required quantity of water to cover the fruit pieces fully.

(2) Tie the apple pieces and the banana in a muslin cloth loosely. Dip this bundle in boiling water.

(3) Cook until the apple pieces are soft and cooked. Remove the bundle from the water. Blenderise it to obtain a pulp.

(4) Add sugar to the pulp. Measure the quantity of sugar. It should be same as that of the pulp. Add citric acid 5 grams for the total weight of sugar and pulp. Cook the mixture on medium flame with occasional stirring.

(5) Cook until most of the water evaporates. Pour the jam into a dry sterilized bottle.

563. Pineapple Jam

Ingredients

(1) 1 ripe pineapple
(2) 500 grams sugar (approximately)

(3) 2 limes
(4) $\frac{1}{4}$ tea spoon edible lemon yellow colour

Method

(1) Select fresh and wholesome pineapple. Peel, clean and grate it. Add sugar (the same quantity as that of the quantity of the pulp and juice obtained).

(2) Mix sugar and pulp and cook the mixture. When half cooked add lime juice.

(3) Mix well. Cook until the mixture thickens. Remove it from the flame. Cool it. Add the colour and pour the jam into a dry sterilized bottle.

Note : The proportion of sugar can be changed according to the size of the pineapple.

564. Mango Jam

Ingredients

(1) 3 alphanso mangoes
(2) 400 grams sugar   (3) 1 lime

Method

(1) Select fresh and wholesome mangoes. Peel and cut the mangoes into small pieces. Add the sugar and cook the mixture on a low flame.

(2) When the mixture thickens a little, add the lime juice. Cook for another few minutes. Remove the jam from the flame.

(3) Cool it and pour into a dry sterilized bottle.

565. Mixed Fruit Jam

Ingredients

(1) 300 grams apples
(2) 1 banana   (3) 1 chiku
(4) 200 grams grapes
(5) 3 oranges

(6) Sugar to taste   (7) 4 limes

(8) Few drops edible red colour

(9) $\frac{1}{2}$ tea spoon mixed fruit essence

Method

(1) Select fresh and wholesome fruits. Peel and grate the apples. Peel banana and chiku and mash them to make a pulp. Extract the juice from the oranges and grapes.

(2) Mix all the fruits. Mix the sugar in the same quantity as that of the total pulp or juice.

(3) Cook the mixture on a low flame. When it thickens a little, add lime juice. Cook for another few minutes until the mixture thickens.

(4) Cool it. Add the colour and essence to it. Pour the jam into a dry sterilized bottle.

566. Tomato Ketchup

Ingredients

(1) 5 kg tomatoes

(2) A small piece of beetroot

(3) 100 grams ginger

(4) Garam masala (cinnamon, cloves, pepper, mace, etc.)

(5) 400 grams sugar

(6) Acetic acid

(7) Sodium benzoate (8) Salt to taste

Method

(1) Select sound ripe tomatoes of deep red colour with less water and more pulp. Chop the tomatoes and steam them in the pressure cooker.

(2) Put them in a sieve and not directly. Place the tomatoes with the cut part on the top. Cut the beetroot into 2 pieces.

(3) Add a little water to the pressure cooker and cook for some time without the whistle until the skin of the tomatoes softens. Remove it from the flame. Place the sieve in a dish in a slanting position to remove the excess amount of water from the tomatoes.

(4) Blenderise the tomatoes and strain the pulp. (Prepare soup from the water extracted from the tomatoes.)

(5) Tie the ginger paste and garam masala into a thin muslin cloth separately. Put these bundles in the tomato pulp extracted.

(6) Add the sugar and mix well. Cook until the mixture thickens. Squeeze and remove the bags. The garam masala from the bag can be used in various other salty preparations.

(7) Add the acetic acid and sodium benzoate. (For 5 kg of tomatoes readymade packets of preservative are available in the market.) Add salt and cool the ketchup. Fill in a dry sterilized bottle.

For extraction of juice

Blenderise all the fruits of which juice has to be extracted. Strain the pulp. Add white pepper powder, salt and black salt powder to it. Add enough sugar. Various fruit juices can be mixed with Limca, Thumps Up, Coca Cola etc. Serve Chilled.

---

567. Raw Mango Juice, Raw Mango Bafala [Serves 5]

Ingredients

(1) 100 grams raw mangoes

(2) 90 to 100 grams sugar

(3) Cardamom

(4) Edible yellow colour

(5) Essence

(6) Few strands kesar

(7) Few drops green edible colour

Method

(1) Wash and boil the raw mangoes. Remove the pulp by squeezing them well. Strain the mixture when cool.

(2) Add sugar, cardamom, kesar strands, essence and edible colour.

(3) Yellow colour and kesar would give yellow coloured juice. Prepare the sugar syrup and cool it. Mix the mango juice with the syrup.

(4) While serving add enough water to the juice, ice cubes, salt and roasted cumin seeds powder.

Note : The proportion of sugar may very depending upon the sourness of the mangoes.

568. Raw Mangoes Bafala

Ingredients

(1) 100 grams raw mangoes

(2) 3 to 4 cups water

(3) 100 grams jaggery

(4) $\frac{1}{4}$ tea spoon red chilli powder

(5) $\frac{1}{2}$ tea spoon cumin seeds powder

(6) Salt to taste

Method

(1) Wash and boil the mangoes. Squeeze and extract the pulp.

(2) Add 3 to 4 cups of water and jaggery to it and mix well until the jaggery dissolves. Mix the mango pulp with it and mix well with a hand mixture.

(3) Add salt, red chilli powder, cumin seeds powder and refrigerate the pulp. Serve chilled. Add cold water if the pulp is too thick or too sour.

Note : The proportion of the jaggery may very depending upon the sourness of the mangoes.

569. Watermelon Juice

[Serves 8 to 10]

Ingredients

(1) 2 kg watermelon

(2) A small piece of ginger

(3) A little pepper and cumin seeds powder

(4) 2 to 3 table spoons juice

(5) 1 cup rose syrup

(6) Ice cubes   (7) Salt to taste

Method

(1) Remove the seeds from the watermelon and scoop out the flesh. Put the scooped portion of the flesh into a liquidiser and take out the juice. Add ginger-juice, salt, pepper and cumin seeds powder. Add the juice and rose syrup and mix well. Serve topped with crushed ice.

(2) Cut the watermelon and scoop out flesh with a melon baller. Extract watermelon juice and mix chilled juice with the melon balls. Serve topped with 1 tea spoon of milkmaid.

Variation

Instead of rose syrup coca cola may also be added.

570. Falsa Juice

[Serves 4 to 5]

Ingredients

(1) 125 grams falsa

(2) 150 grams sugar

(3) Juice of $\frac{1}{2}$ lemon

(4) Few drops edible colour

(5) Salt, black salt and chat masala to taste

Method

(1) Soak the falsa in water for 2 hours. Put the falsa into a liquidiser and take out the pulp. Strain the pulp.

(2) Make 1 thread sugar syrup by mixing sugar and a little water. Add lemon juice to it.

(3) Add the falsa pulp to the sugar syrup and cook for a further 10 minutes.

Cool it. Add a few drops of edible rose red colour and fill it in a clean bottle.

(4) For storing for 1 kg of falsa, add 1 gram of sodium benzoate.

(5) While preparing the drink, take 2 table spoons of the mixture in a glass. Add water, salt, black salt and chat masala. Serve with crushed ice.

Note : (1) Additional sugar may be added if required.

(2) The juice can be strained with a strainer bowl.

571. Amala Juice

[Serves 5 to 6]

Ingredients and Method

(1) Boil 100 grams amala in the pressure cooker. Cut into small pieces and blenderise to make a pulp. Make a sugar syrup by mixing water and 200 grams sugar.

(2) Cool it. Mix the amala pulp to it. Strain it. Add few drops of edible yellow colour.

572. Plum Juice [Serves 3 to 4]

Ingredients and Method

(1) Soak 100 grams plums in hot water for 2 minutes. Remove the skin and the seed. Add salt, 1 tea spoon pepper powder, 50 grams sugar and a little ginger to it. Blenderise it.

(2) Strain the juice. Serve chilled with crushed ice. The proportion of sugar depends upon the sourness of the plums.

573. Pineapple Juice [Serves 6]

Ingredients

(1) 250 grams ripe pineapple

(2) 1 apple (3) 1 limca

(4) Salt to taste

Method

Add 1 tea spoon pepper, 1 tea spoon cumin seeds, $\frac{1}{2}$ tea spoon citric acid and 50 grams sugar to the above mentioned ingredients. Blenderise all ingredients and strain the juice. Serve with crushed ice.

574. Fruit Punch

[Serves 6 to 7]

Ingredients

(1) 1 cup fresh orange juice

(2) 1 cup pineapple juice

(3) $\frac{1}{4}$ cup lime juice (4) 1 cup water

(5) 5 table spoons sugar

(6) $\frac{1}{2}$ bottle soda water or Gold Spot

(7) $\frac{1}{2}$ cup strong black tea

For decoration :

Apple pieces, few mint leaves

Method

(1) Mix the sugar in 1 cup of warm water. Mix well until the sugar dissolves. Cool the syrup.

(2) Mix all the juices and tea together and cool them. Just before serving, mix the sugar syrup, juice and chilled soda water.

(3) Top with apple pieces and $\frac{1}{2}$ mint leaves. Serve chilled.

For preparing the tea : Mix $\frac{1}{2}$ cup hot water and $\frac{1}{2}$ tea spoon tea leaves. Boil it for few minutes and strain. If you don't like tea then it may be avoided.

575. Fruit Cocktail

[Serves 5 to 6]

Ingredients

(1) 1 apple

(2) $\frac{1}{2}$ cup black grapes

(3) $\frac{1}{2}$ cup pomegranate seeds

(4) 1 cup orange juice

(5) ½ cup sweet lime juice

(6) 1 cup pineapple juice

(7) Sugar as required

Method

(1) Mix apple, black grapes, pomegranate and pineapple pieces and blenderise them. Mix orange and pineapple juice to the pulp.

(2) Serve topped with crushed ice and mint leaves.

Variation

250 grams pineapple, 150 grams apples, falsa, orange, 3 to 4 tea spoons sugar and ½ lime. Mix all ingredients and blenderise. If orange or sweet lime juice are not available then the above combination can be used. It makes 11 glasses.

Note : Readymade orange juice can be used. Also orange juice can be prepared from the available powders.

576. Khus, Lemon Juice [Serve 1]

Ingredients and Method

Mix 2 table spoons khus squash with 1 table spoon lime juice and cold water. Serve chilled.

577. Pineapple Juice OR Shake [Serves 4 to 5]

Ingredients

(1) 1 fresh coconut (grated)

(2) Fresh pineapple

(3) Cream   (4) Ice

Method

(1) Add enough water to grated coconut and soak it in water for some time. Blend it in a liquidiser and strain it.

(2) Add 2 slices pineapple and 1 cup pineapple juice. Blenderise it again.

Mix cream, coconut, crushed ice and pineapple pieces.

(3) Serve topped with 1 tea spoon of cream.

578. Chococream [Serves 6]

Ingredients

(1) 4 glasses milk

(2) 5 table spoons sugar

(3) 2 tea spoons coffee

(4) 2 tea spoons Bournvita

(5) 2 tea spoons chocolate powder

(6) 100 grams fresh cream

(7) Cadbury chocolate

Method

(1) Blend milk, sugar, coffee and Bournvita in a liquidiser. Chill it.

(2) Serve topped with crushed ice, chocolate powder, cream and grated chocolate.

579. Cold Chocolate [Serves 2]

Ingredients

(1) 1 cup milk

(2) 1 tea spoon drinking chocolate

(3) 2 tea spoons sugar

(4) 2 table spoons malai

(5) Cadbury chocolate

Method

(1) Blend milk, drinking chocolate, sugar, fresh cream with a hand mixer.

(2) Serve chilled topped with crushed ice and grated chocolate.

580. Thick Shake [Serves 8]

Ingredients

(1) 1 litre milk

(2) 2 tea spoons cocoa

(3) 2 table spoons chocolate powder

(4) 3 table spoons corn flour

(5) 100 grams sugar

(6) 500 grams vanilla or chocolate ice cream

(7) Vanilla essence

(8) 1 cadbury chocolate

Method

(1) Dissolve the cocoa powder, chocolate powder and corn flour in a little cold milk. Mix sugar to the remaining milk and boil it.

(2) When the milk starts boiling add the corn flour mixture. Boil for few minutes. Cool the mixture.

(3) While serving, blend the mixture and ice cream in a liquidiser.

(4) Serve chilled topped with cadbury powder. Instead of ice cream, few drops of vanilla essence can be added. This would make 8 servings.

Ingredients for Chocolate Sauce

(1) 200 ml milk

(2) 2 table spoons cocoa

(3) 2 table spoons sugar

(4) 3 table spoons corn flour

Method

(1) Mix milk, cocoa powder, sugar and corn flour. Boil the mixture until it starts thickening.

(2) Stir constantly. Remove it from the flame. Cool it. Serve as a topping on ice creams.

581. Plum, Cherry Shake
[Serves 6]
Ingredients

(1) 6 plumps

(2) 100 grams cherries

(3) Sugar   (4) 1 cup milk

(5) 200 grams vanilla ice cream

Method

(1) Remove the seeds from the plums and cherries. Cut the fruits into small pieces.

(2) Blend plum and cherries, sugar, milk, and ice cream in a liquidiser. Serve chilled.

582. Peach Cooler
[Serves 6 to 7]
Ingredients

(1) 1 bottle Limca

(2) 2 table spoons vanilla essence

(3) 1 peach (paste) or 3 plums and $\frac{1}{2}$ pineapple slice

(4) $\frac{1}{4}$ tea spoon lime juice

(5) Ice-cubes

Method

Blend all the ingredients in a liquidiser. Serve immediately with lots of crushed ice.

583. Cocoa [Serve 1]
Ingredients

(1) 1 cup milk

(2) 1 table spoon cocoa

(3) 1 table spoon vanilla ice cream

(4) $\frac{1}{2}$ tea spoon drinking chocolate

(5) 1 table spoon sugar

Method

Blend all the ingredients in a liquidiser. 1 tea spoon milk powder can also be added.

584. Pinacolada Cocktail
[Serves 2 to 3]
Ingredients

(1) $\frac{1}{4}$ glass pineapple juice

(2) $\frac{1}{4}$ glass water

(3) $\frac{1}{4}$ glass milk   (4) $\frac{1}{4}$ glass Limca

(5) Coconut water as desired

(6) Vanilla ice cream

Method

Mix all the ingredients to make a thick and sweet shake.

585. Virgin Pinacolada

[Serves 4 to 5]

Ingredients

(1) $\frac{1}{2}$ cup coconut milk

(2) $\frac{1}{2}$ cup fresh cream

(3) 2 pineapple slices (tinned)

(4) 1 cup pineapple juice

Method

(1) Grate the coconut and soak it in water for some time. Blenderise and strain it to prepare the coconut milk. Add cream to it.

(2) Crush the pineapple pieces along with the juice. Strain and add to the coconut milk mixture. Serve chilled topped with crushed ice in long glasses.

(3) If you are not using tinned pineapple then, additional sugar may be added.

586. Hot Kesaria (Saffron)

Milk [Serves 5]

Ingredients

(1) 1 litre milk

(2) $3\frac{1}{2}$ table spoons sugar

(3) 15 almonds   (4) 25 pistas

(5) 10 cardamom pods

(6) 10 kesar strands

Method

(1) Boil the milk. When it starts boiling, add sugar.

(2) Powder 12 almonds and 20 pistas coarsely. Mix cardamom powder and kesar to it. Mix well. Add this masala to the milk and let it boil.

(3) Boil 3 almonds and 5 pistas separately. Peel them and chop them into thin slices.

(4) Almonds and pistas can be soaked in water for 8 to 10 hours instead in boiling them.

(5) Add the chopped nuts to milk. Serve luke warm masala milk.

Variation

1 tea spoon charoli can also be added to the masala milk.

Note : (1) You can powder almonds, pistas, kesar and cardamom together and use this whenever required.

(2) If you don't like a coarse powder then powder it finely.

587. Falsa Cooler [Serves 4]

Ingredients

(1) 2 table spoons vanilla ice cream

(2) 4 table spoons falsa juice

(3) 1 bottle soda

Method

Mix ice cream and juice in a vessel. Add the soda very gradually. Serve in glasses when the froth settles down slightly.

588. Watermelon Cooler

[Serves 10 to 12]

Ingredients

(1) 1 medium sized watermelon

(2) 2 lemons

(3) Powdered sugar as required

(4) 5 table spoons vanilla ice cream

(5) 1 soda bottle

Method

Scoop out the flesh from the melon. Add the remaining ingredients and blend into the liquidiser.

589. Pineapple Cooler

[Serves 10 to 12]

Ingredients and Method

(1) Take 1 pineapple. Scoop out the centre portion from the pineapple and chop the remaining pineapple into small pieces. Blend it into a liquidiser. Chill the pulp.

(2) Chill 1 soda bottle. Place 2 table spoons of ice cream in a bowl. Go on adding the juice to the ice cream gradually and mix well.

(3) Lastly add the soda and mix well. Serve immediately.

590. Lemon Cooler

[Serves 10]

Ingredients 1

(1) 2 big table spoons ice cream

(2) 2 Limca bottles   (3) 1 soda bottle

Method 1

(1) Take the ice cream in a bowl.

(2) Gradually, add Limca and mix well. Lastly add soda and mix well. Serve immediately.

Ingredients 2

(1) 2 table spoons vanilla ice cream

(2) 1 bottle soda

(3) 4 table spoons powdered sugar

(4) 2 limes   (5) 1 cup water

Method 2

(1) Dissolve the sugar in water and add the lime juice to it.

(2) In another bowl place the ice cream and add the lime juice to it. Mix well and add soda. Serve immediately.

591. Espresso Coffee

[Serves 4]

Ingredients

(1) 3 table spoons Nes coffee (or any other instant coffee powder)

(2) 6 table spoons sugar

(3) 3 cups milk   (4) 1 cup water

(5) Cadbury chocolate

(6) 8 to 10 cashewnuts (powdered)

(7) 8 to 10 walnuts (powdered)

Method

(1) Mix sugar and coffee in a cup. Add a little water to it just to soak the sugar and coffee.

(2) Beat it with the hand mixer.

(3) Boil water and milk. Fill the milk in 4 cups.

(4) Add the coffee mixture in equal amounts in all the 4 cups. Sprinkle grated chocolate over it. Garnish with cashewnuts and walnut powder.

592. Ganga Jamuna Juice

[Serves 9 to 10]

Ingredients

(1) 500 grams orange

(2) 500 grams sweet lime

(3) 500 grams pineapple

(4) 1 bottle Limca

(5) Sugar   (6) Salt to taste

(7) Pepper powder

Method

(1) Blend all the fruits in the liquidiser. Add limca to it and all the other ingredients. Mix well.

(2) Chill it in the refrigerator. Serve chilled.

593. Black Grapes and Falsa Juice [Serves 8 to 10]

Ingredients

(1) 400 grams black currants

(2) 350 grams falsa

(3) 1 bottle Thums Up

(4) 200 to 250 grams sugar

(5) A little pepper powder

(6) A little black salt

(7) Salt to taste

Method

Soak the falsa in water for some time. Wash the black currants. Grind both of them into a pulp. Add sugar, salt, black salt and pepper powder. Mix well. Add Thums Up and serve immediately.

Note : The proportion of sugar would depend upon the sourness of the falsa.

594. Black Grapes and Pineapple Juice [Serves 8 to 10]

Ingredients and Method

Substitute falsa with the same amount of pineapple. Other ingredients and method remains the same as given in R. No. 592.

Variation

Watermelon Falsa juice : Soak the falsa in water for some time. Remove the seeds from the melon. Blend them in a liquidiser. Add sugar, salt, black salt and pepper powder according to the taste. Lastly add Coca Cola and serve immediately.

595. Grapes and Apple Juice [Serves 10]

Ingredients and Method

Blend 250 grams grapes and 250 grams apples in a liquidiser. Add sugar, salt and $\frac{1}{2}$ tea spoon pepper powder according to the taste. Lastly add 1 bottle of Limca and serve immediately.

Variation

Black grapes can be taken instead of green grapes.

596. Lemon and Ginger Sharbat

Ingredients

(1) 1 kg lemon   (2) sugar

(3) 250 grams ginger, a few mint leaves

(4) A little black salt

(5) A little cumin seed powder

(6) Salt to taste

Method

(1) Extract the lime juice. Measure sugar (twice the amount of the juice).

(2) Prepare 1 thread sugar syrup by mixing sugar and just enough water. Cool it and mix it with the lime juice.

(3) Extract the ginger juice by grinding the ginger and straining it through a muslin cloth.

(4) Mix it with the sugar syrup mixture. (The remains of ginger can be dried in the sun and used in 'Mukhawas'). Grind the mint leaves and add the paste to the sharbat.

(5) While serving, take 1 table spoon of the sharbat, add chilled water, crushed ice, black salt, cumin seeds powder (roasted) and salt.

597. Choco-Cola

[Serves 6 to 7]

Ingredients

(1) 2 bottles cola

(Thums Up or Coca Cola)

(2) 2 table spoons chocolate ice-cream

(3) $\frac{1}{4}$ tea spoon lime juice

Method

Blend all the ingredients in a liquidiser for 1 minute. Serve topped with crushed ice.

(24) ICE-CREAMS

Points to Remember :

1. Boil the milk properly until it is reduced to half the amount. Stir constantly so that malai or cream is not formed.

2. Add the sugar to the milk and boil it until it thickens. Always taste the ice cream mixture before freezing because freezing absorbs the sweetness also the flavour of the essence, are reduced by refrigeration.

3. Corn flour, gelatine, G.M.S., C.M.C. and stabilizers are used as a thickening agents for the milk.

4. Use shallow metal containers, preferably made of aluminium for freezing ice creams. Freezing is faster in aluminium containers.

5. Keep your ice cream container covered thereby reducing the formation of ice crystals.

6. Always dissolve the corn flour or milk powder in cold milk or water. This would prevent formation of lumps.

7. Set the fridge to its coldest if you plan in advance to prepare the ice cream.

8. Always add the fruits or dry fruits pieces during the churning process after the ice cream is set once. Soak the dry fruits in water for some time before adding.

9. The ice cream box should be kept in direct contact with the bottom of the freezer. If the box is placed over ice trays, the ice cream will not set properly.

Ice creams can be prepared by various methods. Out of which two methods are given below :

(1) By using G.M.S. and C.M.C. powder.

(2) By using milk powder, china grass, corn flour, stabilizer, etc.

When the ice cream is set once, it is churned with an electric egg beater. Then add the fruits or the dry fruits that has to be added.

Method 1 [Serves 10 to 12]

Ingredients

(1) 500 ml milk

(2) 6 table spoons sugar

(3) $1\frac{1}{2}$ table spoons G.M.S. powder

(4) A pinch C.M.C. powder

(5) $1\frac{1}{2}$ table spoons corn flour

(6) $1\frac{1}{2}$ table spoons milk powder

(7) $\frac{1}{2}$ cup malai (cream)

Method

(1) Mix milk and sugar. Boil it. Keep a little cold milk aside.

(2) Dissolve corn flour, G.M.S. and C.M.C. in that cold milk. Add this mixture to the boiling milk.

(3) Boil the milk for a few minutes. Dissolve the milk powder in a little cold milk and add it to the milk mixture.

(4) Boil until it thickens. Remove it from the flame and cool it. Put the same container in the freezer to set.

(5) When it is fully set, take out the ice cream in a bowl. Add $\frac{1}{2}$ cup of malai and beat it well until it is soft and fluffy. Add colour and flavour as required. Mix well.

(6) Pour the ice cream in an ice cream container. Freeze till firm.

Method 2 [Serves 15]

Ingredients

(1) 1 litre milk

(2) 11 table spoons sugar

(3) 2 table spoons corn flour

(4) 3 table spoons milk powder

(5) 1 tea spoon china grass

(6) 1 cup cream

(7) A pinch stabilizer

(8) A few drops edible colour

(9) A few drops essence

Method

(1) Boil the milk.

(2) Add the sugar and boil it for 15 minutes. Dissolve the corn flour in a little cold milk and add it to the boiling milk. Boil again for 10 minutes.

(3) Dissolve the milk powder in a little cold milk. Add it to the boiling milk mixture. Boil the mixture until it thickens. Remove it from the flame. Dissolve the china grass in cold milk and add it to the milk mixture.

(4) Cool it. Add the cream and stabilizer. Stabilizer may be added or avoided as desired. Add colouring and

flavouring as required. Churn it well and pour it into containers and put in the freezers to set.

(5) When it is set, churn it that is, blend it well in the mixer.

(6) Instead of cream, fresh malai can also be used. Take 1 cup fresh malai and add 2 tea spoons of milk to it. Stir well for 7 to 8 times in the same direction. Do not over do it or butter would be formed.

Note : Take 500 ml milk and less then the half of all the quantity. It will enough for 7 to 8 persons.

Various Types of Ice creams

598. Vanilla Ice cream
[Serves 15]

Ingredients

(1) 1 litre milk

(2) 11 table spoons sugar

(3) 2 table spoons corn flour

(4) 3 table spoons milk powder

(5) 1 tea spoon china grass

(6) 1 cup cream

(7) 1 tea spoon vanilla essence

(8) Few drops edible green colour

Method

(1) Boil the milk.

(2) Add sugar and boil it for 15 minutes. Dissolve the corn flour in a little cold milk. Add it to the milk and boil it for 10 minutes. Remove it from the flame.

(3) Add the china grass dissolved in a little cold milk.

(4) Cool the mixture and add the cream to it. Add the colouring and flavouring as required. Churn the mixture in the mixer and pour it in the ice cream containers and freeze it till it sets.

(5) When it is fully set, churn again and set freeze again until it is firm.

(6) Serve topped with chocolate sauce or orange sauce.

Note : (1) This ice cream can be made by method 1.

(2) For preparing quantity enough for 7 to 8 persons take 500 ml milk and take all the other ingredients half of the quantity.

599. Kesar Ice cream
[Serves 15]
Ingredients and Method

(1) Remains the same as in vanilla ice cream. Add $\frac{1}{4}$ tea spoon kesar powder dissolved in milk and add it to the cream. Add $\frac{1}{2}$ tea spoon cardamom powder.

(2) Substitute vanilla essence with the same amount of saffron essence.

(3) Do not add green colour, use yellow colour if saffron is not available.

600. Nutty Ice cream
[Serves 16]
Ingredients and Method

(1) In vanilla ice cream add $1\frac{1}{2}$ cups walnuts, cashewnuts and almonds chopped into small pieces.

(2) Soak the nuts pieces into water for 1 hour. Drain the water before adding the dry fruits to the ice cream.

(3) The proportion of sugar can be increased from 11 table spoons to 16 table spoons according to taste.

601. Pineapple and Nuts
Ice cream [Serves 16]
Ingredients and Method

(1) In vanilla ice cream, add $1\frac{1}{2}$ cups pineapple pieces. Add $\frac{1}{4}$ cups walnut pieces.

(2) Vanilla or ice cream essence may also be added.

602. Chickoo Ice cream
[Serves 16 to 18]
Ingredients

(1) 1 litre milk

(2) 8 table spoons sugar

(3) 4 tea spoons corn flour

(4) 1 tea spoon vanilla essence

(5) 8 chikoos

Method

(1) Boil the milk. Add sugar and boil for 15 minutes.

(2) Dissolve the corn flour in a little cold milk. Add it to the boiling milk.

(3) Boil further for few more minutes. Remove it from the flame and cool it. Add the essence and crushed chikoos.

(4) Churn the mixture in the mixer and keep in the refrigerator to set.

(5) When it is fully set, churn it again and allow it to set again until it is firm.

Note : Take half of the quantity for 8 to 9 persons.

603. Orange Ice cream
[Serves 16]
Ingredients

(1) 1 litre milk

(2) 11 table spoons sugar

(3) 1 tea spoon custard powder

(4) 1 tea spoon china grass

(5) 1 cup cream

(6) $\frac{3}{4}$ cup fresh orange juice

(7) Few drops edible orange colour

(8) Few drops orange essence

Method

(1) Boil the milk until it reduces to half the original amount. Add the sugar and stir until it dissolves.

(2) Add the custard powder dissolved in cold milk. Boil for 2 to 3 times and then add the china grass dissolved in cold milk.

(3) Remove it from the flame. Cool it.

(4) Add cream, orange juice, colour and essence. Churn it and pour it into ice cream containers.

(5) Keep it in the fridge to set. When it is fully set, churn it again and allow it to set again until it is firm.

Note : Take half of the quantity for 8 to 9 persons.

604. Pineapple Ice cream

[Serves 20 to 25]

Ingredients

(1) 1 big pineapple tin (850 grams)

(2) 500 ml milk

(3) 1 tea spoon gelatin

(4) 1 cup fresh cream

(5) 1 tin condensed milk (400 grams)

(6) Few drops yellow colour

(7) Few drops pineapple essence

(8) Cashewnut or walnut pieces

Method

(1) Keep a few pineapple pieces aside. Blend the remaining pineapple pieces along with a little juice and strain it. This juice should be 1 cup.

(2) Boil the milk. Soak the gelatine in water for 5 minutes. Add it to the boiling milk.

(3) Remove the mixture from the flame. Cool it and add cream, condensed milk, pineapple juice, colour and essence. Keep the mixture in the freezer to set. When it is fully set.

(4) Churn again. Add the pineapple pieces, cashewnut and walnut pieces. Pour in ice cream containers and keep in the fridge to set again until the ice cream is firm.

(5) Instead of pineapple, any other fruit can also be added. (alphanso mango, strawberry, banana, chikoo, etc.)

Note : Take half of the quantity for 10 to 12 persons.

Variation

While churning the pineapple ice cream for the second time, small pieces of chocolates can be added. Mix well to make pineapple chocolate chips ice cream.

605. Mango Ripe Ice cream

[Serves 10]

Ingredients

(1) 1 cup mango pulp

(2) 100 ml fresh cream

(3) 1 table spoon corn flour

(4) 500 ml milk   (5) Sugar to taste

Method

(1) Extract the pulp from the mangoes and strain it. Add cream and mix it very well. Chill it in the fridge.

(2) Dissolve the corn flour in a little cold milk. Mix the corn flour paste, milk and sugar. Boil the mixture until it is smooth and thick.

(3) Cool it and keep it in the freezer to set.

(4) When it is fully set, churn it again with the mango pulp and cream mixture. Keep again in the freezer to set until it is firm.

(5) Serve with chopped mango pieces.

Note : This ice cream mixture can be used to prepare ice cream in an ice cream churner.

606. Black Grapes Ice cream

[Serves 15 to 17]

Ingredients

(1) 1 litre milk

(2) 11 table spoons sugar

(3) 2 table spoons corn flour

(4) 1 tea spoon china grass

(5) 4 table spoons milk powder

(6) 1 cup cream   (7) A pinch stabilizer

(8) $\frac{3}{4}$ tea spoon vanilla essence

(9) 1 cup black currants

Note : If you want to add only corn flour, add 4 table spoons of the flour and avoid china grass.

Method

(1) Boil the milk for 15 minutes. Add sugar and boil it for 5 minutes.

(2) Dissolve the corn flour in cold milk. Add it to the boiling milk and boil further for 10 minutes. Remove it from the flame.

(3) Dissolve the china grass and the milk powder in cold milk. Add to the milk mixture. Cool it. Add the cream, stabilizer, colour and essence.

(4) Blend the raisins in the mixer and prepare a thick paste (the skin should be ground properly).

(5) Add this paste to the milk mixture. Churn 3 times for 1 second each.

(6) Pour the mixture into an aluminium container and keep it in the freezer to set.

(7) When it is fully set, churn again in the mixer until a smooth mixture is formed. Keep in the freezer again until it is fully set.

Note : Take half of the quantity for 7 to 8 persons.

607. Custard apple Ice cream
[Serves 15 to 17]
Ingredients and Method

(1) Remove the seeds from the custard apples and take out the pulp. Add this pulp to a little milk. Blend the pulp to a smooth consistency in a mixer.

(2) For 1 litre of milk take 4 big custard apples. The rest of the ingredients and method as same as given in R. No. 606.

Note : Take half of the quantity for 7 to 8 persons.

608. Tender Coconut Ice cream
[Serves 15 to 18]
Ingredients

(1) $1\frac{1}{2}$ cups tender coconut (malai)

(2) 1 litre milk

(3) 11 table spoons sugar

(4) 3 table spoons corn flour

(5) 1 cup cream

(6) Few drops vanilla essence

Method

(1) Chop $\frac{1}{2}$ cup tender coconut (malai) into small pieces. Blend 1 cup tender coconut in the mixer.

(2) Boil the milk for 15 minutes. Add sugar. Add corn flour dissolved in cold milk.

(3) Boil again for 10 minutes. Remove it from the flame and cool it.

(4) Add cream, essence and crushed tender coconut. Churn it and keep it in the freezer to set. When it is fully set, churn again and add the tender coconut pieces. Mix well.

(5) Pour the mixture in the ice cream container and keep it in the freezer to set until the ice cream is firm.

Note : Take half of the quantity for 7 to 8 persons.

609. Rose Coconut Ice cream
[Serves 15]
Ingredients

(1) 1 litre milk

(2) 11 table spoons sugar

(3) 3 table spoons corn flour

(4) 1 cup cream

(5) Few drops rose essence

(6) Few drops rose colour

(7) 4 tea spoons desiccated coconut

Method

(1) Mix milk and sugar and boil.

(2) Add corn flour dissolved in cold milk. Boil again for 10 minutes. Remove it from the flame and cool it.

(3) Add the cream, essence, colour and desiccated coconut. Mix well.

(4) Prepare the ice cream in an ice cream churner. Keep it in the fridge to set. When it is fully set, churn again and set again in the fridge to set until it is firm.

Note : Take half of the quantity for 7 to 8 persons.

610. Kesar Pista Ice cream
[Serves 20 to 22]

Ingredients

(1) $1\frac{1}{2}$ litres milk

(2) 16 table spoons sugar

(3) 2 tea spoons custard powder

(4) 1 tea spoon china grass

(5) $1\frac{1}{2}$ cups cream

(6) Few strands kesar

(7) Few drops kesar essence

(8) Few drops yellow colour

(9) Few drops green colour

(10) Few drops pista essence

(11) Few pista

Method

(1) Boil the milk for 15 minutes. Add sugar and boil until the sugar dissolves.

(2) Add custard powder dissolved in cold milk. Boil for few minutes. Add the china grass and remove the mixture from the flame. Cool it.

(3) Add cream. Divide the mixture into two parts. In one portion add kesar, kesar essence and yellow colour. Churn and allow it to set in the refrigerator.

(4) In the other portion add green colour and pista essence.

(5) Churn and keep it in the fridge to set. When it is fully set, churn again, add the pista slices in the green portion.

(6) First let the yellow portion set. When it is set, churn the green portion and allow it to set. Place it on yellow portion.

(7) Decorate with sliced pistas. Let it set again until the ice cream is firm.

Note : Take half of the quantity for 10 to 12 persons.

611. Anjeer Ice cream
[Serves 20 to 22]

Ingredients

(1) 10 anjeers   (2) $1\frac{1}{2}$ litres milk

(3) 10 table spoons sugar

(4) 2 tea spoons corn flour

(5) $1\frac{1}{2}$ cups cream

Method

(1) Chop the anjeers into small pieces. Boil them in water until the pulp is soft. Cool them.

(2) Add $\frac{1}{2}$ litre milk and keep aside.

(3) Boil 1 litre milk for 15 minutes. Add sugar and corn flour dissolved in cold milk. Boil for few minutes. Cool it. Add cream to it.

(4) Add the milk from the anjeer pieces. Keep the anjeer pieces a side. Do not churn. Mix well and allow it to set.

(5) When it is fully set, churn well and add the anjeer pieces. Mix well and allow it to set until the ice cream is firm.

Note : Take half of the quantity for 10 to 12 persons.

612. Walnut Ice cream

[Serves 15]

Ingredients

(1) 1 litre milk
(2) 11 table spoons sugar
(3) 1 tea spoon china grass
(4) 50 grams mawa
(5) Few drops chocolate colour
(6) Few drops strawberry or orange essence
(7) 4 whole walnuts
(8) Few drops chocolate colour or ice cream essence

Method

(1) Boil the milk for 15 minutes. Add sugar and boil until it dissolves.
(2) Add china grass and remove it from the flame. Cool it.
(3) Add the mawa, colour and essence. Churn well and allow it to set.
(4) When it is fully set, churn again. Add the walnut powder and a few pieces. Mix well and allow it to set until the ice cream is firm.

Note : Take half of the quantity for 7 to 8 persons.

613. Kaju Draksh Ice cream

[Serves 16]

Ingredients and Method

(1) Take 1½ cups cashewnuts and raisins. Chop the cashewnuts into small pieces. Soak the raisins in water for 1 hour.
(2) The rest of the ingredients and method remain the same as that used for vanilla ice cream.

After churning, add cashewnuts and raisins.

Note : Take half of the quantity for 7 to 8 persons.

614. Badam Ice cream

[Serves 15]

Ingredients and Method

(1) Chop the almonds into small pieces and soak them in water for 1 hour. Drain the water when using.
(2) The rest of the ingredients and method remain the same as that used for vanilla ice cream. Instead of vanilla essence, use the same quantity of almond essence.

Note : Take half of the quantity for 7 to 8 persons.

615. Chocolate Ice cream

[Serves 15]

Ingredients

(1) 1 litre milk
(2) 1 tea spoon cocoa
(3) 1½ table spoons drinking chocolate
(4) Few drops of chocolate essence

Method

Same as given in R. No. 598 for vanilla ice cream.

Note : Take half of the quantity for 7 to 8 persons.

616. Coffee Ice cream

[Serves 15]

(1) Substitute chocolate powder with the same quantity of coffee to make coffee ice cream.
(2) The other ingredients and method remain the same as that used to make vanilla ice cream.

Note : Take half of the quantity for 7 to 8 persons.

617. B.P.K. Ice cream

[Serves 16]

Ingredients and Method

According to vanilla ice cream.

Note : (1) To prepare B.P.K. ice cream, add almonds, pistas, kesar strands (powdered) and kesar essence to the ice cream.

(2) Soak the almonds and pista pieces in water for some time. Then drain the water before adding them to the ice cream. Add them to the ice cream after churning it the second time. Mix well and allow it to set until the ice cream is firm.

(3) Take half of the quantity for 7 to 8 persons.

618. Kulfi [Serves 16 to 18]

Ingredients

(1) 1 litre milk

(2) 150 to 200 grams mawa

(3) 125 grams sugar

(4) Few strands kesar

(5) 50 grams mixed dry fruits (almonds, pistas, walnuts, cardamom)

Method

(1) Mix milk and mawa well. Boil it well until it thickens. Add sugar.

(2) Soak the kesar strands in 1 cup of warm milk for some time.

(3) Mix it with the milk and mawa mixture. Mix well. Remove it from the flame. Add all the dry fruits and cardamom powder. Cool the mixture and fill it in the kulfi moulds. Keep them in the freezer to set.

(4) While serving, pour a little water on the kulfi moulds for 2 minutes. Remove the kulfi in the serving dish.

Variation

(1) Almonds, pistas, cardamom powder or biscuit powder can be added to the kulfi mixture.

(2) For preparing kulfi, mawa has to be always added.

(3) For preparing pista kulfi, instead of mawa add pista barfi. For making only mawa kulfi, add plain mawa.

(4) Chocolate kulfi can be made by adding chocolate powder to the kulfi mixture.

Note : Take half of the quantity for 8 to 9 persons.

619. Chocolate Sauce

Ingredients

(1) 200 ml milk

(2) 2 table spoons sugar

(3) 2 table spoons cocoa powder

(4) 3 tea spoons corn flour

Method

(1) Mix milk, sugar, cocoa powder and corn flour. Boil the mixture with stirring it constantly.

(2) When the mixture thickens, remove it from the flame. Cool it.

(3) It can be used as a topping on vanilla, or chocolate ice cream.

(4) It can also be added to the milk.

Note : (1) Various readymade sauces like strawberry, peach, lichi, black grapes, etc. are available.

(2) Pieces of various seasonal fruits can be placed on the top of the ice cream with the sauce of same variety of fruit. For example, serve strawberry ice cream topped with strawberry sauce and decorate it with pieces of strawberry.

620. Mixed Mukhavas

Ingredients

(1) 250 grams roasted coriander seeds dal

(2) 250 grams fennel seeds

(3) 100 grams sesame seeds

(4) 50 grams magatari seeds

(5) 1 tea spoon lovely hiramoti masala

(6) Desiccated coconut

Method

(1) Roast the fennel seeds, sesame seeds and magatari seeds for 5 minutes. Then add the desiccated coconut and roast for a few minutes.

(2) Then add the roasted coriander seeds dal and roast again for a few minutes. Remove it from the flame and cool it.

(3) Then add Lovely masala and mix well.

621. Drakshadivati

Ingredients

(1) 25 grams black currants

(2) 1 lime

(3) 100 grams powdered sugar

(4) 50 grams amchur powder

(5) $1\frac{1}{4}$ table spoons roasted cumin seed powder

(6) 20 to 25 pepper powder

(7) A pinch salt

Method

(1) Soak the raisins in water for some time. Remove the seeds if any. Crush the raisins, lime juice and powdered sugar in the blenderiser. Remove some raisins whole before grinding them.

(2) Place the paste in a dish. Add amchur powder, cumin seeds powder, salt, pepper powder and water just enough to knead the dough. Divide the dough into very small portions.

(3) Make small balls from the dough. Roll the balls in powdered sugar. Colour or essence may be added to prepare drakshadivati of different colours and flavours.

622. Adrakhavati

Ingredients

(1) 500 grams fresh ginger

(2) $1\frac{1}{2}$ table spoons lime juice

(3) $\frac{1}{4}$ tea spoon dry ginger powder

Method

(1) Wash and peel the ginger well. Slice the ginger into thin slices. Add lime juice and dry ginger powder to it.

(2) Mix well. Dry them in the sunlight. A pinch of salt may also be added.

623. Sweet Amala

Ingredients

(1) 1 kg Amala (big sized)

(2) 900 grams sugar   (3) Glucose

Method

(1) Wash the amala and cook them in pressure cooker for 1 whistle or for some time without the whistle.

(2) Remove the seeds and add sugar to it and mix well. (sugar syrup can be also prepared remove the scum from it.) Mix well every day. 2 to 3 times a day.

(3) Do this for 4 to 5 days. Then place them in a sieve like dish. Wash them slightly with water.

(4) Drain all the water and place them on a plastic sheet.

(5) Dry them in direct sunlight. While drying them, add a little glucose powder. Other 500 grams amala can be added to the remaining sugar syrup. (Powdered sugar can be added instead of glucose.)

624. Sweetened Mango

Ingredients

(1) 1 kg rajapuri mangoes

(2) 500 grams sugar

(3) 50 grams powdered sugar

Method

(1) Wash the mangoes and cut them into big pieces. Mix the sugar and keep aside for 3 days. Mix well every day. Place them in a sieve.

(2) Mix powdered sugar.

(3) Other mango pieces can be soaked in the remaining sugar syrup. Dry the mango pieces in sunlight.

(4) These can be also made from Tota variety of mangoes. (Peel them well so that all the green part will be peeled off.)

625. Green Variyali Mukhavas

Ingredients

(1) 150 grams cleaned, fresh, green fennel seeds ($1\frac{1}{2}$ cups)

(2) 15 grams fine perfumed betelnut ($\frac{1}{4}$ cup)

(3) 40 grams powdered sugar (little more than $\frac{1}{4}$ cup)

(4) 100 grams desiccated coconut (little more than 1 cup)

(5) 6 kapoori pan (betel leaves)

(6) 2 tea spoons lovely pan pasand

(7) 15 grams cashewnuts ($\frac{1}{4}$ cup)

Method

(1) Clean the fennel seeds and sieve them and mix all the other ingredients.

(2) Chop the cashewnuts and betel leaves into very fine pieces. Mix all ingredients well.

(3) Decorate with coloured desiccated coconut, cashewnuts and rose petels.

626. Kharek

Ingredients

(1) 500 grams kharek (dry dates)

(2) 750 grams lime or sour mango water

(3) 5 grams lindipiper

(4) 5 grams white pepper

(5) 5 grams akkalgaro

(6) 250 grams powdered sugar

(7) 200 grams pomegranate churan (100 grams + 100 grams)

(8) 5 grams salt or rock salt to taste

Method

(1) Soak the dates in lime or mango water. When they swellup, remove them from water and cut them into 4 horizontal slices.

(2) Mix and powder lindipiper, white pepper and akkalgaro. Add salt, sugar and 100 grams pomegranate churan. Mix well and dry in shadow. Stir it every day.

(3) When the dates are completely dried, (i.e, they do not stick to your hand), add the remaining 100 grams pomegranate churan. Fill in glass bottle.

627. Dried Variyali

Ingredients

(1) 150 grams fennel seeds

(2) 15 grams fine scented betelnut

(3) 40 grams powdered sugar

(4) 100 grams desiccated coconut

(5) 6 kapoori pan (betel leaves)

(6) 2 tea spoons lovely pan pasand

(7) 15 grams cashewnut

Method

(1) Chop the pans very finely (like fennel seeds). Chop the cashew nuts into small pieces.

(2) Mix all the ingredients. Decorate with coloured desiccated coconut.

628. Masala Kaju

Ingredients

(1) 100 grams cashewnuts

(2) Ghee

(3) $\frac{1}{2}$ tea spoon red chilli powder

(4) 1 tea spoon pepper powder

(5) $\frac{1}{2}$ tea spoon chat masala

(6) $\frac{1}{2}$ tea spoon garam masala

(7) 1 tea spoon sugar

(8) 1 tea spoon amchur powder

(9) Salt to taste

Method

(1) Deep fry the cashewnuts in ghee until they become golden brown. Heat a little ghee in a vessel. Add all the masala and fry for 1 minute.

(2) Remove it from the flame and add the fried cashewnuts. Mix well.

Note : Only salt peeper powder can also be used.

629. Masala Badam

Ingredients

(1) 100 gram almonds (2) Ghee

(3) 1 tea spoon pepper powder

(4) Salt to taste

Method

(1) Divide the almonds into two from the centre.

(2) Heat the ghee in a pan and roast the almonds in it. Add salt and pepper powder. Mix well.

(26) SERVING PER PERSON

Dudhapak : 500 ml milk – 300 ml ready dudhapak per person.

Basundi : 500 ml milk – 250 ml ready basundi per person.

Fruit Salad : 250 ml milk per person.

Cream Salad : 100 ml cream, 200 grams fruit per person.

Shrikhand, Mattha : 200 to 250 grams per person.

Pulav : 200 grams uncooked rice for 5 persons.

Alu Muttar : 750 grams potatoes, 450 grams peas for 9 persons.

Dahiwada : (Along with meals) 2 cups chawli dal and 1 cup urad dal for 8 persons.

Patara : (Along with meals) 250 grams colocasia leaves, 225 grams fine chana flour for 6 persons.

Dhokala : (Along with mango juice and puri) $2\frac{1}{2}$ cups flour for 5 persons.

Samosa : (Not along with meals) 1 kg potatoes 250 grams dried peas. Served separately peas for 6 persons.

For 7 persons 500 grams potatoes, 125 grams dried peas. (Along with meals)

Chhole : Per person 75 grams. (Along with meals)

Atom Bomb Pattice : For 5 persons 15 big potatoes, 600 grams green beans.

Corn, Potato Pattice : 1 kg potatoes, $1\frac{1}{2}$ kg corn. This would make 75 pattice.

Potatowada : Along with meals for 6 persons, 1 kg potatoes.

Khichado : For 12 persons 1 kg whole wheat.

Kachori : 1 kg tuver beans — makes 60 kachoris.

Dosa : For 8 persons 6 cups rice and urad dal (total) 15 big potatoes, 250 grams green peas, 15 onions.

Sev Usal : For 7 persons 600 grams dry peas.

Ladava : 100 grams coarse wheat flour makes 3 ladoos.

Ragada Pattice : Per person 2 potatoes and 1 fist dry peas.

Carrot Halwa : For 5 persons 1 kg carrots, 500 ml milk and cream.

Patti Samosa : 175 grams maida, 25 grams wheat flour, 250 grams potatoes, 125 grams peeled green peas — makes 45 pieces.

Punjabi Samosa : 500 grams potatoes, 250 grams peeled green peas, 200 grams maida, 60 grams wheat flour, 1 table spoon rawa, 1 table spoon ghee — makes 40 pieces.

Any readymade sweet : For 10 persons 2 kg.

Kansar : 1 cup coarse wheat flour, 1 cup water.

Fada Lapsi : 1 cup wheat crack, 3 to $3\frac{1}{2}$ cups water.

Khichu : 1 cup rice flour, $1\frac{1}{4}$ cups water.

Upama : 1 cup rawa, 3 cups water.

Sheera : 1 cup coarse wheat flour or (rawa), 3 cups water.

Idli : 3 cups rice, 1 cup urad dal.

Dosa : $3\frac{1}{2}$ cups rice, $1\frac{1}{2}$ cups urad dal.

Dhokala (white) : 3 cups rice, 1 cup urad dal.

Medu Wada : 1 cup rice, 3 cups urad dal.

Khichadi : 2 cups rice, 1 cup mung dal.

Handawa : 2 cups rice + 1 cup tur dal + $\frac{1}{4}$ cup chana dal + $\frac{1}{4}$ cup urad dal.

Khichado : 1 kg whole wheat, 400 grams tur dal.

Uttapa : 4 cups rice, 1 cup urad dal.

Chakali : 3 cups rice flour, 1 cup maida, $\frac{1}{2}$ cup ghee.

Tea : from 500 ml milk we can make 5 to 6 cups.

(27) BEST OUT OF WASTE

(1) The crumbs (sides) of old bread can be cut into medium sized pieces and fried. They can be added in mamara, poha or groundnut chiwada.

(2) The bread sides (crumbs) can be cut into pieces and seasoned. It can be a wonderful snack.

(3) The bread sides (crumbs) can be powdered and mixed with the boiled green peas mixture. It can be shaped like cutlet or round balls and deep fried or shallow fried.

(4) To thickens the gravy for any vegetable, bread (powdered) can be added.

(5) Left out rice cutlets — 1 cup cooked rice, 1 cup toast or biscuit powder, 250 grams potatoes, salt, green chillies, sugar, lime juice, red chilli powder and garam masala. Mix all ingredients.

(6) Left over rice or khichadi can be mixed with dhebaras, pakoras, muthiyas, etc.

(7) Potato poha can be used to make samosa or kachori or bread crumbs can be added to make delicious cutlets.

(8) Potato peas vegetable can be used as a sandwich stuffing.

(9) Add bread crumbs, salt, rawa, maida, ginger, chillies, chutney and sauce to the ragada to make tasty dhokalas.

(10) Use left over vegetables to make dhebaras, muthiyas and handawa.

(11) Methi dhebara flour can be used to make methi gotas. Add a little water to the flour for making gotas.

(12) If you have left over potatowada masala than stuff the stuffing in rotis. Roll it and seal it with water. Fry it and cut into small pieces to make delicious potatowada patara.

(13) To use up old pickles, soak 1 cup black chana. Drain all the water. Add the pickle to it. You can enjoy fresh chana, mango pickle.

(14) After preparing sweet amboliya, the remaining sugar syrup can be used to make mango sharabat adding boiled mango pulp to it.

(15) The left over mint and coriander pulp after preparing pani puri's pani, can be added in preparing punjabi samosas.

(16) Soft or semi-liquid ice cream can be used to make thick shake. Add milk and powdered sugar to it and beat well with a hand mixer. Decorate with small pieces of biscuits.

(17) The remains after extracting ghee from malai, add a little milk and sugar. Heat the mixture for some time. Delicious halwa is ready.

(18) Add all masalas to the remains after extracting ghee from malai. Prepare the stuffing like kachori and stuff this in puris and make kachoris.

(19) Heat 2 tea spoons malai and $1\frac{1}{2}$ tea spoons sugar. Stir in one direction. Cook until ghee separates and it is light brown in colour. Remove it from the flame. Remove the ghee aside. Fresh halwa can be made.

(20) For making soft koftas, soak 6 bread slices in water. Add 1 table spoon chana flour, salt, red chilli powder and garam masala to it.

(21) Boil raw bananas and add chana flour, salt and red chilli powder to it. Shape like koftas and fry them.

(22) To use left over thepalas cut them into diamond shaped shakar paras. Add them to seasonal tur dal. Dal dhokali is ready.

(23) To use left over potato vegetable, remove all the gravy and add all masalas like potatowada. Dip in chana flour batter to make potato wadas.

(24) Stir constantly curdled milk until mawa separates.

28 CELEBRATIONS OF FESTIVALS

KARTAK — New Year

Celebrated by : Making rangolis, lighting up lamps.

Dishes made : Shrikhand, puri, chawlafali vegetable, partra or khaman, dhokala.

Bhaibij

Celebrated by : Worshiping brother.

Dishes made : Dishes and sweets liked by the brother.

Labha Pacham

Celebrated by : Worshiping cow or offering lunch or dinner to any staff member.

Dishes made : Lapsi, bundi, ladoo or jalebi, methi gota or any farsan desired by the individual.

Dev Diwali

Celebrated by : Worshiping Tulsi.

Dishes made : Any fasting dishes, dudha-poha, pattice, pani-puri.

POSHA — Utarayan

Celebrated by : Giving grass to the cow, flying kites.

Dishes made : Coconut and til ladoo, khichado, ravaiya, undhiya, til chikki.

MAHA — Vasant Panchami

Dishes made : Puranpoli, patra.

Shiv Ratri

Celebrated by : Worshiping Lord Shiva. People usually fast on that day.

Dishes made : Boiled sweet potatoes and other fasting dishes.

FAGUN — Holi

Celebrated by : Worshiping Holika in the evenings. Playing holi.

Dishes made : In the mornings Dhani-chana and khajur filled with ghee. In the evening after puja ladoo, dal and val.

Gudi Padava

Importance : People consume juice of neem leaves and kesar, cardamom water.

Ramnavmi

Celebrated by : Worshiping Lord Ram. Visiting temples.

Dishes made : Sheera, puri and bhajiya.

ASHAD — Rathayatra

Dishes made : Kansar and sprouted mung.

Alunuvrata

Dishes made : Moras, machad, luni leaves, sweets, fruits and other food items without salt.

SHARAVAN — Baleva

Dishes made : As liked by the sisters.

Nagpanchami

Celebrated by : Worshiping nag (Cobra snake).

Dishes made : Kuler, Khaja and other dishes depending upon one's own rituals.

SWEETS

1. Kaju Roll 2. Manbhavan Ladoo 3. Roller Coaster 4. Coco Roll
5. Kajukatri 6. Ghughara 7. Mathadi

MUKHAVAS

1. Mix Fruit Toffee 2. Sweetened Mango 3. Masala Badam
4. Masala Kaju 5. Green Variyali

CRISPY SNACKS

1. Mint Chana Dal 2. Chana Jor Garam 3. Green Peas
4. Ratlami Sev 5. Fafada 6. Khasta Kachori 7. Sprouted Mung

SNACKS

1. Atom Bomb Pattice of Peas 2. Aneri Special Lolipop
3. Aneri Special Chatakedar Cake 4. Tri-colour Bread Samosa
5. Green Chutney 6. Ketchup

SOUTH INDIAN

1. Idli 2. Medu Vada 3. Sambhar 4. Upama

SOUTH INDIAN

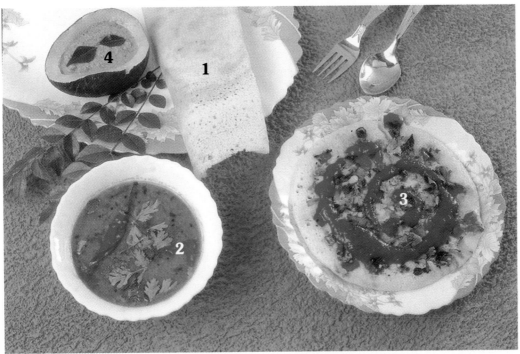

1. Dosa 2. Sambhar 3. Uttappa 4. Chutney

PUNJABI

1. Baby Corn Capsicum Red Masala 2. Tomato Vermicelli Soup

PUNJABI

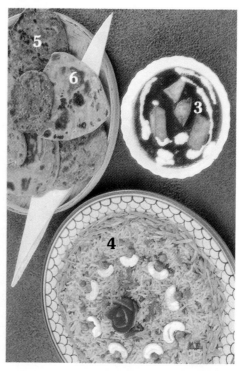

1. Stuff Tomato in Gravy 2. Chhole Takatak 3. Palak Paneer 4. Pulav.
5. Hari Puri Kulcha 6. Paratha

THAI

1. Thai Vegetable in Roasted curry 2. Burmese Khowsuey 3. Pulav

MAXICAN

1. Mexican Cutlet 2. Mexican Tacos 3. Chinese Samosa

SALAD

SALAD

6

PUDDING

1. Fruit Pudding 2. Topping

CAKE

1. Black Forest Cake

ICE CREAMS

Printed by : Chirag Offset Pvt. Ltd.